SOLVING DISCIPLINE PROBLEMS

Related Titles of Interest

Classroom Management for Secondary Teachers, Fourth Edition
Edmund T. Emmer, Carolyn M. Evertson, Barbara S. Clements,
and Murray E. Worsham
ISBN: 0-205-20005-2

Classroom Management for Elementary Teachers, Fourth Edition
Carolyn M. Evertson, Edmund T. Emmer, Barbara S. Clements,
and Murray E. Worsham
ISBN: 0-205-20006-0

**Managing Classroom Behavior: A Reflective Case-Based Approach,
Second Edition**
James M. Kauffman, Mark P. Mostert, Stanley C. Trent,
and Daniel P. Hallahan
ISBN: 0-205-27460-9

A Guide to Positive Discipline: Helping Students Make Responsible Choices
Barbara Keating, Mercedes Pickering, Bonnie Slack, and Judith White
ISBN: 0-205-12152-7

**Principles of Classroom Management: A Professional
Decision-Making Model, Second Edition**
James Levin and James F. Nolan
ISBN: 0-205-16615-6

Discipline for Self-Control
Tom V. Savage
ISBN: 0-13-217431-6

**The Three Faces of Discipline for Early Childhood:
Empowering Teachers and Students**
Charles H. Wolfgang and Mary E. Wolfgang
ISBN: 0-205-15649-5

FOURTH EDITION

SOLVING DISCIPLINE PROBLEMS

Methods and Models for Today's Teachers

Charles H. Wolfgang
Florida State University

Allyn and Bacon
Boston • London • Toronto • Sydney • Tokyo • Singapore

Vice President, and Editor-in-Chief, Social Sciences and Education: Sean W. Wakely
Series Editorial Assistant: Jessica Barnard
Marketing Managers: Ellen Dolberg/Brad Parkins
Manufacturing Buyer: Dave Repetto

Library of Congress Cataloging-in-Publication Data

Wolfgang, Charles H.
    Solving discipline problems : methods and models for today's
teachers / Charles H. Wolfgang. -- 4th ed.
        p.   cm.
    Includes bibliographical references and index.
    ISBN 0-205-28561-9
    1. School discipline.   2. Classroom management.   I. Title.
LB3012.W65   1999
371.5--dc21   98-20692
                                                        CIP

Printed in the United States of America
10 9 8 7 6 5 4 3 2 1   02 01 00 99 98

CONTENTS

PREFACE

This book is for classroom teachers and school administrators who teach and work in elementary, middle, and high schools. In the first few days of the new school year, you quickly learn that one of the children in the class—Walter—is going to challenge your skills as a teacher and a disciplinarian. To put it more bluntly, if less professionally, you know he is going to drive you nuts this year. When fellow teachers see your class roster, they quickly state, "Oh, no, you got Walter! Better you than me! Good luck!" He destroys others' property, fights, uses profanity to the extent that parents and classmates complain, and engages in a host of other misbehaviors that require you to deal with him repeatedly, sapping your energy.

The bus drivers, crossing guards, cafeteria workers, janitors, and other teachers begin a barrage of complaints about Walter, and they expect you to do something about him. Many teaching lessons are routinely disrupted by Walter, and you begin to get the terrible feeling that he is "out to get you." It is as if he deliberately sets "fires" that you are forced to put out, taking up far too much of your teaching time and ruining the pacing and continuity of the schoolday. Other children are stimulated by his misbehavior as they watch his actions, and they are beginning to attempt similar activities just to see if they can get away with it, in a disruptive game of "monkey see, monkey do." Sending Walter to the principal's office doesn't seem to help. Although the principal tries to intimidate Walter by figuratively talking his ears off, three minutes after returning from the office he is up to his old tricks. In fact, he appears to look forward to those "discipline" trips.

We seem to be all alone as teachers in our classrooms. Fellow teachers and school administrators are busy at their own tasks, and we seem to be locked into our "classroom caves" with 30 to 35 children who are beginning to challenge us and our authority, with one child leading the charge by throwing "hand grenades" into our daily classroom routine. We also begin to have the feeling that we are no longer in control of our classrooms; depression and a feeling of "battle fatigue" are quickly setting in, and we are becoming concerned that our professional evaluations might suffer. September isn't even over yet, and we are already thinking about the end of this school year. We have no idea how to regain control of our classrooms and deal effectively with our Walters.

There are many discipline approaches, models, and systems available for teachers to deal with misbehaving children such as Walter. Most of these models (among them *T.E.T.*, reality therapy, control theory, behavior analysis, positive discipline, and assertive discipline) claim to have the "right way" to discipline. They seem to be saying, "Follow my system and I will lead you to the blissful promised land of an educational heaven, a world of perfectly disciplined classrooms populated by happy, cooperative students." All are good models, most of them based to varying degrees on psychological theory. Each has a fairly narrow and differing view of what motivates children and their misbehavior, and each prescribes various techniques for dealing with this. Some models rely on very light requests of the child, while others make clear demands to stop misbehavior; some use strong controlling actions to extinguish the misbehavior, while others suggest methods of dealing with violent-assaultive acts directed at you as a teacher.

These models progress along a continuum from minimum to maximum use of power by the teacher. If you view the continuum of misbehavior in your classroom side by side with the continuum of discipline models with regard to the power these techniques give you as a teacher, you can see that some models may be quite effective with some children but totally ineffective with the very difficult Walters of this world. My position is that no one model can work successfully for all children at all times, nor will the same model always succeed for the same child as he or she experiences different stimuli and exhibits different kinds of misbehavior. In fact, if you observe closely, you will see that you, yourself, do not always use the same techniques with each and every child. Some children who are "out of line" need only to be looked at; if you meet them eye to eye and signal them about their behavior, they will stop. With others, you will need to move more forcefully by confronting them, and then, with some discussion, they will get "back in line." With still others, such as our Walter, you might need to take very strong intervention, even using various forms of encouragement or punishment. Based on a host of variables, teachers tend to change their "faces"—the way they present themselves and the methods they use.

In the real world of Monday morning in the classroom with Walter, one rarely sees a practicing classroom teacher who is a discipline purist—a teacher who uses assertive discipline and only assertive discipline, or Glasser's reality therapy and only Glasser. More likely, one will find the teacher in the practical world using many of the techniques from generally one model, but with his or her own "spin" on the techniques. The teacher adds other techniques previously learned and tested, techniques the teacher has determined can be successful for him or her. Thus, I adopt the approach of the teacher living and working in a practical world— namely: All of the various discipline models in vogue have some strengths and some limitations, so why not learn the best techniques from each of them?

Discipline is the required action by a teacher or school official, toward a student (or group of students), after the student's behavior disrupts the ongoing educational activity or breaks a preestablished rule or law created by the teacher, the school administration, or the general society. The educator's actions may fall into four broad categories of response:

- Relationship-Listening (a therapeutic process)
- Confronting-Contracting (an educational and counseling process)
- Rules and Consequences (a controlling process)
- Coercive-Legalistic* (a restraining, exclusionary, and legal process)

These four processes constitute the *Three Faces of Discipline* and may be placed on a power continuum from minimum to maximum use of power by the teacher. The continuum reflects the level of autonomy and control given to the student to change his or her own behavior or the coercive or aversive actions used by the teacher or school officials to get the desired change in student behavior and reestablish order and safety in the educational setting. Figure A displays the categories, processes, and models that fit this power construct.

These models—based on varying degrees of psychological theory and, to a lesser extent, research-supported knowledge—serve as the knowledge base of practical techniques and skills that are needed to handle the wide variety of discipline situations the educator will face in today's school setting.

Chapter 1, The TBC: The Teacher Behavior Continuum, presents a quick and minor discipline incident and shows how the teacher escalates his or her power across a continuum of teacher discipline techniques, moving from minimum to maximum use of power. The general categories of behavior used by the teacher are placed along a power continuum, called the Teacher Behavior Continuum. This continuum, or TBC, provides a construct that can be used to evaluate the power inherent in the various discipline techniques within these models, which are listed in Figure A and which will be described in more detail later. In essence, the TBC is much like a clothesline onto which all of the techniques from various discipline models may be hung so that the teacher can clearly see the specific and concrete steps suggested by this model as he or she faces another Monday morning with Walter.

Chapters 2 to 11 each presents a popular discipline model (*T.E.T.*, Glasser, behavioral analysis, assertive discipline, etc.) that historically has been used to discipline students at all school levels. I have selected those models that offer clear, practical techniques for what to do with our Monday-morning encounters with the Walters of the world.

Note: Coercive-Legalistic is not a true "face," but is included in most discussions of the Three Faces of Discipline because it represents the final step along a continuum of approaches that may be taken by a teacher or other educator in response to serious disciplinary problems. *Coercive-Legalistic* refers to a preestablished set of procedures that are to be taken to deal with the most serious problems, including assault; some of these procedures involve the law, and teachers generally do not have discretion in dealing with these cases. The actions are restraint, expulsion, and legal proceedings.

TEACHER'S POWER			
Minimum Power			**Maximum Power**
Category	Relationship-Listening Face	Confronting-Contracting Face	Rules and Consequences Face	Coercive-Legalistic
Process	Therapeutic	Educational and counseling	Controlling, rewards, and punishment	Restraining, exclusionary, and legal
Models	Gordon's *T.E.T: Teacher Effectiveness Training,*[1] *Teaching Children Self-Discipline*[2] Schrumpf/Crawford/ Bodine's *Peer Mediation: Conflict Resolution in Schools*[3]	Dreikurs's *Discipline Without Tears*[4] Albert's *Cooperative Discipline*[5] Glasser's *Control Theory in the Classroom,*[6] *Schools Without Failure,*[7] *The Quality School*[8] Gathercoal's *Judicious Discipline*[9]	Madsen/Madsen's *Teaching/ Discipline: A Positive Approach for Educational Development*[10] Alberto/Troutman's *Applied Behavior Analysis for Teachers*[11] Goldstein et al.'s *Skillstreaming the Adolescent*[12] McGinnis/Goldstein's *Skillstreaming the Elementary School Child,*[13] *Skillstreaming in Early Childhood*[14] Canter's *Assertive Discipline,*[15] *Succeeding With Difficult Students*[16] Alberti's *Your Perfect Right,*[17] *Stand Up, Speak Out, Talk Back*[18] Jones's *Positive Discipline*[19]	Nonviolent crisis management and arbitrary preestablished administrative procedures leading to physical restraint, exclusion, and legal actions toward the student or family. CPI (Crisis Prevention Institute)[20]

FIGURE A   Today's Discipline Models

Once you have read these chapters and models, Chapter 12 describes the strengths and limitations of each model to permit reflection and discussion of the specific models and their suggested methods. Chapter 13 introduces a construct of viewing the classroom teacher along a developmental line toward professional maturity. Discussion will also focus on how the student teacher, the first-year teacher, or the teacher new to the classroom might use one or two of these discipline models and their techniques. This chapter also shows how the experienced teacher may create his or her own model by picking and choosing various techniques from among the previously learned models. This eclectic approach becomes the Three Faces of Discipline construct—the Relationship-Listening face, the Confronting-Contracting face, and the Rules and Consequences face, along with coercive-legalistic actions—taking the view that all models have strengths and techniques that can improve the teacher's skill. Through this approach, you can create a pathway of techniques based on escalation or deescalation of your own power as you work with a very difficult child who is disrupting the classroom, such as the notorious Walter.

A style note: In order to avoid the awkward writing construction of constantly using *his or her* and *he or she* to refer to the teacher, I sometimes will simply use one gender at a time. Because teaching is a field shared by women and men alike, both genders will be used at various times throughout this book. The use of only one gender at a time, however, should not be taken as an indication that the concepts and the problems encountered would be more often associated with one gender rather than the other.

ACKNOWLEDGMENTS

A special thanks to all my colleagues and the many teachers who read this manuscript and offered their insights and suggestions; to Cal Johnston for his research work; to Chuck Walsh for his practical examples and vignettes; and to Jon Peck for his excellent editing as well as solid and wise advice. Thank you also to the reviewers of this manuscript for their useful comments: Livingston Alexander (Western Kentucky University) and Roger Cunningham (The Ohio State University).

ENDNOTES

1. T. Gordon, *T.E.T.: Teacher Effectiveness Training* (New York: David McKay, 1974).

2. T. Gordon, *Teaching Children Self-Discipline: At Home and at School* (New York: Times Books, 1989).

3. F. Schrumpf, D. K. Crawford, and R. J. Bodine, *Peer Mediation: Conflict Resolution in Schools* (Champaign, IL: Research Press, 1997).

4. R. Dreikurs and P. Cassel, *Discipline Without Tears* (New York: Hawthorn Books, 1972).

5. L. Albert, *A Teacher's Guide to Cooperative Discipline: How to Manage Your Classroom and Promote Self-Esteem* (Circle Pines, MN: American Guidance Service, 1989).

6. W. Glasser, *Control Theory in the Classroom* (New York: Harper & Row, 1985).

7. W. Glasser, *Schools Without Failure* (New York: Harper & Row, 1969).

8. W. Glasser, *The Quality School: Managing Students without Coercion*, 2nd ed., expanded (New York: Harper Perennial, 1992).

9. F. Gathercoal, *Judicious Discipline*, 3rd ed. (San Francisco, CA: Caddo Gap Press, 1993).

10. C. H. Madsen and C. K. Madsen, *Teaching/Discipline: A Positive Approach for Educational Development* (Raleigh, NC: Contemporary Publishing).

11. P. A. Alberto and A. C. Troutman, *Applied Behavior Analysis for Teachers*, 3rd ed. (New York: Maxwell Macmillan International Publishing Group, 1990).

12. A. P. Goldstein, R. P. Sprafkin, N. J. Gershaw, and P. Klein, *Skillstreaming the Adolescent: A Structured Learning Approach to Teaching Prosocial Skills* (Champaign, IL: Research Press, 1980).

13. E. McGinnis and A. P. Goldstein, *Skillstreaming the Elementary School Child: New Strategies and Perspectives for Teaching Prosocial Skills* (Champaign, IL: Research Press, 1997).

14. E. McGinnis and A. P. Goldstein, *Skillstreaming in Early Childhood: Teaching Prosocial*

Skills to the Preschool and Kindergarten Child (Champaign, IL: Research Press, 1990).

15. L. Canter and M. Canter, *Assertive Discipline: Positive Behavior Management for Today's Classroom* (Santa Monica, CA: Lee Canter & Associates, 1992).

16. L. Canter and M. Canter, *Succeeding With Difficult Students* (Santa Monica, CA: Lee Canter & Associates, 1993).

17. R. E. Alberti, *Your Perfect Right: A Guide to Assertive Living* (San Luis Obispo, CA: Impact Publishers, 1982).

18. R. E. Alberti and M. L. Emmons, *Stand Up, Speak Out, Talk Back* (New York: Pocket Books, 1975).

19. F. H. Jones, *Positive Classroom Discipline* (New York: McGraw-Hill, 1987).

20. National Crisis Prevention Institute, 3315-K N. 124th Street, Brookfield, WI 53005.

1

THE TBC

The Teacher Behavior Continuum

Mr. Leonard's ninth-grade government class has 36 students in it. Every desk in the room is occupied—in fact, two students have to sit at a display table at the back of the room. The class is quietly working on an assignment from the textbook when a commotion erupts in the middle of the room. George, a small, quiet student, is frantically looking around and under his desk. Many of the students around him are watching him, and some are starting to laugh softly. Mr. Leonard moves to George and, speaking softly so others will not be disturbed, asks, "George, what's the matter?" George replies, "Someone swiped my hat!" Kathy, who sits next to George, says, "Mike took it. I saw him!" Mike retorts, "I didn't take it. Check it out. I don't have his stupid hat!" Kathy insists, "You do, too!"

Mr. Leonard moves closer to Mike and makes eye contact (Step 1: *modality cueing or visual looking*). The teacher says, "When teasing by taking someone's property occurs and disrupts the class so that everyone stops their work, we lose valuable time, and I find that quite annoying." Mr. Leonard backs out of Mike's "personal space" and gives him several minutes to respond (Step 2: *nondirective statements*). Mike takes a baseball hat from inside his desk, places it on his head, throws his feet up onto his desk, and smiles broadly at Mr. Leonard.

"What is the rule regarding personal property?" the teacher asks. "What are you going to do to solve this problem, Mike, so that we may all get back to our work?" (Step 3: *questions*). Mr. Leonard is still speaking in a soft voice so only the students near George and Mike can hear.

Mr. Leonard then states, "Mike, put your feet on the floor and return the hat to George" (*directive statement*). There is still no action from Mike, so the teacher adds, "If you cannot quickly put your feet on the floor and return the cap now, I will need to call in Mr. Mack, the assistant principal, and Mr. Baker from across the hall, and we will escort you from the classroom to the

1

"Don't worry, Alfred, it takes time to get a handle on class control."

Cartoon by Ford Button.

principal's office (*preparatory command*). Return George's hat now!" (*directive statement*). The four neighboring students turn to look at Mike, and he slowly pushes the hat toward George and seats himself with his feet on the floor. If Mike had not responded, Mr. Leonard would have followed through on his stated intent to remove the student (*physical intervention*).

For purposes of this example, we have successfully ended the incident with George's hat being returned, with limited disruption to most of the other students and to ongoing classroom activity. However, the experienced teacher realizes that, more likely, this lost hat incident may have degenerated into a situation requiring the teacher's physical intervention to actually remove Mike, to restrain George (who might angrily strike out), or to take some other action to get the students back to their classroom work activity. Later, I will provide methods and constructs for dealing with raw aggression and removal, but first it is important to understand the dynamics of this incident in order to explain the construct of the Teacher Behavior Continuum (TBC) [1, 2, 3] and the concept of escalation from minimum to maximum use of power (see Figure 1–1).

When a student acts in an inappropriate manner in the classroom, the teacher asks, "What should be done to stop this behavior?" The natural tendency, especially for a beginning teacher, is to rush toward the student, state in a loud and forceful manner (*high-profile desist*) what the student must *not* do first ("Don't do

MINIMUM POWER   MAXIMUM POWER
_____

Step 1 Modality Cueing
    Step 2 Nondirective Statements
        Step 3 Questions
            Step 4 Directive Statements
                (preparatory command)
            Step 5 Physical Intervention
                Modeling (reinforcement)

_____

FIGURE 1–1   Teacher Behavior Continuum

that, Mike. Stop clowning around!"), and then, if compliance is not obtained, begin a classroom search for the hat or physically remove Mike. This approach of telling the student what *not* to do is generally ineffective on a number of accounts.

Erikson,[4] a child-development expert, characterized the span of early adolescence as the period of identity versus role confusion. Students at this age appear to be emotionally pulled between two extremes of wanting to be treated as adults while at the same time readily regressing to childish behavior. They are overly sensitive to how they are viewed by peers, especially with a growing new interest in how they appear to the opposite sex. Any confrontation, especially in a context where peers are onlookers, places great pressure on children this age to save face, to avoid being made a fool of, or to sense a challenge to their power thereby requiring them to demonstrate a macho response. When placed in this "spotlight," they emotionally flood with feelings of shame, guilt, and inferiority. Their role confusion is a surface emotion fully ready to effervesce, and can be quickly triggered by any demand. "Don't do it!" brings quick and strong defensive emotional feelings from the student at this particular age and is highly likely to "flood" the student with emotion. This flooding clouds the adolescent's logical thinking on how to respond to a demand. Thus, the "don't do" statements are likely to cause feelings of guilt or inferiority or make the child confused and respond in an aggressive or foolish and destructive manner toward the teacher.

As you view this "don't put your feet on the desk" directive command, keep in mind the way in which students hear and absorb verbal communications when they are emotionally flooded. When emotionally flooded, their thinking regresses to a form of irreversibility[5] of thinking. They do not think through the sequence of past actions and future consequences, but simply feel that they are in the spotlight and everyone is looking at them, and so they must show that they are tough, no matter what. When flooded students hear, "Don't put your feet on the desk," what they often hear and remember is "Put your feet on the desk." Unknowingly, you might actually be suggesting that the students perform the very actions you do not want.

Words also trigger motor-meaning responses in students. If you are reading kindergartners a story that says "The tiger growled and showed his ghastly teeth," a look at the young audience will show most of the students "growling" and showing their teeth. Words suggest, to young students, a motor-meaning response that they seem impulsively unable to control. When adolescent students' thinking is flooded with emotions, their thought process regresses to the young child's way of responding and thinking. Therefore, if you state to a student a sentence that ends with an action or motor meaning, even when the sentence begins with "Don't," you are likely to get the student to perform the motor meaning of the last words. Therefore, teachers should tell the student what to do, not what *not* to do. In this way, you are presenting a reality solution, telling the student what actions you want, and are suggesting the motor meaning of your desired actions ("Keep your feet on the floor").

The final difficulty with the "don't do so-and-so" approach is that if this is a student motivated by the need for power, the student most likely will take you on in a power struggle, especially if he feels a need to save face. As toddlers, children begin to test out their autonomy[6] by attempting to get around limit setting by parents and other adults. If this limit setting by adults has been erratic and inconsistent, by the time children are middle school and high school students these youths might have come to the conclusion that *don't* really is a word that triggers a game of "Let's see if the adult really means what he has said, or if I can beat the adult and do as I wish." The "don't" statement as a directive statement on the Teacher Behavior Continuum places you with your back against the wall, requiring an immediate confrontation or physical intervention with the student challenging your power. The goal in using and understanding the Teacher Behavior Continuum is to grant the student maximum power to change his own behavior by beginning with a *low-profile desist* command. Only when you are not successful in gaining compliance do you then gradually escalate power until you get results.

THE SEVERITY CLAUSE AND "STOP" STATEMENTS

For every rule there is an exception. If a teacher sees a student about to perform some action that is life threatening, is likely to produce injury, or will destroy expensive property, the *severity clause* applies. In such a case, of course, the teacher states firmly or even shouts a "No, Stop!" statement to attempt to get the student to desist immediately. If you have followed the rule and have regularly told the student what to do, and not what *not* to do, your emergency "No, Stop!" statements are more likely to be immediately obeyed. However, if the student has an hourly diet of "don't do this, don't do that" and has been told repetitively "No, don't do so-and-so" a thousand times a day, he is desensitized to the prohibition contained in "No, Stop!" statements and is now less likely to obey an emergency command immediately. Save the "no" statements until they are really needed.

TBC: TEACHER BEHAVIOR CONTINUUM

The confrontation between Mike and Mr. Leonard over a missing hat and the feet-on-the-floor issue contains examples of those myriad small desist requests—which may be called "teachable moments"—that a classroom teacher faces daily in working with students. The incident is dealt with in a matter of minutes, and the teacher escalates up the TBC power continuum as he intervenes, modifying his approach as he receives (or fails to receive) certain responses. With some students, especially physically and verbally aggressive students, these teachable moments may arise five or six times in an hour and occur daily. Teachers may be required over many weeks and months to handle such incidents with one particular student, and the many techniques found in the following chapters can be of great help to you.

What is important here is not this one particular desist request, but rather an understanding of the construct of the Teacher Behavior Continuum. The steps and general categories of behavior on the TBC suggest a power continuum of teacher action moving from the minimum power of modality cueing (Step 1) to the maximum power of physical intervention (Step 5). This escalation to more powerful techniques on the TBC also reflects a very real attitudinal change on the part of the intervening teacher. This attitude change may be characterized as the Three Faces of Discipline: Relationship-Listening, Confronting-Contracting, and Rules and Consequences.

The *Relationship-Listening* "face" involves the use of minimum power. This reflects a view that the student has the capabilities to change his own behavior, and that if the student is misbehaving, it is because of inner emotional turmoil, flooded behavior, or feelings of inner inadequacy. The teacher's goal would be to signal or make the student aware of his actions and get him to talk out his emotional concern. This "talking it out" by the student would lead him to become more purposeful in his behavior, and the misbehavior would stop. The "face" of the Relationship-Listening teacher would rely only on such TBC minimal intervention techniques as modality cueing and nondirective statements (see Figure 1–2).

The teacher's "face" when escalating to a *Confronting-Contracting* method of intervention is one of "I am the adult. I know misbehavior when I see it and will confront the student to stop this behavior. I will grant the student the power to decide how he or she will change, and encourage and contract with the student to live up to a mutual agreement for behavioral change." The Confronting-Contracting position primarily involves the use of questioning techniques found on the TBC (see Figure 1–2).

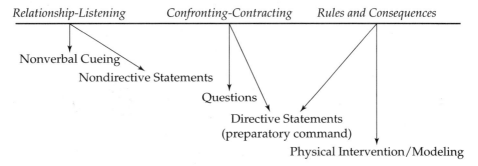

FIGURE 1–2 The Three Faces of Discipline

The more powerful intervention technique is a teacher attitude of *Rules and Consequences*. The teacher's Rules and Consequences "face" is one that communicates an attitude of "This is the rule and behavior that I want and I will set out assertively to get this action. I will teach and reward new positive behaviors acquired by the student." Drawing from the TBC, the teacher's Rules and Consequences "face" will use the powerful techniques of directive statements, physical intervention, and modeling, defined as demonstrating to the student the behaviors the teacher desires (see Figure 1–2).

As discussed in the Preface, Coercive-Legalistic is not a true "face" but should be considered in the context of teacher responses to student behaviors. Coercive-Legalistic involves the physical restraining of an assaultive student and possibly legal actions to remove the student from the school setting. This approach is used only to deal with the most problematic—and potentially dangerous—students, and carries a host of legal implications and predetermined procedural requirements.

The Teacher Behavior Continuum and the escalation and change among these attitudes or "faces of discipline" may be used in two ways to help young students' behavior move to a more mature level:

- First, for the student who is simply having a rare misbehavior, the teacher would escalate across the TBC within a few minutes. This was demonstrated in the example of Mike and the missing hat.
- Second, for the attention-getting, power-seeking, and revengeful student whose life-stance position is one of a day-in, day-out series of classroom disruptions, the teacher may stay with a single "face of discipline"—with its accompanying techniques—for many weeks. The teacher would gradually change this "face" to increase power if these techniques are *unsuccessful* or to decrease power to less intrusive techniques if the student's behavior begins to change and becomes more purposeful and guided.

THE THREE FACES OF DISCIPLINE: A CONCEPT, NOT A RECIPE

The concepts of the Three Faces of Discipline, with the use of the TBC power continuum and its accompanying teacher behaviors, is not for the purpose of giving the teacher a clear-cut recipe for responding to misbehavior. One example of a recipe is suggested in *Assertive Discipline*,[7] which calls for the teacher to place a student's name on the board as a warning of misbehavior, followed by a check mark for each new act of misbehavior; after three checks, the student suffers some form of punishment. This approach takes the skill out of the teacher's hand by assuming that this recipe will be effective with all students. The Teacher Behavior Continuum and the concept of the Three Faces of Discipline simply provide an orderly arrangement of teacher techniques that may be used as they relate to degrees of power. This concept permits the teacher to use her skills to decide how much power is needed for which student under what type of circumstances.

For example, with one misbehaving student, the teacher may choose to state, "Carol, what are you doing? This may not go on!" (Confronting-Contracting techniques). The student, without any undue stress, realizes what she must do to comply, and the discipline incident is over. With another student who is getting out of hand, the teacher may simply need to make eye contact (Relationship-Listening techniques) for the student to gain an awareness of what he is doing wrong and how to stop doing it. Still other students require the teacher to assertively state the rules and demand immediate compliance (Rules and Consequences techniques) before they stop their improper behavior. The teacher, based on past experiences with these students and an intimate knowledge of them, has made a decision as to how much power and which techniques would be most effective with each individual student. The Three Faces of Discipline concept would go one step further. With those students requiring the strong intervention of Rules and Consequences (and to a lesser extent Confronting-Contracting), over many weeks the teacher would gradually teach or lead the students to respond to the teacher's use of less and less power, until they could effectively control themselves. As a result, the teacher would need to use only the Relationship-Listening techniques, or none at all.

Subsequent chapters contain a more detailed explanation of the teacher behaviors found on the Teacher Behavior Continuum, with many new subbehavioral techniques defined and presented under each of these larger behavioral categories. Recall that in the missing hat teachable moment example, the teacher first used the behavioral category of directive statement and then progressed to a subdirective statement under this category called a *preparatory command*. Other behaviors on the TBC will also contain subbehaviors and techniques under these broader categories. The TBC becomes a clothesline related to movable degrees of power. Each of the models presented in the following chapters will use the continuum to display the concrete techniques within that model that are available to the teacher when dealing with a discipline incident.

TEACHER PERSONALITY TYPE

There are many teachers who do not escalate or deescalate their power along a continuum, but instead wear one "face," generally doing two to five discipline actions consistently with most students. This teacher tends to have a set philosophy or orientation.

Each teacher has a deep memory of the child within himself. This memory is an accumulation of how parents, teachers, and other significant adults disciplined him when he was young. Consequently, adults parent the way they have been parented, or teach the way they have been taught. When we set limits with students, we are projecting the degree of autonomy we feel comfortable giving to students to control their own behavior, or how much we wish to be in control as the teacher. Therefore, for some teachers, the Rules and Consequences techniques may be too strong a form of teacher control, or the Relationship-Listening techniques too "touchy-feely" in nature, or the Confronting-Contracting techniques too hokey in bringing discipline issues for group discussion. Based on their personality, then, many teachers are apt to naturally—and unthinkingly—use methods and techniques that tend to cluster under one of these three schools of thought, or "faces."

The question arises: Which one of these "face" philosophies best fits your personality? The Beliefs about Discipline Inventory (presented at the end of this chapter) is a tool that lets teachers answer a series of value questions to help identify which "face" philosophically comes to them naturally—based on the "child" in them. Although teachers would want to know how to deal with situations involving each of the three "faces," the inventory can be useful in helping to identify the launching point from which the individual teacher would naturally begin any approach to discipline. Stop now and complete the inventory, so that after you are more familiar with the methods under each of these positions you will see if your values have changed. Understanding your values will also be helpful in considering Chapter 13, Discipline and Teaching as a Developmental Process, which discusses possible uses of the methods, practices, and "faces" over many years of a teaching career as you mature as a person and as a teacher.

ENDNOTES

1. C. H. Wolfgang, *Helping Aggressive and Passive Preschoolers Through Play* (Columbus, OH: Charles E. Merrill, 1977).

2. C. H. Wolfgang, B. Mackender, and M. E. Wolfgang, *Growing & Learning Through Play* (Poali, PA: Judy/Instructo, 1981).

3. C. H. Wolfgang and M. E. Wolfgang, *School for Young Children: Developmentally Appropriate Practices* (Boston: Allyn and Bacon, 1992).

4. E. H. Erikson, *Childhood and Society* (New York: Norton, 1950).

5. J. Piaget, *The Construction of Reality in the Child* (New York: Ballantine Books, 1971). J. Piaget, *The Language and Thought of the Child* (New York: World Publishing, 1971).

6. Erikson, *Childhood and Society.*

7. L. Canter and M. Canter, *Assertive Discipline: A Take-Charge Approach for Today's Educator* (Seal Beach, CA: Canter and Associates, 1976).

RELATED READINGS

Wolfgang, C. H. *Helping Aggressive and Passive Preschoolers Through Play.* Columbus, OH: Charles E. Merrill, 1977.

Wolfgang, C. H., and Glickman, C. D. *Solving Discipline Problems: Strategies for Classroom Teachers.* Boston: Allyn and Bacon, 1980.

Wolfgang, C. H., Mackender, B., and Wolfgang, M. E. *Growing & Learning Through Play.* Poali, PA: Judy/Instructo, 1981.

Wolfgang, C. H., and Wolfgang, M. E. *School for Young Children: Developmentally Appropriate Practices.* Boston: Allyn and Bacon, 1992.

BELIEFS ABOUT DISCIPLINE INVENTORY

To help you determine where your personality and the techniques you tend to use would fall under the three philosophical positions, or "faces," this 12-question inventory will give you insights about yourself. (Coercive-Legalistic will not be included here because it is a preestablished set of procedures giving the teacher no choice.) In each question, you are asked to choose between two competing value statements. For some questions, you will strongly agree with one statement and disagree with the second, making it easy for you to choose; for others, however, you will agree or disagree with both, and you must select the one with which you more closely identify. There are no "right" or "wrong" answers—but merely indicators of your own personal views.

Forced Choices.   *Instructions*: Circle *a* or *b* to indicate the statement with which you identify the most. You must chose between the two statements for each item.

1. **a.** Because students' thinking is limited, rules need to be established for them by mature adults.
   b. Each student's emotional needs must be taken into consideration, rather than having some preestablished rule imposed on all.

2. **a.** During the first class session of the new school year, the teacher needs to assign each student his or her own desk or table space, and the student should be taught routinely to take that space after transitions.
   b. Groups of students can decide through a class meeting what rules they need to govern themselves.

3. **a.** Students should be given a choice as to which topics for projects they wish to select. Once they choose, they must keep to that decision for most of that grading period.
   b. The material students must learn and the tasks to be performed must be determined by the teacher, and a specific sequence of instruction to accomplish these goals must be followed.

4. The books and similar classroom equipment are being misused, soiled, and at times destroyed. I will most likely:
   a. Hold a class meeting, show the damaged books to the class, and ask them how we may solve this problem, including what action should be taken toward a student found to be misusing books.
   b. Physically remove or limit the number of books available and observe closely to see who is misusing the books. I would then tell that student how such action was affecting other students and how I felt about the loss of such books.

5. Two students of equal power and abilities are in a rather loud verbal conflict over a classroom material. I would:

   a. Attempt to see that this does not get out of control by approaching the students, telling them of the classroom rule, and demanding that they desist in their actions, promising a sanction if they fail to comply.
   b. Avoid interfering in something that the students need to resolve themselves.

6. a. A student strongly requests not to work with the group today. I would permit this, feeling that this student has some emotional concerns related to the group experience.
   b. One student is being refused entry into group activities. I would raise this as an issue in a class meeting and ask for a discussion of the reasons and possible solutions from the student and the group.

7. The noise level in the classroom is at such a high level that it is bothering me. I would:

   a. Flick the classroom lights to get everyone's attention, ask the students to become quiet, and later praise those who are talking quietly.
   b. Select the two or three students really making most of the noise, take them aside to ask them to reflect (think) about their behavior and how it might affect others, and get an agreement from them to work quietly.

8. During the first few days of class, I would:

   a. Permit the students to test their ability to get along as a new group and make no predetermined rules until the students feel that rules are needed.
   b. Immediately establish the class rules and the fair sanction I will apply if these rules are broken.

9. My response to swearing by a student is:

   a. The student is frustrated by a classmate and has responded by swearing, so I do not reprimand the student but encourage him to talk out what is bothering him.
   b. I bring the two students together in a "knee-to-knee" confronting relationship and attempt to get them to work out this conflict while I ask questions and keep the focus on the negotiation.

10. If a student disrupts class while I am trying to lecture, I would:

   a. Ignore the disruption if possible and/or move the student to the back of the room as a consequence of his misbehavior.
   b. Express my feeling of discomfort to the student about being disrupted from my task.

11. a. Each student must realize that there are some school rules that need to be obeyed, and any student who breaks them will be punished in the same fair manner.

    b. Rules are never written in stone and can be renegotiated by the class, and sanctions will vary with each student.

12. A student refuses to put away her work or materials after using them. I would most likely:

    a. Express to the student how not putting her things away will affect future activities in this space, and how frustrating this will be for everyone. I would then leave the materials where they are for the remainder of the day.

    b. Confront the student to reflect on her behavior, think about how her non-compliance affects others, and tell her that if she cannot follow the rules, she will lose the use of the materials in the future.

Scoring Key and Interpretation

Take your responses and circle them on the tables provided:

Table 1		*Table 2*		*Table 3*	
4b	1b	2b	4a	2a	1a
6a	5b	3a	6b	3b	5a
9a	8a	7b	9b	7a	8b
12a	10b	11b	12b	11a	10a

Total number of responses in Table 1 _____
Total number of responses in Table 2 _____
Total number of responses in Table 3 _____

The table for which the total number of responses was the highest indicates the school of thought, or "face," where your values tend to be clustered. Table 1 is Relationship-Listening, Table 2 is Confronting-Contracting, and Table 3 is Rules and Consequences. The table with the next highest score would be your second choice, and the table with the least number may be the "face" that you associate with the least. If your responses are equally distributed across all three tables, you may be an eclectic teacher who picks and chooses from all philosophies. We will return to this inventory in later chapters, after a discussion of the techniques associated with each of the three "faces."

2

THE ROGERIAN (EMOTIONALLY SUPPORTIVE) MODEL

Theorist/Writer: Thomas Gordon

- *Teaching Children Self-Discipline: At Home and at School*
- *T.E.T.: Teacher Effectiveness Training*

The scene is a high school classroom where a student and teacher are involved in a discipline situation. As we watch the situation unfold, we will see the teacher use Rogerian emotionally supportive techniques. (**Bolded** words are names for techniques used by the teacher, which will be defined and explained in fuller detail later.)

The students are talking and laughing as they enter Ms. Walker's chemistry lab. As they move to their assigned seats, Ms. Walker is already checking roll; at the bell, she double-checks and marks two students as absent, sets the attendance book down, and brings the class to order.

Two minutes after the bell, while Ms. Walker is still giving the class instructions, one of her absentees walks in. His clothes are baggy and unkempt as usual, and he is playing "air drums" with two pencils. He heads to his assigned place without looking at the teacher. Ms. Walker states, "Darrin, you're late and I do believe that this is your third tardiness. You know the rule!" Darrin stops and listens to her, with his head dropped and eyes looking at the floor. He turns and yells, "Lay off, bitch. I ain't going to no detention or the office. You think I give a s--- about any of y'all?" He takes his seat and slouches deep into it.

Ms. Walker says, "Class, yesterday, I introduced you to all the concepts you need to know for experiment number 34B on page 120 of the Chemistry

Lab Workbook. I want you to now move to your lab tables and your work groups, and do this experiment like we have done others in the past. Darrin, I need you to stay where you are, at your seat, so that we may talk." The students move to their lab tables and begin to work while Ms. Walker approaches Darrin and seats herself "knee to knee" facing him. She speaks in such a manner that other students cannot hear her words.

> *MS. WALKER:* "When I am called such a name, it shows me much disrespect and causes me to lose respect from other students, and it angers me." **(I-message)**

Darrin slouches deeper into the chair and under his desk.

> *MS. WALKER:* "Darrin, we need to talk. Apparently you are quite upset. Would you like to talk about it?" **(door opener)**

Darrin shifts his weight from hip to hip, makes eye contact with Ms. Walker, and then drops his eyes, saying nothing.

> *MS. WALKER:* "You are obviously having a very bad morning, and are having some difficulty. **(active listening)** I am here to listen to you." **(door opener)**

> *DARRIN:* "Get the f--- out of my face!"

> *MS. WALKER:* "You're angry and upset, and are having a very difficult time talking. **(active listening)** There are a number of ways we can handle this. One, I can call Assistant Principal Mr. Mack and he will remove you from my classroom, which will only result in even more problems for you. **(Method 1: Teacher Wins)** Or, two, I can just ignore this name calling behavior **(Method 2: Student Wins)**, but that is unacceptable to me as a teacher. There is a third way that we can handle this difficulty. If we can talk this out, we might be able to find a 'no-lose' solution where you don't get into more trouble and I can get the respect that I need as a teacher." **(Method 3: No-Lose Problem Solving)**

> *DARRIN:* "I don't want to see 'Mack the Knife' again."

> *MS. WALKER:* "OK, can we talk about this now?"

Darrin shakes his head no.

> *MS. WALKER:* "When do you think you will be ready to talk about this— just before you go to lunch this morning or after school?"

> *DARRIN:* "Before lunch."

> *MS. WALKER:* "OK, I now want you to go quickly to the office and get a late pass and come right back and join your lab table. I will see you here in my classroom at 11:45, just before lunch period."

Darrin nods his head in agreement and departs the classroom; he soon returns from the office with a late pass and joins the other students.

The techniques used by this teacher come from the Rogerian theory and from writers such as Thomas Gordon in his book *T.E.T.: Teacher Effectiveness Training* and Clark Moustakas in *The Authentic Teacher: Sensitivity and Awareness in the Classroom.*

To set the tone for understanding Rogerian theory, consider the words of Moustakas:

> *When the adult [the teacher] loses sight of the child [the student] as a human being, when the adult fails to gather in the child's presence as a person, there is no reality between them, there is no relationship. There is no mutuality.*
>
> *And this is what happens in many situations [such as the Darrin incident] where potential growth and love exist between persons. The persons are lost. The discrepancy or issue [disrespect] becomes all that matters. And the loudest voice, the strongest figure, the person in authority carries out his office of command. Gradually the child [student] is forced into a process of desensitization where feelings and senses are muffled and subdued until eventually he is no longer aware that he is not experiencing from within. When people [teachers] reject, humiliate, hurt, belittle, control, dominate, and brutalize others [students], without any awareness of what they are doing, when there is no concern on the part of others [students] for what is being done to them, there is extreme danger that man will cease to be man, that whatever is distinctly human will be impaired or so significantly reduced that the life of man [teacher] will be as automatic as a self-moving machine and as mechanical as counting beads on an abacus.*[1]

ROGERIAN THEORY

Such popular and practical discipline books as Gordon's *T.E.T.* and Moustakas's *Authentic Teacher* are based on a school of thought first conceptualized and popularized by Carl R. Rogers in his books *Client-Centered Therapy, On Becoming a Person,* and *Freedom to Learn.* Rogers's therapeutic concepts, focused on self-concept and emotional development, marked a departure from the highly deterministic Freudian psychology therapy based on innate inner-aggressive drives.

Although the belief in the inner-person remained, Rogers did not accept the positions that the child is inherently ruled by destructive forces. Instead, he aligned with A. H. Maslow's belief that the child is born "prior to good and evil,"[2] a belief that would suggest that what a child grows to become will be a summation or embodiment of the child's experiences. The child does have an inherent capacity, but it is a capacity for being rational and capable. Rogers believes that given empathetic understanding, warmth, and openness, one will choose what is best for oneself and will become a fully functioning person, constructive and trustworthy. The child is seen as "exquisitely rational," and it is believed that problems arise from the conflict that occurs when the inherent rationality is stifled. It is felt that this "stifling" happens in the classroom when teachers set about to order, direct, or force a student to behave according to the teacher's will.

The underlying assumption of Rogerian theory is that each person is unique and thus it is impossible for one person to make appropriate decisions for another. Any two people in a given situation will experience that situation in different ways. This is because people experience and interpret stimuli based on prior encounters, goals, expectations, and attitudes. Each person will "screen" the event according to who he or she is as a person, and this screening, to a great extent, occurs at the unconscious level. Life, then, according to Rogerian theory, is a process of continually changing situations and continually changing problems in which one must make a multitude of decisions based on individual experiences and perceptions. Many of these factors about making personal decisions are hidden from one's consciousness. Therefore, within the Rogerian theoretical framework, the process or goal for the individual experiencing problems is consciously to process his or her difficulties through the vehicle of language. By expressing feelings and concerns, an individual can make decisions that will result in the most appropriate rational solution.

Let's return to our earlier example of Ms. Walker and Darrin's statement, "Lay off, bitch. I ain't going to no detention or the office. You think I give a s--- about any of y'all?" This statement and Darrin's repeated lateness are seen by Rogerians as just the tip of the iceberg. Underneath these aggressive words and behavior is a collection of fears, disappointments, and deeply angry feelings of not belonging or being rejected. "You think I give a s--- about any of y'all?" might be more appropriately interpreted as a message to the teacher and anyone willing to listen that "I am deeply unhappy, isolated, and cut off from others, and I don't expect anyone to concern themselves with me!"

A teacher such as Ms. Walker, if she is using this Rogerian model, would hear a wider message and would not fall into the trap of denying the child's underlying message by lecturing or responding with similar hostility. This model requires a very secure teacher who isn't frightened by such hostility, especially if it is expressed in front of an entire class of onlooking students.

The teacher, as we saw, took an empathic, nonjudgmental position. She simply mirrored the student's statement, behavior, and feelings ("You are obviously having a very bad morning, and are having some difficulty"), attempted to encourage the child to "talk out" his concerns, offered to share her power (Method 3: No-Lose Problem Solving), and offered her listening and empathetic help. The Rogerian teacher such as Ms. Walker believes that, given a supportive, nonjudgmental climate, the student will be able to express his problem(s) and feeling(s) and then suggest his own solutions. Whether the solutions are successful or not is not as important as the student being able to trust his own capacities to eventually master his problems.

This theory holds that a faith in the student's own problem-solving capacity relates directly to the idea of self-concept. *Self-concept* can be defined as a set of ideas and feelings that one holds about oneself as a person. A person may see himself or herself as basically competent or incompetent in meeting life's continual challenges. It is only through the opportunity to wrestle with one's own daily problems that a person becomes master of his or her own destiny. In the Darrin example, the student can enhance his self-concept only by realizing that he can define his own problems and make attempts to solve them. If the teacher had lectured or advised him, the opposite effect might have occurred and Darrin's self-concept would have been weakened in the process.

Based on this theoretical position, the teacher's role is primarily one of being a supportive, noncritical facilitator with a total commitment to the rational ability of a child to identify and solve his or her own unique problems. With this understanding, we may now turn to the techniques of Gordon and observe how he has operationalized Rogerian theory into specific teacher practices, as described in *T.E.T.: Teacher Effectiveness Training*. We will follow Gordon's procedures, using the Teacher Behavior Continuum (TBC) as our organizer in comparing the central elements or behaviors. Keep in mind that these behaviors are (1) silently looking on, (2) nondirective statements, (3) questions, (4) directive statements, (5) reinforcement, (6) modeling, and (7) physical intervention and isolation. The ranked order of these behaviors suggests an increasing use of power by the teacher and a decrease on the part of the student. It should be obvious that, given Gordon's theoretical framework, he will stress those behaviors (1, 2, and 3) that give most control to the child. With this in mind, let us begin.

T.E.T. *AND THE TEACHER BEHAVIOR CONTINUUM*

Looking On

Central to the *T.E.T.* model is the expression of open and authentic communication between teacher and student. By definition, the word *communication* suggests an exchange of ideas between people. Obviously, there is a difference between talking and hearing versus communicating. Communicating is a process whereby each party understands what the other has to say and formulates responsive messages in a way to create further understanding. Of course, all teachers will "hear" what a child says. The child who screams an obscenity is clearly heard, but, according to Gordon, the child is often not understood in terms of the meaning of the "real" message and the impact of strong feelings being expressed. Stress is placed on the teacher to use the least control possible in the process of understanding a student. That minimal control is described as *silently looking on* as the teacher *critically listens* to what a student is trying to say.

The first step on the Teacher Behavior Continuum is for the teacher simply to look at a misbehaving child. The look should be one of saying, " I see what you are doing. I have trust in your ability to correct yourself. If you need my help, I am here." The student who cannot achieve his or her own immediate solution to the problem should then be encouraged to verbalize the issue. The teacher gives the student much time and encouragement to express what is troubling him or her, with the teacher nodding or using various gestures to encourage the child to continue.

STUDENT: "Janie is a stuck-up snob. She wouldn't go to the game with us!"

TEACHER: "Uh-huh." (teacher nods while looking at the child)

Gordon, in *T.E.T.: Teacher Effectiveness Training*, stated, "Saying nothing actually communicates acceptance. Silence—critical listening—is a powerful nonverbal message that can make a student feel genuinely accepted and encourages him to share more and more with you. A student cannot talk to you about what is bothering him if you are doing the talking."[3]

Questioning (Skipping Nondirective Statements Temporarily)

At times, when students are talking to teachers they seem to have trouble beginning, or, once started, they pause in the middle of what they are saying and cannot appear to get started again. In these instances, it may be necessary to use what Gordon called "door openers or reopeners." Examples would be such questions as "I'm interested, would you like to talk more about that?" or "Would you like to go on?" Such door openers (questions) are of a nonevaluative nature. They encourage the student to explore his or her feelings more fully.

TEACHER: "Hello, Tommy. I think I see a worried look on your face. Would you like to talk about it?" (This is the use of *questioning* as a door opener.)

STUDENT: "Someone stole my pencil. This has happened three times this week!"

TEACHER: "Uh-huh." (nods while *silently looking on*—critical listening)

Using these supportive questions as door openers is quite different from using those kinds of questions that Gordon calls "roadblocks to communication." The latter are questions that probe, cross-examine, or accuse and are of little help to a student trying to find his or her own solutions. For example, "How much time did you spend on this project?" or "Did you ask permission before you did that?" are questions that impose the teacher's will and dominance. These are really camouflaged directive statements that say, "You are wrong. You need me to tell you what to do." Gordon is adamantly opposed to the use of questions or directive statements that diminish the student's capacity to rationally alter his or her own behavior. On the other hand, making nondirective statements is seen as a more active way of helping the student.

Nondirective Statements

The question now arises as to exactly how to use language to communicate with students most effectively. The most important use of language by the teacher within the *T.E.T.* model is called *active listening*. To employ silence, to acknowledge responses by silently looking on, or to use door openers as questions has a positive but limited use and, in general, reflects passive behavior on the teacher's part.

Effective communication between teacher and student involves a much more active response by the teacher through active listening and the use of *nondirective statements*. The teacher can actively communicate to the student that he or she is being understood by summarizing or mirroring the student's feelings or problems as the teacher comprehends them.

It may be helpful to look more closely to see how true communication really works, or, in short, "why people talk." Gordon says that people talk when they have an internal need, either physical or emotional, and that people encode that need in the form of spoken language so that they can be understood by others. Unfortunately, many needs, especially those related to feelings, are difficult to express in language.

The philosophical orientation of these Rogerian techniques views the child as an inherently good and rational being. If his behavior is destructive, the Rogerian explanation would be that the child is having some form of inner turmoil, which is called *flooding,* and this inner tension comes out as "acting-out" behavior. Thus, the student, under the Rogerian position, should never be viewed simply as being naughty. The teacher's helping role is to establish a nonjudgmental supportive relationship with the child and to encourage the child to communicate these feelings in words, by using the teacher as a sounding board.

Communication is a very difficult process among adults, but it can be even more difficult for students, with their limited intellectual knowledge and verbal ability. Gordon suggested that teachers and students constantly maintain one of two internal states: They are at either equilibrium or disequilibrium. A child who is full and not hungry, and who is playing happily, is at equilibrium. An hour or two later, the child begins to tire and gets inner-messages that she is beginning to get hungry, indicating a growing disequilibrium. When this hunger is very strong, the child attempts to communicate this inner need to her mother. As seen here, the first and surface communication, when heard by the mother, is not always what the child really means.

CHILD (in a whining, demanding voice): "Mom, when is dad going to get home from work?"

MOTHER: "Ann, you know that dad always gets home at six o'clock."

The child has failed to communicate her real need and the mother has failed to hear what was *really* being said—thus poor communication. What the child really meant to say was, "Mom, I am very hungry and I don't think I can wait until dad gets home to eat." When the child has an inner-need, she must express it externally, and so she tries *verbally encoding* that need to express her wants.

Now, let's replay the discussion, this time with the mother using *active listening*:

CHILD (in a whining, demanding voice): "Mom, when is dad going to get home from work?"

MOTHER: "At six o'clock, but you would like dad to get home sooner?" (*active listening*)

CHILD: "Ah, he'll be late again!"

MOTHER: "You are worried that he might not be on time today." (*active listening*)

CHILD: "I don't think I can wait for dad if he's going to be late."

MOTHER: (looks at child, nods, and smiles—*acknowledgments*)

CHILD: "I'm starving!"

MOTHER: "You are very hungry, and you'd like to eat now and not wait for dad because he might be late?" (*active listening*)

CHILD: "Yeah. Uh-h-h... "

MOTHER: "Would you like to tell me more?" (*door opener*)

CHILD: "Yeah, while I was waiting for the bus it rained and I forgot to bring my lunch into the shelter. It got wet and was ruined, and all I had to eat for lunch was a banana."

MOTHER: "Oh, that *does* make a difference. The rule is that we wait for dad so we can all eat dinner together, but because you missed out on lunch today why don't you have a glass of milk and two oatmeal cookies to tide you over."

Active listening is a technique for improving communication between child and teacher whereby the child is encouraged to repeatedly "talk out" a problem, and the adult's role is to attempt to mirror back to the child the emotional feelings the adult thinks he or she is hearing from the child. If you take first or surface communication statements from the child as fact, especially when the child is flooded, you may not hear what the child is really attempting to communicate. The adult's nonverbal behavior of nodding the head (called *acknowledgments*) and asking questions such as, "Would you like to tell me more?" are called *door openers,* and simply serve to encourage the child to continue to talk in an attempt to truly communicate (see Figure 2–1).

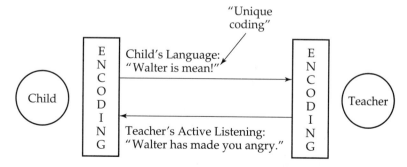

FIGURE 2–1   Student and Teacher Communication

Let's return to the opening vignette, where Darrin asked his teacher, "You think I give a s--- about any of y'all?" We must realize that it will only be after much active listening that we may discover Darrin's real feelings and the problems he is facing. The student's first attempt to *encode* his feelings by using this hostile verbal aggression is considered a *unique coding* and reveals only the surface of the deeper problems he is facing. We must not take such uniquely coded statements at face value, but permit the student to continue expressing through language while we mirror with active listening (nondirective statements) our understanding of what the child is attempting to really say. Figure 2–2 provides examples of feeling words that the teacher may use when doing active listening and mirroring the student's feelings.

Ms. Walker enters her empty classroom at 11:45 and finds Darrin, as they had agreed, seated at his desk, with his lunch and soda unopened before him.

MS. WALKER: "Oh, Darrin, I see that you have brought your lunch—well, I have mine too."

She seats herself knee to knee (*knee-to-knee conferencing*) before the boy.

"Feel free to eat your lunch. I'm going to eat mine as we talk. I'm stuck with a peanut butter and jelly sandwich today. What do you have?"

DARRIN: "Meat, I guess . . . baloney."

MS. WALKER: "Well, I think that's better than mine. Gee, you were angry this morning. We need to talk about what is going on!"

DARRIN: (drops eyes)

MS. WALKER: (Three very long minutes pass with total silence—*critical listening*) "Would you like to tell me what is happening with you these days?" (*door opener*)

DARRIN: "I hate this f-----' school."

Negative Feelings		Positive Feelings	
confused	sad	appreciate	happy
disappointed	scared	better	joyful
frightened	sorry	cheerful	like
hate	unfair	enjoy	love
hurt	unhappy	excited	pleased
left out	want to get even	glad	proud
mad	want to give up	good	successful
	worried	great	wonderful

FIGURE 2–2   Example of Feeling Words

MS. WALKER: (silence as she munches on her sandwich—*critical listening*)

DARRIN: "Everybody's on my case!"

MS. WALKER: "You feel that everyone is telling you what to do." (*active listening*)

DARRIN: "Yeah, I get crap from my mom, and crap at school!"

TEACHER: (silence—*critical listening;* makes eye contact with Darrin and nods her head—*acknowledgment*)

DARRIN: "Jeez, the crap my mother makes me do!"

TEACHER: "Your mother is requiring you to do things that you dislike." (*active listening*)

DARRIN: "S---, Jimmy isn't my kid! Why do *I* have to watch him?"

TEACHER: "You are responsible for Jimmy and must take care of him." (*active listening*)

DARRIN: "The guys are always bustin' my chops about that. Yeah, I never get to hang out."

TEACHER: "You are required to watch Jimmy, and your friends tease you about it."

DARRIN: "Yeah, and that damn bus."

TEACHER: (silence—*critical listening*)

DARRIN: "This is the fourth freakin' time it's been late!" (three minutes of silence) "Damn bus!"

TEACHER: "Would you like to tell me about that?" (*door opener*)

DARRIN: "Well, I'm stuck with watching my little brother when my mother leaves. That damn day-care bus was late picking him up. Now I'm late and get detention after class. I ain't going to no detention—my mother will whip my ass."

TEACHER: (nods—*acknowledgment*)

DARRIN: "My mother will whip my ass if I don't watch Josh."

TEACHER: "Let me see if I understand what you are telling me. You must watch Jimmy, and the day-care bus is late, which makes you late for school, and you also have to watch Josh or you will be in big trouble with your mother." (*critical listening*)

DARRIN: "I can't stay in no detention. I have to get Josh or the big kids will pick on him."

"Douglas, what I think I hear you saying..."

John Anfin, from *Phi Delta Kappan.*

> *TEACHER:* "Oh, I see. Staying after school for detention keeps you from picking up and watching Josh, and that will get you in trouble with your mother." (*critical listening*)

In the preceding dialogue, we see the teacher helping the student express feelings that were uniquely "encoded" and unclear at first ("Damn bus!"). Through critical and active listening, the teacher finally hears the student's central problem and the feelings that were deeply troublesome.

Now that the teacher has some understanding as to the problems of her student, what should the teacher do? Should she call Darrin's mother, tell a school counselor or administrator, or give Darrin a solution for his difficulties? Gordon would not advise any of these alternatives. He would describe such a response as a "roadblock," called "advising, offering solutions, or suggestions." *T.E.T.* provides a helpful construct for the teacher to use in answering these questions and in defining what the teacher's response should be.

Who Owns the Problem?

The key to these issues in *T.E.T.* is: Who owns the problem—the teacher or the child? As shown in Figure 2–3, all behaviors of the student can be placed on a "window" and divided into three areas: (1) those behaviors that indicate the student is having a problem (i.e., other students will not pick him as a team member); (2) a no-problem behavior (i.e., a child works quietly at his desk); (3) those behav-

Gordon

Student owns the problem	← Student is angry because he or she is not chosen by the team.
No-problem behavior	← Student works quietly at desk.
Teacher owns the problem	← Student interrupts.

FIGURE 2–3   Problem Ownership

iors by the student that have a direct and concrete effect on the teacher, causing the teacher to "own" the problem (i.e., student interrupts while another child is being helped).

When the problem belongs to the student ("I can't find my pencil" or "Mrs. Jones won't let me do so-and-so"), the role of the teacher is to use critical listening (silently looking on) and door openers (questions), and to periodically mirror the child's concerns or messages with active listening (nondirective statements). If the problem is owned by the teacher, in that it has a concrete effect on the teacher, then she may introduce an I-message. This is a matter-of-fact directive statement containing the word *I* that expresses to the student the description of the student's behavior and how it is having a negative effect on the teacher. It also tells the student how the teacher feels about these actions; for example: "When gym equipment is left in the aisle, I might trip, and I'm afraid I might fall and be hurt." The I-message must contain the sequence of *behavior, effect, feeling.* Once an I-message is expressed and the student has heard how her behavior is interfering with the teacher's needs, the teacher returns to critical listening (silently looking on), active listening (nondirective statements), and, if need be, door openers (questions). The following dialogue provides examples of each of these behaviors.

TEACHER: "Carol, when lunch trash is left on the table instead of being thrown away, I must pick it up before the next lunch group can be seated. I find this frustrating!" (*I-message*)

STUDENT: "I'm always getting picked on! Everyone *always* picks on me!"

TEACHER: "You feel that everyone is making unfair demands on you." (*active listening, nondirective statement*)

STUDENT: "Well, everyone picks on me."

TEACHER: "Uh-huh." (*critical listening, nondirective listening*)

STUDENT: (Silence)

TEACHER: "Would you like to tell me more?" (*door opener, question*)

STUDENT: "Well, Mrs. Jones makes me pass out the papers and lots of other dorky jobs for her, and Mrs. Anderson has made me clean out the animal cages in the biology lab for the last two weeks."

TEACHER: "You feel that it is unfair for you to be given extra jobs by teachers, and therefore you do not need to clean up after yourself at lunchtime." (*active listening, nondirective statement*)

STUDENT: "Well, it is unfair, but I guess I could throw my lunch trash away. Gee, I didn't know it was such a problem for you. But I'm going to tell Mrs. Anderson, 'No more hamster cages for me!'"

The preceding dialogue reveals a problem clearly owned by the teacher. The student's *behavior* (leaving behind lunch trash) had a concrete effect on the teacher (the teacher had to pick it up and it interfered with her ability to seat other children), and in turn the teacher described her feelings (frustrated). We can also see that the teacher did not use any forms of power-related behavior to manipulate the outcome. After delivering an I-message, the teacher returned the problem to the student, and the teacher maintained a nonjudgmental stance (see Figures 2–4 and 2–5).

There are other behaviors engaged in by students about which a teacher might hold very strong feelings. However, when these are investigated closely, it may be found that they do not have a concrete effect on the teacher, in which case an I-message would have little impact. Students' hairstyles, short dresses, hand-holding in the halls, poor posture, and the choosing of friends all may evoke strong feelings in a teacher, but these student behaviors involve clashes in values and cannot be said to affect the teacher directly. They are simply matters of personal taste. Gordon has warned against trying to change students to conform with a teacher's values by I-messages or "roadblocks." Gordon suggested the use of values clarification, one of our models described in Chapter 3, to deal with problems concerning differences in values.

Notice that in the earlier vignette Darrin had two problems—he wanted to "hang out" with his friends and he was late for school—but the teacher did not solve the problems for him. Darrin owned these problems; the teacher facilitated Darrin's process of thinking through and then acting on the problems. We as teachers are solidly motivated to nurture and help children. We may wish to be Superteachers and see our role as the person who solves all problems in the classroom. If we do that, however, we rob the children of the real experience of clashing and interacting with others—an essential process that enables them to acquire the skills necessary to solve their own problems and become autonomous. In dealing with problems that involve students, it is important to determine whether it is the student or the teacher who owns the problem. These questions will help:

1. Does the student's action or problem take away the teacher's or classmates' rights?
   (Jeff takes three handouts while others have only one or did not get one. By his actions, Jeff is moving to take a fourth. This requires teacher intervention.)

Poor Example: "I want you to get your feet off that table now!"
This is a you-message implying guilt. It contains a poor definition of the improper behavior, no example of the effect, and a lack of expression of the teacher's feelings.

Good Example: "When feet are put on the table (behavior), they scratch and destroy the table surface, and I am responsible for protecting school property. I get in trouble with my administrators (effect), and I therefore am fearful and annoyed (feelings)."

Poor Example: "When students run in the hall (behavior), I don't like it!"
The message starts effectively with a good statement of behavior, but no effect is given. "I don't like it" is a value judgment rather than an expression of the teacher's feelings.

Good Example: "When students run in the hall (behavior), they may fall and get injured or injure others, and I am responsible for keeping students safe (effect), and that makes me frightened (feelings)."

More Examples of Good I-Messages

"When tables are not cleaned after lunch (behavior), it will make these tables unusable for the next group of students (effect), and I am afraid (feelings) the extra cleaning will slow down the cafeteria schedule and everyone will not have time to eat."

"When I am told to 'shut up' when I am carrying on a discussion with the class (behavior), I am not able to explain the lab rules to everyone (effect), and I am fearful (feelings) that someone will get hurt using the acids and chemistry equipment."

"When students lean out the classroom windows (behavior), I am afraid (feelings) that they will fall out and get seriously injured (effect)."

"When trash paper is left on the floor (behavior), I am responsible for cleaning up my classroom for the next teacher before I leave and it causes me lots of extra work and makes me late for my next class (effect), and I get annoyed and exhausted (feelings)."

"When people scream indoors (behavior), it hurts my ears (effect) and I get angry (feelings)."

"When people write or scribble in our good schoolbooks (behavior), it destroys them (effect). I am responsible for their care, and I am afraid (feelings) we soon will have no books to share or read."

"When objects are thrown (behavior), they may hit people's eyes and hurt them (effect), and I am the teacher who must keep people safe, and that worries (feelings) me."

"When students are late to class (behavior), I need to repeat my first instructions, which wastes of lot of classroom time (effect), and that exhausts and frustrates (feelings) me."

FIGURE 2–4   Example of Poor and Good I-Messages

Student's ACTION	Teacher's I-MESSAGE
Joe starts to talk to Ryan while the teacher is lecturing. He talks loudly enough that he starts to disturb everyone listening to the story.	"When students talk while I am lecturing (behavior), I have a hard time speaking so everyone can hear (effect), and that makes me frustrated (feelings)."
Katy leaves her equipment scattered across the lab table when she returns to her seat and readies herself to depart.	"When students leave equipment out on the lab tables (behavior), I am fearful (feelings) that others will knock them over and get hurt (effect), and I am responsible for keeping equipment and students safe."
When the school bell rings, Caroline runs at full speed through the door and down the stairs.	"When students run down the stairs (behavior), I am fearful (feelings) that people will fall and get injured (effect), and my job is to keep people safe."
Mary appears in front of the teacher and, with hysterical excitement and rapid-fire delivery, begins to talk so loudly and at such a pace that the teacher cannot comprehend.	"When students shout (behavior), I can't understand what is being said (effect), and I am disappointed (feelings) that I can't help."
The teacher is talking to a parent when Carlos interrupts her and starts talking.	"It makes it hard for me (feelings) to understand two people who are talking to me at the same time (behavior), and I become confused (effect)."
Mark deliberately pushes Tim while lining up at the water fountain.	"When students are pushed (behavior), it is dangerous (effect), and that frightens me (feelings) because I am in charge of safety."
Ali and Chris fight over a book, pulling it back and forth.	"When books are pulled (behavior), I am afraid (feelings) that they will get damaged and destroyed and we will not have them anymore (effect)."

FIGURE 2–5   I-Messages

2. Is the safety of materials, classmates, the teacher, or the student himself involved?
   (In industrial arts class, Sean uses the band saw without wearing protective glasses. This requires teacher intervention.)
3. Is the student too young and thus incapable of "owning" or solving this problem?
   (Christine wishes to move a friend's car on the school parking lot but does not have a driver's license. This requires teacher intervention.)

If the answer to any of these questions is *yes*, then the teacher owns the problem and must respond. Response techniques will be I-messages, active listening, door openers, acknowledgments, and possibly the Six Steps to Problem Solving (discussed later).

The concept of problem ownership clearly tells teachers to inhibit their "rescuer" tendencies.

STUDENT: "Mr. Johnson, my pencil is missing!"

TEACHER: "What are you going to do to get another?" *(door opener)*

In reality, 80 to 90 percent of all problems faced by students in the classroom belong to them. The guidelines for problem ownership suggest that we as teachers must not allow our need to help or our fear of chaos to prompt us to move too quickly and without thinking, thus robbing the children of the experience of solving their own problems.

Emotions, Anger, and Feelings

Many of us have suffered the experience of another driver cutting in front of us too quickly or having a similar near-accident because of another driver's poor driving actions. We quickly respond by swerving out of the way, and then perhaps sounding our car horn, visually glaring, shouting, or even swearing at the other driver. For the next 10 minutes, we remain very angry, before gradually calming down. Our actions—sounding the horn, glaring, shouting, even swearing at the other driver—were for the purposes of making the other person feel guilty for the careless behavior and clearly sending a message of anger—"you dummy."

In sending an I-message to students that expresses anger, we will produce guilt in those students and they will hear this message as a You-message. Anger is almost always expressed and directed at another person and involves guilt.

There are two forms of feelings: primary feelings and secondary feelings. Looking at the dangerous driver example, we may really see that our first or *primary feeling* was fear, arising from the genuine risk of an accident. Then once the incident has passed and we are relieved to see that we have avoided the accident, we now become angry. We want to show our *secondary feeling* of anger to the "dummy" as a way of punishing that driver. In dealing with students, then, Gordon[4] requires us first to determine our primary feelings and then express the I-message with the use of a primary feeling, rather than expressing it with anger—a secondary feeling—in order to minimize the guilt that the student will feel.

Recall the opening vignette: "Darrin stops and listens to her, with his head dropped and eyes looking at the floor. He turns and yells, 'Lay off, bitch. I ain't going to no detention or the office. You think I give a s--- about any of y'all?' He takes his seat and slouches deep into it."

Much like the close call while driving, we may feel—and rather quickly—the secondary feelings of anger at Darrin, but there was a primary feeling of embarrassment or fear that preceded the feelings of anger. It is this primary feeling that needs to be delivered in an I-message, rather than anger. "When I hear such harsh fighting names directed at me (behavior), I am embarrassed and fearful (feelings) that this will hurt my relationship with the person and hurt my authority and respect with the students in my class (effect)." (See Figure 2–4 for examples of feeling words that may indicate primary feelings.)

Directive Statements

I can imagine some of you shaking your heads in amazement and thinking, "Do you mean to say that this fellow Gordon says for me never to tell students what to do? He must be some kind of a crazy guy!" Never fear. Actually, Gordon does believe that there are times when teachers must use very strong directive statements with students, such as the giving of orders, directions, or commands. When directive statements are used correctly, they are described by Gordon as strong "influencing attempts" by the teacher. If a student is in some immediate danger, naturally it is appropriate for the teacher to command, "Turn down that flame quickly. It is in danger of exploding" or "Don't jump now—someone is climbing underneath!" or "Watch your head!" Such "influencing attempts" are generally acceptable to students, and they are willing to comply. No true conflict arises between teacher and student as a result. The difficulty occurs when teachers overuse commands or direct too strongly. Then, in reaction, students begin to resist and the teacher and student find themselves in conflict. When this occurs, such directive statements again become roadblocks, and the teacher will need to return to active listening to reestablish the relationship.

Gordon cited the following examples of directive statements that should be avoided by teachers.

1. Ordering, commanding, directing. *Example: "You, stop playing with your pencil and finish that test right now."*
2. Warning, threatening. *Example: "You had better straighten up, young man, if you want to pass this course."*
3. Moralizing, preaching, giving "shoulds" and "oughts." *Example: "You know what happens when you hang around with 'that gang'—you get into trouble. You ought to choose your friends more wisely."*
4. Advising, offering solutions or suggestions. *Example: "What you need to do is to make a list and then put yourself on a time schedule to get these things done on time."*
5. Teaching, lecturing, giving logical arguments. *Example: "Let's look at what is going to happen. If you do not bring your gym clothing you will not be able to take PE and you will fail that class."*

(Each of the preceding roadblocks presents a teacher's solution to a student's problem. The next five communicate judgments, evaluations, and, at times, put-downs.)

6. Judging, criticizing, disagreeing, blaming. *Example: "You're just not the student that your sister was."*

7. Name-calling, stereotyping, labeling. *Example: "You're always acting like the class clown. When are you going to grow up?"*
8. Interpreting, analyzing, diagnosing. *Example: "You're always trying to find the easiest way to get around your homework."*
9. Praising, agreeing, giving positive evaluation. *Example: "You are the best student I have in this class. I'm sure you will want to be chairperson of this committee."*
10. Reassuring, sympathizing, consoling, supporting. *Example: "I also found that course difficult when I first tried it, but once you get into it you'll find it easier."*[5]

The last two roadblocks (numbers 9 and 10) are examples of strong reinforcing techniques that are central to some of the models that will be summarized in the following chapters. It is interesting to note that certain strategies held to be of utmost importance to some experts are scorned by others. Gordon's interpretation of reinforcement must be closely read to understand the later differences with other writers.

Reinforcement

The resolution of conflict within the *T.E.T.* models relates to Gordon's definition of two types of authority and how the teacher uses his or her power with students. *Type I authority* is desirable and is based on a person's expertise, knowledge, and experiences. An individual obtains the power inherent in Type I authority by being judged as one who is wise and expert enough to be listened to by students, and is an individual sought after for advice. *Type II authority* is undesirable. It is aligned with a power-based position that enables a teacher to (1) dispense certain benefits that students need or want (reward or positive reinforcement) or (2) inflict discomfort or painless punishment on students (negative reinforcement). Later we will discuss how those who endorse the Rules and Consequences face use reinforcement and rewards as a central tool in techniques to get students to change. The Relationship-Listening writers such as Gordon dramatically disagree with such an approach. Gordon sees the use of both positive and negative reinforcements as a manipulation and misuse of power by a teacher, which will eventually produce defensive reaction mechanisms in students to deal with such authoritarian power. Gordon would suggest that if we see the following behavior in our students, we may need to investigate our use of power. These following behaviors indicate the use of Type II authority:

- *Rebelling, resisting, defying*
- *Retaliating*
- *Lying, sneaking, hiding feelings*
- *Blaming others, tattling*
- *Cheating, copying, plagiarizing*
- *Bossing, bullying, pushing others around*
- *Needing to win, hating to lose*
- *Organizing, forming alliances*

- *Submitting, complying, buckling under*
- *Apple polishing*
- *Conforming, taking no risks, trying nothing new*
- *Withdrawing, dropping out, fantasizing, regressing*[6]

Finally, even the teacher who has Type I authority and uses silently looking on, nondirective statements, door openers, and I-statements will still run into conflict with an individual child. The occasions will be less frequent but still inevitable. The *T.E.T.* model provides a resolution for such conflict. Gordon has defined *conflict* as a collision occurring between teacher and student where their *behaviors* interfere with each other's attainment of their own needs, and thus *both parties own the problem*. For example:

TEACHER: (returns to the classroom to discover a student taking a pencil from the teacher's desk) "When pencils are taken from my desk, I cannot find one to do my work and I must pay to purchase new ones. This has happened a number of times, and I find it annoying." (*I-message, directive statements*)

STUDENT: "Well, each time I return from music class I find someone has taken my pencil. This has happened three weeks in a row."

In this example, both teacher and student own the problem and they find themselves in conflict. Gordon suggests that such problems are usually resolved by using two methods that result in either the teacher or the student winning. In *Method I,* the teacher wins by using authority and power, and the student loses.

TEACHER: "Well, you're just going to have to learn that you cannot be permitted to steal from the teacher's desk. For the remainder of this week you will not be permitted to go for recess (or to the pep rally)." (Judging, criticizing, blaming, and punishing are creating an obstacle to the student's rational capacity to solve his or her problems.)

We can restate the dialogue to show *Method II,* where the student wins and the teacher loses.

TEACHER: "Someone has taken your pencil."

STUDENT: "Yes, and if you had not left class to go to the teacher's lounge, you would have been here to prevent someone from taking my pencil. My father is really angry, and he said if I have one more thing stolen from my desk he is going to come to see the principal."

TEACHER: "Well, uh, I don't ever want you to take things from my desk again."

This is an example of *Method II,* where the student wins when the teacher gives up or ignores the student's actions. These win-lose methods both center on a "power struggle" between teacher and student, and in each case the loser goes away feeling angry and resentful. Many teachers unknowingly use one of these methods. Some teachers use both, which is even more destructive, as the teacher swings from an authoritarian position to one of being permissive. They appear highly erratic and unpredictable and leave the student confused. Gordon proposes an alternative solution called *Method III*, where the conflict is resolved without the teacher or student using or losing power.

TEACHER: "Someone has taken your pencil." (*active listening, nondirective statement*)

STUDENT: "Well, I probably shouldn't have taken yours, but I really need a pencil for the test next period—and someone keeps stealing mine."

TEACHER: "Can you think of how we may solve this problem for now so we will both have our pencils and both feel OK?"

STUDENT: "Well, it only happens on Tuesday when I go to music class. I could take my pencil with me, but I don't use pencils in music class, and I really don't want to carry it around."

TEACHER: "Taking your pencil to music class does not seem to be the solution." (*active listening, nondirective statement*)

STUDENT: "Yeah, I wonder if I could put my pencil somewhere else in the classroom on Tuesdays when I go to music—somewhere where it will be safe. And I'm going to bring this problem to our class meeting to see if we can get people to stop taking my pencil."

TEACHER: "It sounds like you have begun to solve your problem." (*active listening, nondirective statement*)

STUDENT: "Could I put it in your desk?"

We can see that *Method III*—"no lose"—is a conflict-solving process in which the teacher does active listening and uses I-messages until he or she fully hears what the child's problems and needs are, and then they "put their heads together" until a solution can be found that is acceptable to both. *Method III* creates a "no-lose" result, and no power struggle is involved. The solution can be suggested by either the student or the teacher, but the final agreement must be acceptable to both members involved in the conflict.

In the opening vignette, we saw Ms. Walker use these three methods of problem solving with Darrin. "There are a number of ways we can handle this. One, I can call Assistant Principal Mr. Mack and he will remove you from my classroom, which will only result in even more problems for you **(Method 1: Teacher Wins).** Or, two, I can just ignore this name calling behavior **(Method 2: Student Wins),** but that is unacceptable to me as a teacher. There is a third way that we can handle this difficulty. If we can talk this out, we might be able to find a 'no-lose' solution where you don't get into more trouble and I can get the respect that I need as a teacher" **(Method 3: No-Lose Problem Solving).**

Explaining these three methods to Darrin is not a threat but simply a reality explanation to give him a perspective on the use of power. It is an invitation by Ms.

Walker to share her power and enter into an authentic relationship of shared problem solving.

Gordon also suggests that to create a "no-lose" climate, the teacher can introduce the following six steps as a process for *Method III* problem solving:

The Six Steps to Problem Solving

- *Step 1. Defining the Problem:* With the use of active listening and I-messages, the teacher helps a student or an entire class focus on a problem that affects them. During this defining step, the teacher should not attempt to provide a solution or make an evaluation, but instead simply attempt to get everyone involved, to clarify their needs.
- *Step 2. Generating Possible Solutions:* During this second step, the goal is to brainstorm many different solutions for the problem, again without attempting to make an evaluation of the ideas presented. Premature evaluation of solutions will limit creativity, and the teacher might need to use I-messages to keep the discussion guided toward brainstorming.
- *Steps 3 and 4. Evaluating and Deciding on Solution(s):* Having made a list of the possible solutions in Step 2, the teacher and student, or group, need to go over each solution to determine which ones can be agreed upon by all involved. If the teacher or student cannot live with the solution being considered, they can express this through I-messages. It is important that all solutions be considered fully. The teacher will have to use much active listening to achieve this end.
- *Steps 5 and 6. Implementing and Evaluating Solution(s):* During the final steps, a clear agreement must be established as to who will do what and when they will begin. At this time, those involved should set a time to meet again to reevaluate the results.[7]

In using the *Method III* ("no-lose") conflict-solving process, Gordon suggests that there are some problems outside the teacher's "area or spheres of freedom." He provides a chart that looks much like a target with a bull's-eye, and places the teacher in the center. This center area represents activities—such as classroom organization, rules, assignments, and so forth—that are within the teacher's "area of freedom." In turn, each circle moving out from the center is labeled "principal," "superintendent," "school board," and so on (see Figure 2–6). Each new circle represents a higher level of authority that can limit the teacher's freedom to make certain decisions. For example, the state law requires compulsory education for all students, so if by *Method III* the teacher and class were to decide that school attendance should be elective, there would be no way to implement their decision. This issue is simply outside their realm of decision making. In other words, there are certain social constraints within which both the student and teacher must live.

Although *T.E.T.* rejects the systematic use of *reinforcers*, which we will see described later, Gordon does acknowledge the need to create a classroom that is supportive of various activities. He suggests that the classroom environment can be modified in a systematic and creative way to alleviate student disruption. It can

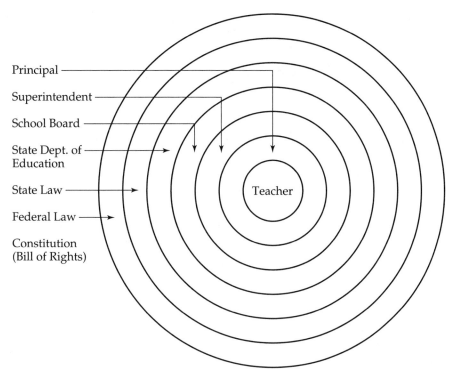

Principal

Superintendent

School Board

State Dept. of Education

State Law

Federal Law

Constitution (Bill of Rights)

Teacher

Each outer sphere limits the teacher's authority to permit certain student behavior or to make certain rules.

FIGURE 2–6   Spheres of Authority

be changed to enrich the learning space and activities. In modifying the environment, time is another variable that relates to certain student problems. The effective teacher knows that at certain times in the day it is better to introduce difficult concepts to students, while at other times students tend to be irritable, which can make such learning difficult. Time, within the *T.E.T.* model, is organized and viewed in three ways: (1) diffused time, (2) individual time, and (3) optimum time.[8]

When students are working closely with others in a busy classroom, they need to use a lot of energy for screening out stimuli in order to concentrate on such work as reading or working a math problem. *Diffused time* is the time period in which students work in close social contact. Students can effectively function only for a limited time in such a stimulating environment before becoming fatigued. It is necessary, therefore, for students to have some *individual time* where they can be by themselves for a short period (for example, a "quiet corner" or an individual study carrel). The third classification, *optimum time*, is a period during the day when a student is able to meet individually with the teacher or a fellow student. If this time is not provided for, the child might attempt to fulfill his need for personal attention by being disruptive. This misbehavior forces the teacher to deal with the student and in turn gives the one-to-one contact that is desired. With these time classifications in mind, the teacher is encouraged to plan the day deliberately to create a balance of all three forms of time to maintain a teaching-learning environment that maximizes a "hassle-free" climate for child growth.

THREE SPHERES OF RELATIONSHIPS[9]

Just as students need to deal with others through three types of time, so too does the teacher need to deal with the class through three spheres of relationships.

Adults who are placed in charge of institutions (e.g., hospitals, prisons, schools) or business sites (e.g., airline counter, store check-out line), when under day-in and day-out stress, can begin to show *institutional behavior*. They begin to deal with the public in a mechanical (nonauthentic) manner, showing curt speech, flat expressionless behavior, and an unthinking administration of the rules. They exhibit little consideration of the needs of the individuals with whom they are dealing and they communicate no warmth. If we are not very careful, this same attitude begins to be seen in the behavior of teachers in the middle and high school classroom, especially if there are too many students, too few supervisors (such as in the cafeteria or study hall), and too little equipment and classroom materials.

The airline counter attendant is burned out because she has to manage too large a number of passengers. A snowstorm has grounded five flights and she must deal with literally hundreds of angry passengers; the situation is obviously out of balance. Teachers working in an imbalanced classroom (too many kids, not enough materials) begin to become burned out and take on institutional behavior. Students spend many hours in school and classroom settings, and they must have a significant emotional investment by teachers. To go days, weeks, or months dealing with teachers or staff (including office personnel) who are depressive and burned out can have a real and lasting destructive effect on students. Even a busy parent caring for a very small number of her own children, after a few busy weeks, suddenly stops and asks herself, "When is the last time I just stopped and totally listened to my child?" She feels guilty when she realizes that it has been many weeks or that she cannot remember how long it has been. We cannot permit this to occur in today's classrooms. Thus, we use the three spheres of relationships construct to determine how we use our time with students.

There are three basic spheres in a teacher's relationships with students: *Sphere 1: one to one, Sphere 2: one to group,* and *Sphere 3: one to all* (see Figure 2–7). Viewed in reverse order, we see that the *one-to-all sphere* is a lecture format where the students must sit passively, refrain from communicating, and listen to the teacher speak. They feel no affection coming from the teacher and feel depersonalized—thus, one teacher to all students. In the classroom, this might occur during a classroom lecture.

One to One	A teacher interacts with one student (knee to knee).	The students receives near total emotional attention by the teacher and may dominate the conservation.
One to Group	A teacher interacts with a small group of four to eight students.	The student feels more emotional connection with the teacher and peers, but needs to share conversation with peers.
One to All	A teacher speaks to or teaches the entire group of students.	The student feels little emotional contact through spatial distance with the teacher and must generally inhibit the desire to talk rather than simply listen.

FIGURE 2–7   Spheres of Relationships

The *one-to-group sphere* occurs where the teacher is seated together with a group of six to eight students and there is conversation among all members of the group. An example of this would be when the teacher is seated with students at lab or group work. There is much more warmth felt among this smaller group, but students do have to share the teacher's warmth and attention with their tablemates— thus, one teacher to a group of up to eight students.

The *one-to-one sphere* is the time where the teacher and student are totally alone with one another, as with knee-to-knee conferencing. The student can receive total warmth and attention from the teacher and is free to dominate the conversation. Rogerian techniques—such as active listening, door openers, and acknowledgments—can be very helpful in communicating with the student during this one-to-one sphere of relationship.

We cannot leave it to chance and hope that every student will get sufficient personal time with a teacher. If we do this, the quiet and less assertive students will fall through the cracks. In staff meetings and during teacher planning time, we must use this three spheres construct in planning the students' semester to assure that each student will have a relationship with the teacher in each of the three spheres. Some schools accomplish this through academic advisement groups. A school system can have a rich collection of materials and well-designed classrooms but still have teachers who are spending 100 percent of their time dealing with students in the third sphere of *one to all*. These teachers are "lifeguarding," directing traffic and activities and dealing with the students in a custodial manner. In such a case, they are expressing cold, institutional behavior. Test to see if this is occurring in your school by asking: What are the teachers doing during nonclassroom time, such as in the cafeteria, during sporting events, and so on? If no adult is seated with the students, then the teachers are merely playing "lifeguard."

Modeling

Although the use of modeling is more systematically used in the Confronting-Contracting techniques, the *T.E.T.* model acknowledges its importance. For the teacher using *T.E.T.*, the rule of thumb is: Do it, don't talk about it! Practice, don't preach! In other words, the teacher, by her every action, is modeling to the students behaviors that reflect the teacher's values. Greater problems arise when the teacher attempts to "teach" students to behave in one way while she behaves in an opposite manner. The injunction to "Do as I say, not as I do" produces a double standard that is easily recognized by students. Gordon would suggest that we as teachers look closely at our school and class rules and ask: Do the rules allow the adults to behave in one way while denying the same behavior to nonadults? Can teachers hit students (corporal punishment), whereas acts of fighting among students are severely punished? Do teachers "cut" the lunch line, whereas students must wait their turn? Are teachers permitted to smoke in school, whereas students are not? Such questions require us to introspect closely and ask ourselves what exactly are the values that we are modeling. A teacher's modeled behavior has a powerful effect on student behavior.

T.E.T. also addresses the modeling of behavior that a teacher uses while resolving a conflict with a student. Do we retreat to *Method I* power behaviors that enable only the teacher to employ his authority to win? Or do we give in and use *Method II*, wherein we become permissive, and lose to the student? The *Method III* ("no-lose") technique of problem solving models the type of authentic behavior that helps relationships between the teacher and students. A youngster, having seen *Method III* techniques modeled by the teacher, may then begin to use similar techniques with adults and peers.

Physical Intervention and Isolation

The use of physical behaviors by the teacher, such as inhibiting a disruptive child by removing her from the classroom, is not explicitly dealt with in *T.E.T.* We may infer, though, that such strong measures would not be acceptable within the *T.E.T.* framework, except in a case where a student physically endangers herself or others. A reasonable teacher would be justified in intervening to keep students safe. The use of isolation or physical force to coerce students would be an extreme form of a "roadblock" to communication and would be clearly rejected by *T.E.T.*

SUMMARY

By using the Teacher Behavior Continuum (TBC) in Figure 2–8, we may now summarize and outline the "tools" that Gordon has provided to the teacher in his *T.E.T.: Teacher Effectiveness Training* model. Figure 2–8 classifies those tools as overt teacher actions and covert preplanning activities.

The overt behaviors are those outward actions taken by the teacher that can be clearly observed and defined. These are (1) critical listening, (2) acknowledgments,

Looking On	Nondirective Statements	Questions	Directive Statements	Modeling	Reinforcement	Physical Intervention/ Isolation
(1) Critical listening (2) Acknowledgment-type responses (gestures)	(4) Active listening (mirroring feelings): "You're worried about getting an exam soon." (5) I-messages (behavior-effect-feeling): "When I find paper left on the floor..."	(3) Door openers: "Do you want to talk more about it?"		(6) *Method III:* "no-lose" problem solving (7) Six Steps to Problem Solving 1. Defining 2. Generating 3. Evaluating 4. Deciding 5. Implementing 6. Evaluating (a) Daily actions	(b) Reorganizing space (c) Reorganizing time (diffused, individual, optimum) (d) Three Spheres of Relationships 1. One to one 2. One to group 3. One to all	
			(8) Influencing: "Watch your step!"			

numbers = overt teachers actions

letters = covert preplanning or reflection

FIGURE 2–8   Teacher Behavior Continuum (TBC): Rogerian Model

(3) door openers (or reopeners), (4) active listening, (5) I-messages, (6) Method III "no-lose" problem solving, (7) Six Steps to Problem Solving, and (8) influencing statements.

The covert behaviors suggested by *T.E.T.* and the Rogerians are actions that run through the teacher's mind in reflecting, planning, predicting, and preventing, and that do not deal with direct action or conflict resolution between student and teacher. These covert actions can be listed as (1) daily actions ("Do as I do!"), (2) reorganizing space, (3) reorganizing time (diffused, individual, and optimum), and (4) the Three Spheres of Relationships.

ENDNOTES

1. C. Moustakas, *The Authentic Teacher: Sensitivity and Awareness in the Classroom* (Cambridge, MA: Howard A. Doyle Publishing, 1966).

2. A. H. Maslow, *Towards a Psychology of Being, 2nd ed.* (New York: D. Van Nostrand, 1968), p. 3.

3. T. Gordon, *T.E.T.: Teacher Effectiveness Training* (New York: David McKay, 1974).

4. Ibid.

5. T. Gordon, *Teaching Children Self-Discipline: At Home and at School* (New York: Times Books, 1988), pp. 127–128.

6. Gordon, *T.E.T.*

7. Ibid.

8. Ibid.

9. Moustakas, *The Authentic Teacher*.

EFFECTIVENESS TRAINING: INSTRUCTOR TRAINING WORKSHOPS

Name	Minutes	Format	Address of Distributor
Instructors Training Workshops: *T.E.T.: Teacher Effectiveness Training* The Workshops historically have been given in major cities such as San Diego, Boston St. Louis, San Francisco, Washington, D.C., and Los Angeles.	5½ days	Workshops	Effectiveness Training International 531 Stevens Avenue Solana Beach, CA 92075-2093 (619) 481-8121 FAX (619) 481-8125

Workshop: *T.E.T.: Teacher Effectiveness Training*
T.E.T. teaches the necessary interpersonal communication skills for teachers to develop warm and friendly relationships with students and prevent disruptive behavior.

Workshop: *No-Lose Conflict Resolution Training*
This course offers new insights and skills on how to get out of a win-lose power struggle posture, how to defuse anger so people can use their heads and be rational, how to brainstorm many possible solutions and then decide on the best, and how to make sure the solution is carried out.

The promotional brochure for the Effectiveness Training workshops reads as follows:

> *Purpose*
> *"Enroll in one of our comprehensive 5½ day Instructor Training Workshops where you will learn for yourself and be prepared to teach others the Effectiveness Training System—a proven model offering self-disclosure, listening, and conflict resolution skills. Several million parents, women, men, youth, teachers and leaders throughout the world have benefitted from learning this system, which was developed by Dr. Thomas Gordon over 30 years ago. Whether you choose to teach our Parent Effectiveness Training, Effectiveness Training for Women or Effectiveness Training course, you will gain personal satisfaction, increase your job skills, provide a valuable community service and supplement your income as an authorized Effectiveness Training Instructor!"*

Books That Can Be Ordered from Effectiveness Training International

Order from Effectiveness Training International, 531 Stevens Avenue, Solana Beach, CA, 92075-2093.

> *Teaching Children Self-Discipline: At Home and at School* by Dr. Thomas Gordon. Dr. Gordon's book presents new strategies for parents and teachers to prevent self-destructive and antisocial behaviors of youth.
>
> *Parent Effectiveness Training (P.E.T.)* by Dr. Thomas Gordon. Read the book that pioneered a new and more effective parenting method.
>
> *P.E.T. in Action* by Dr. Thomas Gordon and Judy Gordon Sands. Parents tell how they transformed family life with P.E.T.
>
> *Effectiveness Training for Women (E.T.W.)* by Linda Adams with Elinor Lenz. For women who want relationships that feel fair.
>
> *Be Your Best* by Linda Adams with Elinor Lenz. Reach your personal goals and deepen all your relationships.
>
> *Leader Effectiveness Training (L.E.T.)* by Dr. Thomas Gordon. One of the first books to identify the necessary skills to make "participative management" work.
>
> *Padres Eficaz y Tecnicamente Preparados* by Dr. Thomas Gordon. The Spanish language version of the *P.E.T.* book.

Other Items Recommended as Related to the Rogerian Philosophy

Order from Effectiveness Training International, 531 Stevens Avenue, Solana Beach, CA, 92075-2093.

> *Feeling Marketplace* designed by Steven Emmons. A deck of cards that fosters open communication and warms everyone up. Improve communication with your children, students, or group members using cards that illustrate 140 different feelings. Use them as a springboard to get people to express deeper feelings about themselves. They're fun yet effective. #1006010
>
> *Discipline: 101 Alternatives to Spanking* by Alvin Price. A child psychologist and consultant to Head Start offers creative and effective alternatives to discipline and punishment—at home and at school. A supplement to the *T.E.T.* book. #1003510
>
> *ABC Feelings: A Coloring/Learning Book* by Alexandra Delis-Abrams, Ph.D. *ABC Feelings* makes it easy and fun for children ages 3 to 8 to share their feelings. Appropriate and fun during playtime with parents, grandparents, relatives, teachers, or other caring adults, this coloring book links different emotions to the 26 letters of the alphabet. #1000510

Anger: The Misunderstood Emotion by Carol Travis. A landmark book that explodes conventional assumptions about anger and presents a deeper and fuller understanding of this complicated emotion. It offers strategies for handling anger when you have to live with it for dealing with difficult people or aggressive children, and for solving family battles, especially those after divorce or victimization. #1001010

Strategies for Classroom Discipline by Meryl E. Englander. Proves how traditional discipline and control fail to influence students to be responsible. It offers remedies and strategies ranging from changing how institutions function to changing the way teachers teach. It also deals with morals, self-discipline, and raising students' self-esteem while developing effective rule setting and problem solving. #0250030

INSTRUCTIONAL MEDIA: THE ROGERIAN MODEL

Name	Minutes	Format	Sound	Address of Distributor
Teacher Effectiveness Training	25	Audio-tapes	yes	Effectiveness Training International 531 Stevens Avenue Solana Beach, CA 92075-2093

Successful Parenthood—Tape 1
Side 1: Misleading Myths about Parents
Side 2: The Problem-Solving Family: Why It Works So Well

Successful Parenthood—Tape 2
Side 1: Two-Way Communication Skills
Side 2: The No-Lose Method of Resolving Family Conflicts
#1023510

The Everyday Genius by Peter Kline.
Those who want to bring out the infinite possibilities of children are shown how not to discourage them from taking control of their own unique learning process. #1005510

Siblings Without Rivalry by Adele Faber and Elaine Mazlish.
Learn easy and practical ways to help your kids develop cooperative and living relationships with their brothers and sisters. #1014010

Name	Minutes	Format	Sound	Address of Distributor
Teacher Effectiveness Training	29	16 mm	yes	Films Incorporated Video 5547 N. Ravenswood Ave. Chicago, IL 60640-1199 (800) 343-4312 Ext. 388 (312) 878-2600 FAX: (312) 878-0416 (Human Relations and School Discipline Series)
A compete outline of the methods created and developed by Dr. Thomas Gordon, originator of *Teacher Effectiveness Training*, a system of techniques now widely used by teachers in building more effective classroom relationships. Dr. Gordon illustrates and explains the concepts of active listening, I-messages, and the no-lose method for resolving conflicts. Public school teachers who regularly practice *T.E.T.* techniques share their classroom experiences.				
Be an Effective Teacher	55	16 mm	yes	Films Incorporated Video 5547 N. Ravenswood Ave. Chicago, IL 60640-1199 (800) 343-4312 Ext. 388 (312) 878-2600 FAX: (312) 878-0416 (Human Relations and School Discipline Series)
This film on teacher effectiveness training (*T.E.T.*) provides a sound basis for promoting a learning environment in the classroom. In reel 1, role-play demonstrations portray the *T.E.T.* approach in action through active listening when the child has the problem and I-messages when the teacher has the problem. In reel 2, conflict-resolution skills are presented and Gordon discusses the origins and underlying philosophy of the control concepts, as well as the techniques of implementation. (Order no. 77533C)				
T.E.T. in High School	29	16 mm	yes	Films Incorporated Video 5547 N. Ravenswood Ave. Chicago, IL 60640-1199 (800) 343-4312 Ext. 388 (312) 878-2600 FAX: (312) 878-0416 (Human Relations and School Discipline Series)
Demonstrates the "no-lose" method of resolving conflicts and improving human relations in the secondary-level classroom.				

Carl Rogers on Education (Parts 1 and 2)	30	16 mm	yes	American Association for Counseling and Development 5999 Stevenson Avenue Alexandria, VA 22304

(*Part 1*) Carl Rogers describes how people acquire significant learning and indicates the directions in which the educational system must change to have a real impact on students. The film covers such topics as the role of the student in formulating his or her own curriculum, the circumstances under which learning will be a lasting and meaningful process, the activities a teacher should engage in to be a facilitator of learning, and the qualities in the interpersonal relationship between facilitator and students that foster and encourage the learning process. (Order no. 77526C)

(*Part 2*) Carl Rogers continues his analysis of the educational system by focusing on the following topics: implementing "freedom to learn" within the restraints and obligations imposed on teachers in the usual educational setting, coping with the different expectations students have of what they want or need from a teacher, the role of the educational system in transmitting society's values and in helping young people resolve value questions, and the characteristics in young people that are fostered by teachers who facilitate "freedom to learn." (Order no. 77527C)

3

THE PEER MEDIATION MODEL

Theorists/Writers: Fred Schrumpf, Donna K. Crawford, and Richard J. Bodine

- *Peer Mediation: Conflict Resolution in Schools*
- *Creating the Peaceable School: A Comprehensive Program for Teaching Conflict Resolution*

The scene is a small conference room where three middle school students are seated around a square table. As we watch the interaction progress among these three students, we will see that Roger is the leader, or mediator, seated between the two other students, James and Mike, the disputants, who have some conflict between them. We see that in attempting to mediate the dispute between his peers, Roger will follow a series of predetermined steps and procedures as he performs his role. We will see this process unfold and then later describe how the Peer Mediation Model can contribute to good discipline in schools and classrooms, whether in a middle school setting (as in this illustration) or even with younger children.

THE SIX STEPS OF MEDIATION

Step 1: Agree to Mediate (Open the Session— Introductions, Setting Ground Rules, and Agreeing to Mediate)

MEDIATOR ROGER: "I welcome both of you to this mediation session. I'm Roger and I'll be your mediator today. What's your name?"

MIKE: "Mike Gates."

MEDIATOR ROGER: "What is your name?"

JAMES: "James Allen."

MEDIATOR ROGER: "The rule is that I won't take either of your sides and I will remain neutral. *(Ground Rule #1: Mediator remains neutral)* I'll keep our conversation private because what is said here should remain in this room and I'd like you to do the same! *(Ground Rule #2: Confidentially)* Everyone gets to talk. When James is talking, Mike you can't interrupt him, and when Mike is talking, James you can't interrupt him. *(Ground Rule #3: Take turns talking without interruptions)* Will you accept these rules, and are you willing to work for an agreement?"

JAMES: "Yes."

MIKE: "Yes."

Step 2: Gather Points of View
(Gather Information—Each Side Presents Its View)

MEDIATOR ROGER: "Mike, tell me your side of this problem."

MIKE: "Well, for the last two weeks, James has constantly been putting me down, and today he grabbed my shirt, pushed me against the lockers, and threatened me. I can't understand it. He tells me to stay away from his girl and keeps accusing me of attempting to hit on her."

MEDIATOR ROGER: "Is there more you can tell us?"

MIKE: "No, he just better get off my case!" (While Mike was talking, Mediator Roger faced him and stayed visually focused on him—Communication Skill: Attending)

MEDIATOR ROGER: "So, James is accusing you of hitting on his girlfriend and is putting you down and got physically rough today?" (Communication Skill: Summarizing)

MIKE: "Yes! But he's not so tough."

MEDIATOR ROGER: "James, what is your side to this?"

JAMES: "Well, he *is* hitting on my woman, Carolyn. Natoya told me he had his arm around her in Health class, and he was hitting on her again in chemistry."

MIKE: (interrupts) "I ain't hitting on his girl!"

MEDIATOR ROGER: "Just a minute, Mike. It's James's turn to talk. Remember the rule—everyone gets to talk uninterrupted. You'll have a chance to talk later."

JAMES: "And today I find him carrying her books and being at her locker."

MEDIATOR ROGER: "Is there anything else?"

JAMES: "No. But he is going down!"

MEDIATOR ROGER: "Well, James, you feel that you're hearing from others that

Mike is showing too much attention to your friend Carolyn, and today he was at her locker. You are angry about this. Is that it?" (Communication Skill: Summarizing)

JAMES: "Yeah."

MEDIATOR ROGER: "Is there anything else you want to tell us?"

JAMES: "No."

MEDIATOR ROGER: "Your turn, Mike."

MIKE: (Roger turns to face Mike—Communication Skill: Attending) "Well, in Health class, the teacher paired me up with Carolyn, and we were practicing the Heimlich maneuver for helping people who are choking. Carolyn was my partner and I had to put my arms around her to practice the maneuver. James's friend ragged me when I did this. I didn't choose Carolyn; the teacher assigned us as a pair. Since both of our last names begin with Z, we are at the end of the alphabet, and when the teachers sit us in alphabetical order I'm always at the end with Carolyn. It's the same way in Chemistry. All the Zs are seated at the same lab table, and I'm next to Carolyn and again she's my partner. I like Carolyn as a friend but I don't want to date her! In fact, she tells me she likes James and wants to go to the dances with him. Same thing with the lockers—they're assigned alphabetically, and Carolyn's is next to mine. She had to go to band practice, which is on the other side of the building, so she asked me to do her a favor and put her books in her locker. I'm not hitting on Carolyn."

MEDIATOR ROGER: "So you're not interested in dating Carolyn, and because of the letters of your last names being the same, you are placed together and paired up for activities." (Communication Skill: Summarizing)

MIKE: "That's it."

JAMES: "Well, if she needs her books taken to the locker, I'll do it."

MEDIATOR ROGER: "James, you see it as your role to help Carolyn." (Communication Skill: Clarifying)

JAMES: "Yeah."

Step 3: Focus on Interests (Identify Common Interests)

MEDIATOR ROGER: "James, *what is it that you want?*"

JAMES: "I want Mike to stay away from my girl!"

MEDIATOR ROGER: "So, you want Mike to stay away from Carolyn, and Mike, *what is it that you want?*"

MIKE: "I want to be friends with Carolyn, but just friends, and I want to be able to work with her in school without James getting jealous. I want to be able to feel safe and that he isn't gonna jump me, punch me, or push me against the locker. I don't want to be James's enemy and also have his friends turn against me."

MEDIATOR ROGER: "You want to be working friends with Carolyn and feel safe with James and his friends."

MIKE: "Yes."

MEDIATOR ROGER: "James and Mike, what do you think might happen if things continue this way and this isn't settled?"

MIKE AND JAMES: (in unison) "We'll get in a fight and get suspended."

MEDIATOR ROGER: "Do you both want this?" (Goal: Establish a common interest)

MIKE AND JAMES: "No."

MEDIATOR ROGER: "Then it's in your best interest to find a solution to the difficulties between you. (Determine the interest of each disputant.) I hear Mike saying that he has no interest in becoming Carolyn's boyfriend, but finds himself required to work closely with her, and he can't stay away from her all the time. And neither of you wants to fight and get into big trouble."

Step 4: Create Win-Win Options
(No Criticism, Evaluation, or Discussion)

MEDIATOR ROGER: "We will now brainstorm some solutions, but we have a rule for brainstorming: We just say anything that comes into our minds, and we will not criticize the ideas or discuss them. Just say any solution, no matter how silly or ridiculous it might sound, and let's come up with as many ideas as we can."

JAMES: "Well, I could agree to meet Carolyn in the hall at end of fifth period and get her books and take them to the locker for her."

(Mediator Roger writes down this and all other possible solutions.)

MIKE: "I'm going to talk to Carolyn and tell her that James wants to carry her books. I could talk to Mrs. Herrington and get her to move me to a different lab table, but in Health class, Carolyn and I have a cooperative learning activity. We're halfway done with it, and if we stop working together, we'll lose too much."

JAMES: "Well, I guess I can stop listening to rumors and things my friend tell me about Mike and Carolyn."

MIKE: "I know that Carolyn's dad has given her four tickets to the rock concert, and I know she wants to take James. Maybe I could get a date and all four of us could go together. And if he has an issue or problem with me, he should *talk* to me about it instead of manhandling me—I need to feel safe."

Step 5: Evaluate Options

MEDIATOR ROGER: "OK, here are some possible solutions. Let's evaluate them and decide on a solution." (Roger turns his notepad so both boys can read the solutions that have been proposed)

JAMES: "I'd like to go to the rock concert with Carolyn, and double with Mike—but only if I drive." (Mike nods in agreement.) "I could carry Carolyn's books on Monday through Wednesday, but I can't do it on Thursday because I have practice—maybe Mike could take her books to the locker on that day. And I could tell him if he's doing something that I don't like, instead of pushing him."

MIKE: "I could ask the teacher to change my lab partners."

JAMES: "That's not necessary. Carolyn tells me that she needs your help on difficult problems."

MEDIATOR ROGER: "OK, are these solutions fair? (Both nod yes.) Mike, will you now feel safe?"

MIKE: "Yes."

MEDIATOR ROGER: "James, do you still think Mike is hitting on Carolyn?"

JAMES: "No, but I'll be watching."

Step 6: Create an Agreement

MEDIATOR ROGER: "OK, now let's formalize this agreement by writing it down and signing a contract. The problem was that James thought Mike was hitting on his girlfriend, but Mike only wanted to be friends with her and had to work with her on many projects because the teachers put them together. James, you agreed to do this: (1) Talk to Mike if you have a problem with him and (2) talk to Carolyn about working out carrying her books, with Mike helping on Thursdays. And Mike, you'll talk with Carolyn about doubling for a date to the rock concert. Are you both in agreement with this contract? (Both agree.) I'm going to sign this contract and I want each of you to do the same. (Both sign.) Now, I'd like to thank you for letting me be your mediator, and I want to shake your hands. Thanks. Would you like to shake each other's hand?" (They do so.)

UNDERSTANDING PEER MEDIATION AND DISCIPLINE

What you have just read is one incident where a student mediator attempted to follow a predetermined structured procedure for getting two students to settle a dispute that, if it continued, could have resulted in both boys being suspended for fighting. The Peer Mediation Model belongs among the collection of discipline models presented in this book and can be clearly classified and a Relationship-Listening Model, since the mediator spatially brings potentially hostile disputants together, stays neutral in the process, encourages each person to listen and communicate with each other, and then finds a solution that satisfies each. The mediator does not impose his or her own solution and does not take action involving any punishment.

Peer mediation is not a reactive tool; a delineation must be made between conflict resolution and a discipline program. Mediation is a proactive approach that helps set the school climate, so that many of the self-destructive and violent behaviors requiring discipline action will not occur. It is not well suited to handling disputes after incidents have gotten out of hand or the misbehavior has occurred. However, this mediation process can be used to mediate between students after everyone has calmed down and to lessen the likelihood that future incidents will occur.

Theorists and writers Fred Schrumpf, Donna K. Crawford, and Richard J. Bodine do not see peer mediation working with forms of discipline they call "obedience training," whereby students' behavior is maintained by teachers following the role of enforcer through coercion. The key to positive behavioral change is not to simply say "Don't do that!" Instead, the key is for students to be educated to alternative ways to behave. The positive discipline as a program of behavior management relies on a program "dependent upon students' ability to evaluate their own behavior and generate alternative behavioral choices, ones accepted in the system"[1] and is not involved in fault finding and punishment for past behaviors.

RATIONALE FOR PEER MEDIATION

Today, every child is affected by violence, whether or not physical harm is evidenced.[2] Acts of physical violence in school are seen repeated in the public media, and students increasingly find themselves overwhelmed by those who are hostile, aggressive, violent, and disconnected. For many students today, the only way they know to handle varying degrees of conflict is through violent actions. Many schools that take pride in the idea that they do not experience overt violent confrontations are unaware that their students may be experiencing passive psychological violence through intimidation. Peer mediation, as a proactive process, can help eliminate discipline incidents as a "result of jealousies, rumors, misunderstandings, bullying, fights, misuse of personal property, and the ending of friendships."[3]

The Peer Mediation Model is executed by training a cadre of peer mediators, as a third parties, who can be called on to mediate disputes among students. Generally, the faculty helps administer the program, but teachers are not the mediators, thus taking the educator out of the time-consuming role of arbitrating sanctions that rarely resolve the real conflict among students. Students are seen as more effective mediators because (1) they are able to connect with peers in a way that adults may not; (2) peer mediators can frame disputes in language that may be more understandable to peers; (3) students, using peer mediators will not feel that adult authority figures are judging them; (4) peer mediators are respected; (5) the process self-empowers youths; and (6) when students are in control, they feel more committed to solutions.

The philosophical position of peer mediation is

Schools must be places from which viable, positive future pathways for young people can be built. They must, above all, be places where youth can learn to live and get along with one another, as well as to become ready to assume their future roles as responsible citizens of a democracy, as parents, as community members and leaders, and as productive members of the work force. Many students have no other place from which to gain these experiences. Only schools can extend these possibilities equally to all students—this is the constitutional mandate to the schools.[4]

UNDERSTANDING CONFLICT

Peer mediators are trained to understand conflict as a natural process of living. Conflict occurs when there is a discord between two individuals or between groups of people related to blocked needs—the needs for belonging, power, freedom, or fun.[5]

Responses to a conflict may be viewed as three different types: soft responses, hard responses, and principled responses. The *soft response* occurs when people attempt to avoid conflict by withdrawing from the situation, by ignoring the problem, or by denying that a conflict exists. When this occurs, one person adjusts to the position of the other and does not get his needs met or served within the relationship. This person's passive response will produce feelings of disillusionment, self-doubt, fear, and anxiety about the future, thus this soft response is not a healthy or productive response. The *hard response* is when one individual applies pressure to win a contest of will. Hostility, physical damage, and violence can often result from this type of response to a conflict, and it is destructive to cooperation. The *principled response* to conflict occurs when communication between disputants is established. Through this communication, each person has the opportunity to create a resolution through which both parties get their needs met and blame is eliminated.

The soft response is a lose-lose approach in which both parties deny the existence of the conflict and issues are not resolved. The hard response produces a lose-win outcome in which one individual gets what she wants while the other does not. Finally, the principled response produces a win-win situation where both disputants get their needs met by focusing on the interests of both, bringing people to a gradual consensus rather than an emotionally destroying relationship.

PROGRAM ORGANIZATION AND OPERATIONS

The implementation, design, and operation of a peer mediation program involves a six-phase plan:

- Phase 1: A staff and student conflict resolution program team is created and trained. A program coordinator is designated, a needs assessment is conducted, and a faculty consensus is built for the program.
- Phase 2: A time line for implementation is established. An advisory committee is formed, policies are developed, and funding sources to support the program are identified and developed.

- Phase 3: Student peer mediators are recruited through nominations and are then selected and trained.
- Phase 4: Workshops are held for staff, students, parents, and the community so that a critical mass of people within and outside the school understand the mediation process.
- Phase 5: A promotional campaign is carried out through various communication sources, including the news media.
- Phase 6: The daily operation of the program is designed, including requests for mediation, scheduling of mediation and mediators, supervision of mediators, recording of data, provision of training and support, and finally evaluation of the program.

The peer mediation text and Student Manual contains training procedures, forms, and all other necessary materials to carry out these six organizational phases.

Steps and Procedures

The role of the peer mediator is to follow a prescribed procedure of steps and guidelines to create an atmosphere that fosters cooperation and problem resolutions. A mediator must be impartial, empathetic, a good listener, respectful, trustworthy, and able to get peers to work together. The mediator arranges the physical space, normally a private room with a square table and three chairs, with the disputants seated opposite each other and the peer mediator in the middle. The materials needed are the peer mediator request (filled out by the parties beforehand), a brainstorming worksheet, a peer mediation agreement form, a pencil or pen, and an easel pad and marker.

We will now examine in detail each of the six steps for effective peer mediation. (See Figure 3–1 for a summary of how these six steps are reflexed on the Teacher Behavioral Continuum.)

Step 1: Agree to Mediate

The peer mediator introduces himself or herself and each disputant, as mediators usually are assigned to disputants who they do not know personally. The ground rules are stated: (1) the mediator remains neutral; (2) the mediation is private; (3) the disputants must take turns talking and listening; and (4) the disputants must cooperate to solve the problem. The peer mediator gets a clear statement from the disputants that they will commit themselves to mediate the dispute and obey the ground rules.

Now that we understand the components of an effective peer mediation program, let's look back on the earlier illustration:

MEDIATOR ROGER: "I welcome both of you to this mediation session. I'm Roger and I'll be your mediator today. What's your name?"

MIKE: "Mike Gates."

Looking On	Nondirective Statements	Questions	Directive Statements	Physical Intervention
		Step 1: Agree to Mediate Open Session (a) "What is your name?"	(b) "Here are the rules." (neutral mediator, congenial, and no interruptions) Step 2: Gather Points of View (a1) "Tell me what happened."	
	Communication Skills (a2) Attending Looks at Speaker (a3) Clarifying "So, I hear you saying ___." (a4) Summarizing "These are your points and position __."	Step 3: Focus on Interests "What is it that you want?"		
		(a1) Goal—Establish a Common Interest "Do you both want __?"	Step 4: Create Win-Win Options (no criticism, evaluation, or discussion) "Each of you tell me solutions." (write them down)	
			Step 5: Evaluate Options "Let's evaluate these options."	
			Step 6: Create an Agreement (write it down, and sign contract) "All shake hands."	

FIGURE 3–1 **Teacher Behavioral Continuum (TBC): Peer Mediation Model**

MEDIATOR ROGER: "What is your name?"

JAMES: "James Allen."

MEDIATOR ROGER: "The rule is that I won't take either of your sides and I will remain neutral. *(Ground Rule #1: Mediator remains neutral)* I'll keep our conversation private because what is said here should remain in this room and I'd like you to do the same! *(Ground Rule #2: Confidentially)* Everyone gets to talk. When James is talking, Mike you can't interrupt him, and when Mike is talking, James you can't interrupt him. *(Ground Rule #3: Take turns talking without interruptions)* Will you accept these rules, and are you willing to work for an agreement?"

JAMES: "Yes."

MIKE: "Yes."

Step 2: Gather Points of View

The peer mediator now asks each disputant (one at a time) to tell his point of view about the problem. The mediator listens to each disputant and summarizes after each statement. This is when the mediator uses her communication skills. The mediator does not interrupt, offer advice, judge, ridicule, criticize, distract, or bring up her own experiences. The peer mediator uses the communication skills of (1) *attending* (looking at and listening to the speaker with accompanying nonverbal gestures to encourage the speaker to talk), (2) *summarizing* (active listening techniques, whereby the facts are restated and feelings are reflected, as previsouly presented in the T.E.T.[6] model), and (3) *clarifying*, through which the peer mediator deliberately asks open-ended questions to get additional information, such as, "How did you feel when this happened? Do you have more to add? What happened next? What do you think is keeping you from reaching an agreement?"

Again, returning to the dialogue from our example:

MEDIATOR ROGER: "Mike tell me your side of this problem."

MIKE: "Well, for the last two weeks, James has constantly been putting me down, and today he grabbed my shirt, pushed me against the lockers, and threatened me. I can't understand it. He tells me to stay away from his girl and keeps accusing me of attempting to hit on her."

Step 3: Focus on Interests

Next, the peer mediator attempts to get the disputants to find a common interest. The mediator may ask, "What do you want? Why do you want that?" The mediator will listen and summarize. To clarify, the mediator may ask:

- What might happen if you don't reach an agreement?
- What would you think if you were in the other person's shoes?
- What do you really want?

Finally, the mediator summarizes with a statement that defines the speaker's interest, such as "Your interests are _____."

Again, returning to the introductory example, we may recall the interaction.

MEDIATOR ROGER: "James, *what is it that you want?*"

JAMES: "I want Mike to stay away from my girl!"

MEDIATOR ROGER: "So, you want Mike to stay away from Carolyn, and Mike, *what is it that you want?*"

MIKE: "I want to be friends with Carolyn, but just friends, and I want to be able to work with her in school without James getting jealous. I want to be able to feel safe and that he isn't gonna jump me, punch me, or push me against the locker. I don't want to be James's enemy and also have his friends turn against me."

Step 4: Create Win-Win Options

When people are in a dispute and angry, they tend to be in either an offensive or defensive position. The win-win options are created through a brainstorming process that encourages everyone to think creatively, without concern for judgments and criticism. The peer mediator explains the brainstorming rules:

- Say any ideas that come to mind.
- Do not judge or discuss the idea.
- Come up with as many ideas as possible.
- Try to think of unusual ideas.

The mediator writes these ideas down on a brainstorming worksheet and may ask additional questions to help generate even more ideas.

Step 5: Evaluate Options

The goal in this step is to have the disputants evaluate and improve on the ideas listed in Step 4. The mediator may ask each disputant to name the options or parts of options that they approve of. These are circled on the brainstorming form. Then the peer mediator can go back over the circled items, asking such questions to the disputants as "Is this fair? Can it be done? Do you think it will work?" and so on.

Step 6: Create an Agreement

After the discussion in Step 5, the mediator uses those options that have been agreed upon and pushes for a plan that is satisfactory to both disputants and to which they will commit themselves—including a willingness to sign a contract. Once the agreement is written, the mediator will review the central points, have it signed by all parties, thank the disputants, and shake hands.

SUMMARY

In today's schools, much of the misbehavior that leads to discipline incidents that must be dealt with by teachers or school authorities stems from conflict between individuals. This conflict is inevitable and is part of life's experiences, but many of today's students are growing up without the communication skills and abilities to deal with their blocked needs. They are left having to choose between responding in an aggressive hostile manner (hard resolution) or passively withdrawing into a shell of insecurity and having feelings of not being safe (soft resolution). Peer mediation is not a reactive process but rather proactive, utilizing a schoolwide mediation program to foster an atmosphere that says "Our school is a place where we can talk over our differences. We don't have to fight to get justice."

ENDNOTES

1. F. Schrumpf, D. K. Crawford, and R. J. Bodine, *Peer Mediation: Conflict Resolution in Schools* (Champaign, IL: Research Press, 1997), p. 10.

2. Richard J. Bodine, Donna K. Crawford, and Fred Schrumpf, *Creating the Peaceable School: A Comprehensive Program for Teaching Conflict Resolution* (Champaign, IL: Research Press, 1994).

3. Schrumpf, Crawford, and Bodine, *Peer Mediation.*

4. Ibid., p. 13.

5. Glasser, W., *Control Theory* (New York: Dell, 1984).

6. Gordon Thomas, *T.E.T.: Teacher Effectiveness Training* (New York: David McKay, 1974).

4

THE SOCIAL DISCIPLINE MODEL OF RUDOLF DREIKURS (ADLERIAN THEORY)

Theorist/Writer: Rudolf Dreikurs

- *Psychology in the Classroom: A Manual for Teachers*
- *Encouraging Children to Learn: The Encouragement Process*
- *Discipline Without Tears: What to Do with Children Who Misbehave*

New Writer (for Classrooms): Linda Albert

- *A Teacher's Guide to Cooperative Discipline: How to Manage Your Classroom and Promote Self-Esteem*

New Writer (for Parents): Donald Dinkmeyer

- *Systematic Training for Effective Parenting (STEP)*

It is the first day of winter semester after the holidays and Mr. Garcia is casually observing his new class as the high school students enter the room for third-period chemistry class. He finds nothing particularly distinctive about this new group, until Ronald appears. This student is dressed in faded jeans covered with sign patches bearing the trademark of the Harley-Davidson motorcycle company. Even more noticeable are the two patches running across the seat of the pants with the words "Screw You" on one hip pocket and "Mother F-----" on the other. The rest of Ronald's attire includes a T-shirt and a western-style hat pulled down over his eyes. In order for him to see while walking, he has to lead with his chin and look out over his nose.

Mr. Garcia gradually loses sight of Ronald as he visually skims over the remaining faces in the classroom. Suddenly, he hears a girl's scream and another student's laugh, and then the classroom quiets. Everyone's attention focuses on Ronald, who is slouched down in his seat with his hat pulled over his face. The class glances from the teacher to Ronald and back to the teacher. Seeing that neither the teacher nor Ronald is going to make any further move, the class members return to their chatting. A few minutes later, Mr. Garcia begins reading through the class roster, calling each student's name and receiving in return a proper acknowledgment such as "I'm here." When he calls out "Ronald Foster," there is no response. He repeats it a second time to no response, but all eyes turn toward Ronald. The teacher asks, "Isn't Ronald Foster here?" Ronald replies, "Yo, chill, man!" The teacher states, "You're Ronald?" Ronald gives the slightest "yes" nod of his head.

Mr. Garcia ignores Ronald's lack of a solid response, finishes calling the roll, and finally introduces himself and the content of the course. He turns his back to the class and begins to write the name of the textbook across the chalkboard. Before he can finish, the same girlish scream is heard, but this time with such intensity that it signals something more serious. The girl seated in front of Ronald jumps to her feet, crosses her arms across her chest and runs frantically to the classroom door. As she passes before Mr. Garcia and the front of the class, everyone can see that her bra is open in the back. A few nervous giggles come from the class, and now all eyes focus on Ronald and then, unfortunately, *back to Mr. Garcia.*

Mr. Garcia is quite obviously "on the spot." It is the beginning of the semester, and he faces a troublesome male student, a distraught female student, and a class of 31 teenagers waiting to see what will transpire. What specific steps should he take to defuse this situation, get the class back on track, help the girl, and eventually aid Ronald in improving his behavior? This chapter will explain Rudolf Dreikurs's techniques as we apply them to Mr. Garcia's treatment of Ronald. As the techniques are explained, you will see a particular application of the teacher's behavior as it relates to Ronald's misbehavior and motivation.

DREIKURS AND ADLER'S SOCIAL THEORY

Dreikurs's writings flow out of the work of the noted social psychologist Alfred Adler. Adler believed that the central motivation of all humans is to belong and to be accepted by others. Humans are foremost social animals. Books written by Dreikurs and his various associates (*Children: The Challenge; Logical Consequences; Encouraging Children to Learn; Psychology in the Classroom;* and *Discipline Without Tears*) all have a common bond with Adler. This bond is that all behavior, including misbehavior, is orderly, purposeful, and directed toward achieving social recognition.[1] Each action taken by such students as Ronald Foster is goal directed. The "inner" goal results in the "outward" behavior. The teacher must have a student like Ronald recognize his inner-goal and then help the student change to the more appropriate goal of learning how to belong with others. This is the rationale for placing Dreikurs under the Confronting-Contracting orientation. He believes in an underlying cause for misbehavior (similar to Relationship-Listening), yet he believes that its correction is the result of a teacher actively showing a student how to belong.

Since Dreikurs's death in 1972, two writers have built on his work and expanded on it. They are Linda Albert, whose *A Teacher's Guide to Cooperative Discipline: How to Manage Your Classroom and Promote Self-Esteem* presents readable and practical suggestions for classroom teachers, and Donald Dinkmeyer, author of *Systematic Training for Effective Parenting* (STEP), who has written a host of books for parents dealing with differing ages of children and has conducted many valuable workshops for parents. Both writers build their suggestions, techniques, and practices solidly on the Adlerian-Dreikurs theoretical constructs, with Albert's work speaking clearly to the classroom teacher. The following is a presentation of Dreikurs's methodology as it relates to discipline; where Albert has expanded the practical methods, I have added her suggestions in an outline-block format throughout this chapter.

DREIKURS'S METHODS AND PHILOSOPHY

When a student is unsuccessful in obtaining social acceptance (sometimes as early as her infant or toddler years at home), a pattern of misbehavior begins. One way of analyzing this is through a sociogram (see Figure 4–1). The student is left with the recourse of trying to fulfill inner-needs by annoying, destructive, hostile, or helpless behavior. If we, as teachers, can help misbehaving students understand their mistaken, faulty goals and provide them with avenues for group acceptance, then such students will rationally change their own behaviors. These subconscious goals that motivate misbehavior are (1) attention getting, (2) power and control, (3) revenge, and (4) helplessness.[2]

   1. *Attention Getting:* This is evident when a student is constantly looking to belong and be recognized in the class. Instead of receiving such recognition through productive work, often a student will resort to acting in ways that demand incessant praise or criticism. Both praise and criticism of an incessant nature are equally undesirable.

   2. *Power and Control:* This is a goal for a student who feels inferior, who feels unable to measure up to the expectations of others or of self. It makes no difference whether the student is actually handicapped in some way or has only a false perception of being inferior. In either case, the youngster will try to remedy this perception of inferiority by trying to get his own way, by being the boss, by forcing himself onto others, or by bragging or clowning.

   3. *Revenge:* This is a goal for the student who feels unable to gain attention or power. This student sees herself as having unequal status because of what others have done to her. This student places the blame for her plight on those outside. She

Since Adlerian-Dreikurs theory places membership and belonging as the primary motivator, teachers may wish to study the social makeup of the class with use of a Friendship Chart (sociogram). This may be done by asking the students to state preferences for other member of the class in response to such questions as: Who would you like to sit beside? Who would you like to work with in a study group or laboratory? Which student would you most like to visit at home? Which boys or girls do you like least? Based on the results, the teacher constructs a diagram similar to this:

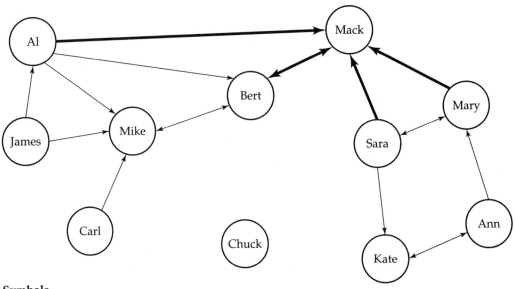

Symbols

A ◀────── B   B chooses A, but A does not mention B

A ◀──────▶ B   A and B choose each other

A ──────▶ B   A dislikes B

A ◀──────▶ B   A and B dislike each other

Explanation
There is a clique centering around Mike, as leader.
Al is a *fringer* in this group; only James has chosen him.
Carl and Chuck are both *isolates*; neither has been chosen by other students.
Mack is a *reject*; two boys and two girls dislike him, and he has no friends.
There are three pairs of mutually chosen friends (Sara and Mary, Kate and Ann, and Mike and Bert).
There are two boys who mutually dislike each other (Bert and Mack).
Definition of Terms: fringers-may consider themselves a member of a group but only chosen by one member of the group; isolates-have no close friends; rejects-disliked by others.

FIGURE 4–1   Friendship Charts (Sociograms)

feels hurt by others and compensates by following the philosophy "an eye for an eye." In other words, "If I'm hurting, then I have the right to make others hurt." The student goes beyond the desire for attention and power, beyond the desire to win. She resorts to achieving status not by merely winning over others, but by beating others with maliciousness and humiliation.

4. *Helplessness or Inadequacy:* The student operating with this goal is the most pathetic. He has given up on the possibility of being a member of or of gaining any status in the group. This student not only feels uncared for, unequal, and wrongfully treated but also feels incapable of doing anything (either constructively or destructively) about it. The student has accepted the feeling of being a nobody and no longer cares what happens.

With this beginning understanding of Dreikurs, let us move to the Teacher Behavior Continuum with Mr. Garcia and Ronald Foster.

THE TEACHER BEHAVIOR CONTINUUM

To begin, the teacher must determine which of the four faulty goals is motivating the student. This determination is basically a four-step process, as follows:

1. The teacher observes and collects information about the student in situations involving peers and family.
2. After gathering information about the student, the teacher can then hypothesize or guess which of the underlying goals is held by the student.
3. This goal can be verified by the teacher by reflecting on what feelings arise within the teacher as a result of the student's behavior.
4. Final verification is achieved by confronting the student with a series of four questions and looking for the student's recognition reflex.

In carrying out this procedure, the teacher moves through *silently looking on, questions, directive statements,* and back to *questions.*

Looking On

Mr. Garcia, in the immediate situation with 31 pairs of eyes peering at him, disinvolves himself emotionally from Ronald's behavior. He has noted the first impression of rudeness, braggadocio, and flashiness that Ronald has created. Mr. Garcia makes a mental note to himself to search for more information by looking at school records, talking to former teachers, and possibly making a home visit. For now, though, with limited information, he suspects that Ronald's goal may be attention getting, power, or revenge. It certainly is not helplessness!

It is important to remain calm during the beginning encounter with a student operating under any of the faulty goals, and not to give the student what he seeks. For example, the worst thing Mr. Garcia could do would be to call out loudly and angrily to Ronald. To do so would give Ronald the attention he seeks (attention getting), or it would accelerate the battle of who will win out (power), or it would drive Ronald into physically lashing out (revenge).

Mr. Garcia can remain calm because he knows rationally that Ronald's behavior is not directed at him personally but is simply the student's previously learned mode of responding in groups. Of course, a quite human reaction from a teacher would be to explode, but this urge must be held in check. Examining this emotional urge or feeling toward the student will be most helpful in narrowing down and identifying the student's goal.

Questions (Covert)

Now Mr. Garcia can assess the inner emotions that Ronald's behavior has evoked. Dreikurs suggested that teachers covertly ask themselves four questions related to the goals.[3]

Introduction: Teacher Beliefs on Discipline

1. Do I feel annoyed? If so, you may have reason to suspect *attention getting* as a goal.
2. Do I feel beaten or intimidated? If so, you may have reason to suspect *power* as a goal.
3. Do I feel wronged or hurt? If so, you may have reason to suspect *revenge* as a goal.
4. Do I feel incapable of reaching the child in any way? If so, you may have reason to suspect *helplessness* as the goal.

Mr. Garcia analyzes his feelings as "annoyed," to say the least, and even slightly intimidated, which suggests that Ronald's goal was attention getting or power.

Let's see what Ronald's probable responses would have been if the teacher had given free rein to his first impulses. If Mr. Garcia had yelled at him, Ronald might have responded with, "Chill out, chill, man, no need to lose it, just chill!" In other words, if Ronald's goal was power, he would have won at that point. He would have "shown up" Mr. Garcia in front of the class as a teacher who becomes easily flustered while he, a 17-year-old student, was more of a man, with calm and collected reactions. If Ronald's goal was to get attention, he would have responded in a different way. Mr. Garcia's yells might have caused Ronald to put his head down sheepishly and grin to himself. The rest of the class would be observing Ronald, and as soon as Mr. Garcia turned away, Ronald's head would be back up, face smiling and looking around to make sure that everyone had seen him. In both cases, Mr. Garcia's primary reaction would have done little to prevent numerous future occurrences. Mr. Garcia knows he can't play into the student's scheme and is ready now to take specific action. He makes a guess that Ronald's primary goal is to seek attention.

Directive Statements

The previous reflective and covert behaviors of silently looking on and questions were primarily enacted to gather information, to narrow down and identify the student's possible goal, and to make a tentative plan for action. A teacher trained in Dreikurs's approach would take only a split second from first witnessing the girl running out of the classroom to begin action with Ronald.

> Having identified attention getting as Ronald's underlying goal, Mr. Garcia acts in a way that deprives Ronald of the attention related to his misbehavior. Mr. Garcia turns to the girl and quietly tells her to come back in the classroom when she is ready and to take another seat away from Ronald. He then turns to the class and states, "Class, I would like to introduce you to some of the laboratory equipment you will be using this year. In a few minutes I would like you to break up into groups of four people and gather around the lab tables at the back of the room. When you get settled, open to the first page of your lab manual, where you will find pictures of the various kinds of equipment. As a group, see if you can first learn the equipment names, then I will join each group briefly to demonstrate how to use some of the more dangerous equipment, such as the Bunsen burner. OK, class, find your groups of four and move to your tables." Turning to Ronald, he adds, "Oh, Ronald Foster, your behavior has told me that you are not ready to work with others. I want you to remain in your seat. When you think you can join a group without being disruptive, you may do so."

Having attended to the class, Mr. Garcia gives Ronald a directive statement. He has told Ronald that he can join the group if and when he is ready to contribute in an appropriate way. This is an example of a teacher applying logical consequences rather than punishment. (I will explain this difference more fully later. For now, let us say that Mr. Garcia has employed as a logical consequence the loss of the student's right to engage in an activity as a result of behavior that would be counterproductive to performing that activity.) Before Mr. Garcia can conclude definitely that attention getting is Ronald's goal and then continue with a long-range plan based on that goal identification, he needs further verification. He can achieve this by returning to overt questioning with Ronald.

Questions (Overt)

Ronald has stayed by himself, slouched down with his hat over his face for nearly half the period. This is a further sign that Mr. Garcia has correctly identified Ronald's goal. If Ronald had wanted power, he would have continued to defy the teacher's rules. If Ronald had wanted revenge, he would have physically retaliated against the girl or teacher.

> Mr. Garcia eyes Ronald slowly getting out of his seat and moving toward the lab table. There is only one spot open in the groups of four, and he heads

toward that spot. When this group of three notices that he is ready to join them, one of the girls at the table (the very one that Ronald bothered) begins to complain and shout, "No, no, you don't! You're not joining our table." Ronald then turns to another nearby group and is greeted with, "You're not coming into our group. There is dangerous stuff here—you'll get us killed!" With a parting shot, "You're all a bunch of jerks," Ronald returns to his desk. Mr. Garcia moves toward him, takes a seat nearby, and in a voice that cannot be heard by anyone else begins to question Ronald.

> *TEACHER:* "Do you know why you acted like you did this morning?" (*confronting*)
>
> *RONALD:* (Simply shrugs his shoulders)
>
> *TEACHER:* "I have some ideas. Would you like to know?"
>
> *RONALD:* (Nods yes)
>
> *TEACHER:* "Could you want special attention?" (*verifying*)
>
> *RONALD:* (For the first time, his eyes look directly at Mr. Garcia, and he gives a slight smile.) (*recognition reflex*)

During a discussion in a calm setting, Dreikurs proposed that the teacher do as Mr. Garcia has done.[4] The teacher should ask the student if she is interested in knowing why she behaves as she does. If the student does not resist, the teacher asks one of four questions. Dreikurs listed them as:

(Attention)	1. Could it be that you want special attention?
(Power)	2. Could it be that you want your own way and hope to be boss?
(Revenge)	3. Could it be that you want to hurt others as much as you feel hurt by them?
(Helplessness)	4. Could it be that you want to be left alone?[5]

After the teacher asks each of these questions, he looks (*silently looking on*) for behavioral verification. If the student smiles, laughs, looks up suddenly, moves her shoulders, or shows other signs of response to the implied goal, then the teacher has conclusive evidence that his hypothesis is correct and treatment can proceed. The teacher formulates a plan and returns to appropriate directive statements.

Directive Statements

Now that Ronald has given the "recognition reflex" to question number 1, Mr. Garcia can be confident that attention is Ronald's goal. Mr. Garcia's task now becomes one of finding ways for Ronald to receive attention through constructive social behavior. In other words, he needs to give Ronald the attention that he craves. Following are descriptions of treatment for each of the four goals that correspond with Dreikurs prescriptive chart for teachers.[6]

Attention.   A student who seeks attention should not receive it when he acts out. To give attention to the student for inappropriate behavior would be playing into the student's plan and would not help the student learn how to behave productively in the group. Instead, the teacher might do some of the techniques shown in Figure 4–2.

Student's Motivation	Behavior Characteristics	Teacher's Feelings
Attention getting	Repetitively does actions to make him the center of attention. When asked to stop, will comply but will start again later.	Annoyed

Techniques with the Attention-Getting Student

Minimize the Attention
   Ignore the behavior
   Give "The Eye"
   Stand close by
   Mention the student's name while teaching
   Send a secret signal
   Give written notice
   Give an I-message

Legitimize the Behavior
   Make a lesson out of the behavior
   Extend the behavior to its most extreme form
   Have the whole class join in the behavior
   Use a diminishing quota

Do the unexpected
   Turn out the lights
   Play a musical sound
   Lower your voice to a whisper
   Change your voice
   Talk to the wall
   Use one-liners
   Cease teaching temporarily

Distract the Student
   Ask a direct question
   Ask a favor
   Change the activity

Notice Appropriate Behavior
   Thank the students
   Write well-behaved students' names on the chalkboard

Move the Student
   Change the student's seat
   Send the student to the thinking chair

FIGURE 4–2 Nonsocially Adaptive Students: Attention Getting

Source: Albert, L. (1989). *A Teacher's Guide to Cooperative Discipline: How to Manage Your Classroom and Promote Self-Esteem.* Circle Pines, MN: American Guidance Service, Inc., pages 31–41. Reprinted with permission.

Power.   A student who wishes to possess power should not be able to engage the teacher in a struggle. The teacher who falls for this "bait" and gets pulled into the battle is merely continuing the excitement and challenge for the student. The student becomes increasingly bolder and pleased with trying to test the teacher. The teacher should attempt to remove the issue of power altogether and force the student to look for some other goal for behaving.

Revenge.   In this case, the teacher is dealing with a more difficult task. A student who feels hurt and wishes to retaliate must be handled in a caring, affectionate manner. It is probable that this student appears unloving and uncaring, and is very hard to "warm up to." But this is exactly what the student needs—to feel cared for. Figure 4–3 discusses some techniques that are helpful with students who are seeking power and/or revenge.

Helplessness.   The student who shows inadequacy or helplessness is the most discouraged. She has lost all initiative of ever trying to belong to the group. The teacher must exercise great patience and attempt to show the child that she is capable. Some practices that might assist a helpless student are discussed in Figure 4–4.
Returning now to the vignette:

> Ronald is obviously interested in Mr. Garcia's idea that Ronald is seeking attention, but he jars Mr. Garcia back to the immediate situation with a sarcastic, "Well, that sounds cool, but there's one big problem. I can't do all these things without equipment, and no one wants me in their group. What do you suggest? Maybe you'll buy me my own laboratory?"

Mr. Garcia, as a Dreikurs teacher, knows that he must capitalize on using the group as a model to help Ronald adjust.

Modeling

> Mr. Garcia informs Ronald that at the end of class today, and on every Friday, there will be a short class council meeting to discuss problems that are of concern to the members of the class. He adds that Ronald could bring up his problem at that time and see what he and the class might work out.

Dreikurs believed that Western schools and classrooms, as part of a democratic society, need to be models or laboratories of that society.[7] In other words, students need to practice democratic principles in school in order to learn how to contribute later to society as a whole. The central process for carrying out this modeling of democracy is the use of the class meeting, which Mr. Garcia refers to as the class council. Regular meetings should be held to discuss everyday occurrences as well as long-range policies. We will see in the next chapter how William Glasser has further refined and elaborated on this concept of classroom meetings.

Student's Motivation	Behavior Characteristics	Teacher's Feelings
Power	Repetitively does actions to make him the center of attention. When asked to stop, he becomes defiant and escalates his negative behavior and challenges the adult.	Annoyed
Revenge	Hurts others physically or psychologically.	Hurt

Techniques with the Power and Revengeful Student

Make a Graceful Exit
    Acknowledge student's power
    Remove the audience
    Table the matter
    Make a date
    Use a fogging technique:
        Agree with the student
        Change the subject

Use Time Out
    Time out in the classroom
    Time out in another classroom
    Time out in the office
    Time out in the home
    Enforcing time out
        The language of choice
        The Who Squad
    Setting the duration for time out

Set the Consequence
    Establishing consequences
    Presenting consequences
    Guidelines for effective consequences
        Related consequences
        Reasonable consequences
        Respectful consequences
    Consequences versus punishments
    Choosing the consequence
        Loss or delay of activity
        Loss or delay of using objects or equipment
        Loss or delay of access to school areas
        Denied interactions with other students
        Required interactions with school personnel
        Required interaction with parents
        Required interaction with police
        Restitution:
            Repair of objects
            Replacement of objects
    Student response to consequences

FIGURE 4–3 **Nonsocially Adaptive Students: Power and Revenge**

Source: Albert, L. (1989). *A Teacher's Guide to Cooperative Discipline: How to Manage Your Classroom and Promote Self-Esteem.* Circle Pines, MN: American Guidance Service, Inc., pages 72–83. Reprinted with permission.

Student's Motivation	Behavior Characteristics	Teacher's Feelings
Helplessness	Wishes not to be seen, passive and lethargic, rejects social contact, refuses to comply or try most educational demands.	Inadequate-incapable

Techniques for the Helpless (Avoidance-of-Failure) Student

Modify Instructional Methods
Use Concrete Learning Materials and Computer-Assisted Instruction
   Attractive
   Self-explanatory
   Self-correcting
   Reusable
Teach One Step at a Time
Provide Tutoring
   Extra help from teachers
   Remediation programs
   Adult volunteers
   Peer tutoring
   Learning centers
Teach Positive Self-talk
   Post positive classroom signs
   Require two "put-ups" for every put-down
   Encourage positive self-talk before beginning tasks
Make Mistakes Okay
   Talk about mistakes
   Equate mistakes with effort
   Minimize the effect of making mistakes
Build Confidence
   Focus on improvement
   Notice contributions
   Build on strengths
   Show faith in students
   Acknowledge the difficulty of a task
   Set time limits on tasks
Focus on Past Success
   Analyze past success
   Repeat past success
Make Learning Tangible
   "I-Can" cans
   Accomplishment albums
   Checklists of skills
   Flowchart of concepts
   Talk about yesterday, today, and tomorrow
Recognize Achievement
   Applause
   Clapping and standing ovations
   Stars and stickers
   Awards and assemblies
   Exhibits
   Positive time out
   Self-approval

FIGURE 4–4   Nonsocially Adaptive Students: Helplessness (Avoidance of Failure)

Source: Albert, L. (1989). *A Teacher's Guide to Cooperative Discipline: How to Manage Your Classroom and Promote Self-Esteem.* Circle Pines, MN: American Guidance Service, Inc., pages 98–104. Reprinted with permission.

Meetings can be conducted informally without a designated leader, or formally with a rotating president, recorder, and treasurer. Voting should be avoided, as it has a tendency to alienate the minority. Instead, decisions should be made through arriving at a consensus of all members. When many people agree with a decision, peer pressure tends to influence the one or two "holdouts" and thus makes the decision unanimous. (We see this at political party conventions. After a hard battle among several candidates, one individual finally emerges a winner and all opposition evaporates. A united party once again emerges.) Let's see how Mr. Garcia capitalizes on the group process.

> Mr. Garcia calls the class back to their seats and tells them that, in his classes, he always has a class council meeting on Fridays for the last 20 minutes of the period. However, since this is the first week of a new semester and they have a lot of problems to work out, they will have a meeting every day this week, beginning today. The class is then encouraged to begin an open general discussion. One or two students bring up different problems pertaining to missing lab equipment, how they are going to be graded, and whether the lab could be open during their free period after lunch. Finally, Ronald raises his hand, and everyone turns to look at him. "I have no equipment and I'm in no group." The girl he previously embarrassed shouts, "Serves you right." Mr. Garcia interjects, "What Ronald has done is in the past. What can we do about his not having a group to join?" The class begins in earnest to discuss the issue. Most students express the feeling that if Ronald has no equipment, then he cannot pass the course and that would be unfair. Some members ask the three-member group if they would let Ronald into their group. Again, the girl that had been embarrassed states, "No way! He will bug us and keep us from our work. Those chemicals are dangerous!" However, the other two members of the group say that they would be willing to work with him on a trial basis. Finally, after much discussion, it is decided that the girl will change places with a student in another group and Ronald would now have three people with whom he could work at the laboratory table. Ronald appears greatly relieved to hear this decision.

Up to this point, everything seems to have been resolved. But what happens if Ronald continues to misbehave? What recourse does the teacher or class have? We need to look at Dreikurs's interpretation of logical consequences to answer these questions.

Reinforcement

Dreikurs did not believe in the use of punishment, negative reinforcement, praise, or positive reinforcement. Instead, he substitutes natural/logical consequences and the process of encouragement. Each of these will be explained as it applies to Ronald.

Natural/Logical Consequences

If Ronald should create a commotion after becoming accepted in the group, he could be disciplined as a result of some of the following logical consequences:

- Have the group of three decide what should be done with Ronald.
- Have Ronald work alone and have him use the laboratory equipment on his own time (at lunch, study hall, after school).
- Bring Ronald's misbehavior back to the entire class in a classroom meeting to decide on future consequences.

Specifically, for Ronald, this means:

- If Ronald has been causing a disturbance by poking students with a pencil, take away all his pencils and tell Ronald that whenever he needs to write, he'll have to come to the teacher's desk to ask for a pencil.
- If Ronald has been constantly moving out of his chair and distracting others, tell Ronald that he does not seem to need a chair and take it away from him. Let him stand until he requests to have it back and to stay in it.

A *natural consequence* is defined as that which happens as a result of one's behavior. If a student is rushing to get into line and trips and falls, we call this a natural consequence. On the other hand, if a student is rushing and pushing others in order to be first in line and is removed by the teacher to a place at the end of the line, then this would be identified as a *logical consequence*. In other words, a natural consequence is an inevitable occurrence that happens by itself, whereas a logical consequence is arranged but directly related to the preceding behavior. Dreikurs believes that, in a democratic society and in a democratic classroom, students must be responsible for how they behave. There is no room for autocratic punishment, as such punishment further alienates and discourages a child. Extensive punishment serves as a force to drive a student toward the goal of revenge. Punishment is not seen as being logically related to a student's behavior. It is inflicted as a reaction to personal dissatisfaction felt by the teacher. Punishment says to the student, "You had better behave or I (the teacher) will make life miserable for you." If the student does "knuckle under," it is because of the power of the teacher and not because the student has learned how to be a productive member of the group. If one accepts Dreikurs's definition of human behavior as a purposeful attempt to belong, then a teacher who uses punishment blocks a student's purpose. Punishment "plays back" into the student's misdirected goals. It gives attention, enhances the power struggle, stimulates further revenge, and keeps the helpless child in his or her place.

Additionally, Dreikurs rather pragmatically pointed out that, in today's age of equal rights and militancy, students are not easily coerced by the use of authoritarian power. Not only does punishment thwart a student's ambition but it simply does not work.[8] Let us further explore the operational distinction between punishment and natural/logical consequences. Sending a student home with a note, keeping her after school, paddling, scolding, ridiculing, or standing the student in a corner are all forms of physical or psychological punishment. The teacher's actions are aimed at hurting the child or making her feel bad. Punishment is the teacher's vengeance for a committed crime. On the other hand, students who clean up the mess they created, who are put at the end of the line for shoving, who miss a pep rally because of tardiness with their assigned work, or who are barred from using certain materials until they choose to use them properly are all actually involved in the effects of logical consequences. Logical consequences are not always easy to tailor to every disruptive action. However, it is the teacher's task to arrange the situation that follows the disruption in a way that the student can see a relationship between the consequences and her behavior. (This is a further break from the Relationship-Listening position, particularly Gordon's, which would criticize logical consequences as being false, contrived, and manipulative.)

Finally, it is important to note the differences in a teacher's attitude and manner in the application of logical consequences as opposed to the act of punishment. Two teachers might arrive at the same solution for a problem caused by a child's behavior, but one will be an example of logical consequences and the other will be an example of punishment. Sounds confusing, but it really isn't! For example, during quiet work time, Sue Ann continually pokes Ernie with a pencil. One teacher, "Mr. Matter-of-Fact," tells the girl, "Sue Ann, if you do that again, you are showing that you cannot control your pencil, and I will need to take it from you. You will be able to finish the pencil and paper task here in this classroom while others are at the pep rally." The other teacher, "Mr. How-Dare-You," says, "Sue Ann, I have told you a thousand times not to do that. Can't you understand anything? If I catch you once more, I'll take all your pencils away and you'll stay in at recess. Maybe being alone is the only way that you can work!" Mr. Matter-of-Fact has calmly told the student to use the pencil correctly or give it up. Mr. How-Dare-You acts as though he has been personally affronted and that Sue Ann's misbehavior is a direct challenge to his authority. He tries to hammer her down by scolding, questioning her competence, and challenging her. The same outcome has occurred, the student has had the pencil confiscated, but Mr. Matter-of-Fact has used logical consequences and Mr. How-Dare-You has applied punishment.

Encouragement

At the same time that the class and Mr. Garcia are applying logical consequences to Ronald's behavior, Mr. Garcia is also using the encouragement process. Mr. Garcia asks Ronald to keep inventory of all laboratory equipment and to prepare an order of new supplies for the class. Mr. Garcia also makes a mental note to greet Ronald warmly each day.

The encouragement process is an attitude taken with a misbehaving student that results in a climate of respect and optimism.[9] One must remember that a student whose goal is *attention* feels stifled by authority, and may retreat to the even more destructive goal of *power*. When that goal is "beaten down" by an overbearing, punitive teacher, the student may then resort to the goal of *revenge* to retaliate. When revenge is crushed by even more coercive means, we may finally have the most pathetic result, a student who has simply given up and has internalized the goal of *helplessness*. This lowering of goals is the result of a student becoming further discouraged. Not only does the student retreat further back into gloom and despair but so does the teacher. The vicious cycle compounds the problem.

The role of the teacher is to stop this dissipation of hope by using encouragement. This is accomplished by teacher action such as:

- *Emphasize improvement rather than a perfect product.*
- *Criticize the student's actions, but not the student* (i.e., "I like you but I don't like to hear you shouting").
- *Keep the student in a group with other students who are willing to help.* Determine those peers who are most accepting and tolerant of the student in question. Seat the student with them and arrange for him to work with them in groups. Find a companion or friend for the student.
- *Refrain from having the student compete against others.* Do not compare the student to others ("Why can't you behave like Rufus?") or constantly single out for praise others who outperform the youngster. Deemphasize grades; try to grade the student on effort, not her rank in relation to others. Avoid contests for the best-behaved student or citizen of the week, where the student has little chance of winning.

Dreikurs believes that the provision of positive reinforcement is generally not a desirable method. Encouragement is much broader than in the Rules and Consequences use of verbal praise, materials, or situational rewards as conditioning to achieve appropriate behavior. In 1963, Dinkmeyer and Dreikurs wrote:

> *Unfortunately, even the well meaning and sincere educator may often fail to convey much needed encouragement if he tries to express his approval through praise. . . . Praise may have a discouraging effect in the long run, since the child may depend on it constantly and never be quite sure whether he will merit another expression of special approval and get it.*[10]

Dinkmeyer and Dreikurs were not saying that praise should be totally avoided, but what they were suggesting is that too much praise makes a child dependent on the teacher. The student who is "won over" by the teacher to work quietly due to the teacher's praise ("Oh look at Hillary! What a fine student to be working so quietly! I am so proud that you're being so quiet") has not learned social behavior. Instead of learning how to act out of consideration for others, the child instead is learning how to act for purposes of receiving the teacher's special compliments and dispensations. In other words, the child behaves well, but for all the wrong reasons. If the teacher is removed from the scene, the child's behavior will deteriorate. The child needs to internalize the correct motivation for being well behaved (acting as a productive member of the group) in order for it to be lasting.

In addition, the child who sees himself as a failure and is motivated by revenge or helplessness will tend to disbelieve the authenticity of the teacher's words. A child who refuses to work and "gives up" on carrying out any order may have reason to speculate on why the teacher makes such an effort to praise her ("Oh, Sam, look what a good job you did! You make me so pleased when you hang your coat up!" Or, "Margie, it's great the way that you answered that question!"). The student will, in effect, believe that the teacher is overcompensating and that she is being singled out because she is indeed inferior. The child may think, "Why make such a big deal about hanging my coat up or answering a simple question? The teacher must think I'm a real nincompoop (idiot, jerk, bozo, etc.)." Thus, the opposite effect of what the teacher intended will result—a further sign that reaffirms the child's inferiority. In this vein of thought, Dreikurs and Grey wrote that there is a fundamental difference between the act of reward and the act of encouragement. Few realize that, at times, success can be very discouraging. The child may conclude that, although success was achieved once, it could not happen again. The student's recent "success" may become a threat to her future ability to succeed. But what is worse, such an event often conveys to the child the assumption, which actually is shared by most of her teachers and fellow students, that she is worthwhile only when she is successful.[11]

What we have, then, is the premise that praise or other forms of reward seem to heighten a child's anxiety always to have to "measure up." It puts constraints on a child who feels such pressure. He feels comfortable only when being successful. The discomfort with being unsuccessful further discourages a child from feelings of being accepted and of being an acceptable person. He feels accepted only when successful, but not when something less than success occurs as a result of efforts expended. The child who needs to learn to be a member must learn to accept his individual self as being a person capable of both success and failure but who, despite outcomes, is still worthy of being loved and accepted by others.

A child who is always dependent on being rewarded for what he does is in a bind when it comes to taking a risk. The child who is learning how to belong must be encouraged to try new ways of behaving. The student who learns that it is safe and rewarding to be meek and passive will not easily venture into the unknown by being assertive and active. He won't venture into untried areas. This is the danger of having "failure-proof" programs or "praise-laden" teachers.

The teacher must not stress the concept of success but, instead, promote a climate of always accepting the student as worthwhile. This happens when a teacher uses encouragement rather than such reinforcement as praise.

Following are two contrasting lists that give examples of praise versus encouragement. Praise focuses on the teacher being pleased by the child and on the child achieving a completed product. Conversely, encouragement focuses on the student and on the process of the student trying.

Praise	*Encouragement*
1. "I (teacher) like what you have done."	1. "You're trying harder."
2. "Great job! What a smart person."	2. "You must be happy with (playing that game, being with others, etc.)."
3. "You get a star (token, free time) for doing that."	3. "It must be a good feeling to know you're doing well."
4. "I'm going to tell everyone how proud I am of you."	4. "You have every reason to be proud."

Physical Intervention and Isolation

Forms of teacher intervention such as paddling or shaking a student would be rejected by Dreikurs. Such treatment would be seen as a form of punishment that would drive a student further away from social cooperation. Pain experienced as a natural consequence (without the possibility of serious harm) could be allowed. Some examples of this might be the student who recklessly rushes to be first in line and falls and is bruised, or the student who repeatedly provokes the science class gerbil and is bitten. On the other hand, there are some natural consequences that can eventuate when a student precariously tilts back in her chair, or when a "90-pound weakling" begins to taunt and enrage a 250-pound high school football tackle. These could be dangerous consequences, and the teacher would be wise to prevent them from occurring. It is important to note that a teacher should carefully judge the natural consequence before deciding to act or not act in a given situation.

Isolation must also be used judiciously by the teacher. Dreikurs advocated the use of isolation only as a logical consequence. We saw that Ronald was isolated temporarily by Mr. Garcia when his behavior was immediately disruptive of others. However, Ronald was given the opportunity to join the group once he decided that he wished to belong.

It is obvious that if being part of a group is the ultimate goal for all individuals, then each person needs to learn to relate successfully to others. One only learns such relationships by practicing appropriate behaviors with others. One does not learn cooperation by being lectured to or having to sit by oneself. For these reasons, instead of relying on isolation, the teacher is required to look constantly for ways to encourage attachments between the offending child and other members of the class.

THE "OUTSIDE AGGRESSOR" PHENOMENON

In the eleventh-grade art class, the students are allowed to select their own seats among the many tables in the room. Five girls have sat together at a round table for four weeks so far. Amy, an attractive new student at the school, has been sitting by herself but has started to become friendly with some of the girls at the "in" table. After class, Marcia, one of the girls at the table, tells Amy to make sure to get to class early tomorrow and grab a seat at the round table. She confides that she and three others will also be early so they can all sit together. The next day, Amy and the four girls are already seated by the time Julie, a past member, walks in. She seems startled and walks up to Amy and says, "Pardon me, but you're in my seat!" Amy isn't too sure what to say and looks around at the other girls, who are smiling at her. Marcia looks up at Julie and says, "We've invited Amy to join us. I'm sure you can find somewhere else to sit where you'll fit in." Stunned, Julie walks away.

During the class that same day, Julie's teacher, Mrs. Anderson, is placing paints before her on her table when one pot accidentally tips and spills, making a small yellow paint mark on Julie's blouse. Julie shouts at her teacher, "Look what did, you damn stupid old cow!" The entire class quiets while "the gang" giggles and laughs at Julie.

The incident with Julie and "the gang" shows clearly that Julie has lost her past friends and companions, and is now being socially isolated. The Confronting-Contracting position would be that Julie's "acting out" (the verbal aggression, "you damn stupid old cow") was a result of built-up "revengeful" feelings being directed at an innocent party: the teacher. All misbehavior by students in the classroom—whether attention-getting power acts, revengeful acts, or passive behavior—is seen by Confronting-Contracting as a failure to find social acceptance. However, we rarely get such a clear observation as in the Julie incident to actually verify this position. Instead, we typically see a repetitive host of misbehaviors and aggressive actions that on the surface do not appear to be related to immediate behavior by other children (e.g., "He hits other students without any provocation"). Students' first feelings of acceptance come out of the home setting with parents and siblings. If they felt they were rejected in early family interaction, they will assume that they will be rejected in a classroom situation and will set out with negative actions *to prove* that others do not like them.

The less skilled teacher might bring "the gang" aside and verbally reprimand and lecture them for their actions, applying large doses of guilt for their behavior. Such actions might unknowingly make members of "the gang" even more hostile to Julie, and now they will be revengeful toward her in more subtle ways that the teacher will not see or detect. Julie needs to acquire social skills that will enable her to find acceptance.

There are a number of techniques that enable the teacher to be proactive in helping students to acquire social skills. Before they are presented, however, it may be helpful to first explain the *"outside aggressor" phenomenon.*

A visitor to an early childhood center is asked on the playground by a 3-year-old, "What's your name, Mister?" The man responds, "Mr. Wolfe." The child, hearing woof, jumps up and runs screaming to the opposite end of the playground, shouting, "Woof, Woof!" Then each member of his group picks up a light twig that had fallen during a storm the night before. They "stalk" the visitor, walking up behind him on tip-toe, and then each child forcefully strikes the man in the back with the sticks. They run off, again screaming, "Woof!"

We have just witnessed the phenomenon of the "outside aggressor."

Since young children still have two large islands of emotional extremes—when they love, they love totally, and when the hate, they hate totally—and their feelings of rivalry are still very strong, they have a difficult time coming together in groups. One of the more primitive and base levels of social interaction, which first begins during the early years, is coming together in a group and finding an outside person, object, or fantasy object against which to project their strong competitive feelings and aggression. This creates an implicit agreement not to aggress against each other and establishes a temporary feeling of belonging. Julie became the common outside aggressor object to "the gang," just as Mr. Wolfe did to the 3-year-olds.

Although the "outside aggressor" phenomenon begins in early childhood,[12] examples can yet be seen among adolescents and adults. One can recall the interaction at a dinner party when one person must depart early, leaving everyone else behind to talk about him in the most negative manner. The "leaver" becomes the dinner group's outside aggressor. Members of the group, by default, have informally agreed to project their aggressive criticism at the departed person, and not to speak ill of each other. The game works if nearly everyone says something derogatory. Thus, for a short period of time, the members of the "dinner gang" have a superior feeling of being above someone else—a feeling of primitive belonging to this "in" group. Politicians throughout history have used this outside aggressor phenomenon to gain control of groups; perhaps the most glaring and frightening example was the way in which Hitler controlled an entire nation by casting one ethnic group as the outside aggressor.

Banding together against an outside aggressor is normal for many adolescents. Our role as teachers, of course, is to engineer ways through which students can learn to be social in a more healthy manner and to help children like Julie acquire social skills and feel like they belong.

Social Engineering

Mrs. Anderson calls Julie to the art table. She has seen Julie being made the outside aggressor, and she summons her in a voice loud enough for "the gang" to hear. She states, "Julie, we are going to make the centerpiece for the Christmas dance, and I am going to let you be the chairperson of this project. I will arrange with the principal and your study hall supervisors to have this committee released from study hall for the next three weeks. You may choose helpers to work with you!" Every member of the class is eager to be on this committee, and everyone begins waving their hands to be chosen. Julie chooses six nearby students. "The gang" sees what is happening. Their facial expressions show that their excitement has been deflated, and they begin to wander over to the art table and look on as this new project is being organized. They loiter about, and then gradually plead in a whining voice, "Mrs. Anderson, can we be on the committee, too?" The teacher responds, "I don't know. I am not the chairperson of this project—Julie is! You will have to ask her." The gang approaches Julie and asks, "Can we join your committee?" Julie hesitates for a few seconds, then smiles and says yes. The teacher hovers nearby, watching all the committee members working on the art arrangement, her presence helping Julie to maintain her power. Later, when the dance programs are made, Julie's name will be listed as the chair of this committee. In addition, she has her photograph taken while working on the project for the local newspaper and for the class yearbook. Later, during the class discussion, Mrs. Anderson will encourage other students to express their joy at being a part of the project and working under Julie's leadership (*encouragement*).

In the use of social engineering, we consider that a misbehaving child is powerless, lacking the skill to find social belonging. We deliberately "engineer" or set up activities whereby we empower children such as Julie and help them enjoy the experience of successfully working within a group. We deliberately point out to classmates how she has given and contributed to making the classroom a happy and accepting place. Thus, we deliberately engineer positive experiences for misbehaving children. After the centerpiece experience, we may question Julie with Confronting-Contracting "What" questions, such as, "Julie, what did you do as committee chair? What worked for you as you worked with friends? What did not? What will you do next time when you want friends?" Notice that we did *not* tell Julie how well she did, or make any value judgments, or offer a prescription for her in further interactions. Through our questions and counseling of children who are having social difficulty, we want them to become reflective after social experiences, to become consciously aware of their own behavior, to evaluate their success, and to come up with ideas of how they may be even more effective the next time.

Disengaging

Teachers are not robots who are emotionless, who never get angry, and who always have good feelings toward all children. Some children are appealing and some are very unappealing; the unappealing children generally are the ones who cannot find acceptance in their homes and from fellow classmates. As previously stated, the nonsocially adjusted misbehaving child in the classroom, because of feelings of rejection, begins to seek excessive attention and power, becomes revengeful and, finally, retreats into a passive state of helplessness. If we as teachers acknowledge that we are human beings with a range of feelings, we will allow that the excessive attention-getting child produces feelings of annoyance in us, that we feel at times beaten by the power-needy child, that we feel hurt by the revengeful child, and that we feel inadequate in working with the helpless child.

We must acknowledge to ourselves that we have these feelings toward these children. Our feelings only become a problem when we ourselves begin to regress into becoming revengeful or feeling helpless toward these children. Therefore, we now have a good reason to use isolation techniques—that is, to get ourselves *disengaged*. If we are angry and overcome by our own feelings because of the repetitive demands that the problem child is presenting to us (being called an "old cow") we may become emotionally flooded in the middle of a teachable moment. We need to do skilled confronting, yet we are not able to handle this successfully and professionally because our clear thinking has been flooded by emotions. We then may consider placing the misbehaving child in isolation for a period of time, or moving the child temporarily to another room or into a different room or building area under the supervision of another teacher or school authority. As emotionally flooded individuals, we must spatially move away from this student for a period of time until we have disengaged from these strong emotions. Once we are calm and relaxed, we will have energies to reapproach the difficult child to begin our steps of confronting. *We cannot do Confronting-Contracting when angered.*

Unknowingly, the entire school staff can collectively begin to have these same angry, revengeful, and helpless feelings toward this one student. The child with an attitude of, "If I can't be the best good student, I will be the best bad student" is known in schools by the bus driver, guidance counselor, cafeteria worker, and even the parents of other students. The student has a reputation that precedes him or her. If we analyze the staff and the reaction of the problem child's classmates, we begin to see that after a period of time, we have made the "Ronalds" of this world the outside aggressor in our classroom. He gets blamed by *all* students and staff for *all* accidents and negative occurrences. Others, including teachers, do not want him at their table or sitting near them at social events. Most everyone, including adults, has unknowingly begun a process of "shunning" the problem student. This shunning and being the object of the outside aggressor phenomenon now severely complicates the intervention and dynamics of ever helping this child to change. The difficult child has dug a deep social hole that he or she will never be able to climb out of by himself or herself.

Besides disengaging (if necessary) before confronting such a child, how then do we handle this collective anger and shunning toward the child?

The Most Wanted

A staff meeting must be called involving all adults who come into daily contact with the difficult student. (If you are one teacher by yourself, you may need to sit down during a quiet period and in essence have this meeting with yourself.) At the start of this meeting, it might be helpful if members of the group of adults are permitted some time to express their honest feelings toward the student. Staff members who are frightened by their own negative feelings toward the difficult child might receive some reassurance if they hear a skilled and respected teacher state, "I am wondering how you are feeling about Ronald Foster these days. I must confess that at times I find myself getting angry and even frightened by him. At times I don't want him in my class, and at times I am having a hard time liking him." The first step in changing staff's negative behavior toward a difficult student is to get honest feelings "out on the table."

As we noted, the problem student has dug a deep social hole that he cannot climb out of alone. Feeling rejected, the student sits about day in and day out, his negative actions evoking further rejection from classmates and adults. After all, adolescents are still children. A problem student is still in the formative years of development, and these stormy adolescent years are the most robust years for making a positive impact on the child's development that will serve—or misserve—him for a lifetime. As the expression goes, "Love begins with love!" The very nature of our jobs, and *the central role as teachers,* is to make a lasting contribution to these difficult children. Almost all adults can recall one significant experience where a teacher has befriended and helped a struggling child at a difficult point in his life. We must understand what a lasting impression this can have and how it can make long-term positive results for the child's well-being.

That is the challenge—and the opportunity—before us as we deal with this one particular difficult problem child. If we do not do it, who will? Literally, anyone can teach the child who has been well mothered and fathered, but it is the difficult child who enables us to "earn our stripes" as teachers. This is a big responsibility but we may be their only and last hope, because once they get into the real adult world, rarely will they find another person willing to take the time to help them.

Now, exactly how do we do this? We do it in a staff meeting by using the Confronting-Contracting procedures on ourselves, much as Glasser reality therapy questions. We ask, What are we and his classmates really doing to Ronald Foster? The answer is that we are, unknowingly, shunning him and making him the outside aggressor. We want most staff members to verbally express past incidents in which they have moved away from this problem child. Mrs. Anderson confesses, "I am embarrassed to admit it, but one time when I was seated at the table with a group of students, we had one chair remaining at our table. I saw Ronald approaching, and—again, I'm embarrassed to admit it—I grabbed another student and had him take the free seat so that Ronald would not be at my table." This outward admission is most important! (The teacher working alone might want to write this out.) Mrs. Anderson's candor may then encourage other staff members to share similar experiences or feelings.

The next question to ask is, What will we do to change? The answer is that for the next two weeks we will put Ronald, as our difficult problem child, on the Most Wanted list. Unlike a police Most Wanted list, however, this list will single Ronald out for special *positive* behavior. Have you ever witnessed the behavior of staff and students when the school has a visiting student, perhaps visiting from another country? Visitors enjoy special status while spending the day in the classroom. The "red carpet" is rolled out for them: They are greeted warmly at the door, shown where to be seated, and told how and where things work. Placing our difficult student on our Most Wanted list means treating him as an honored guest throughout the two-week period. When every staff member—even those who do not have him in their group or classes—sees the difficult child passing by, they are to give him the "time of day." The teacher says hello, makes eye contact, says the child's name, and makes some pleasant verbal overture. The teacher helps the student and invites him to be a part of any group activities. During *every* time period throughout the day for the two weeks, some adult should be helping the student as if he were new to school procedures and practices—a stranger visiting without friends. At any discussion groups involving the entire class, the teacher will provide statements of encouragement by pointing out to classmates any and all positive behaviors by the difficult child.

Almost as if a whistle has been blown, all adults deliberately change their behavior toward the difficult student. If we as the teacher don't change, then classmates as well as the student cannot change. We help the problem student "climb out" of the deep social hole in which he was imprisoned by changing the entire social environment in the school. At first, you will feel phony acting in such a manner, but you must push and commit yourself to perform such "motor actions." A campaign of welcoming the child day in and day out can have a real impact to change a problem student's behavior and help him gain a feeling of acceptance. In contrast, if the social engineering techniques described previously are employed but the school climate (the actions of the adults and classmates) still shuns the difficult student as an object of outside aggression, it will be unlikely that progress can be made. At the end of the two-week period of the Most Wanted program, another staff meeting must be held. This will be a follow-up meeting to evaluate the success or lack of success of the welcoming process. The remainder of the staff meeting should follow the Six Steps to Staffing (described in later chapters), through which the staff focuses on the child's problem behaviors and addresses what actions can be taken individually by a teacher or the staff in dealing with misbehavior. Also, it is a given that the welcoming and accepting attitude toward the difficult child should and must continue.

SUMMARY

We have positioned Dreikurs as the initial example of Confronting-Contracting for three reasons. First, closely aligned with the Relationship-Listening orientation, he had an optimistic belief in the child's rational capacities. Second, unlike those under Relationship-Listening, he believed that such a development must occur in a social milieu where adults or peers need to intervene and redirect the child's misplaced goals. Third, Dreikurs instructed the teacher to use specific actions to redirect the child's misdirected goal. The use of such actions is much more assertive than the Relationship-Listening orientation's nonjudgmental approaches. Dreikurs has directed the teacher to use strategies that personally combat the child's game and aim consciously to pull the group to her side. The teacher then arranges logical consequences for the offending student to experience. Dreikurs believed that every student can attain her place in life but needs the active help of the adult. His approaches therefore are more intrusive than with Relationship-Listening, but could hardly be described as the shaping mechanisms of Rules and Consequences.

Looking at Figure 4–5, we can now identify the covert and overt behaviors of a teacher using this model. The teacher begins by covertly observing and collecting information about the student by (a) silently looking on. This is followed by the teacher's analysis of his or her own feelings toward the student's behavior by (b) asking himself or herself such questions as "Do I feel…annoyed (reflecting the student's goal of attention getting); beaten (the goal of power); hurt (the goal of revenge); or incapable (the goal of helplessness)?" The teacher can then make an immediate guess at the student's goal and respond with (1) an appropriate directive statement that includes a logical consequence. In order to determine the student's goal and to plan accordingly, the teacher will choose a calmer moment and

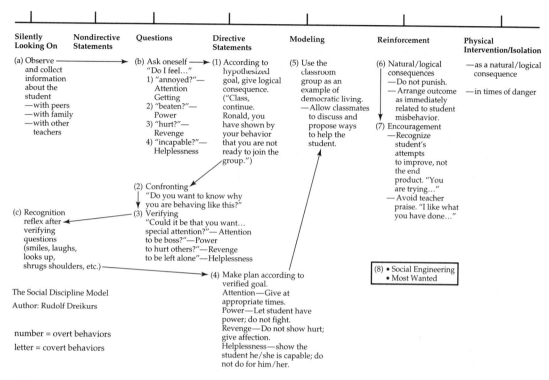

Silently Looking On	Nondirective Statements	Questions	Directive Statements	Modeling	Reinforcement	Physical Intervention/Isolation

(a) Observe and collect information about the student
—with peers
—with family
—with other teachers

(b) Ask oneself "Do I feel..."
1) "annoyed?"— Attention Getting
2) "beaten?"— Power
3) "hurt?"— Revenge
4) "incapable?"— Helplessness

(1) According to hypothesized goal, give logical consequence. ("Class, continue. Ronald, you have shown by your behavior that you are not ready to join the group.")

(5) Use the classroom group as an example of democratic living.
—Allow classmates to discuss and propose ways to help the student.

(6) Natural/logical consequences
—Do not punish.
—Arrange outcome as immediately related to student misbehavior.

(7) Encouragement
—Recognize student's attempts to improve, not the end product. "You are trying..."
—Avoid teacher praise. "I like what you have done..."

—as a natural/logical consequence

—in times of danger

(2) Confronting "Do you want to know why you are behaving like this?"

(c) Recognition reflex after verifying questions (smiles, laughs, looks up, shrugs shoulders, etc.)

(3) Verifying "Could it be that you want... special attention?"— Attention to be boss?"—Power to hurt others?"—Revenge to be left alone"—Helplessness

The Social Discipline Model
Author: Rudolf Dreikurs

number = overt behaviors

letter = covert behaviors

(4) Make plan according to verified goal.
Attention—Give at appropriate times.
Power—Let student have power; do not fight.
Revenge—Do not show hurt; give affection.
Helplessness—show the student he/she is capable; do not do for him/her.

(8) • Social Engineering
 • Most Wanted

FIGURE 4–5   Teacher Behavior Continuum (TBC): Social Discipline

use questions that (2) confront the student as to whether the student wishes to know why she behaves as she does, and then (3) verify the suspected goal by asking one of the four questions that correspond to the elements of attention, power, revenge, and helplessness. Immediately after each question, the teacher will be silently looking on for the student to exhibit a "recognition reflex" identifying her goal. With the goal verified, the teacher can (4) initiate a long-range plan by conferring with the student and describing, through the use of directive statements, how the student can successfully have her needs met through socially appropriate ways. The classroom group can serve as a model of democratic living by (5) proposing ways to help the student. Finally, the teacher builds the use of (6) natural/logical consequences for those misbehaviors that may continue into the plan, while simultaneously using the process of encouragement. This combined approach prevents the student from becoming discouraged, even though there may be future instances when natural/logical consequences occur as a result of socially inappropriate behavior.

ENDNOTES

1. R. Dreikurs, *Children: The Challenge* (New York: E. P. Dutton, 1964).

2. R. Dreikurs, *Psychology in the Classroom: A Manual for Teachers,* 2nd ed. New York: Harper & Row, 1968), pp. 16–17.

3. R. Dreikurs and P. Cassel, *Discipline Without Tears: What to Do with Children Who Misbehave,* rev. ed. (New York: Hawthorn Books, 1972), pp. 34–41.

4. Dreikurs and Cassel, *Discipline Without Tears,* p. 41.

5. Dreikurs, *Psychology in the Classroom,* p. 55.

6. Dreikurs and Cassel, *Discipline Without Tears,* p. 42.

7. Dreikurs and Cassel, *Discipline Without Tears,* p. 44.

8. Dreikurs, *Psychology in the Classroom,* pp. 71–73.

9. Dreikurs, *Children: The Challenge,* p. 76.

10. D. Dinkmeyer and R. Dreikurs, *Encouraging Children to Learn: The Encouragement Process* (Englewood Cliffs, NJ: Prentice Hall, 1963), pp. 45–56.

11. Dinkmeyer and Dreikurs, *Encouraging Children to Learn,* p. 121.

12. R. Dreikurs and G. Loren, *Logical Consequences* (New York: Meredith Press, 1968), p. 157.

RELATED READINGS

Albert, L. *A Teacher's Guide to Cooperative Discipline: How to Manage Your Classroom and Promote Self-Esteem.* Circle Pines, MN: American Guidance Service, 1989.

Dinkmeyer, D., and Dreikurs, R. *Encouraging Children to Learn: The Encouragement Process.* Englewood Cliffs, NJ: Prentice Hall, 1963.

Dreikurs, R. *Children: The Challenge.* New York: E. P. Dutton, 1964.

Dreikurs, R. *Psychology in the Classroom: A Manual for Teachers,* 2nd. ed. New York: Harper & Row, 1968.

Dreikurs, R. *Discipline Without Tears: What to Do with Children Who Misbehave.* New York: Hawthorn Books, 1972.

Dreikurs, R., and Loren, G. *Logical Consequences.* New York: Meredith Press, 1968.

Books for Parents on the STEP Program (Adlerian-Dreikurs Based Theory)

Dinkmeyer, D., and McKay, G. D. *Systematic Training for Effective Parenting (STEP).* Circle Pines, MN: American Guidance Service, 1976.

Dinkmeyer, D., and McKay, G. D. *Padres Eficaces con Entrenamiento Sistematico (PECES).* Circle Pines, MN: American Guidance Service, 1981.

Dinkmeyer, D., and McKay, G. D. *Systematic Training for Effective Parenting of Teens (STEP/Teen).* Circle Pines, MN: American Guidance Service, 1983.

Dinkmeyer, D., and McKay, G. D. *Systematic Training for Effective Parenting (STEP) of Children Under Six.* Circle Pines, MN: American Guidance Service, 1989.

Dinkmeyer, D., Sr., McKay, G. D., Dinkmeyer, D., Jr., Dinkmeyer, James S., and McKay, J. L. *The Next STEP.* Circle Pines, MN: American Guidance Service, 1983.

INSTRUCTIONAL MEDIA: ADLERIAN-DREIKURS THEORY

Name	Minutes	Format	Sound	Address of Distributor
Adlerian Family Counseling	35	16 mm	yes	Educational Media Corporation 2036 Lemoyn Avenue Los Angeles, CA 90026

The Adlerian model holds that the difficulties with children, being experienced by parents and other adults, are primarily due to a lack of education. Dr. Oscar Christensen of the University of Arizona works with the Lohman family in front of an audience of parents and adults and discusses the impact of the ordinal position. He hears the parents' concerns and validates these by checking with the children. He then summarizes the session and provides encouragement and gives recommendations for the parents.

Name	Minutes	Format	Sound	Address of Distributor
Coping with Kids	26	Video ¾ inch	yes	Films Incorporated Video 5547 N. Ravenswood Avenue Chicago, IL 60640-1199 (800) 343-4312 FAX (312)878-0416

Dr. Thomas Sweeney demonstrates the Adlerian principles. The students representing the four mis-motivations are interviewed.

In-Service Training

Name	Time	Format	Sound	Address of Distributor
Cooperative Discipline (Adlerian-Dreikurs Oriented), Linda Albert	105 minutes	Kit, text, video cassette ¾ inch	yes	AGS—American Guidance Service 4201 Woodland Road P.O. Box 99 Circle Pines, MN 55014–1796 (800) 328-2256

A video-based training program using a Cooperative Discipline Kit, the test, *A Teacher's Guide to Cooperative Discipline, Teacher's Handbook,* and two video cassettes. Also included is a *Leader's Guide,* with a *Leader's Guide Booklet,* video cassettes with script booklet (105 minutes in all), text, and 18 blackline masters (reproducibles). Finally is *An Adminstrator's Guide to Cooperative Discipline.* Training can be provided at the school site.

Name	Time	Format	Sound	Address of Distributor
Stet: Systematic Training for Effective Teaching, Don Dinkmeyer	14 sessions	STET Participant's Packet, includes teacher's handbook and teacher's resource book	yes	AGS—American Guidance Service 4201 Woodland Road Circle Pines, MN 55014–1796 (800) 328-2256
Designed for preschool through grade 12 teachers, this is a flexible training format letting the school personnel vary the schedule of training. Topics: Why students misbehave; Motivation through encouragement; Communication skills; Discipline; Working with a group; Understanding students with special needs; and Working with parents. (Dr. Dinkmeyer has written a number of books for parents on discipline, and offers training for parents in his *STEP: Systematic Training for Effective Parenting.*)				

ADLERIAN-DREIKURS ACTION PLAN

Steps follow those from the TBC (see Figure 4–5)	
Name of Student	Date
Step (a): Observe and describe the child's behavior	Step (b): Ask yourself, Do I feel...
1.	
	(check one) __annoyed? __beaten? __hurt? __incapable?
2.	
	(check one) __annoyed? __beaten? __hurt? __incapable?
3.	
	(check one) __annoyed? __beaten? __hurt? __incapable?
Steps (1) and (2): Confront the student (write your verbal statements):	
Step (3): Verify the goal: "Could it be that you want: special attention / to boss / to hurt others / to be left alone?"	What is the student's goal: (check one) __annoyed? __beaten? __hurt? __incapable?
Step (4): Make a plan	
Step (5): Use the classroom group: How could a class meeting/discussion enlist peers to help?	
Step (6): State natural/logical consequences to be used:	Step (7): State encouragement strategies:
1.	1.
2.	2.

(continued)

3.	3.
Step (8): Describe social engineering strategies:	Describe a Most Wanted strategy:

5

GLASSER'S REALITY THERAPY, CONTROL THEORY, AND THE QUALITY SCHOOL

Theorist/Writer: William Glasser

- *Reality Therapy: A New Approach to Psychiatry*
- *Schools Without Failure*
- *Control Theory in the Classroom*
- *The Quality School: Managing Students Without Coercion*

Mr. Roberts's eleventh-grade literature class was discussing the short story they had read the previous day. There were only 19 students in this class and it was turning out to be a very enjoyable experience for Mr. Roberts. He didn't have any problems, and the students were friendly and seemed genuinely interested in the themes he had selected so far. During the discussion, he noticed Doug, a tall angular boy who plays basketball, passing a note to Sophia, a very pretty young lady who sits next to him. Mr. Roberts decided to ignore the note and kept the class discussion going. Sophia looked at the note and then quickly crumpled it up and made the short toss to the rear trash can. Doug smirked a bit and kept his eyes mostly on Sophia. A very short time later, Sophia quickly stood up, looked directly at Doug and then turned to Mr. Roberts and said, "He's disgusting. Make him stop it!" Mr. Roberts responded, "Stop what? What's going on back there?" As he was saying this, Mr. Roberts looked at Doug in time to see the boy quickly pulling his hand away from his crotch, where only a moment ago it was firmly grasped. "It's just filthy!" Sophia said, and then looking back at Doug added, "You make me sick. I wish you would just leave me alone!" Smiling, Doug said, "C'mon Sophia, it was only a joke, I thought you... (now looking at Mr. Roberts). It wasn't anything—it's between me and her. I didn't do anything wrong." Mr. Roberts then remembered the note in the trash can.

MR. ROBERTS: "Doug and Sophia, I can see that there is some difficulty between you. Sophia, if you wish, you may move over here to the empty desk. I will meet with both of you after class to see what the problem is and how we may work this out. I now need to return to our discussion."

DOUG: (in a loud defiant voice) "I didn't do anything wrong—I didn't do anything wrong! She is telling me dirty jokes!"

MR. ROBERTS: "I want to help you work this out. I am not looking to punish you. Doug, I want you to calm down, and as soon as I have time when the class is over, I will talk to you and we can work it out."

DOUG: "It's not my fault—she started it!"

MR. ROBERTS: "Since you won't calm down, I can't get back to my teaching. If you are not willing to settle down, it will be better if you leave. Settle yourself and let me return to teaching, or go to the school's time-out room and check in with Mr. Sanders, the assistant principal."

Sophia moves to the free desk, Doug slumps down into his desk and becomes quiet, and Mr. Roberts finishes the remainder of the class without any disturbance. When the bell rings, the class is dismissed to go to the cafeteria for lunch. Doug and Sophia are asked to remain behind. Mr. Roberts calls them to the back table, seats them facing each other but with the table between them, and takes a seat between them at the short side of the rectangular table. The teacher has retrieved the note from the trash can, and lays it unopened before them.

MR. ROBERTS: "What did you do, Doug?"

DOUG: "I dunno."

MR. ROBERTS: "What did you do, Sophia?"

SOPHIA: "He is disgusting!" (She drops her head and becomes introverted.)

MR. ROBERTS: "It is obvious that there is a problem between the two of you. I am not here to find fault or to punish, but I am here to help the two of you work this out. We need for everyone to understand what they did and what the rules are, and come to some agreement among the three of us that this problem is worked out." (silence)

MR. ROBERTS: "What did you do, Doug?"

DOUG: "Nothing, nothing, nothing!"

MR. ROBERTS: "Well, I did clearly see you pass this note to Sophia, and then later you were holding your crotch, as you giggled and stared at her."

SOPHIA: "He sent me that paper with a dirty picture drawn on it—it's disgusting! And then he starts to play with himself in class and make dirty remarks to me."

MR. ROBERTS: "What did you do, Doug?"

DOUG: "She started it. She sent me a dirty joke first."

SOPHIA: "No, I didn't. You're a liar!"

DOUG: "Yes, you did, in study hall—yesterday."

SOPHIA: "That was *not* my note! Andy asked me to pass you his note. That wasn't my note—I don't write notes at school, especially dirty notes. All morning you have been acting weird to me. You're harassing me!"

MR. ROBERTS: "Is there more you want to say?"

SOPHIA: "Yes, I have a right to feel safe in this school. It scares me when boys act like Doug is acting. I become frightened, and I don't want to hear sexual things or see sexual drawings. I have the right to be safe, and those things frighten me."

MR. ROBERTS: "What did you do, Doug?"

DOUG: "I don't know!"

MR. ROBERTS: "I think it's clear that you *do* know. You gave Sophia a note with a sexual drawing on it and you made sexual gestures and sexual remarks toward her. Am I correct—do I have a clear understanding of what occurred here?"

DOUG: (sinks deep under the table, drops his eyes, turns sideways) "I didn't mean to scare her, I was just teasing—she sent me a note."

MR. ROBERTS: "But now it appears that it was not her note, but Andy's note. Well, we have a problem here. How can this be worked out between the two of you, so that Sophia can feel safe and not harassed and the class is not disrupted again in the future?"

SOPHIA: "I think he owes me an apology, and I want to be sure that he never harasses me again. We have a nonharassment policy here at Moorage High, and if I file a grievance he'll be in big trouble. But I don't want to get him in trouble. I just want to feel safe."

DOUG: "I'm sorry, it's no big deal!"

MR. ROBERTS: "No, it *is* a big deal to Sophia. She needs to feel safe in this school. Is this a sincere apology?"

DOUG: "Yes, I am sorry. I didn't know I was scaring her. I was just trying to have some fun."

MR. ROBERTS: "Maybe it was fun for you, but I hear Sophia saying that she was frightened. What about in the future? Can Sophia feel safe when she is around you?"

DOUG: "I am sorry. I won't do it again. I really didn't mean to scare her."

MR. ROBERTS: "Sophia, do you accept Doug's apology, and do you have anything more to say?" (He looks at both students for a few moments face to face.) "Then we have an agreement—a contract. Doug apologizes and Sophia accepts the apology, and Doug agrees not to make such actions toward Sophia again. Are we in agreement, Doug? (Doug nods his head yes). Are we in agreement, Sophia? (Sophia nods her head yes) Good, then this problem is solved. Why don't you both hurry on to the cafeteria— there's still time to have your lunch."

GLASSER'S DISCIPLINE MODEL

This case illustrated some of the steps of reality therapy, as espoused by William Glasser. Glasser is a psychiatrist who was trained in, but later broke from and rejected, the Freudian concepts of psychoanalysis and views of behavior. He maintained that the traditional clinical approach to working with disturbed patients was seriously deficient. He also maintained that Freudian and play therapy encouraged dependence. He believed that the approach of allowing a person to give free vent to her emotions and to dissect and analyze her personal history, with the psychoanalyst then giving interpretations and labels to the individual's inner-conflicts, was an inefficient one and did not help patients live in the real world. In Glasser's view, individuals who were escaping reality by behaving in inappropriate ways do not need to find a rationale and defense for their illogical behavior. Instead, people must be helped to acknowledge their behavior as being irresponsible and then to take action to make it more logical and productive. As a psychiatrist, Glasser does not believe in working with the unconscious, or of being nonjudgmentally accepting (such as the Rogerians believe) of a person's action. His statement, stripped to its essentials, is that human beings must live in a world of other human beings. Each individual must satisfy his own needs in a way that does not infringe on another's.[1] He clearly states that each individual is responsible for his own actions and, regardless of how disturbed or dependent he claims to be, each person must bear the consequences of his own behavior and make a commitment to act in a responsible manner toward others.

This might read as a rather harsh manner of treating inappropriate behavior, but Glasser's work and writings are not cold and dictatorial. Rather, the reverse is true. He has applied his psychiatric concepts of reality therapy to work with delinquent girls (as cited in *Reality Therapy*) and to work with children in public schools (as cited in *Schools Without Failure*). In both settings, he is found to be one who practices and advocates for others a personal and caring relationship with misbehaving students. He sees the establishment of care and warmth as a necessary human pre-

"Then after Billy Hunt pushed you off the monkey bars, all WHAT broke loose?"

Cartoon by Ford Button.

requisite for an individual who hopes to begin to come to grips with the sometimes awesome responsibility of being planner, manager, and executor of one's own actions.

Old Wine in New Bottles

Schools Without Failure, published in 1969, was a popular book that helped educators reevaluate just what they were doing to students and how they could create schools where students felt accepted and did not fail. Glasser's two newer books, *Control Theory in the Classroom* and *The Quality School: Managing Students Without Coercion,* may be characterized as old wine in new bottles. This is not a criticism—because the "wine" Glasser produces from his philosophical vineyard is very good indeed and has changed very little. However, in these two books he has picked up the preaching, theory, and vogue terminology of W. Edwards Deming[2] to give a modernized justification to the Glasser outlook and philosophy.

Deming was the industrial managerial theorist who was sent to Japan after World War II to teach the Japanese how to democratize their factories. He succeeded so well that the Japanese industries in many ways have surpassed their U.S. and other Western counterparts. Many of today's businesses, as seen in the book *In Search of Excellence,*[3] are attempting to catch up with the Japanese by learning to use Deming principles to get the best from Western and U.S. workers. Glasser draws a direct parallel between the old factory model of industry that has failed our nation and the way our schools and classrooms traditionally have been run. He calls for schools and teachers to begin to apply the Deming principles of *Quality Systems* to classroom practices.

Historically, workers—and, Glasser would suggest, students—were viewed by industrial psychologists as either Theory X or Theory Y. Theory X holds that workers (students) cannot be trusted and must be watched every minute. These workers are paid (given grades) for the amount they produce and are punished if they fail to meet time schedules or otherwise fail in their narrowly defined duties. This is an extreme militaristic position where top-down, chain-of-command executives make all decisions and where line workers have an unthinking job that makes them merely parts of a machine. Consider the example of the worker whose job it is to put hundreds of hubcaps on cars as they move down the assembly line. Sometimes the assembly line is functioning so poorly that the hubcap worker has a car appear before him on the line with no wheels—the fault of another person before him up the line—so he has no wheel to put his hubcap on. In a top-down mentality, of course, this is not his problem. So, since he is paid for the number of hubcaps he gets "rid of" daily, he simply throws the hubcaps into the backseat of the wheelless car. Both Deming and Glasser would say this illustrates what is wrong with recent American and Western industry and today's schools. Just like the assembly line worker, today's students are giving teachers "what they want"—producing mindless work with little or no real learning taking place. We hear students say, "How many pages does the report have to be?" and the teacher replies, "I want a minimum of a five-page paper!" Just like the hubcap worker, students fill up paper, using double spacing, big print, and any other device they can think of to meet the requirement—much like the factory worker filling up the backseats of new cars with hubcaps.

Theory Y is based on the belief that workers can be trusted. The theory maintains that if people work in a supportive environment where they "punch in and punch out" at will and are respected, they will invest in the job and return the goodwill to the company by working hard.

The newest cast on the Deming-Japanese theory is Theory Z, which holds that individuals are social beings who prefer to work in intimate groups of people with whom they can depend daily. The factory is organized into Z groups of four to six employees, with a group given the responsibility for assembling, for example, the entire front of the car and not just the hubcaps. Jobs are rotated and shared. The bosses, with the help of the consumers, define the job that needs to be done by the group, but the group is given great freedom in deciding how the job is to be done and—more importantly—in evaluating the quality of their job performance. Built into the quality systems approach is a measurement system whereby the workers within the group can see how well they are meeting the highest standards. If they are not meeting these standards, they can actually shut down the entire assembly line until the job is done right—a concept simply unheard of in the Theory X management system. Why does a car reach the end of an assembly line without wheels? How many other parts are missing? The group's goal as a team is to continually improve its performance by working smarter and gaining more and more quality in the productions.

A Japanese bar that uses a Quality Systems approach has each group of waitresses count tips every evening and graph the amount on a chart over a span of many days, weeks, and months to measure quality performance or service to the customer. Naturally, the waitresses would continue to think of methods to increase customer satisfaction and thus improve their tips. They would also record the amount of drink left in the glasses, to determine which drinks are not liked by the customers, who is purchasing what and so on, so the bar can know more about its customers in order to better meet their needs.

Glasser has used Deming's popularity and philosophical position to give new justification to old but very worthy constructs that he has always promoted. His view is that grades are destructive to students' motivation, and schools are set up to be uninteresting places that bore students, who cannot see any connection between what is being taught and what is meaningful in their own lives. He rejects the Theory X top-down approach to running schools through a state Department of Education that mandates standardized testing and school districts and principals who demand certain test results from schools and students as a measure of success. The use of standardized tests—especially when comparative scores are reported school by school or teacher by teacher in local newspapers—would be akin to reporting how many hubcaps were used in the Theory X factory, with no mention that the factory was not making a quality product. Such a reporting system would easily disregard the fact that little learning was really taking place.

Teachers have often confused *measurement* by interpreting it as meaning the same thing as *testing*, which they generally dislike. But there must be a moment-by-moment measuring process, not for the teacher to give grades but for the students to assess themselves on a Quality Systems measurement of their work and learning so they may continue to improve.

In a second publishing of *The Quality School* in 1992, Glasser presented almost 20 bulletins written for the practicing teacher or principal who wishes to put the Quality School concepts into practice. These bulletins are short theory-to-practice suggestions that attempt to describe clearly how to carry out practical matters. Many of his ideas on grading, homework, curriculum, and a host of other practical topics will be covered later, but here I will attempt to pull out any new constructs on discipline and add them to Glasser's reality therapy[4] practices widely used by teachers and schools.

Using the Quality Systems thinking, Glasser would view the misbehaving student in today's Theory X authoritarian school (based on rewards and punishment) as follows:

> *Right now the system tells the teacher to deal with disruptive students punitively and show them who's boss. Punishment, however, is not a part of a Quality School Program. If you are a teacher in a Quality School and you are confronted by a disruptive student you would 1) not immediately defend yourself as if you were being attacked personally and 2) not angrily counterattack as if you could squelch their behavior. As abusive as students may be, they are not really attacking you personally. Their rebellion is against a system of education that does not sufficiently take*

their needs into account. To them, you represent this system. Therefore, if the system is to be changed, you must change what you do.[5]

As indicated by these remarks, Glasser is calling for a fundamental change in how classrooms and schools are managed through application of quality systems methods. He makes a distinction between *discipline problems* and *discipline incidents*. Of discipline incidents, he seems to say, "Ye shall always have them among thee." These are short flare-ups that can be handled through learned techniques. But the major discipline problems are a product of the current school systems in which students are not engaged in a quality experience in which they can challenge themselves to grow and learn.

Our main complaint as students (and this has not changed) was not that the work was too hard, but that it was boring, and this complaint was and still is valid. "Boring" usually meant that we could not relate what we were asked to do with how we might use it in our lives. For example, it is deadly boring to memorize facts that neither we, nor anyone we know, will ever use except for a test in school. The most obvious measure of the effective teachers we remember is that they were not boring; somehow or other what they asked us to do was satisfying to us.[6]

Figure 5–1 shows the concepts originally found in Glasser's reality therapy methods, as well as any new practical techniques and methods found in his later writings. Glasser's positions on grading and other classroom management issues will be addressed in later chapters on management.

GLASSER'S METHODS AND THE TEACHER BEHAVIOR CONTINUUM

Looking On

Silently looking on is not in the Glasser model as a specific overt step by a teacher in working with a child, as it is with the Relationship-Listening orientation. Rather, Glasser asks the teacher to assess the situation covertly. This is a three-part process. As the teacher, you need to:

1. Reflect on your past behavior with this student.
2. Start with a fresh approach. (If your actions haven't been successful in the past, why think that they will work in the future?)
3. Expect a better tomorrow. (Since the past has not been effective, the teacher can be optimistic. After all, the situation can hardly get much worse!)

Nondirective Statements

Again, Glasser is too much of a Confronting-Contracting believer to use this central behavior of the Relationship-Listening orientation. He does not agree with

Step 1: What am I doing? (The teacher asks this question of himself or herself to gain an intellectual awareness of self, rather than a stereotypical reflex response involving a narrow set of predictable teacher behaviors that are not working and may be making things worse.)

Step 2: Is it working? If not, stop doing it. (A directive by the teacher to himself or herself based on Step 1.)

Step 3: Recognition. (The teacher should give the student "the time of day" and establish an informal relationship with the misbehaving student during the times the child is not misbehaving, in order to personalize himself or herself to the child.)

Step 4: What are you doing? (This question is directed to the child, delivered without guilt as a genuine request for the child to reflect cognitively on his or her own behavior. If the child cannot remember, remind the student what he or she did.)

Step 5: Is it against the rules? (The teacher asks the student this question, again for cognitive reflection.)

Step 6: Work it out and make a plan. (The student is counseled on how he or she may act whenever this incident occurs again. The teacher and student now have an agreement on what the student's behavior will be in the future. The plan may be solemnized with a handshake or written out and signed by both parties.)

Step 7: Isolate from the class: Within the classroom. (Used only in elementary school— what Glasser calls "off to the castle" or to a chair at the back of the classroom.)

Step 8: Isolate from the class: Out of the classroom. (In-school suspension or a time-out room in the building.)

Step 9: Send the student home.

Step 10: Get professional help. (Ask parents to get psychological help for the child, and possibly improve parenting skills through counseling for themselves.)

FIGURE 5–1   Glasser's 10 Steps to Discipline

empathetic, all-supportive acceptance of the child. He makes this quite apparent when he discusses one of his first cases as an intern working with an emotionally disturbed young boy. After weeks of using play-therapy steps of visually looking on and nondirective statements, he became increasingly frustrated with the child's continuing egocentric and destructive behavior. Finally, he wrote:

> *I began a kind of Reality Therapy. I told him (the child) to shut up and for once in his life to listen to what someone had to say. I informed him that the play was over, and that we would sit and talk in an adult fashion, or if we walked we would walk as adults. I explained clearly that I would not tolerate any running away or even any impolite behavior while we were walking. He would have to be courteous and try to converse with me when I talked to him. He was to tell me everything he did and I would help him decide whether it was right or wrong.*[7]

Directive Statements

As is evident in the previous quote, Glasser believes in defining clear boundaries of acceptable behavior. Further, he suggests that the teacher's role is to enforce and encounter, with directive statements or commands, the student who transgresses. When a child steps out of line, the teacher confronts the student and tells the student to stop transgressing. Examples of such directive statements might include:

- "Johnny, put that ruler down and get back to work."
- "Felix, if you are going to talk, you must first raise your hand."
- "Selena, this is quiet reading time, so open your book and begin reading."
- "Antonio, give me that slingshot. A slingshot is not to be used around people or animals that can be hurt by it."
- "Johanna, keep your hands off that mural! It was just painted and it must dry."

The teacher does not berate the student with such warnings as "Don't you dare do that again," or insults like "You are acting like a little baby!" or such negative speculations as "There must be something wrong with you to act that way." Instead, Glasser wishes the teacher to express directly the misbehavior and then to follow with a description of an appropriate behavior. The issue at stake is the student's *irresponsible* behavior. Therefore, the teacher needs to tell the student in effect to stop the wrong irresponsible behavior and to act correctly and responsibly. If this does not achieve results, then the teacher is to follow such directive statements with questions.

Questions

The teacher frames questions for the student to make the child think rationally about his or her actions and eventually verbalize concerning these irresponsible behaviors. The teacher might confront the offending child at the time of disruption with a question such as: What are you doing?

The teacher is not interested in excuses or reasons; she simply wants the child to verbalize what is happening. The teacher is not to ask the student *why* he is doing something. A "Why" question simply gives the student the opportunity to disown the behavior with such excuses as "Oh, I was mad (tired, hungry, etc.)," "He made me do it," "They're always picking on me," and so on.

We saw how Mr. Roberts avoided a "Why" question, yet Doug still wanted to rationalize his behavior with "But Sophia made me. . . ." Mr. Roberts would not accept such excuses. The confronting adult attempts to keep the student's discussion of the problem within the present, in order to get the issue of misbehavior out on the table, and then presses for a plan to be made.

After the question, What are you doing? the teacher asks the child to tell in what ways this behavior fulfills the child's needs. For example: How does (spitting, fighting, coming in late, etc.) help you?

The student is thus asked to think of the consequences of her own actions. Usually, the student will not be able to give a ready answer. The last objective of the teacher is to press for a plan or contract and commitment by the student by asking: What are you going to do about your behavior? or What is your plan going to be so that you don't break that rule again? These questions are crucial to reality therapy because they force responsibility back on the student. Many students get into a "cat-and-mouse" game with their teachers by constantly challenging the teacher to do something. By turning this challenge for action back to the student, there is no game left to play. Now the student's irresponsible actions will be dealt with according to the student's own plan. They will not be dealt with according to the dictates of an adult who has been forced to play supervisor. It is not the teacher who is responsible for the child's behavior, but the child who is responsible for that behavior. This does not mean that the teacher is passive in the student/teacher interaction; rather, the teacher becomes an active partner with the student in making a plan and then provides the student with the help necessary to implement the plan, which reflects the student's own feelings and thoughts.

Modeling

Glasser does not address this behavior as a specific step in working with a disruptive child. He would, however, surely agree that a teacher should set an example of being responsible to others and of being committed to carry out any stated pledge to students.

Reinforcement

Reinforcement is not advocated by Glasser in terms of schedules and concrete rewards, as seen by the Rules and Consequences advocates. Yet Glasser does agree with the use of reinforcement as it applies to the loss of privileges for breaking one's plan or contract. In this respect, he and Dreikurs are in agreement. A student needs to have logical consequences follow his behavior, whether that behavior is positive or negative. The student is encouraged to decide what those privileges or negative results should be.

It is not for the teacher to impose his praise or punishment because, in so doing, the teacher lets the student off the hook. Rather, the student must accept the natural repercussions of the misbehavior and should not be shielded from them. If the student does not respond to the question, What are you going to do about it? then the teacher can help by suggesting a plan that the student can agree to, or by sending the student away until she comes up with an acceptable alternative plan. Once a plan is agreed on, Glasser goes so far as to tell the teacher to have the student sign a written pledge to honor her plan.[8] The student agrees in writing to lose the privileges if she should falter and break the agreement. *Commitment* is Glasser's key word!

For example, a student named Merle had agreed to a plan with his teacher that he would not fight during study hall. Merle knew and agreed to the terms of the plan, which meant that to fight would mean the loss of study hall. If having study hall was, in fact, more reinforcing to Merle than the pleasure of fighting, then in time the teacher would expect that the loss of that privilege would rationally alter the student's behavior. Merle would be expected eventually to realize that his physical aggression was not helping him have the advantages of study hall, and that to fight would mean that he had broken his commitment. The message became simply: If you really like to have study hall, then behave in ways that will make going there a certainty.

Of course, you might wonder how this strategy, which appears so foolproof in theory, would work with the student who couldn't care less about study hall or who never thinks about any of his or her actions in terms of the consequences they might have. Glasser would admit that the student who couldn't care less will be a more difficult case to treat.[9] It is obvious that, to a student such as this, being able to go to study hall is not sufficiently motivating. The student would rather fight and miss study hall than not fight and go to study hall. So what do you do? The answer, which might well appear somewhat simplistic, is merely to find some other activity or situation that is more valued by the child than fighting. Some alternatives for younger children might be the following:

- Awarding the job of classroom helper
- Granting free time for personal projects
- Permitting the child to work with the school custodian
- Allowing time to listen to tapes
- Making the child the "official" messenger to the school office for the day or week

Some possibilities for older students might be the teacher granting permission for:

- Receiving free time for personal projects
- Listening to popular tapes or compact discs
- Reading popular movie or sports magazines
- Playing a game (electric football, hockey, chess)
- Watching television

If it is determined that the student cannot engage in any activity that is more personally reinforcing than his misbehavior, then the problem falls into one of two categories. Either the classroom situation is in need of being drastically over-hauled, or the student is beyond the help of the school.[10] In other words, if the child is experiencing no success and finds no relevance in what he is doing, then the teacher must stand back and assess the entire classroom curriculum and organization.

Glasser believes that misbehavior of most students results from the failure of teachers and schools to fulfill their needs. He believes that students want to experience success, they want to have feelings of self-worth, and they want to learn. In too many situations, students are obstructed by such practices as:

- Grades that label a few as successful and many as failures
- Constant teacher lectures to be sat through passively
- Reading materials that are geared for the average student and are thus too hard for the slower ones and too easy for the brighter ones
- Classroom topics or subjects that are irrelevant to the students
- Too much memorizing and recitation of facts instead of discussions and experiments

With such conditions, it is a wonder that more students don't misbehave. School for students in such classes is simply an unhappy, unsuccessful, irrelevant, and boring place to be. On the other hand, if the classroom is an exciting place for all but one student, and the teacher cannot find (after numerous attempts) any activities that interest this misbehaving child, then the teacher has further grounds to suspect that the child's problems are beyond the scope of the immediate classroom. Such a student might need to be referred for outside psychological or social help.

There are some students who simply are unaware of consequences, and dealing with these youngsters is an easier matter. A student perhaps has always exploded with rage whenever her "feathers have been ruffled." The aftereffect of this temper may never have been consciously processed by the student. As this student is still liable for her actions, regardless of the internal degree of cognizance, it is therefore the teacher's role to:

1. Raise the child's level of awareness by pointing out the immediate behavior and consequences.
2. Commit the student to creating a signed plan.
3. Enforce the natural consequence of loss of privileges if the plan is violated.

For example, it might take months of repetitive loss of study hall before a student such as Merle (in the earlier illustration) becomes aware of what his behavior is doing to him. In time, with consistent application, the lesson cannot help but be learned. Glasser suggests that the teacher begin anew by (1) reflecting on past behavior, (2) starting fresh, and (3) expecting a better tomorrow. The student is given as many chances as have been agreed on with the teacher.

Physical Intervention and Isolation

Physical Intervention

Glasser is not a believer in the teacher's use of physical control. He is certainly not an advocate of paddling or spanking. He has even more concern with the psychological damage that adults do to children by using humiliation and ridicule. He does not believe that any form of punishment, whether physical or psychological, is appropriate. He does not justify his position on moral grounds, but on the grounds that punishment simply is not effective. To paraphrase a statement he made to a group of school teachers and administrators: If punishment really worked, we should have no delinquents or criminals. After all, as children, most of today's convicts have been punished and abused frequently. If punishment worked, then we should now have a perfect society. We obviously don't and we obviously need to look for other methods.

Isolation

Glasser sees the use of isolation not for the purposes of punishing a student, but instead, for providing a place for the student to sit quietly and think about a plan for reentering the classroom milieu. When a student persists in breaking her commitment, or refuses to make one, then the student is removed to a place so that she can begin again. The first step of isolation takes place "in class." Glasser calls this "off to the castle." The student should be able to observe or listen to what is going on, but her placement should not interfere with the classroom routine. In the elementary school, such a place is easily made in the classroom; in the junior high or secondary school, such a place, if not available within the room, can be set up in close proximity (e.g., the hall). The student is told to stay in the designated area until she has made a plan to ensure a successful return to the group. This plan, again, has to be agreeable to both student and teacher. If the student bothers others while in the isolation area or persists in acting out after returning to the classroom, then the teacher could move to the second step of isolation, which leads away from the classroom to an "in-school" suspension room.

The teacher would need to have the principal's and faculty's support to free the necessary space for such a purpose. If an extra room is not available, a large storage area or a seldom-used office would be suitable. The environment should provide a relaxing place that is physically apart from the busy school activities. Movement to this area means that the student is being treated in a realistic manner. Until she takes the responsibility to plan and implement acceptable behavior in the classroom, she cannot participate in such activities. Glasser would suggest that, after all, this is the basis for societal enforcement of reasonable law and order. If one breaks the rules, then one is removed from the larger society. During the periods of in-school suspension, the principal or guidance counselor will need to be involved, but the parents will not. The teacher need not be concerned with the student's past, home life, or what her parents can do about the student's behavior. The teacher is only concerned with what can be done within the context of school. Not until the teacher has to resort to out-of-school isolation is it essential to involve the parents. This does not mean that the teacher must keep parents ignorant of their child's behavior. However, it does mean that the teacher should not look to the child's home as a source of help. The student's problem is in school, and it is the school's responsibility to handle it.

The child needs to learn to live appropriately in a classroom and to deal with the immediate consequences of her behavior in that room. Therefore, sending warning notes home or asking parents to punish the child would make the parents responsible for a problem that is not theirs. In effect, making the parents accountable to "shape up" their youngster removes that responsibility from the school and, more importantly, from the child.

The next form of isolation is suspending the student from school. If the student cannot show minimal control in an in-school suspension, then she may no longer attend school. The student can return when a plan is made.

Throughout each form of isolation (in-class, in-school, out-of-school), the teacher remains a helping person, one who is not afraid to tell the student where she has transgressed, one who is willing to ask pointed questions as to what the student is doing, and one who will encourage the student to commit herself to a plan. The teacher never lets the child get away with breaking her commitment and the teacher never lets the student shift responsibility for her behavior to others. At the same time, the teacher is not a mechanical enforcer of law and order. The teacher constantly tells the student, "I want to help you to become more in control of your own actions. I will talk, listen, give opinions, and offer advice, but in the end it is you who has to make the decision and commitment. I cannot and will not do that for you." So, as can be seen, the teacher becomes personally involved with his student. The teacher cares, and that caring is clearly shown by the teacher never allowing the child to transcend the boundaries of the commitment that the child has made. The teacher remains as one who will enforce reality behavior and the student remains as one who must learn the meaning of that reality.

In fully explaining the mechanism of isolation, recall the previous behaviors of questions and directive statements. These teacher behaviors do not stop when isolation begins. Rather, the teacher continues to ask the student through each stage of isolation to reply to such questions as: What are you doing? What rules are you breaking? In what way is this behavior helping you? What are you going to do about it? and What is your plan? The teacher also tells the student directly what his or her transgressions are and what the consequences of these behaviors are. Any interaction with the student should contain such direct confronting statements as: "Stop doing that! The rule is. . . . You are breaking the rules and therefore cannot be part of the group. You cannot have back your privilege (or return to the group) until you tell me your plan. Don't give me any excuses; tell me what you did!" Therefore, questions and directive statements are interspersed throughout the process of isolation and are essential in aiding the child to become aware of his actions, the consequences involved, and the responsibilities that need to be met. Glasser also pointed out that there may well be a few students who will actually need to be referred to an outside agency, such as a treatment center for delinquent children, when they engage in types of criminal behavior and none of the previous steps has met with any success.

THE CLASSROOM MEETING

It would be a disservice to omit one of the major formats for applying the teacher behaviors of reality therapy. What Glasser is perhaps best known for among school practitioners is the classroom meeting.[11] This practice of holding regular meetings provides a structure both for dealing with an individual student's problems and for revising the overall organization and curriculum of the class. The teacher meets with the entire class on a regular basis. They always sit in a circle facing each other, usually on a rug, sometimes in chairs. The teacher stresses to the class that during this meeting there are no wrong answers, and that each child should feel free to express his ideas, opinions, and feelings. The teacher is expected to express her ideas, opinions, and feelings in the same manner. The students are told that they are to talk about the present and the future, not to dwell in the past. The teacher further adds that students are not "to put down" or use insulting terms when speaking to or about others.

Since there are no "wrong" answers, every child in the meeting has the opportunity to be successful. A child need not fear being corrected for what he says. The teacher (silently looking on) encourages everyone, with nods and words of approval, to speak, but does not force anyone who resists. The teacher may ask a student for his ideas, and if no reply is forthcoming, may say (nondirective statement) something like, "Well, you think about it and let me know if you come up with an idea that you would like to discuss. I'd like to hear it."

Glasser discussed three types of meetings: (1) open ended, (2) educational/diagnostic, and (3) problem solving. Open-ended meetings are held for students to create their own fantasies and to explore imaginary problems—for example: What would we do if we were stranded on a tropical island? The educational/diagnostic meeting is one where the teacher discusses a curriculum topic in order to find out what students already know about it, what they don't know, and what further interests they might have—for example: What is pollution? Where does it come from? Why is it a problem? The teacher then uses that information to make curriculum decisions as to what aspects of the topic would be most essential to cover and what activities would be most relevant to the students. The third type of meeting is the problem-solving one, in which the class focuses on a real problem that affects all of them. They clarify the problem, add information, propose alternative solutions, and finally commit themselves to a plan of action. Examples of such general problems might be:

- How the athletic equipment is to be distributed at gym class
- What to do about missing items in the class
- How to cut down on asking the teacher questions when he is busy
- What to do about name calling among the students
- What to do about the length of time it takes to get the whole class settled before starting the next lesson
- What to do about graffiti and littering problems in the restrooms

Specific problems concerning individual students are also a topic for problem-solving meetings. The use of this kind of meeting as a vehicle for working with student misbehavior is an application that will now be discussed. Behaviors by an individual that would be relevant as topics for a classroom meeting might include:

- A student who "hogs" the gym equipment (balls, bats, frisbees, and the like)
- A student who physically pushes other students around

- A student who constantly distracts others from working (by making loud noises, talking, and so forth)
- A student who takes items from others
- A student who plays cruel "tricks" on others (locks children into closets, writes on others' homework, and so on)
- A student who tries to be boss all the time, who is always telling others what to do but will not accept any criticism of self

As we have seen, integral to Glasser's approach is for a student to be made aware of and become responsible for the consequences of her actions. When a student has behaved in ways that are constantly disruptive to the majority of other students, and the problem has escalated from one that is solely between student and teacher, then Glasser believes that the student needs to be confronted and helped by the entire class. Therefore, the problem-solving classroom meeting is held, and the misbehaving student hears what others think of her behavior.

The teacher holds a firm rein on this type of meeting to ensure that it does not become a name-calling free-for-all. The teacher explains the reason to discuss a student who has been destroying classmates' property. The teacher then suggests that, as a group, perhaps the class can help the student to act more appropriately.

1. The teacher asks each student to express openly what this student has recently done to interfere with him or her personally. The students are asked to tell that student, face to face, what those behaviors are and what effects they have had on them (emotionally and/or physically).
2. After all have had their chance to speak (including the teacher), the misbehaving student is given an opportunity to explain what others have done to interfere with him or her.

At this juncture, the meeting swiftly swings from "getting all the cards out on the table" to doing something constructive with the information that has been gleaned.

3. The teacher suggests that the class and the offending child may be able to offer some possible solutions to the problem—ones that would be agreeable to all. The teacher listens to all ideas and then asks the group to narrow down the alternative plans and ideas that were offered.
4. Finally, the student is asked to select a plan and commit himself or herself to it. At the same time, the members of the class (including the teacher) commit themselves to carrying out any actions that will help the student in implementing his or her plan.

The conclusion of such a meeting is the achievement of an agreed-upon, manageable plan. The participants leave the meeting with a feeling of positive action.

Note that the teacher's role in such a classroom meeting is identical to the role required in dealing with a child on a one-to-one basis. The same techniques of

"What" questions and directive statements are used to keep the discussion on target and within the boundaries of rules. All verbalizations are designed to help the class and child come to grips with the reality of behavior and for them to "get on" with a course of action. The offending child is kept in the "straitjacket" of responsibility, and, after a plan is agreed on, the teacher remains as the enforcer of logical consequences. Breaking of such a commitment could result in the student being led through the three levels of isolation.

To many teachers, the use of a classroom meeting for the confrontation of a child by his peers seems to be a harsh approach. Many would feel that, for some children, there is the danger of emotional harm and the reinforcement of a child's negative self-concept in such a confrontation. Glasser is careful to point out that such a meeting needs to be carefully guided by the teacher to avoid any such destructive outcome.[13] The teacher needs to move the discussion carefully from the phase of eliciting peer perceptions to that of developing helpful solutions. The classroom meeting is purposefully used to show the offending child that he cannot act in an egocentric vacuum of being oblivious to the effects of his behavior on others. If the teacher shields the disruptive child from feedback from peers, then that child has little opportunity to explore the reasons for cooperative behavior. If the child is really bothering his peers, as well as the teacher, then the student needs to know this directly from those affected. If the student is to live with others, then there is nothing more realistic than for others to inform the student when his actions are transgressing on their rights. The meeting is not designed, or held, to blame or punish the child, but to *find solutions* that will help the child.

SUMMARY

Glasser's procedures for dealing with disruptive children are placed along the Teacher Behavior Continuum of Figure 5–2. In *Schools Without Failure*, Glasser has gone beyond the specifics of working with disruptive, "unrealistic" students and addresses what he considers to be the major source of inappropriate behavior. In doing so, he speaks of covert behaviors that the teacher might use with such students. Students, like all humans, wish to fulfill their needs, and misbehavior can be explained as a person's unsuccessful attempt to succeed in these efforts. Glasser sees schools as institutions that breed failure and irrelevancy.[13] Most misbehaving students do not feel successful in school. They are not involved in what they learn, and therefore they erect a shield of defiance, apathy, and unconcern to protect them from the further hurt of inadequacy. Consequently, when a misbehaving student is expected to give up privileges (or successful experiences) as a result of wrong action, the student has none to give up and the defiant behavior continues. So, in these situations, Glasser tells the teacher to be covert about silently looking on with the student while:

1. Observing the student and the situation
2. Assessing what the teacher herself is currently doing and what success the student is having

Looking On	Nondirective Statements	Question	Directive Statements	Modeling	Reinforcement	Physical Intervention/ Isolation
a) Observe —the student —the situation b) Assess —what the teacher is currently doing —what success the student is having c) Classroom reorganization and activities d) Move to overt behaviors —if step c does not work —if present teacher behaviors are unproductive	(2) "What" questions: "What are you doing?" "What are the rules?" "In what ways is your behavior helping you?" "What is your plan?"		**(1) Confront transgressor. "Stop that, the rule is . . . " (3) Press for a plan. "You must make a plan; I will help but you are responsible."	(4) Reap the consequences of plan.		(5) "Off to the castle" (classroom isolation); repeat 1,2,3,4 (6) Off to the office (with principal doing 1, 2, 3, 4) (7) Removal from school; repeat 1, 2, 3, 4, 5, 6 (8) Referral to outside agency

The Reality Model   **Steps 1–4 can be carried out in class meetings.

Author: William Glasser

numbers = overt behaviors

letters = covert behaviors

FIGURE 5–2   Teacher Behavior Continuum (TBC): Reality Therapy

3. If necessary, starting fresh by reversing classroom organization and/or activities

Only at this point, if failure continues, does the teacher begin the process of overt behaviors.

The central technique for the teacher to use is an approach that confronts the student and makes him responsible for his own behavior. A student, upon violating rules, is:

1. Confronted and told to stop (directive statements)
2. Asked "What" questions (questions)
3. Pressed for a plan and commitment (directive statements)
4. Faced with logical consequences that have been agreed upon (reinforcement)

ENDNOTES

1. W. Glasser, *Reality Therapy: A New Approach to Psychiatry* (New York: Harper & Row, 1975), p. 13.

2. Deming information is published in Dr. Myron Tribus, Selected Papers on *Quality and Productivity Improvement.* National Society of Professional Engineers, P.O. Box 96163, Washington, DC 20090-6163. W. Edwards Deming, *Out of the Crisis* (Cambridge: Massachusetts Institute of Technology, Center for Advanced Engineering Study, 1982.)

3. T. G. Peters, *In Search of Excellence* (New York: Warner Brothers, 1984).

4. Ibid., p. 13.

5. W. Glasser, *The Quality School: Managing Students Without Coercion, 2nd ed. expanded* (New York: HarperCollins, 1992), p. 265.

6. Glasser, *Reality Therapy,* p. 170.

7. W. Glasser, *Schools Without Failure* (New York: Harper & Row, 1969), p. 126.

8. W. Glasser, "Disorders in Our Schools: Causes and Remedies," *Phi Delta Kappan* (January 1978): 331.

9. W. Glasser, "Glasser's Approach to Discipline," pamphlet published by the Educator Training Center, Los Angeles, CA, 1978, step 10, pp. 8–9.

10. W. Glasser, "Glasser's Approach to Discipline," step 7, p. 6.

11. Glasser's presentation to the School Council of Ohio Study Group, December, 1974, Delaware, OH.

12. Glasser, *Schools Without Failure,* chapters 10 and 11.

13. Ibid., p. 129.

RELATED READINGS

Glasser, W. *Schools Without Failure.* New York: Harper & Row, 1969.

Glasser, W. *Reality Therapy: A New Approach to Psychiatry.* New York: Harper & Row, 1975.

Glasser, W. *Control Theory in the Classroom.* New York: Harper & Row, 1986.

Glasser, W. *The Quality School: Managing Students Without Coercion, 2nd ed. expanded.* New York: HarperCollins, 1992.

INSTRUCTIONAL MEDIA: THE QUALITY SCHOOL TRAINING PROGRAM

The Quality School Consortium and Quality School Training Program was conceived by Dr. William Glasser to offer schools that wish to become trained to work within the Quality Schools orientation the opportunity to join and be trained in this process. Those interested may write or fax to the Institute for Reality Therapy, 7301 Medical Center Drive, Suite 104, Canoga Park, CA 91307, (818) 888-0699; fax (818) 888-3023.

Name	Minutes	Format	Sound	Address of Distributor
Classroom Meetings on Class Meetings	28	16 mm	yes	Films Incorporated Video 5547 N. Ravenswood Avenue Chicago, IL 60640-1199 (800) 343-4312 FAX (312) 878-0416
Demonstrates the dramatic results that class meetings can produce as sixth-graders think about intellectual questions, listen to others, and search for reasonable alternatives to problems. School Practices and Schools Without Failure Series.				
Reality Therapy Approach	29	16 mm	yes	Films Incorporated Video 5547 N. Ravenswood Avenue Chicago, IL 60640-1199 (800) 343-4312 FAX (312) 878-0416
Selected documentary of elementary teachers successfully using concepts developed by Dr. William Glasser to achieve effective school discipline, along with a full explanation of Dr. Glasser's five-part approach to discipline and the seven steps reality therapy. Together, these elements provide the basis for building individual responsibility and self-motivated productive behavior. Human Relations and School Discipline Series.				
Reality Therapy in High School	29	16 mm	yes	Films Incorporated Video 5547 N. Ravenswood Avenue Chicago, IL 60640-1199 (800) 343-4312 FAX (312) 878-0416
Shows Glasser's reality therapy approach to discipline in authentic situations and examines the dramatic effects on the total school climate. Describes how a principal and staff introduced the approach and how during the first year it resulted in more than an 80 percent decrease in discipline problems. New Approaches to High School Education Discipline Series.				

6

THE JUDICIOUS DISCIPLINE MODEL
School Rules, the Bill of Rights, and Student Misbehavior

Theorist/Writer: Forrest Gathercoal

- *Judicious Discipline*

Theorist/Writer: Barbara McEwan

- *Practicing Judicious Discipline: An Educator's Guide to a Democratic Classroom*

Sam is a large, muscular senior high school student with a consistent B average and no record of any discipline difficulties. His father currently is an unemployed aeronautics worker in his late 40s who is beginning to drink heavily during late evenings. When intoxicated, the father begins a taunting harassment directed at Sam. Last night, the verbal conflict degenerated into an actual physical assault, with both Sam and his father exchanging blows. The father literally kicked Sam out of the house, telling him, "Get out and stay out!" This occurred a 10:30 P.M. on a cold January evening, and Sam found himself on the street without money or adequate outer clothing. He walked to a public bus station, where he attempted to sleep most of the night. He arrived at school hungry, cold and tired the next morning.

It is now 12:45 P.M. and Sam is standing in the school cafeteria line, having borrowed lunch money from a friend. As he patiently waits for the line to advance, two other students cut in line directly in front of him. Sam shouts at them and pushes them out of the line. A shoving match begins between Sam and one of these boys, escalating to the point that Sam strikes the schoolmate. Mrs. Adams, the cafeteria supervisor, attempts to stop the fight but is accidentally hit in the face by the back of Sam's hand, crushing her glasses into her face. Sam is taken to the assistant principal's office, where he is told that the school rule calls for a three-day suspension for fighting. Less than 15 minutes after the fight, Sam finds himself out of the school, wandering down one of the city's back streets on his way to the arcade and game room in a nearby mall. He has no idea where he will sleep that night.

If we ask why Sam was suspended, we would be told that the school administration understandably feels that fighting is one of the most serious discipline offenses. The school has a rule that has been approved by the school board, published in the student handbook, and widely publicized to all students: Fighting results in a three-day suspension—clear and simple. The administration feels that rules need to be fair, clear, and applied to all students evenly. Everyone who fights in the school is suspended, and making an exception for Sam would not be fair to other students—in short, a rule is a rule and it must be enforced.

Was the school administration right in its action? Were all the students of this school well served by this discipline action? Was Sam well served by the action? What rights do we have as citizens, and what rights do students have in schools? Who will pay for Mrs. Adams's broken glasses and any medical needs? These are not easy questions to answer, but the discipline model *Judicious Discipline,* written by Forrest Gathercoal, may give the educator much help in answering these questions.

Before we can talk about rules and discipline, we must have a beginning understanding of children's moral growth and understanding—their sense of right or wrong—as a developmental process. Why do people obey rules? If people do break rules, what is appropriate punishment? The questions apply at all ages, including adulthood. Suppose you are rushing home, driving your car down a busy street when the traffic light turns red, requiring you to stop. What is your reasoning if you see no one around and proceed through the light? What is your reasoning if you instead stop at the light and obey the law? If a police officer writes a citation for violating the traffic law, what is appropriate punishment for the violator?

MORAL GROWTH AS A DEVELOPMENTAL PROCESS

From a child-development perspective, based on psychological theory, there are two basic motivators: Level 1: Fear of Authority and Level 2: Feelings and Understanding of Social Responsibility. Stop now and score yourself on the Authoritarian/Democratic Teaching Scale (Figure 6–1) so that you may gain a new perspective on your own teaching style to better understand the concepts that you will learn later in this chapter.

Place a check for each statement that describes what you do in your classroom and fits with your beliefs.

(✔)   **Classroom Practice or Beliefs**

1. Rules are written with a specific punishment, incorporating the degrees and number of times a rule is broken.

2. When assignments are late, the student's grade is lowered or a set number of points are lost toward the final grade on that assignment.

3. I agree that some schoolwide rules are necessary, so that when certain behaviors occur, every student breaking the same serious rule should be suspended.

4. Punishment has a very central role in teaching students responsible behavior.

5. I keep an open gradebook, meaning that students may ask at any time to see the data, comments, or grades I am keeping on them.

6. If a student is found cheating, I would have him or her retake another test or be tested by writing a paper or other alternative method.

7. If a student did not come to class with pencil, paper, and appropriate books, he or she would miss out on the classroom activity and be graded down for failing to do the work.

8. I will not, under most circumstances, send a student out of my classroom because of misbehavior.

9. Passing notes among students is OK with me but it must be done in a manner that does not disturb others and follows our classroom rules.

10. I have rules that toys, such as squirt guns and similar items, are not permitted in my classroom, and if found, I confiscate them and they are lost to the student forever.

11. As a general practice, I would not search a student's locker.

12. Hats, message buttons, and similar items may be worn in my class.

13. If a student was discovered skipping school, I would permit that student to make up a test or work that he or she missed.

14. A good rule is to predetermine, so everyone knows ahead of time, that if a student comes x number of times late for my class, he or she will receive y number of detention hours.

A	☐	In the space next to the letter A (for Authoritarian), place the number of checks you made next to items 1, 2, 3, 4, 7, 10, 14.
Subtract D	☐	In the space next to the letter D (for Democratic), place the number of checks you made next to items 5, 6, 8, 9, 11, 12, 13.
Total	☐	Subtract D from A to obtain a total. Note this may be a negative number (e.g., –1, –2, –3, –4, –5, –6, –7).

FIGURE 6–1   Scale of Authoritarian vs. Democratic Teaching Style

Next, use this total (number) on the Authoritarian/Democratic scale and circle that same number on the scale below. From the descriptive words above the scale, you may now determine to what degree you are a Highly Authoritarian, Somewhat Authoritarian, Somewhat Democratic, or Highly Democratic teacher.

Authoritarian/Democratic Scale

Democratic								Authoritian						
Highly				Somewhat					Somewhat					Highly
–7	–6	–5	–4	–3	–2	–1	0	1	2	3	4	5	6	7

FIGURE 6–1   (continued)

Fear of Authority

When we as adults stop our cars at a traffic signal, what is our reason? Is it a fear of being punished—ticketed and fined, arrested, perhaps even deprived of the opportunity to drive? Or in stopping the car do we recognize that in our society we are dependent on others and that rules are necessary to keep us safe so that life's activities may proceed in an orderly, safe, and productive manner?

Fear of authority is the first moral understanding of very young preschool-age children (ages 2 to 7); they intellectually cannot understand how their actions can deprive others of their rights, and they simply obey parents' rules out of fear of losing their parents' love.[1] In this first childish moral position, what is right or wrong is not related to motive, but is tied to Mom and Dad's punishment or reprimand. As soon as children are out of the sight or supervision of the parent or other adult authority, they lose the ability to control themselves. When their wants and selfish needs are in conflict with the established rules, selfishness wins out and the rules are broken.

There are many students in elementary and secondary school, and even adults, who grow up but never grow out of this first moral position—fear of authority. They will obey rules only under the strict monitoring of a strong authority figure, and when out from under the close supervision of that authority, they will quickly break society's rules (such as stealing or lying) and will take destructive actions to serve their selfish and self-centered needs. It is in the elementary and middle school years that children grow into an understanding of how their actions affect others in society. Gradually, with the right educational experiences, they move to the second moral position: feelings and understanding of social responsibility and empathy for others.

Feelings and Understanding of Social Responsibility

It seems that in the natural order of human development, a growing child who learns a new developmental skill is nearly obsessed with practicing it. Once the 12-

month-old can walk, she is consumed with movement, constantly preoccupied with walking. Near the age of 7, at the beginning of the elementary school years, the child has fully developed a conscience, as can be attested to by the kindergarten or first-grade teacher who hears a constant stream of tattling on the playground: "Teacher, Tommy did so-and-so!" The natural order of development permits the early elementary child to practice, without risk, how to obey rules through her games and activities. This elementary school-age child is consumed with wanting to play games with rules—sports such as softball or soccer, board games such as Candy Land, checkers, and Monopoly, or card games. This elementary school-age child will constantly seek out peers and make demands of her parents to join in these rule-governed games. While playing these games, which appear to be just using up spare time, the child of this age is really practicing the moral position Level 2: Feelings and Understanding of Social Responsibility. The child is learning how to obey rules, what happens when she breaks rules, and the social responsibility and joy of being a cooperative participant in rule-governed activities. The child is gaining an empathetic understanding of others (see Figure 6–2).

From a child-development perspective, it is our role as teachers to build our discipline plans on an understanding that students are still in transition from this immature *fear of authority* (first moral position) and are growing to a more mature *social responsibility* (second moral position). They are gaining empathy for others and a social conscience to understand that their actions can endanger others and disrupt the social society in which they live. If our discipline actions are based on fear, power, and unilateral authority to simply bend the will of students and coerce them to perform under strict rules and severe punishment, we will retard the children's moral growth and development. Highly authoritarian school discipline procedures not only mis-serve the student but also mis-serve the democratic society in which the student will become an adult and assume responsibility as a citizen. A democratic society requires the student to develop to the second moral

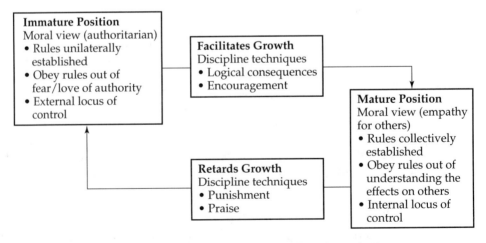

FIGURE 6–2   Moral Development: A Concept of Right and Wrong

position of feelings and understanding of social responsibility. Children must develop the abilities to inhibit their self-centered approach of wanting it now, being first, and being childishly indulged. As they grow and mature, they must develop an understanding of a moral view. This moral view holds that rules that are collectively established by citizens serve to give everyone an equal chance (equal rights), that these rules are for safety and society's good (property loss or damage and health and safety), and that they permit an opportunity for everyone to find a chance for their needs to be adequately met (obtain an education).

Why do students obey rules? We want our students, after their educational experience in our *judiciously* oriented schools, to answer this question with a second moral position answer reflecting an intellectual understanding of society's rules and feelings and understanding of social responsibility.

What Actions Should Be Taken When Rules Are Broken?

When rules are broken by students, the teacher, principal, and parents need to take actions. The actions taken can be morally directive and controlling, as *punishment*, or educational and supportive, as *logical consequences*.[2] A food fight among students occurs in the cafeteria. One possible set of sanctions includes two weeks of detention after school (or some similar deprivation). This is a punishment and keeps the students in the first moral position of being *externally* controlled by fear of authority. Instead, the school authority could require the food-fighting students to lose their after-lunch recess period and clean up the cafeteria floor and tables for a three-week period—a logical consequence of their actions.

Punishment, then, is an authoritarian action requiring the educator to take a position that the students are "sinful" or are unworthy because of their misbehavior and therefore must suffer some degree of discomfort in the form of punishment action. A logical consequence, in contrast, is educational. It takes the position that the student is still immature and growing, and will make mistakes. The mistake, which appears as misbehavior by the student, is an educationally valuable *judicious* teachable moment for the school and parents. The actions that adults take toward that misbehaving student will serve to enable the student to gain a new perspective on his behavior and actions. Such students can learn how they may have taken away the rights of others, and they can become more aware of their social responsibility toward others.

The punishment response to the food fight, such as detention, requires only a passive response from the misbehaving students. They simply have to "grin and bear it" and soon the discomfort will be over. While the students are "suffering" the punishment, they can and will have strong feelings of resentment toward the educator and school, and might feel martyred for being treated "unfairly." Usually, punishment such as detention has no logical relationship to the previous misbehavior.

Logical consequences, as in the example of the food fight, require the students to be active, and by this action make amends or "give back" to society or others for the negative behavior and actions (e.g., cleaning up the cafeteria for three weeks). Logical consequences as a sanction, in direct contrast to punishment, are directly and logically related to the misbehaving act of the students. The students, through their misbehavior, trashed the cafeteria; now, logically, as a consequence, they must clean it up and continue to clean it up for three weeks. Society—in this instance, the school and the school cafeteria—has predictable and reasonable rules that make it safe and comfortable for people to eat in this space. The misbehaving students have broken the social contract and thus lose their right to act in such a manner; they must now make amends or take actions to make things right again (clean up the cafeteria). Through suffering the logical consequences directly related to the misdeed, the students are educated as to the cause and effect of their misbehavior.

In many ways, punishment, as a authoritarian procedure or process, is *easy* for the student and *easy* for the adult educator. When suffering a punishment, the student simply has to accept it and it will soon pass. For the educator, punishment requires little or no thinking. The student did *x* (misbehaved) and therefore, based on the "rule book," must suffer *y* (two weeks of detention). This punishment stance by the educator eliminates any real thinking on the educator's part. The result of this punishment is resentment by the student toward the educator and the school, and little or no educational growth or benefit will occur.

Perhaps you are thinking, "Yes, but after that harsh punishment, the students never got into another food fight." Normally, this is true only to the limits of this one narrow misdeed, but is not true at a deeper level because new behavior will result unseen by the adult. Punishment rarely educates and stops misbehavior; rather, it simply causes the student to respond passively out of resentment. The student may become lethargic and passive at school, and at the first opportunity drop out from what she considers a punishing environment (school). Or the student may become active by engaging in other misbehaviors to get even with the educator or school (such as putting inflated condoms on the teacher's car antenna, destroying school property, or becoming more sneaky or skilled at continuing the same misbehavior as before). A motorist who is fined for speeding on the interstate highway rarely stops speeding—he simply purchases a radar detector and becomes more skilled at breaking the law.

If we return to the opening vignette of Sam and the fight in the cafeteria line, we now see that the administration's arbitrary rule calling for punishment in the form of a three-day suspension was representative of Level 1: Fear of Authority. Putting Sam out on the street with a suspension is clearly punishment that bears no logical relationship to his action. Also, because of Sam's negative home situation, the punishment was quite illogical—the action was of no educational value to Sam and was destructive to his well-being. Previously a good student, he may now feel resentment toward school as a place that has compounded his problem of lack of home security and his anxieties over how to handle a serious life problem. The school's action may be characterized as the "principle of the tyranny of fairness," which holds that the school must deny or punish everyone equally out of a warped sense of fairness. In a similar unilateral fashion, we see the same reasoning regarding rules and punishment when we have schools enforcing compulsory attendance requirements by telling students, "You'd better come to school or we will kick you out!"[3] The student is truant for one day, so we suspend him for three days; this punishment is not a logical consequence. There are a host of similar rules and punishment events that do not follow the notion of a judicious school discipline program.

Our goal in school, then, is to work with staff and parents to move to a school discipline plan that attempts to use, as far as possible, creative and imaginative thinking in the form of logical consequences and judicious discipline toward the students' misbehavior. Through education, we try to help the child develop maturity in moral reasoning and become an individual who has empathy for others and understands that rules are needed in a productive democratic society.

The model of *Judicious Discipline* would suggest, from a feelings and understanding of social responsibility position, that the question the school must ask is: What is it that Sam must learn in this "teachable moment"? The answer is that he must learn that the school is not a knowledge "gas station" where he pulls in and fills up, with only a narrow selection of services available at one or two pumps. These pumps may or may not meet his needs, and if he has other needs he is simply out of luck because this educational filling station neither provides nor cares to provide that service. He must instead learn that, in a judicious school, he will be permitted to make mistakes and that this does not make him unworthy of the school's services and school membership. He must also learn that he will be given due process with empathetic educators who wish to help and counsel him in finding answers to his problems and needs, and that he should handle stress and tension in a nonviolent manner. If sanctions are needed, they will be ones that teach rather than punish.

CONSTITUTIONAL RIGHTS

For students and adults who have learned the skills and reasoning of Level 2: Feelings and Understanding of Social Responsibility, the dilemma for true moral reasoning is the conflict between "the good of all" and "the rights of the individual." Sam's school administrators had the "good of all" in mind when they created their rules about fighting. But what are Sam's rights in such situations? Generally, one's concept of democratic rights dictates that the majority rules. When we decide what game to play, which film to see, or what colors and mascot will represent our school, we vote on it and follow the majority's decision. But there is another, second aspect of democracy that is not easily understood or often taught, and that is *individual rights*. If Sam insists on wearing his hair a certain style or length, wearing certain nonstandard clothing, displaying highly unpopular political buttons, refusing to say the pledge to the flag, or choosing not to read certain school-assigned books because his church says they are sinful, laws should protect his individual rights from being taken away by the majority.

The standard for judging individual rights in a democratic nation is its constitution. In the United States, of course, the key provisions are contained within the Bill of Rights, particularly the First, Fourth, and Fourteenth Amendments.

The First Amendment

Congress shall make no law respecting an establishment of religion, or prohibiting the free exercise thereof; or abridging the freedom of speech, or of the press; or the people peaceably to assemble, and to petition the Government for a redress of grievances.

In a school context, this amendment would raise such questions as:

- Does a student have a right to publish and distribute material on school premises? (freedom of press)
- Can a student refuse specific assigned reading based on religious practices and beliefs? (freedom of religion)
- Can the child wear clothing that is outside the school handbook rule but is an expression of his religious faith?
- Can the student be absent from school for religious practices without losing the opportunity to learn the educational content and avoiding punishment with regard to his or her grade for this absence?

The Fourth Amendment

The right of the people to be secure in their persons, houses, papers, and effects, against unreasonable searches and seizures, shall not be violated, and no Warrants shall issue, but upon probable cause, supported by Oath or affirmation, and particularly describing the place to be searched, and the persons or things to be seized.

This amendment would raise such questions as:

- Can a teacher or school official search a student's property, including lockers, purses, pockets, or vehicles in the parking lot?

The Fourteenth Amendment

All persons born or naturalized in the United States, and subject to the jurisdiction thereof, are citizens of the United States and of the State wherein they reside. No State shall make or enforce any law which shall abridge the privileges or immunities of citizens of the United States; nor shall any State deprive any person of life, liberty, or property, without due process of law; nor deny to any person within its jurisdiction the equal protection of the laws.

This lengthy amendment, parts of which are quoted here, contains the key due process and equal protection clauses, which would raise such questions as:

- Can a teacher, as a discipline action, put a student in a hall or isolated room, or suspend or expel the student, thereby depriving the student of the property right to be educated, without a due process hearing? May legal counsel be present to represent the student?

- Can the student's grade—described by Gathercoal as a student's "property"—be lowered or withheld because he or she is late to class or truant?

In Loco Parentis

Prior to 1969, these amendments simply were not applied to students in public schools. Before that date, teachers and school officials were considered to be *in loco parentis*. This meant that schools were granted the same legal authority over students as that of a parent. Gathercoal noted that minor children who live with parents or legal guardians enjoy no constitutional rights. For example, parents may search their daughter's bedroom without a search warrant and would not be violating her Fourth Amendment protections against unreasonable search or seizure. A son denied the keys to the car would have no Fourteenth Amendment right to appeal his parents' decision.[4] Because of *in loco parentis*, schools historically enjoyed the widest power and authority—just like parents—to impose their will on students, as long as it was not capricious, arbitrary, malicious, or in bad faith.

This changed in 1969 with the case of *Tinker* v. *Des Moines Independent School District* (393 U.S. 503), a landmark decision that set the precedent for present-day school practices, especially those related to discipline. In the *Tinker* case, a high school student was suspended by his principal for wearing a black arm band to school to protest the United States involvement in Vietnam. The student won the right to express his political beliefs, with the U.S. Supreme Court holding that "First Amendment rights, applied in light of the special characteristics of the school environment, are available to teachers and students. <u>It can hardly be argued that either students or teachers shed their constitutional rights to freedom of speech or expression at the schoolhouse gate</u>" (emphasis added).

Parents today may still dictate to their children that they will obey certain rules because those rules represent the parents' values. Under *in loco parentis*, most schools previously acted in a similar fashion, unilaterally making rules that fit the values of the school, the teachers, and the administrators—a Level 1: Fear of Authority position. Now, in the wake of *Tinker*, courts have forced the school authorities to work in a Level 2: Feelings and Understanding of Social Responsibility system based on constitutional rights. As a result, school officials are faced with the moral dilemma of balancing "the good of all" against "the rights of one."

Due Process

"...nor shall any State [the school] deprive any person [student] of life, liberty or property [an education], without the due process of law." If we return to the case of Sam, we will see that the school—an extension of the state—deprived Sam of his education (property) by suspending him for three days. This is a serious matter because the state has deprived him of his rights. Was this done legally?

The state, in the form of the school, may deprive someone of established rights if it can show a *compelling state interest*. To do this, the school must demonstrate that one of four interests is involved:

State Interest	*Examples of Student Violation*
Property loss or damage	• Putting graffiti on classroom walls • Destroying the property of others • Walking on the gym floor with cleated shoes
Legitimate educational purpose	• Failing to bring a textbook, pencil, and notebook paper to class
Health and safety	• Failing to wear eye and ear protection while operating the drill press in the industrial arts class • Running down the "up" stairs • Failing to obtain a doctor's examination before playing school-sponsored sports
Serious disruption of the educational process	• Rough-house behavior that prevents other students from concentrating • Setting off firecrackers in the stair wells • Food fights in the school cafeteria

If the student's behavior violates one of these four state interests, the school has a responsibility to prohibit the behavior because it affects the welfare of the school. Sam's behavior did violate a number of these state interests. He caused the loss and damage of property, endangered the safety and health of a student and teacher, and seriously disrupted the educational process (the cafeteria). Where the school may have failed, however, is in the *due process* steps.

The state, through the school, may not arbitrarily deprive a student of his or her property (education) without a number of procedural due process criteria being met:

• Adequate notice—an oral or written notice of the charges, such as a description of the rule the student violated
• A fair and impartial hearing
• Evidence—a summary of the evidence against the student, such as a report of a teacher who witnessed the student's behavior
• Defense—an opportunity for the student to be heard (i.e., the student has an opportunity to tell his or her side of the story)
• The right to appeal any decision

The school clearly gave adequate notice, having previously published the rule and corresponding punishment in the student handbook as well as verbally notifying all students. However, it did not provide a fair and impartial hearing during which Sam would have been notified of the specific rules he broke, a witness (preferably a teacher) who might have described the incident, and, finally, the opportunity to tell his side of the story. All levels of state government have administrative offices above them in a chain of command, and Sam would have the right to appeal the principal's decision to the superintendent or school board, and eventually even to the state or federal courts. This is rarely done, but the right for Sam (or any other student) to do so remains in place.

It is these due process steps that are required to give fairness to discipline actions as a sanction. The basic rule that fighting in school means a three-day suspension was wrongly stated and conceived from a Level 1: Fear of Authority position. Rules such as "If you do x, then you will suffer y" provide no judicious flexibility during the due process steps to enable sanctions to be fair. The school wrongly boxed itself in by establishing an arbitrary rule framed for punishment—fear of authority—rather than for purposes of educating a student. Discipline incidents are never "cut and dry"; they always involve extenuating circumstances. In Sam's case, the fact that he has no home to be sent to when suspended must be taken into consideration.

Gathercoal wrote clearly to this matter:

> *One of the problems educators often express when considering individualizing consequences is the fear that students will fault them as being unfair if others are treated differently. Those employing punishment models are forced to be consistent, as students are usually quick to remind educators their punishment was not the same as that which others received for the same offense. [The students are trained to also think in a Level 1: Fear of Authority position of reasoning.] On the other hand, judicious consequences by definition respect individual differences among students and allow more flexibility by styling consequences to meet the educational and self-esteem needs of all parties involved. When students perceive consequences as educational in nature, feel they make sense for them and are acting on their own volition, they should show little interest in comparing their situation to that of others. The variety of educational methods educators employ to remedy individual* learning *problems* are seldom questioned by students. Why, *therefore, should students object to educators employing different consequences as they work with the many different individual needs and attitudes their fellow student bring to* behavioral problems?[5]

The use of judicious discipline by Sam's school principal after the fighting incident would be guided by the following questions:

- What needs to be learned here?
- How would an educator manage the problem?
- Do I need more information about the student or the student's family?

- What strategies can be used to keep this student in school?
- How will the student perceive the consequence?
- How will it affect the school community?

In order for the important issues of the problem to unfold and for workable solutions to take form, the following question must be answered:

- How can I keep intact the mutual respect needed for a strong student/educator relationship through the life of the consequence?[6]

If these questions had been addressed, the discipline actions regarding Sam would have been resolved in a judicious and educational manner so that any action would have been taken to help Sam gain security and confidence in his future.

Let's take another discipline action—that of revising grades based on behavior—and think it through from the judicious perspective of Level 2: Feelings and Understanding of Social Responsibility. These ideas may surprise the large number of educators who still rely on established tradition despite *Tinker*.

GRADING

Historically, teachers have "docked" students' grades or subtracted points that lead to grades because of tardiness, unexcused absences, late papers, insolence, and a host of deportment behaviors that are not acceptable to educators. In practice, educators have intertwined achievement with behavior, but courts have ruled that a grade is perceived by society as a summation of academic achievement.[7] The letter grade on a report card or transcript is perceived by employers or university admissions officers as reflecting a level of skill and knowledge. A gifted student's English grade may be lowered because of unexcused absences, resulting in his rejection by a university with competitive admissions standards. However, the gifted student may have read extensively and mastered the entire course content, as demonstrated on a standardized national English test.

Many courts today are saying that the school's grade, which mixed behavior with achievement, was highly unfair. The authoritarian teacher who arbitrarily decides that a letter grade will be a mix of achievement and behavior assessment, in order to control students, is violating the students' rights. A grade is seen as property, as defined by the Fourteenth Amendment, and the students have earned this property by the mastery of academic skills and knowledge. Thus, this property cannot be denied as a part of a discipline action to control behavior. This discipline action of lowering the grade may also deprive the student of the opportunity to get into a prestigious university that would ensure a higher income for the remainder of his or her life. This touches on the cherished phrase "*nor shall any State deprive any person of life, liberty, or property.*" This does not mean that there may not be consequences for misbehavior—merely that these consequences or punishments must be kept separate from the student's letter grade.

Teachers might be quite surprised to learn that proponents of *Judicious Discipline* suggest that homework should not be graded or reflected in the final letter grade. According to this thinking, students who come from homes with many resources—including money and parental guidance and time—will also show superior performance with homework when compared with a child whose home situation is antithetical to homework. Thus, if we grade this homework, we are not grading the student's knowledge but rather the supportiveness of his home context. In such a case, the grading discriminates against the child based on a home situation that he or she cannot control and violates the student's equal opportunity guarantees. Where homework is still used in the classroom today, the teacher and school must find creative ways for students to complete these assignments supported by the school structure and not solely dependent on parents. No matter how homework is used, according to this philosophy, the grading of the homework should not be mixed with more objective measurements of what the child has learned. Figures 6–3 to 6–10 provide a quick-reference summary of classroom and school practices that may be impacted when using judicious thinking similar to the grading example just discussed.

Discipline Issue	Level 1: Authoritarian Position	Level 2: Judicious Position	Judicious School Procedures (Gathercoal, 1991)
Unexcused absences or tardiness	The school provides students an education and if they fail to take advantage of what is provided by skipping class and showing academic deficiencies, bad attitude, and offensive cultural values, the school and teacher have no further responsibilities to the student. By his or her actions, the student is less worthy and the school will not serve him or her. Law requires mandatory days of school attendance.	The gates will be open, a commitment to help all students will be given, and the school will place no walls to bar those "less worthy." The focus of mandatory school attendance should not be on days of attendance, but on whether the student has acquired the knowledge and skills needed to graduate and succeed in life.	Under no circumstances are grades lowered because of lateness or absences. Alternative times, such as evenings and weekends, will be offered and special tutoring may be available to enable the student to learn the material.

(continued)

FIGURE 6–3 Compulsory School Attendance: "You'd Better Come to School or We Will Kick You Out"

Discipline Issue	Level 1: Authoritarian Position	Level 2: Judicious Position	Judicious School Procedures (Gathercoal, 1991)
Denying credit and dropping students from classes	After a specific number of absences, the student will be dropped from the class. This will apply to everyone.	The essential question is not the rule itself but the individual circumstances that serve as the substance of appeal. Each case must be looked at individually to determine whether the student is capable of completing satisfactory classwork.	Students may be assigned to alternative education classes with tutors for the remaining grade period, and individualized instruction would be available. Students should not be punished for nonattendance, and should be given credit for the course if they demonstrate that they have obtained the knowledge by other means. Alternatives include a term paper covering the subject matter missed, a book review on the subject, or several pages outlining the chapters missed. Schools could also provide flexible schedules, including after-school and weekend programs, to alleviate overcrowding in alternative programs. If one student is ill and a second simply skipped class, should both be allowed to make up the work? Judiciously, the answer is yes, because both are still in need of an education regardless of the reason for nonattendance; each should have equal educational opportunity (Gathercoal, 1991, pp. 65–66).
Tardiness	The tardy student must be sent to the office for an excuse. After three unex-cused incidents of tardi-ness, the student is suspended for one or two days. Problems: students losing more class time by going to the office; disruption for a second time; students playing games with rules by being tardy twice but never the third time (what if all 30 students in the class played this game?); difficulty in judging and proving acceptable excuses; students learn more about following rules than about responsible behavior.	Each case must be handled individually. The student who is tardy needs to be taught the skills of getting organized and being punctual. Tardiness should be approached as an educational instance, not as a moral judgment.	The teacher should be well prepared, start class promptly, and model behavior congruent with expectations of students. The teacher should have the responsibility of handling tardiness as an educational learning problem, with administrators becoming involved only in the most chronic cases.

FIGURE 6–3   (continued)

Discipline Issue	Level 1: Authoritarian Position	Level 2: Judicious Position	Judicious School Procedures (Gathercoal, 1991)
Suspension (a short-term denial of the student's right to the benefits of public education; because of the brief duration, the student would not suffer substantial loss of his or her educational opportunity) (Gathercoal, 1991, p. 67)	Rules are written, and breaking them will result in judicious suspension. A Level 1 Authoritarian position is: This will teach you a lesson.	The attitude of the educator is critical to a judicious suspension. The Level 2 Judicious position is: We could both use time away from each other. The school would offer weekend and after-school tutoring to help the student make up missed content. A fostering of the student's self-esteem is critical, and the administrator calls the student during the suspension to offer encouragement, indicate that the student is wanted back, and maintain a student/educator relationship.	*Gross* v. *Lopez* (419 US. 565) requires due process: • *Notice:* an oral or written notice of the charges (e.g., the rule the student violated) • *Evidence:* a summary of the evidence against the student (e.g., a teacher witnessed the student's misbehavior) • *Defense:* an opportunity for the student to be heard (e.g., the student has an opportunity to tell his or her side of the story) (Gathercoal, 1991, p. 167). (An administrator does not have to comply with a student's request for an attorney or presence of a witnesses. The courts have judged that this overburdens the school.).
Expulsion (a longer duration than suspension; usually results in the loss of grades and credit, thereby substantially depriving the student of educational opportunity)		As above, the administrator must attempt to project an attitude that maintains a student/educator relationship.	The school must provide substantive and procedural due process rights, offering charges, evidence, and a hearing to substantiate the reasons for its action. The student has the right to be represented by counsel, to receive a complete and accurate record of the proceedings, and to appeal the decision.
Suspension or expulsion of student with a disability			Students with disabilities have additional rights that are not necessarily extended to others. If the condition is the cause of the removal, other procedures legally come into play. Since these laws change quickly, up-to-date legal advice should be sought from an appropriate attorney.

FIGURE 6–3   (continued)

Discipline Issue	Level 1: Authoritarian Position	Level 2: Judicious Position	Judicious School Procedures
Withholding privileges	Would be considered the teacher's right.	Participation in the graduation ceremony, for example, is a privilege and can be withheld. The student, however, does have a right to graduate; that right is not to be taken away as a consequence of unacceptable behavior.	Must be clearly in perspective with the gravity of the offense proportionate to the age and mental, emotional, or physical condition of the student. The school must give adequate notice, written or oral. Punishment must be judicious.
Corporal punishment	Has long been used to punish students for unacceptable behavior and is still legal in many states. However, many new state child abuse laws are making principals and teachers subject to abuse charges because of corporal punishment.	Would be rejected as noneducational. However, reasonable physical force may be necessary at times to maintain order.	Follow these guidelines with parent approval: • A due process procedure with charges, evidence, and the student's right to be heard • Reasonable administration with moderation, prudence, and consideration of the gravity of the offense, and physical condition and size of the student • Privately administered, out of the presence or hearing of other students • Witnessed by a certified staff member • Properly recorded and placed on file as a matter of record • Notification to parents or legal guardian (Gathercoal, 1991, p. 78)
Punishing the group for the acts of one student	If no one admits to the "crime," the whole group suffers.	Not permitted.	The judicious attitude is to take steps to prevent the action from occurring.
Punishing the student for the acts of his or her parents	The student may be disciplined because the parent brought him to school late.	The student is not responsible for the acts of people beyond his or her control, such as parents.	It is not permitted to punish the student for the actions of parents.
Sitting outside classroom doors, names on the blackboard	If the student fails to perform as required, this is the deserved punishment.	This type of punishment would do damage to the student's self-esteem.	May be considered holding the child up to ridicule by peers and may have detrimental psychological effects.

FIGURE 6–4   Forms of Punishment

Discipline Issue	Level 1: Authoritarian Position	Level 2: Judicious Position	Judicious School Procedures
Keeping students after school	Often used as punishment; students will suffer public ridicule for unworthy actions.	Not educational; only serves to lower self-esteem.	Safety concerns about the child returning home in nontraditional time and manner.
Not permitting student to participate in class because of not having pencil/ school supplies	"If you are unprepared, you may not participate."	Inconsistent with the child's right to equal educational opportunity.	Have community equipment that may be "borrowed."
Detention rooms	"Doing time" is seen as an appropriate punishment.	Seen as a form of jail and may require due process criteria to be met; does not correct the behavior but causes resentment from the student; hurts the student/educator relationship.	Rename detention rooms to correction rooms or problem-solving rooms with tutors for learning.

FIGURE 6–4 (continued)

Discipline Issue	Level 1: Authoritarian Position	Level 2: Judicious Position	Judicious School Procedures
Destroying school property	The student must conform to behavior that will not do damage to school property, whether or not these expectations have been modeled in the student's home environment.	The judicious consequences must be proportionate to the severity of the loss incurred and the student's feeling of remorse.	Requires adequate notice; requires public service. Parents are liable for damage done by their child. The school may use small claims court to recover costs.
Student's personal property loss		Efforts will be taken to help make personal property secure.	Inform parents and students of the risk involved in bringing objects from home. Educators and parents must explore alternative methods for securing items that must be brought. Parents of a student suffering property loss may take a classmate and his or her parents to small claims court to recover loss caused by that classmate.

FIGURE 6–5   Property Loss and Damage

Discipline Issue	Level 1: Authoritarian Position	Level 2: Judicious Position	Judicious School Procedures
Dress and appearance	The school usually will provide a long list of specifics: no short shorts, frayed trousers, shirttails outside pants, bare midriffs, etc.	Have one broad rule covering the importance of dress in the educational environment; parents of the offending student would be notified that if the dress was patently vulgar or clearly inappropriate, it would be prohibited.	First Amendment rights do protect a certain amount of self-expression. Students should be handled individually through educational means, and schools should enlist the help of parents; the educational means will serve as prior notice because of the vague broad rule.
Public displays of affection	Unacceptable in public.		Notify parents and enlist their help.
Student's refusal to say Pledge of Allegiance	Each student must recite the pledge.	First Amendment guarantees the student a choice.	Protected by the Constitution; students may not be forced or punished.
Reading materials brought from home or pictures displayed in lockers			In the student's free time, the right to read these materials is protected as long as they are not patently vulgar.
Wearing robes for graduation; wearing shoes at all times; wearing protective gear for industrial arts, athletic activities, etc.			May be required as a legitimate educational purpose.
Insubordination and open diffidence; profane language; indecent gestures; bigoted statements	Punishment would be administered.	The teacher would not be offended, but would confront the student and attempt to determine what is behind the verbal aggression in an educational way.	Rarely if ever is punished.
Free speech activities		Predetermine a place and location for such independent expression.	Place a bulletin board in hallways and classrooms for displaying free speech materials; "controlling the reasonable time, place, and manner of student expression" (Gathercoal, 1991, p. 86) or the distribution of expressive materials.

FIGURE 6–6   Speech and Expression

Discipline Issue	Level 1: Authoritarian Position	Level 2: Judicious Position	Judicious School Procedures
Searching lockers, purses, bags, or students' cars in the parking lot	Teachers may open desks, bags, etc. on any occasion that they think they might find something that is not allowed.	Teachers must have reasonable cause to search; no search warrant is needed (e.g., during the last week of class in an attempt to find missing school property).	Must have witnesses and, if possible, the student should be present and given prior notice.
Searching the body or conducting "strip searches"		Risky if the student fails to cooperate; avoid if possible. Reasonable cause must exist and be considered when determining legality of the search.	The school may wish the parent or police to perform such searches if the situation is serious.
Random searches		The searches are legal if a "compelling state interest" can be shown.	Not permitted unless there is prior notice or authorities are looking for misplaced school property or spoiled food that might cause health problems; bomb threats make such searches legal for safety reasons.
Seizure by school authorities of a student's property that disrupts the classroom or school environment (toys, fad items, and similar "brought from home" items)	Student's property may be confiscated because students were warned not to bring such items. These items are lost to the student forever.	A teacher may confiscate disruptive items. These items shall be returned as quickly as possible.	A teacher may give a receipt for the items, showing respect for ownership.

FIGURE 6–7   Search and Seizure

Discipline Issue	Level 1: Authoritarian Position	Level 2: Judicious Position	Judicious School Procedures
Prior restraint mandating in advance what someone may publish	The administration has the right to restrict content of students' speech.	Students only enjoy some substantive rights because of their age and impressionability, and the fact that they are not legally liable for what they publish.	Create a publication advisory board composed of a student editor, advisor, student-body representative, teacher, administrator, school board member, and possibly local newspaper editor. Review editorial problems within 48 hours. Write publication guidelines.
Passing notes	Passing notes is not acceptable.	May be viewed as a matter of civil rights if not disruptive to the educational process.	Teacher works with students to find an acceptable manner for note passing, showing the learning of responsible behavior.

FIGURE 6–8   Press

Discipline Issue	Level 1: Authoritarian Position	Level 2: Judicious Position	Judicious School Procedures
Religious celebration/ advocating religion; prayer at assemblies within school	The school has always done this, and large numbers of the public would complain if it stopped using prayers, religious symbols at Christmas, etc.	Advocating religion in a school context is clearly forbidden, but the study of religion as an academic study is permitted.	Religion and related activities are approached from an educational perspective.
Not participating in classes on religious grounds	All classes must be attended or the student fails the course.	If a student or parent feels the class is contrary to his or her religious beliefs, the student may be excused from attending the class without having his or her grade lowered.	Assigning alternative work is advisable to serve an educational purpose, not for punishment.
Wearing religious attire	School dress code must be observed.	This is clearly a student right, but a teacher may not wear religious dress if it appears to advocate a particular religious belief.	

FIGURE 6–9   Religion

Discipline Issue	Level 1: Authoritarian Position	Level 2: Judicious Position	Judicious School Procedures
Religious themes/music	Christmas and other Christian holidays may be observed in school.	Religious music, etc., may be used in a secular manner. The attitude of the teacher and leadership is critical. Religious beliefs may be unacceptable to the minority, and therefore are not to be advocated by the school.	Students will have bulletin board space allocated to express religious preferences, and students are allowed freedom to express religious beliefs.
Religious decorations	Christian holiday symbols have always been allowed, and to stop such practice would offend the majority.	Particular religious decorations are not advanced.	Not permitted as a wide distribution through the school, but may be allocated space for student expression.

FIGURE 6–9   (continued)

Discipline Issue	Level 1: Authoritarian Position	Level 2: Judicious Position	Judicious School Procedures
Required payment for school supplies	All are required to pay; if one person is given an exemption, it would be unfair to the rest.	Make all efforts to eliminate such fees, because of possible discrimination against those students whose families may not be able to afford them.	When fees are needed, have other funds available for those who cannot afford to pay, and be very discrete in awarding this.
Access to the student's school records		Parents or the student (18 years or older) may not be denied an opportunity to review records.	Student/parents must be able to view, make copies at their own expense, and challenge the content of the student's records.

FIGURE 6–10   School Fees and Records

RULES

Public schools may not create rules unilaterally just because a teacher or administrator values certain kinds of behavior and deportment. But fair rules *are* necessary and schools are often required to put a discipline statement and plan into writing; these are usually placed in student handbooks to provide a guideline and *prior notice* for students and parents. (This does not necessarily pertain to private schools that receive no public money.) Substantive due process means a rule must (1) have some rational basis or need for its adoption, (2) be as good in meeting this need as any alternative that a reasonable person might have developed, and (3) be supported by relevant and substantial evidence and findings of fact.[8] In other words, substantive due process means the rules and decisions must have a legal basis before the school may deny a student the opportunity to act in a specific manner.

Next, the judicious rules should be written with the justification that depriving students and prohibiting their behavior is necessary because of the compelling state interest test of (1) property loss or damage, (2) legitimate educational purpose, (3) health and safety, or (4) *serious* disruption of the educational process. The written rules, in a Level 1: Fear of Authority manner, establish a one-to-one relationship between a rule and a specific punishment or degree of punishment, thus boxing in the administrator or teacher and not permitting a judicious due process determination of a sanction or consequence. These rules should also reflect a Level 2: Feelings and Understanding of Social Responsibility (judicious) attitude by having them stated in positive terms rather than negative "thou shalt not" decrees. The student should be told what to do rather than told what *not* to do. Level 1 negatively states the rule as "Don't run in the hall!" or "Don't shout in the hallways!" or "Don't walk on the gym floor with street shoes!" These same rules can be positively stated, reflecting a Level 2 attitude, as "Move in a safe manner through the halls" or "Keep your voice down so that others are not disturbed" or "Wear appropriate footwear when walking or playing on the gym floor." See Figure 6–11 for an example of a rule preamble statement that may appear in a student handbook written from a positive judicious perspective.

JUDICIOUS DISCIPLINE AND THE TEACHER BEHAVIOR CONTINUUM

Most discipline models provide the teacher with specific techniques to use in dealing with a student during and after an incident of misbehavior, while the teacher is feeling the "heat" and stress of the situation. Judicious discipline, however, essentially is a reflective and teaching model requiring the teacher to think out cognitively her general approach and pass nearly all school practices through the filter of democratic rights. Once this is understood, the teacher will change rules, sanctions, grading, and a host of other procedures to create a more fair, nonauthoritarian classroom. The judicious classroom will present a climate of acceptance in

Kent High School is a learning community where students feel accepted and the teachers value each child's abilities and rights. Members of this community of learners are interdependent and must work to show others that they are respected for their distinct and unique differences. Every member must strive to make this school a community that is healthy and safe for all, and a place where everyone can learn. As a student-citizen of this community-school, each person will be guaranteed the right to know the reason for rules and actions that personally effect him or her, and will have the responsibility to contribute and participate in procedures ensuring these rights. The student will respect the rights of all members and the school will take actions to stop students who willfully attempt to take away others' rights by their behavior. The major goal of Kent High School is to educate students as citizens who understand and can contribute to a democratic way of governance and living. The school, as a democratic laboratory, will teach academic and social skills that will serve its students as mature citizens.

Signed:

Written by the 1994 faculty and
administration of KHS

School Rules:
Act in a Safe and Healthy Way.
(Use furniture appropriately, walk when inside the building, etc. Compelling State Interest: Safety)

Treat All Property with Respect.
(Take care of textbooks, library books, school materials and equipment, etc. Compelling State Interest: Property)

Respect the Rights and Needs of Others.
(Show courtesy, cooperate, use appropriate language, etc. Compelling State Interest: Serious Disruption of the Educational Process)

Take Responsibility for Learning.
(Work hard, come prepared, be on time, etc. Compelling State Interest: Legitimate Educational Purpose)[9]

FIGURE 6–11   Kent High School—Student Handbook Preamble

which the teacher focuses on maintaining the student/teacher relationship. The teacher will also teach the class about constitutional rights, either by having the students create their own judicious classroom rules or, if limited by short classroom periods, announcing rules founded on these same democratic amendments.

Judicious discipline is not a "stand-alone" discipline model, but must be used interactively with other more proscriptive discipline models. The ideas, techniques, and models of Dreikurs, cooperative discipline, Glasser, and, to a lesser extent, Gordon's *T.E.T.* philosophy would add strength to this model. In Dreikurs, Glasser, and other models, rules are necessary but the teacher must decide which rules are fair, necessary, and acceptable; clearly, judicious discipline answers these questions and makes a major contribution to an understanding of rules and democratic fairness.

Judicious discipline is not a discipline model that prescribes a formula or specific procedures for handling discipline incidents in the classroom. Rather, it is a preventive guide and a teaching model that uses legal rights and laws to give democratic perspective to the framework for creating rules (Do the rules meet our nation's legal standards?). It also gives the teacher steps and procedures, called *due process*, for dealing with the student after a discipline incident. The following is a step-by-step process that attempts to make this model clear for the user. Again, the Teacher Behavior Continuum is used.

The primary elements used from the Teacher Behavior Continuum (see Figure 6–12) are questioning and directive statements. First, the teacher questions his own orientation to authoritarian and democratic procedures, and then reflects on the fairness of each set of procedures. When a discipline incident occurs or a rule is broken, the teacher asks questions to help ensure due process for the student while determining actions that will maintain a judicious attitude and healthy student/

Looking On	Nondirective Statements	Questions
Step 1: Teacher Commitment to Democratic Classroom		Step 2: Teach Principles—students list their individual rights: • What rights do you have in this country? • What rights do you have in this school? Compare to list (on board): Are these rights the same? (skip to Step 3 for teacher with limited class time) Step 4: Establish Class Rules—related to the three amendments: Which of our rules are justified by the amendments? Step 5: Teach "Compelling State Interest" Teacher: When can society take away individual rights?—compelling state interest • Property loss/damage • Legitimate educational purpose • Health and safety • Serious disruption of educational process

FIGURE 6–12   Teacher Behavior Continuum (TBC): Judicious Discipline

teacher relationship. (Visually looking on and nondirective statements are not used in the judicious discipline's TBC.)

Question/Directive Statements

Step 1: The teacher commits. The teacher must question her own procedures and behaviors and commit herself to running a democratic classroom by teaching principles of constitutional amendments, due process procedures, and the difficulties of group versus individual rights. The teacher would change a host of general practices in order to advance democratic practices.

Step 2: Teach democratic principles. (*Note:* Step 2 is for the teacher who is not confined to a 50-minute period with her students and has time to teach this inductively through activities and discussion. The teacher who has limited time should skip Step 2 and go to Step 3.) The teacher asks the class to list what

Directive Statements	Modeling	Reinforcement (Judicious Consequences)	Physical Intervention/ Isolation
		Step 7: Teach examples of judicious consequences, apology, conference with parents, etc.—see Figure 6–13.	
Step 3: Teach 1st, 4th, & 14th Amendments directly (property loss/ damage, legitimate educational purpose, health/safety, serious disruption of educational process).			Consequences: • Time-out • Loss of privilege • Suspension • Expulsion • Others
Write, post, sign rules.	Step 6: Give examples of group vs. individual rights.		

FIGURE 6–12 (continued)

rights they have in their country. She then asks the class to list what rights they have in school as students. These two lists are compared by placing them both on the board, with the teacher asking questions.

Step 3: Teach the First, Fourth, and Fourteenth Amendments through directive teaching (directive statements).

Step 4: Establish class rules. Through questioning, the class now compares the amendments and democratic rights with the previously established rules. (Note: The deductive teacher will announce and explain predetermined rules based on judicious guidelines.) The class then discusses and reflects until the students agree on all the salient rules needed to guide them in their classroom activities and social interactions. The rules are posted, signed by each student, placed in the student handbook, and sent home to parents (due process: prior notice).

Step 5: Teach "compelling state interest" (property loss/damage, legitimate educational purpose, health and safety, and serious disruption of educational process).

Modeling/Physical Intervention

Step 6: Teach rules of the group vs. individual rights. The teacher provides examples of students' rights that cannot be taken away (e.g., speech, how to wear hair and clothing, etc.). The students will learn at what point the teacher and school administration will prohibit and intervene (physical intervention) by taking away the individual's rights in order to stop inappropriate behaviors or, when needed, to protect a compelling state interest.

Reinforcement

Step 7: Teach/explain judicious consequences and attitude. With the use of Figure 6-13, the teacher will describe the types of consequences a student might experience (loss of privileges, required apology, restitution, suspension, expulsion, and others) if the student's behavior takes away others' rights. Just as important is to show that the teacher will always work to maintain a student/teacher relationship and will attempt to provide educational consequences when rules are broken. The teacher explains that in the application of judicious consequences, not all children will get the same consequence for breaking the same rule; rather, the response will be individualized.

SUMMARY

The teacher must use his manner of establishing rules and awarding sanctions to model a Level 2: Feelings and Understanding of Social Responsibility approach. This also means that the teacher cannot allow himself special privileges (such as cutting in line in the school cafeteria when there is a rule against cutting by students, smoking when students may not, or failing to wear safety glasses in the

Property Loss and Damage	Legitimate Educational Purpose	Health and Safety	Serious Disruption of the Educational Process
apology	apology	apology	apology
clean it up	redo the assignment or	complete a research report	private conference
give it back	take another test	community service project	mutual agreements
restitution	complete an alternative	private conference	time out
mutual agreements	assignment	mutual agreements	problem solving room
community service	study with a tutor	counseling	counseling
project	private conference	conference with parents	mediation
counseling	mutual agreement	reassignment	conference with parents
conference with parents	counseling	loss of privileges	reassignment
reassignment	conference with parents	suspension	community service
loss of privileges	reassignment	expulsion	loss of privileges
suspension	loss of privilege		suspension
expulsion	suspension		expulsion
	expulsion		

FIGURE 6–13   Examples of Consequences Suggested by *Judicious Discipline* (Gathercoal, 1991)

industrial shop when students are required to do so). The teacher must take a "do as I do" approach rather than just one of "do as I say."

Finally, when a teacher or administrator is faced with a situation where the student has broken a rule and has to be prohibited from acting in a manner that impinges on state interests or the rights of others, the attitude utilized is critical. It is important to teach constitutional rights, rules, compelling state interest, and due process, but the cement that holds all of this together to build a solid and democratic classroom or school is the attitude of Level 2: Feelings and Understanding of Social Responsibility. It is critical for the educator to take the time, when preparing to discipline a student, to utilize due process and to ask:

- What needs to be learned here?
- How would an educator manage the problem?
- Do I need more information about the student or the student's family?
- What strategies can be used to keep this student in school?
- How will the student perceive the consequence?
- How will the consequence affect the school community?
- How can I maintain the student/teacher relationship?[9]

Sam, with his fight in the school cafeteria, would have been better served if he would have had a more judicious school that did not have as its rule a punishment statement that boxed in the educators to a unilateral authoritarian position. The preceding questions would have permitted the school administration to recognize Sam's family situation. This in turn would have enabled them to take actions that might work to improve the father/son relationship, strengthen Sam's ability to handle his own behavior under stress, and maintain a relationship with him through which he would feel that he is not in a "them-versus-me" relationship. This would allow the student to feel that school is a place that cares about him and his needs, and that really wishes to help him become a more complete, better educated person during these important adolescent years.

ENDNOTES

1. J. Piaget, *Moral Judgment of the Child* (Trans. Marjorie Gabain) (New York: Free Press, 1965).

2. R. Dreikurs, *Psychology in the Classroom: A Manual for Teachers, 2nd ed.* (New York: Harper & Row, 1968).

3. F. Gathercoal, *Judicious Discipline* (Davis, CA: Caddo Gap Press, 1991).

4. Ibid.

5. Ibid., p. 44.

6. Ibid., p. 42.

7. Ibid.

8. Ibid.

9. Ibid.

RELATED READINGS

Dreikurs, R. *Psychology in the Classroom: A Manual for Teachers, 2nd ed.* New York: Harper & Row, 1968.

Editors of Deskbook Encyclopedia of American School Law. Information Research Systems, P.O. Box 409, Rosemount, MN 55068 (yearly).

Gathercoal, F. *Judicious Discipline.* Davis, CA: Caddo Gap Press, 1991.

Kern, A., and Alexander, M. D. *The Law of Schools, Students and Teachers in a Nutshell.* St. Paul, MN: West Publishing, 1984.

Kirp, D. L., and Jensen, D. N. *School Days, Rule Days.* Denver: Falmer Press, 1986.

McEwan, B. *Practicing Judicious Discipline: An Educator's Guide to a Democratic Classroom.* Davis, CA: Caddo Gap Press, 1991.

Piaget, J. *Moral Judgment of the Child* (trans. Marjorie Gabain). New York: Free Press, 1965.

Yudolf, M. G., Kirp, D. L., Geel, T. V., & Levin, B. *Educational Policy and Law.* Minneapolis, MN: McCutchan Publishing, 1982.

For a list of law-related textbooks, write to: West Publishing Company, Attn.: Law-Related Education, W. Kellogg Blvd., P.O. Box 64779, St. Paul, MN 55164.

For a monthly publication summarizing recent court cases, write to: National Organization on Legal Problems of Education (NOLPE), Southwest 29th, Suite 223, Topeka, KS 66614.

7

THE BEHAVIOR ANALYSIS MODEL

Cowritten with Mark Koorland

*Professor and Chair, Department of Special Education,
Florida State University*

Theorist/Writer: B. F. Skinner

- *Science and Human Behavior*
- *Beyond Freedom and Dignity*

Theorists/Writers for Teachers: Paul A. Alberto and Ann C. Troutman

- *Applied Behavior Analysis for Teachers*

Theorists/Writers for Teachers: Charles Madsen and Clifford Madsen

- *Teaching/Discipline: A Positive Approach for Educational Development*

The Behavior Analysis Model, sometimes called *behavior mod*, requires strong intrusion and management techniques that demand that the teacher plan a systematic shaping process to help misbehaving students gain self-control and a reawakening sense of control. Key to this model is the use of reinforcers, both positive and negative, to obtain desired behavior and to extinguish inappropriate behavior. Let us see the teacher in action, first *without* using behavior analysis techniques.

Jimmy, a kindergarten student, stands before the paint easel. Using a large, thick paintbrush, he dips the end into the paint pot. Soon the brush reappears, dripping with a large glob of paint. As Robert walks by, Jimmy turns and sticks out the brush as if it is a sword and attempts to "stab" his schoolmate. The peer screams and runs off, much to the delight of Jimmy. Smiling, Jimmy "El Zorro" dips his brush into the paint pot and looks about for a new target.

Robert huddles with two friends in the block corner to tell them of Jimmy's "paint stabbing." The three classmates smile broadly as they move as a group, much like a military assault squad, tentatively and defensively approaching Jimmy to see if they can get the same results. Jimmy eagerly complies by dipping his brush into the red paint and stabbing out toward the approaching boys. The three boys gleefully scream and flee through the classroom, knocking over another student's block building. This creates a loud crash and screams of distress from the student using the blocks, as the boys take up a hiding position behind the block shelves.

The teacher quickly approaches "El Zorro" and orders, "Jimmy, behave yourself!" Jimmy drops his head before the easel and, placing the brush on the paper, makes circular scribbling actions as if he is painting. After the teacher returns to her previous activity, Jimmy—aware that he has four paint pots each with a vivid color—begins to pump the paintbrush up and down in each pot. He rotates his paint-covered brush from one pot to the next until the colors in all four pots become a blended mess of muddy brown. The teacher reprimands, "Jimmy, look what you have done. You have mixed all four paints together. You have made them look like mud, and people can't paint with colors like this!" The teacher takes away the pots of muddy brown paint and replaces them with fresh pots taken from a nearby easel.

The teacher stresses, "Now, Jimmy, do not mix these colors!" The teacher then departs, leaving Jimmy with a supply of fresh colors. He watches closely to see that the teacher is involved with another student, and then moves his body so that his back is to the teacher, blocking her view of the paint pots. He dips his brush into the blue paint, then slowly sinks it into the yellow pot, making a blue swirl in the yellow paint. Giggling, Jimmy brings out the brush, inspects it closely, and reaches over to his neighbor's easel and makes a blue-and-yellow streak down the right side of the student's paper. The neighboring painter now screams at Jimmy, and the teacher once again appears before Jimmy.

BEHAVIOR ANALYSIS TECHNIQUES

In previous chapters describing other models, we have seen how the techniques of the Relationship-Listening and Confronting-Contracting faces can modify routine misbehaviors in many cases. However, some students present extremely difficult discipline problems that call for strong escalation along the Teacher Behavior Continuum. Through the techniques of behavior analysis, the teacher plays a more specific role in shaping appropriate behavior by these students.

How shall we view the interaction between Jimmy and the teacher, and how could the teacher have more successfully intervened by using behavior analysis? The answer is that we begin to arrange consequences and measure behavioral change to help the student acquire the more positive behaviors.

Behavioral Objectives

When dealing with a student's misbehavior, it is imperative that you clearly define the behavior that you wish to change so that you may be clear about the *target behavior*. This target behavior may be selected for change because (1) it is a behavioral deficit, something lacking in the student's daily activities (using the paintbrush and paints incorrectly; can't get to class on time; etc.) or (2) it is a behavior that is correct in form or function but is displayed excessively or at the wrong time (asking so many questions in class that no one else has a chance to ask a question; talking during test taking; taking all the art supplies so there are none left for peers; etc.).

To decrease an inappropriate target behavior exhibited by a difficult student who fails to respond to your initial intervention efforts, and to increase his use of desirable behaviors, you must begin by choosing and defining *behavioral objectives* for this student and committing these objectives to writing. In order to understand the behavioral changes that you want and to communicate them to other staff members, you must establish a behavioral objective that identifies the following components:

1. The learner
2. The antecedent conditions under which the behavior is to be displayed
3. The target behavior
4. Criteria for acceptable performance

Returning to our example of the kindergarten child, Jimmy "El Zorro," with his repeated attempts at "stabbing" others, we now take the first step in a behavior change program by engaging in *pinpointing*—specifying in measurable, observable terms a behavior targeted for change—by establishing a behavioral objective. "Jimmy (1. *identify the learner*), while at the easel (2. *identify the antecedent conditions*), will use the brush by marking paint on the paper (3. *identify the target behavior*) for three of the next four times he uses the easel (4. *identify criteria for acquisition*)." Now that the behaviors are pinpointed, the teacher may move to the next step of behavior analysis, collecting data to help the student acquire this behavioral objective (see Figure 7–1).

Other Examples of Behavioral Objectives

Beth cries, has a temper tantrum, or becomes inactive and sucks her thumb when her mother departs each morning.

1. Identify the learner (answers "Who?").
   "Beth..."

Identify the *Learner* (answers "Who")	Promotes individualization of instruction, requiring the teacher to specify the targeted student or group of students.	*Jimmy* will . . . (state action). *Students* in the block corner will . . . (state action).
Identify the *Antecedent* conditions	Description of the preceding activity, condition, or stimuli (antecedent stimulus that sets the occasion for occurrence of the target behavior).	Jimmy, *when using the paint easel*, will place his paintbrush on the paper and paint. Debbie, *when sitting at the table*, will put her feet on the floor. Kevin, *when finished at the snack table*, will stand, pick up his trash, and place it in the waste basket.
Identify the target *Behavior*	What will the student be doing when the desired change is achieved? The words chosen should lead to behavior that is observable, measurable/countable, and repeatable.	Good verbs: to mark, to remove, to put on, to label, to place, to say, to cross out, to take, to hand up, to point *Poor verbs*: to apply, to appreciate, to analyze, to understand, to select, to perform, to become competent
Identify *Criteria* for acceptable performance	Sets the standard for evaluation and defines what will be measured to determine completion of the desired behavior; may also include how long the student will perform the desired behavior (duration) or length of time from start signal or cue before the student actually starts (latency).	*Acquisition criteria:* . . . four days out of five . . . . . . on each occasion . . . . . . completes all five steps independently . . . *Duration criteria:* . . . role-play in sociodramatic play for 10 minutes . . . . . . stay seated in circle time for 5 minutes . . . *Latency criteria:* . . . after waking up, the student will put on her socks and shoes within three minutes. . . . within 60 seconds after being seated, the student will place food in his mouth.

FIGURE 7–1   Components of a Behavioral Objective: "Learner A-B-C" Criteria

2. Identify the conditions.
   "when parting from her mother in the mornings . . . "
3. Identify the target behavior.
   "will pick up toys or materials (or speak to another person) . . . "
4. Identify criteria for acceptable performance.
   "within five minutes after her mother leaves." (*latency*)

Judy constantly talks to her neighbors during seatwork.

1. Identify the learner (answers "Who?").
   "Judy . . . "

2. Identify the conditions.
   "while doing seatwork..."
3. Identify the target behavior.
   "will work silently..."
4. Identify criteria for acceptable performance.
   "for a period of 10 minutes." (*duration*)

Cal refuses to stay in his seat while the class is working.

1. Identify the learner (answers "Who?").
   "Cal..."
2. Identify the conditions.
   "during the work period..."
3. Identify the target behavior.
   "will stay in his seat..."
4. Identify criteria for acceptable performance.
   "for at least two 30-minute periods for the next three days." (*acquisition criteria*)

Collecting Data

In the opening vignette, we saw a hard-working, well-meaning teacher attempt to intervene with Jimmy "El Zorro" and stop his stabbing with the paintbrush. She reprimands him, physically appears before him, and changes the paint pots, even as other students run or become upset because of his actions. When we closely examine exactly what is going on—in this case, understanding the technical concept and operation of positive reinforcement—we discover that the teacher is actually a large part of the problem. The teacher's reinforcement, in conjunction with the reinforcement from classmates and the materials themselves, served to reward misbehavior. Unfortunately, this is not an isolated incident. It is rather typical of what, at times, is really occurring when misbehavior is repeated—the teacher's behavior unknowingly is exacerbating the situation.

For us as teachers, the classroom is a very dynamic situation requiring attention to a host of stimuli coming from students, as well as attention to safety concerns with the objects and materials being used. On top of all that, we have a student like Jimmy, who is like a hand grenade ready to go off at any minute. Time and again these overwhelming activities may require us to take some action. Unfortunately, the behavior and actions of others might be shaping and controlling our behavior, when instead we should be in control of them. We will never know if this is really true until we collect reliable data that can give us a perspective on just what influential events are occurring in our classroom and school. But most importantly, data will tell us if our intervention is working. If it is not, then this is a signal for us to try to improve our intervention.

It is the third week of the new school year and Jimmy "El Zorro" has made these last three weeks a living hell for his teacher, Mrs. Anderson. She realizes that she cannot continue through an entire school year putting out all the "fires" and disruptions that Jimmy starts. She challenges herself to get on top of the "Jimmy problem" and really think through the situation. She makes a list of the misbehaviors she can recall from the first two weeks. She finds that:

- Four out of five days a week, there is a temper tantrum exchange between Jimmy and his parent (usually his mother) when he is dropped off in the morning.
- He has knocked over the block structures of a group of boys on four occasions. The boys involved were Mark, Robert, Walter, and Barry.
- Three out of five days, he was part of food-throwing activity that turned to aggressive biting during snack time. At the table were Barry, Carol, Robert, and Kevin.
- During one circle time, he began violently kicking those sitting near him, Janet and Robert.
- Nearly every playground period there is a fight over who can ride on the rickshaw, which carries three students, with Jimmy pulling the rickshaw and hitting other students. Those usually involved were Mark, Steven, and, always, Robert.

From this list, the teacher begins to see that the *antecedent condition* leading to some form of misbehavior, aggression, and disruption always involves Robert— who the teacher considers a generally well-behaved student—and involves an arrival period in which the mother brings Jimmy to school. Mrs. Anderson may decide to attempt to collect reliable data on Jimmy's behavior for the following reasons: (1) she wants precise observations and measurements of behavior, which may enable her to determine the best way to change Jimmy's misbehavior and to give information about Jimmy to other teachers, his parents, school administrators, and, if need be, school counselors or psychologists; and (2) the observation/ data collecting will establish a *baseline,* enabling her to accurately determine if her particular intervention is really working over time.

Almost desperate, Mrs. Anderson decides that Jimmy "El Zorro" will be her special project for a one- or two-week period. She recognizes that the commitment of time on his problem is justified because Jimmy is already dominating her time as she tries to "put out the fires" that he causes, at the expense of time for other students. Therefore, for a one- to two-week period, she will give Jimmy this time and focus on him proactively, rather than focus reactively as she had before. On Friday, she meets with her aide, Ms. Walker, and they agree that together they will begin gathering data on Jimmy using a number of measurements: (1) *event recording,* (2) an *anecdotal report,* and (3) *time sampling,* which indicates stages of play ranging from isolated to cooperative play. The measurements will be conducted by the aide between 10:00 and 10:30 A.M. for five days.

Event Recording

Since Mrs. Anderson works with an aide, at times the aide is required to intervene with Jimmy in dealings that are not seen by Mrs. Anderson. Therefore, a cooperative system is created to count and record Jimmy's disruptive actions (*events*) over an entire week. On a centrally located shelf out of the reach of the students, they place two plastic cups, one labeled "clips" and containing a supply of paper clips (or some other readily available item), and the second marked "disruption." When Jimmy acts in a manner disruptive to his peers or destroys materials, the teacher or aide—whoever sees the event and is closest to the cups—takes a paper clip from the supply cup and puts it in the "disruption" cup. While on the playground, where the cups are not in easy reach, the adults simply move a paper clip from their right "supply" pocket to their left pocket, which serves as a temporary "disruption" container. A *data sheet* is created with the five days listed and divided into four time periods: Arrival to Snack (10:00 A.M.), Snack to Beginning of Rest Time (12:30 P.M.), Rest Period to Midafternoon (3:30 P.M.), and Midafternoon to Departure. At the end of each of these time periods, Mrs. Anderson counts the number of paper clips in the "disruption" cup and records that number on the data sheet (see Figure 7–2).

Graphing

The total number of disruptive events for each day is graphed (see Figure 7–3). Looking at the graph of disruptive events over the week, it is obvious that Monday, Wednesday, and Friday were very difficult days for Jimmy, whereas Tuesday and Thursday were much easier days. Various kinds of graphic displays can be used to show a student's behavior. Often, line graphs with data points and connecting lines are used. See Figure 7–3 for an example of Jimmy's data in line graph form.

Student: <u>Jimmy</u>
Observer(s): <u>Mrs. Anderson</u>   <u>Ms. Walker</u>
Behavior: <u>disruptive behavior toward others and objects</u>

	Monday	**Tuesday**	**Wednesday**	**Thursday**	**Friday**
Arrival to 10:00 A.M.	3	0	3	0	3
Snack to 12:30 P.M.	1	0	3	0	2
12:30 to 3:30 P.M.	1	1	0	1	3
3:30 P.M. to departure	1	1	0	1	2
Total	6	2	6	2	10

FIGURE 7–2   Event Recording Data Sheet

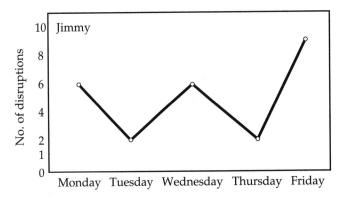

FIGURE 7–3   Graph of Daily Number of Disruptions

In addition, Jimmy's behavior appears to have worsened by the end of the week, as Friday easily showed the greatest number of disruptions. The question that arises in the teachers' minds is: What was different—the antecedent stimulus—that set him off into disruptive behavior on Monday, Wednesday, and Friday, as compared to the other two days of the week? The teachers could also tell from the four time intervals on the data sheet that Tuesday and Thursday mornings went quite well for Jimmy, with only two disruptive incidents—both after rest period. His afternoon disruptions were steady for Monday, Tuesday, and Thursday, but there were none on Wednesday afternoon—and Friday afternoon was filled with almost as many disruptions as Jimmy committed in all the other afternoons of the week. What changed? What antecedent stimulus was absent on Wednesday afternoon or present on Friday afternoon?

Anecdotal Report

To shed even more light on Jimmy's behavior, Mrs. Anderson decides to keep an anecdotal report on Jimmy's behavior for these same five days. She focuses on arrival, snacking, circle time, napping, and outdoor play as she attempts to describe the disruptive events generally in writing. Because Robert appears to be a consistent peer associated with Jimmy's disruptions, the teacher attempts to make note of Robert's location during any of Jimmy's misbehaviors. When possible, she also records her location and that of her aide, Ms. Walker.

For five days (Monday through Friday), Mrs. Anderson ends each day writing a daily *anecdotal report* on Jimmy, focusing on any events of misbehavior. Her report shows:

Monday

Arrival: 7:45 A.M.

Mother brings Jimmy to school carrying 6-month-old baby brother. Jimmy has a temper tantrum and pouts passively after mother leaves, and does not begin active play until 9:30. *Note:* He is passive for approximately 1½ hours.

Snack: 10:00 A.M.

Knocks over Andy's milk glass, and screams and throws food at those students at his table. Complains that he is not seated by Robert.

Circle time

Kicks Carol, who is seated between him and Robert.

Nap: 12:45 P.M.

Makes noises and disturbs other students during nap time; is defiant when told to desist. Ms. Walker was supervising.

Playground: 3:30 P.M.

Fights over tricycle with Andy. Wants the red tricycle just like Robert's.

Playground: 3:50 P.M.

Goes the wrong way on the path and runs into other cyclists, who scream at him and finally knock him over for blocking their way.

Playground: 4:00 P.M.

After tricycle conflict, Jimmy cries, goes to tire structure, and sits in tire while sucking thumb or biting his sleeve for 45 minutes.

Pickup: 5:15 P.M.

Reunites well with father.

Tuesday

Arrival: 7:45 A.M.

Mother brings Jimmy to school; no infant is with her. Jimmy arrives well and begins playing with Robert, building a block structure immediately after mother departs.

Snack: 10:00 A.M.

Eats well at snack. At his table are Mark, Walter, Carol, Andy, Roosevelt, and Judy (no Robert).

Circle time

Handles himself well at circle time. Robert is seated at the furthest end of circle from him.

Nap: 12:45 P.M.

Naps well, but awakens defiant and moody. Refuses to put on his shoes or put his blanket in the storage box. Ms. Walker was supervising.

Playground: 3:05 P.M.

Sits passively in the sand box, slowly digging with a small shovel in the sand. For no immediately apparent reason, throws sand in Mary's face. Runs to the opposite side of the playground and hides in bushes. Hides in bushes for 35 minutes.

Snack: 4:00 P.M.

Refuses to eat snack; sits and pouts.

Pickup: 5:15 P.M.

Reunites poorly with father by kicking at him when he attempts to put coat on Jimmy.

Wednesday

Arrival: 7:45 A.M.

Mother brings Jimmy to school, again carrying 6-month-old baby brother. Jimmy has a temper tantrum and pouts passively after mother leaves; does minor injury to his hand while hitting the front door as mother departs. Does not begin active play until 8:30.

Free play period: 8:45 A.M.

Using the paint easel and brushes, repetitively attempts to stab passerby with the paint-covered brush. Paints on neighboring student's paper, to the displeasure of the classmate.

Snack: 10:00 A.M.

Is first at snack and grabs the snack basket; shoves much of the snack into his mouth and refuses to relinquish the basket so others may share the food. During tussle, he knocks milk container from Ms. Walker's hand, spilling milk over one-third of dining area floor.

Circle time

Jimmy sits in a back corner by himself; appears withdrawn and sucks his fingers.

Nap: 12:45 P.M.

Falls asleep quickly and is slow to wake up. Mrs. Anderson was supervising.

Playground: 3:30 P.M.

Spends most of the outdoor time on a swing by himself.

Pickup: 5:15 P.M.

Reunites well with father without speaking, but appears flat and expressionless as father takes his hand to go.

Thursday

Arrival: 7:45 A.M.

Father brings Jimmy to school with no infant in hand. Jimmy departs well and begins building with Legos with Robert and three other boys immediately after father departs.

Snack: 10:00 A.M.

Eats well at snack, sitting with Robert at a two-person table.

Circle time

Handles himself well at circle time. Robert is seated beside him and they chat in a friendly manner.

Nap: 12:45 P.M.

Naps well, but awakens defiant and moody. Refuses to put on his shoes or put his blanket in the storage box. Begins a game of "catch me if you can" by jumping dangerously from cot to cot out of Ms. Walker's reach. One cot he jumps onto turns over and strikes him in the face (nosebleed quickly stopped when attended to). Ms. Walker was supervising.

Afternoon

Sits in the outdoor truck tires passively, sucking his thumb with a flat expression; participates in no activities.

Snack: 4:00 P.M.

Refuses to eat snack; sits and pouts.

Pickup: 5:15 P.M.

Reunites warmly with father, indicating that he wishes to be carried to the car "like a baby."

Friday

Arrival: 7:45 A.M.

Father brings Jimmy to school, carrying 6-month-old baby brother. Jimmy has a temper tantrum over who will open the classroom door. Refuses to hang up his coat, and lays on the floor crying as father departs.

Snack: 10:00 A.M.

Pushes Wayne out of the chair next to Robert, which develops into hair-pulling fight with Wayne. Calls other students at his snack table "butt-face" and "fart-breath." Takes large bite out of Ellen's fruit, upsetting her.

Circle time

Pinches and pulls others' hair, makes noises with such volume that group activities cannot go on. He is removed from circle time and moved to another area of the room by the aide, whom he attempts to bite.

Nap: 12:45 P.M.

Makes noises and disturbs other students during nap time. Is defiant when told to desist. After nap time, refuses to put on socks, shoes, and coat. Ms. Walker was supervising.

Playground: 3:30 P.M.

Starts "run and chase" game, putting himself into dangerous positions (attempts to climb over the school fence, runs into path of students on swings, and jabs the pet rabbit with a stick). When Ms. Walker approaches, he runs to the other side of the playground and starts game again.

Playground: 4:00 P.M.

Falls on the playground steps, scratches his knee and cuts his chin (both bleed slightly).

Pickup: 5:15 P.M.

Cries when father appears, and continues crying as father carries him to the car.

The anecdotal data, when added to the event recording accounts of daily disruptions, suggest a number of hypotheses to the teacher:

1. Generally, the arrival was difficult and would involve a temper tantrum or negative behavior if Jimmy's infant brother was in a parent's arms when Jimmy was brought to school. This suggests a series of *antecedent events* before Jimmy arrived at school in the morning that sets a negative tone for him for the entire day. This possibly calls for a conference with the parents to show them these data and perhaps suggest that a morning arrangement without the infant sibling might create a less disruptive process of departing home and arriving at school for Jimmy.
2. Waking up from rest period was a difficult process for Jimmy, although the one day that Mrs. Anderson supervised his awakening (Wednesday) he had no trouble as compared to the awakening process when it involved Ms. Walker. More data are needed on this before any conclusions can be drawn.
3. Jimmy appears to want to be friends with Robert, and their relationship can be warm and cooperative at some times but hostile at others. More data and observation are needed on the Robert/Jimmy relationship, but at this early stage we might see the need for a goal of teaching the two boys how to work together.

After doing the event recording and the anecdotal record, the teacher now has solid data related to Jimmy's level of functioning and the events (antecedent stimuli) leading to Jimmy's misbehavior. With this knowledge, she can establish goals for dealing with Jimmy and out of these goals establish clear *behavioral objectives*. The objectives, which should be stated positively, might involve helping Jimmy:

- Arrive at school more effectively.
- Play and work with Robert.
- Wake up from rest period in a cooperative manner.
- Acquire social skills as identified by social competency levels.

• Follow group rules in group settings such as circle time and snack.

Understandably, the teacher cannot achieve all of these goals and objectives at once. But she can use her professional judgment to select the more immediate behavior to work on and then, over a period of many weeks, gradually make real and lasting growth gains with Jimmy by achieving each of the goals.

The teacher should continue collecting and graphing data regarding Jimmy. Valuable insights may be obtained regarding the frequency of conflict with Robert; how long Jimmy can play with blocks (*duration recording*) or paint, or engage in sociodramatic play; how long it takes him to wake up (*latency recording*) and become productive; how long it takes in the morning to begin productive activity after the parent departs (*latency recording*); the loudness of his rest-time noises that disturb others (*measure of intensity*); and whether he has acquired certain defined skills, such as tying his shoes, pouring juice at snack, and so on (*simple yes-no measurement-criterion recording*). All of these measurements can be graphed to display the data in a manner that enables the teacher to see if the behavior is changing in the desired direction over time.

Note: Generally, classroom teachers would rather have root canal surgery than comprehensively assess a student's behavior. This is most likely the case because assessment is time consuming, and most assessment has typically been for the simple purposes of awarding a letter grade. However, the effective application of behavior analysis with the use of the Rules and Consequences techniques requires scientific and systematic data collection that enables the teacher to understand just what reinforcers or other stimuli are at work in the classroom; to display the data in ways that will suggest goals and objectives; and, finally, to show that the behavioral procedures are effective and behavior really is changing.

Reinforcement and Other Consequences

The basic view of behavior analysis is that human behavior—both *good behavior* and *misbehavior*—is learned. Jimmy's behavior occurs as a result of the consequences of his very behavior. Behavior that is followed by a desired consequence—for that particular person a *positive reinforcer*—tends to be repeated and thus learned. Behavior that is followed by an unpleasant consequence—*a punisher*—tends not to be repeated and thus one learns not to perform that behavior.

Jimmy's stabbing with the paintbrush, destructively mixing paint colors together, failing to follow the teacher's commands, and painting on the neighbor's paper were all a result of Jimmy having learned to do these destructive actions. The peers (Robert and the attack squad), the screaming neighbor, and—most importantly—the teacher have unknowingly reinforced Jimmy's misbehavior by giving him the attention he was seeking.

Reinforcement is a behavioral principle that describes a direct relationship between two real events: a *behavior* (any observable action: "Jimmy stabs at Robert with a wet paintbrush") and a *consequence* (a result of that act: "Robert screams and runs away"). There are two kinds of reinforcement: positive and negative. Care should be given in using these terms, for positive reinforcement is not always good for a student and negative reinforcement is not always bad. The key to these behavioral principles is what kind of behavior increases when these different reinforcers are applied.

Positive Reinforcement

Positive reinforcement is observed when a behavior is followed by a consequence that increases the behavior's likelihood of occurring again ("Jimmy looks for a new target for stabbing"). Jimmy draws a strong response by his actions, and his actions increase; thus, the actions have been positively reinforced and he is now likely to repeat them to get this predictable payoff.

In the opening vignette, Jimmy was reinforced on at least 10 occasions in a very short time period. (The *italicized statements* in the following examples identify the reinforcer.)

- Behavior: Jimmy turns and sticks out the brush as if it is a sword and attempts to "stab" his schoolmate.

  Consequence: *The peer screams and runs off, much to the delight of Jimmy.*

- Behavior: Jimmy dips his brush into the red paint and stabs out toward the approaching boys.

  Consequence: *The three boys gleefully scream and flee through the classroom,* knocking over another student's block building and causing a loud crash.

  Consequence: The teacher quickly approaches Jimmy and orders, *"Jimmy, behave yourself!"* (This may appear to be negative statement, but Jimmy's continuing actions indicate the teacher has unknowingly reinforced his behavior by attending to him.)

- Behavior: Jimmy pumps the paintbrush up and down in each color pot and rotates his paint-covered brush from one pot to the next.

  Consequence: *The colors in all four pots become a blended mess* of muddy brown.

  Consequence: The teacher reprimands (provides attention, a positive reinforcer for Jimmy), *"Jimmy, look what you have done.* You have mixed all four paints together. You have made them look like mud, and people can't paint with colors like this!" (Again, this may appear to be a negative reprimand, but Jimmy's actions indicate that the teacher's acknowledgment has unknowingly positively reinforced his behavior.)

  Consequence: The teacher takes away the pots of muddy brown paint and *replaces them with fresh pots taken from a nearby easel.* (By replacing the paints, the teacher has unknowingly positively reinforced and concretely rewarded Jimmy for his inappropriate actions.)

  Consequence: The teacher stresses, *"Now, Jimmy, do not mix these colors!"* (By talking and interacting with Jimmy, the teacher is rewarding him.)

- Behavior: Jimmy dips his brush into the blue paint, then slowly sinks it into the yellow pot.

Consequence: He *makes a blue swirl in the yellow paint and giggles.* Jimmy brings out the brush and inspects it closely.

- Behavior: He makes a blue-and-yellow streak down the right side of the student's paper.

Consequence: The *neighboring painter now screams* at Jimmy.

Consequence: The *teacher* once again *appears* before Jimmy. (The neighbor's scream and the teacher's attention that follow are positive reinforcers for Jimmy.)

A reinforcer can only be judged as positive or negative based on its effect on an individual student in a specific time context and situation. We have heard the term *positive reinforcement* used widely by the general public, and may have heard it used to describe such common examples as "Clean up your toys and you will get a lollipop'" (with the lollipop supposedly being the positive reinforcer). However, if, unknown to the adult, the student has just eaten four lollipops, he will be *satiated* at that particular time by this taste and the consequence of the candy will not serve to reinforce the student. The adult will not get the desired behavior—cleaning up the toys—thus, the candy is not a positive reinforcer at the moment.

In another example, an adult may say, "Do your homework and then you may go outside for the playground period." If, however, outside is a threatening place that the student wishes to avoid, then going outside is not a positive reinforcer—being indoors with the teacher is. In fact, the student might not do the homework specifically so he will not be made to go outside. Teachers may have to experiment and must clearly observe to truly determine whether their actions as offered consequences are in fact positive reinforcers, negative reinforcers, or punishers.

On the surface, all of the teacher's reprimanding statements ("Jimmy, behave yourself!" "Jimmy, look what you have done. You have mixed all four paints together. You have made them look like mud, and people can't paint with colors like this!" "Now, Jimmy, do not mix these colors!") may be seen as negative reprimands or punishing statements. For this particular student, however, they are really positive reinforcers. The true test for defining a consequence as a positive reinforcer, then, is if the behavior followed by a consequence increases in rate of occurrence over time.

Punishment

An event or behavior is seen as being punishment only *if it is followed by a consequence that decreases the behavior's future rate of occurrence.* It is best to keep in mind that any consequence to a behavior is defined by its effects on that behavior. Thus, paddling may be seen by the general public as punishment, but for some students getting paddled enables them to gain status in the eyes of their peers, so the action may actually be a positive reinforcer resulting in increased misbehavior. A student whose father rarely gives her attention might be very positively reinforced by a paddling for misbehavior, even though she cries during and after her father's actions. But if she continues the "punished" behavior, then punishment is really not taking place—reinforcement is actually occurring.

Note: Negative reinforcement, explained later, and punishment are generally confused by the wider public use of these two different terms. Remember that any time the term *reinforcement* is used—whether positive or negative—it means some behavior will increase. When the term *punishment* is used, it means a behavior will decrease. The punishment and negative reinforcement produce very different outcomes.

Behavior analysts use the word *punishment* as a technical term to describe a specific, observable, and concrete relationship: *Punishment has only occurred when the behavior followed by punishment has decreased.* Again, just because you think you have responded with an unpleasant event or consequence, this may not be punishment. Much of the so-called punishment delivered in schools today is ineffective because it generally does not decrease target behaviors and there is little observation done to determine the real effects in terms of the student's actions. The common use of time out, for example, can be considered punishment only if a functional relationship can be established between the student's behavior and the application of the consequence, resulting in a decrease in the behavior's rate of occurrence. In such a case, the action can be classified as punishment because the behavior that was followed by an unpleasant consequence was not repeated or occurred less frequently.

Negative Reinforcement

Punishment is said to occur only if behavior is followed by a consequence that decreases the behavior's future likelihood of occurring. The concept of *negative reinforcement* is somewhat more difficult to define. Essentially, it involves steps designed to lead the student to appropriate action (i.e., increase certain kinds of behavior) in order to escape or avoid an unwanted consequence. For example, Margaret is a student who, when awakened from her nap, is generally noncompliant and refuses to leave her cot, put on her shoes and socks, go to the toilet, and move outside for the daily routine of playground period and snack. The teacher says, "Margaret, we are having juice popsicles (a favorite of hers) at the picnic table on the playground today. If you get up and move soon, you can get to the playground before the juice popsicles melt or have to be put away, and you won't miss out on your treat today."

The use of negative reinforcement enables the teacher to avoid or terminate an unpleasant situation if the behavioral goal is achieved. In technical terms, it is the contingent removal (if you get up and act, this will not occur) of an aversive stimulus (missing out on the treat) that increases the future rate or probability of the response (the student gets up, uses the toilet, and quickly moves outside). For negative reinforcement there is an aversive stimulus—missing out on the treat—but the situation requires the student to behave or act to avoid that aversive stimulus. In this way, appropriate behavior—the behavior desired by the teacher—will increase in its rate of occurrence. In contrast, punishment is intended so that the consequences (e.g., time out) will *decrease* the future rate of occurrence of the inappropriate behavior (e.g., stabbing with the paintbrush). Another way to think of negative reinforcement is that the student does a behavior in order to *subtract* (avoid or escape) some undesirable situation.

Other Examples of Negative Reinforcement

- The student is required to pick up his art supplies or materials (waste paper, puzzles, etc.) at the end of period before he may move to the playground. "Tommy, these are your (materials, etc.) to pick up and put away. If you move quickly, you won't miss out (aversive stimulus) on playing on the playground today."
- The student refuses to put on his coat to go outside in cold weather. "Coats keep us warm so that we will not get sick. If you put your coat on, you won't have to stay inside. We have a new sled outside for students to ride, and if you do not go outside, you will miss having your turn on the snow sleds. Inside toys are closed and cannot be used while the class is outside playing."
- The student refuses to wash her hands before snack. "Sarah, hands must be washed before snack so we don't get sick from germs on our hands. If you move quickly and wash your hands, you won't have to miss out on today's special snack (or have to eat snack by yourself)."
- "We are running late this period, and I need to ask you to clean up your work area very quickly. The last five people to finish will be asked to stay and sweep the floor."

Use Negative Reinforcement and Punishment Sparingly

Suppose you, the teacher, describe the classroom behavior of a student who is causing you considerable difficulty (i.e., bites other students, willfully destroys other student's objects, swears in very strong sexual language, etc.). If you ask for solutions from other adults, including teachers, many of their "solutions" are likely to involve punishment. In some cases, these suggestions will involve aversive stimuli following inappropriate behavior, such as striking the back of the student's hands with a ruler, squeezing the student's shoulder, verbally giving the student a "dressing down," or sending the student to the principal. When such aversive stimuli are used heavily, the student may begin to flinch when the teacher approaches or the principal appears.

In the short term, negative reinforcement and punishment are the easiest solutions to think up and often they get immediate results. However, there are long-term side effects to the use of negative reinforcement and punishment. The negative consequences—especially if the actions are strongly aversive—are paired through associative learning with the teacher, the classroom, and the school itself.

Margaret, the student who refused to awaken properly from her nap, was told she would miss a juice popsicle as a snack treat. She now watches to see what snack is going to be given that day; if it is something she likes, she refuses to take a nap, and may even refuse to remain in the room where the other students are napping. In the short run, we have won a "cheap" quick victory by getting the student to get up from a nap promptly. But in the long run, we have lost the "campaign" because the student has learned a different lesson of avoiding a nap altogether. The student who refused to clean up the blocks before participating in a special activity refuses to play with blocks altogether; the student who refused to put on his coat now demands to wear his coat all day inside the classroom; the student who refused to wash her hands for snack now screams at the school door and refuses to come to school, seeking to avoid the place where she is required to wash.

Negative reinforcement can be an effective tool if used correctly with students, but it must be used (1) sparingly and (2) with an awareness of the degrees of intrusiveness associated with different aversive techniques.

Emphasize Positive Reinforcement

Students learn more positive behaviors by seeing positive models from teachers or peers. These models teach the student, inspiring him to comply with and follow these positive models. The classroom filled with positive reinforcement creates an environment where strong emotional attachment is given to the teacher and fellow classmates. The experiences and materials are welcoming and satisfying to the student, and the student loves to come to school to be with teachers and peers. So, on balance, *positive reinforcement should dominate the classroom behavioral procedures,* with punishment and negative reinforcement used sparingly.

For the noncompliant student who refuses to join activities after getting up from nap, one teacher may be freed up to stay with that student after nap time for a few days. During this time period, the teacher gives this difficult riser more time to really wake up, perhaps reading a favorite reinforcing story and cuddling with her on the floor near the student's cot. In subsequent days, the teacher moves to an adult rocking chair, and the student gets up and goes to the chair to be read to and cuddled. Next, the teacher takes the student to the toilet and then reads. Then the student uses the toilet and goes outside for the teacher to read the story on the school steps. Eventually, the reading is phased out; the student can now follow the normal routine of getting up from nap. In a similar fashion, the student refusing to put on her coat can become the target of a "putting on coats" game accompanied by a humorous song, or the student who refuses to wash her hands may be allowed to choose an attractively colored soap bar as a reinforcer for washing her hands.

Negative reinforcement and punishment can spread quickly and unknowingly into daily classroom procedures. Hence, teachers may be advised at monthly faculty meetings to make a list of all the punishment and negative reinforcement being used that month in order to design *shaping strategies* to teach the desired behavior through positive reinforcement.

Types of Reinforcers

Primary Reinforcers

The student's natural, unlearned, or unconditioned reinforcers are called *primary reinforcers.* These include edible reinforcers (food and liquids) or sensory reinforcers that appeal to the student's five senses (the sight of a favorite character, the sound of music or mother's voice, the taste or smell of food, the feel of the student's favorite silky blanket, etc.). These reinforcers are central to the student's basic and early survival needs and life experiences, and provide the student with pleasure. This makes them very powerful reinforcers for the student (see Figure 7–4).

The strength of the primary reinforcer will depend heavily on the extent to which the student has been deprived of this reinforcer. The student who has been reinforced with a primary reinforcer—for example, small sugarless candies—for 10 or 15 minutes will become *satiated*, a condition of nondeprivation. In other words, the reinforcer has lost its strength for the student at that particular time. This student will reject the candies or even spit them out, showing that for now these candies are weak as a reinforcer.

Both edible and sensory reinforcers can quickly satiate. In addition, they can be awkward and time consuming to deliver repeatedly, and may use up much of the time that should be spent on the learning activity. The overuse of treats such as small candies as primary reinforcers has brought much criticism to behavioral professionals. The use of primary reinforcers is only a temporary measure to enable rapid acquisition of appropriate behavior, but the primary reinforcer quickly needs to be replaced by a secondary reinforcer.

Secondary Reinforcers

Secondary reinforcers include tangible reinforcers, such as stickers and badges; privilege reinforcers, such as the opportunity to be first or to use a one-of-a-kind toy; activity reinforcers, such as the chance to help make cookies; generalized reinforcers, such as tokens, points, or credits; and social reinforcers, in which the teacher gives her attention and reinforces the student through such things as her expres-

Taste	Smell	Sound	Sight	Touch
fruit juice	garlic clove	party blowers	flashlight	balloons
flavored gelatin	vinegar	push toys	mirror	breeze from electric
raisins	coffee	whistles	pinwheel	fans
cereal	perfume	bells	colored lights	air from hair dryers
honey	cinnamon	wind chimes	bubbles	(on low)
pickle relish	suntan lotion	tambourines	reflector	body lotion
peanut butter	oregano	harmonica	strobe lights	electric massager
toothpaste	after-shave lotion	car keys	Christmas tree	body powder
lemon juice	flowers	kazoo	ornaments	feather duster
bacon bits	vanilla extract	bike horn	wrapping paper	water
apple butter			rubber worms	sand
				burlap
				silly putty

FIGURE 7–4   Sensory Reinforcers

Source: D. L. Westling and M. A. Koorland, *The Special Educator's Handbook.* Boston: Allyn and Bacon. Reprinted by permission.

sions, proximity to the student, words and phrases, feedback, and similar social interaction. Social reinforcers may also be given by classmates in a similar manner.

Secondary reinforcers are not basic to the student's survival, and initially may be of little interest to the student. The value that students place on them is acquired, not inherent. After some previously neutral event or stimulus is learned to have reinforcing value, it is said to be a *conditioned reinforcer* (conditioned means learned). In rewarding successful behavior, the teacher may state how successful the student has been, may gently stroke the student's back as she cuddles the student, and may place a sticker on the back of the student's hand. Soon the statements and the sticker will become powerful secondary reinforcers.

Another approach to secondary reinforcement would be to have the student wear a filing card on his shirt, attached by a safety pin or ribbon around the student's neck. When the student is successful, he is permitted to reach into a fish bowl containing trinkets and claim a reward. At the same time, the teacher uses a paper punch to make a hole in the student's card to serve as a "diary" of the successful behavior. The student is soon required to have two punched holes in his card before he can go to the treat bowl, then four punches, then eight; the number continues to increase, requiring a greater delay of gratification on the student's part.

Since the primary and secondary reinforcers have been *paired* in their early and repetitive presentation, the primary reinforcer can be gradually dropped. The secondary reinforcer is now *conditioned* and is just as powerful as the original primary reinforcers. If the secondary reinforcer begins to lose its effectiveness, it can be paired again with a primary reinforcer every now and then. This is sometimes necessary until the secondary reinforcer regains its strength for the student. Figure 7–5 summarizes the types of reinforcers.

Thinning Reinforcement by Using Schedules

Let's now consider a case in which we have established a target behavior (e.g., have the student complete a six-piece puzzle, drink all the milk at snack, or interact at the sand table by sharing toys) and written a behavioral objective. The student does perform the behavior and we positively reinforce it, possibly with a primary reinforcer (edible or sensory) or a secondary reinforcer (token or social reinforcer). As a result of our reinforcement, the student repeats the desired behavior. We now reinforce again and again. Soon, however, the process gets too time consuming and exhausting to keep up such a repetitive routine of reinforcement. Yet if we abruptly stop the reinforcement, the student's performance of the desired behavior will begin to weaken.

Instead, we turn to the behavioral procedure of *thinning* the reinforcement. We gradually make the reinforcement available less often for a given behavior or else contingent on a greater amount of appropriate behavior, until eventually the need for the reinforcement is eliminated altogether. We do not deliver or withdraw a reinforcer at whim just because we are busy or it just seems like the thing to do at the moment. The reinforcer must be thinned based on a methodical process using

Class	Category	Examples
Primary Reinforcers	1. Edible reinforcers	Foods and liquids (e.g., pieces of cracker, sips of juice, pudding, juice popsicles)
	2. Sensory reinforcers	Exposure to controlled visual, auditory, tactile, olfactory, or kinesthetic experience (e.g., face stroked with furry puppet, the student's security blanket, taped music through head-phones, mixing colors of paint)
Secondary Reinforcers	3. Tangible (materials) reinforcers	Certificates, badges, stickers, balloons, status clothing (e.g., a police hat)
	4. Privilege reinforcers	Being first to share at circle time, setting the table for snack, holding the teacher's big book while she reads, sitting near friends or on the teacher's rocking chair, being first to use a new toy
	5. Activity reinforcers	Play activities, special projects such as making cookies
	6. Generalized reinforcers	Tokens, points, credits, reinforcers that can be traded in for other valuables
	7. Social reinforcers	Expressions, proximity, contact, words and phrases, feedback, seating arrangements

FIGURE 7–5   Types of Reinforcers

Source: Adapted from P. A. Alberto and A. C. Troutman, *Applied Behavior Analysis for Teachers, 3rd ed.* New York: Merrill-Macmillan, 1990, p. 201.

intermittent schedules where reinforcement is given following some, but not all, appropriate responses (see Figure 7–6).

Shaping

Behavior analysis is employed to bring behavior under the control of time, place, and circumstances. Outside on the playground, yelling with "outside voices" is perfectly acceptable, yet at nap time loud talking, even with "inside voices," is unacceptable. Varying types of reinforcers, as previously described in this chapter,

Name	Description/example	Advantage/disadvantage
Fixed-ratio schedule	The number of times the student performs the target behavior will determine when he will receive the reinforcer (e.g., for every four worksheet math problems completed, the student is reinforced; every third time the student hangs up her coat, she is reinforced). Thinning may now occur by increasing the number of times the student must perform (from four math problems to six) in order to receive the reinforcement.	Since time is not critical, the student might take far too long between tasks (e.g., complete a puzzle and then pause for an hour before starting the next puzzle). If the number of tasks is too large, the student may even stop responding. The key is to seek the right amount of work given the reward schedule. Normally a ratio schedule produces consistent work.
Variable-ratio schedule	The target response is reinforced on the average of a specific number of correct responses—sometimes after the 3rd, 5th, 9th, 10th, 13th, 17th, or 20th, but on the average of once for every 10 times. This makes it unpredictable for the student.	A student operating under a fixed-ratio schedule may realize that it will be a long time between reinforcers, and may therefore work slowly. The variable-ratio schedule is done in such a manner that the reinforcer is not predictable, so the student maintains or increases the pace of his output. Normally under this kind of schedule behavior is persistent.
Fixed-interval schedule	The student must perform the behavior at least once, and then a specific amount of time must pass before his behavior can be reinforced again. The student is reinforced the first time (does one puzzle), and then a specific time must pass (four minutes); on the very next puzzle completed after the four-minute wait, the student is again reinforced. This reinforcement arrangement will be thinned by increasing the wait to six minutes, then eight, and so on.	The student can become aware of the time length and, knowing he has to perform just once, will wait for the time schedule to almost run out before beginning his next task. This kind of schedule is easiest for teachers to use, since it is based on the passage of time. A teacher does not have to monitor each piece of work, only the clock and the work performed at the moment.
Variable-interval schedule	The interval between reinforcers will vary and be unpredictable to the student, with the interval differing but maintaining a consistent average length.	The student's behavioral performance is higher and steadier because he cannot determine the next time interval that will be used to make reinforcement available.

FIGURE 7–6   Types of Schedules

can help bring students' existing behavioral skills under the control of the teacher and will result in well-disciplined behavior.

A second part of behavior analysis is the teaching of new behaviors that are not in the student's existing repertoire. How, for example, can the teacher positively reinforce the skill of putting puzzles away into their rack if the student has never before used the rack or put the puzzles away? New behaviors are acquired often through a process called *shaping*. Shaping is much like the children's game in which one person is "it" and others hide an object, such as a coin under a chair cushion. The person who is "it" wanders around the room and when he moves in the direction of the hidden coin, all the students shout, "You're getting hotter!" (a positive reinforcer). When "it" turns away, the response is, "You're getting colder!" The verbal feedback has now shaped "it" to move in the correct direction. As the person approaches the chair, everyone screams, "Hotter, hotter, hotter!" until "it" passes the chair and the screams change to "Colder, colder." The person who is "it" turns around to a new chorus of "Hotter, hotter," until finally the student locates the chair, moves his hands around the cushion (while being reinforced by repetitive statements of "Hotter, hotter"), and finds the hidden coin. The students' reinforcements have shaped a new behavior, leading the subject student to new positive actions.

After saying good-bye to her parent in the morning, Adrienne spends an hour or even two hours doing nothing but sucking her thumb, her behavior flat and expressionless. When the teacher goes to her and attempts to "dazzle" her with good cheer to perk the student up, Adrienne only sucks her thumb more vigorously and withdraws further. The teacher's target or pinpointed behavior is to get Adrienne to leave her parent and go to activity objects and materials or to classmates and be playfully active. When shaping, it is very important for the teacher to have chosen a clearly stated terminal behavior, in the form of a behavioral objective: "Adrienne (1. *identify the learner*), when departing from parents in the morning (2. *identify the conditions*), will go to materials and objects and begin to use them, or verbally interact with a classmate (3. *identify the target behavior*) within five minutes (4. *identify criteria for acquisition*)." With the terminal behavior stated in the form of a behavioral objective, the teacher is ready to reinforce Adrienne as her behavior gradually changes step by step into the specific target behavior (touching objects or speaking to playmates).

The shaping process unfolds in successive approximations of the terminal behavior as follows:

1. Adrienne leaves her parent but is in tears and sits passively.
2. She stops crying. (The teacher socially reinforces.)
3. Her eyes drop and she turns her face into the wall. (The teacher withdraws her presence and stops reinforcement.)
4. Hearing students laugh, Adrienne turns and looks intently at what is occurring. (The teacher catches her eye and smiles, stating, "Friends are doing fun things"—social reinforcer.)

5. Adrienne stands to get a better view of the classmates' activities. (The teacher stands by the play activity and holds out her hand—social reinforcer.)
6. Adrienne walks across the room and grasps the teacher's hand with both of hers and buries her face behind the teacher's back, away from the classmates. (The teacher stands still and does not reinforce the "looking away.")
7. Adrienne stands erect, still holding the teacher's hand, and takes a sustained look at the play of the classmates. (The teacher states, "Ah, see what they are doing—Carol is a nurse, Jane is the doctor, and Mary is the patient, and they are pretending to wrap Mary's injured arm.") At the same time, the teacher drops Adrienne's hand and affectionately strokes her head; the student cuddles into her as the teacher sits herself on a small chair nearby (social reinforcement).
8. Adrienne runs to the play area, picks up the stethoscope, and runs back to the teacher, attempting to crawl onto the teacher's lap. (The teacher subtly closes her lap, denying Adrienne the use of it, and places her hand in her pocket—differentially stopping reinforcement that would continue to permit Adrienne to be dependent.)
9. Finally, Adrienne moves into the play area, picks up a toy doll, pretends to listen to its heartbeat with the stethoscope, and plays *parallel* with the classmates. (The teacher catches her eyes, smiles warmly [social reinforcement], looks on at Adrienne, and then moves to another area of the room to help another student [the natural reinforcement of playing with others takes over—the target or terminal behavior has been obtained].)

The skills needed for the use of shaping are to state clearly a behavioral objective with a target (i.e., terminal) behavior, to know when to differentially deliver or withhold reinforcement, and to be able to shape the student in gradual successive approximations toward the target behavior. It is important not to move too quickly or too slowly when shaping. The experienced teacher eventually can anticipate the steps of successive approximation, but for the newer teacher attempting to use shaping, it might be helpful to attempt to write out the steps on a shaping planning worksheet, such as that seen in Figure 7–7. It is important to keep in mind that although these steps are likely to be followed in a shaping process, they may not develop in this exact form.

DECREASING MISBEHAVIOR: STEPS AND PROCEDURES

When we want to *increase* a student's behavior, we present a positive reinforcer after the behavior. In contrast, when we want to *decrease* a student's misbehavior, we present an aversive stimulus after the behavior occurs; if it is aversive for that student, the behavior will stop or decrease. We have seen that *aversion* associated as punishment or negative reinforcement can have its fallout effects (a student who must eat alone because he didn't pick up the blocks quickly now refuses to play with blocks at future times) and we are thus required to cautiously limit the use of

Space is provided below to help the teacher determine what gradual step-by-step actions a student might take toward acquiring target behaviors. Go first to Step 7 and write a behavioral objective, then return to Steps 1 to 6 to project shaping steps that the student might take. Also write at the bottom the types of reinforcers you will use. As an alternative, it often helps to work backwards and think of the behavior that comes just before the last one you want. Continue this process until you are at the student's current behavior.

Shaping Steps:

1. _____

   _____

2. _____

   _____

3. _____

   _____

4. _____

   _____

5. _____

   _____

6. _____

7. (Behavioral Objective)

   (a) Identify the learner _____

   (b) Identify the conditions _____

   (c) Identify the target _____

   (d) Identify the criteria for acquisition _____

FIGURE 7–7   Shaping Planning Worksheet   *(continued)*

What Reinforcer(s) Will Be Used?

(Check)   (Describe)

1. Edible reinforcers

2. Sensory reinforcers

3. Tangible (materials) reinforcers

4. Privilege reinforcers

5. Activity reinforcers

6. Generalized reinforcers

7. Social reinforcers

FIGURE 7–7   (continued)

any form of aversion. To give us guidelines in applying the varying procedures in an attempt to decrease a misbehavior, we may establish a continuum consisting of five steps, moving from the use of minimally intrusive procedures to the use of maximally intrusive procedures (see Figure 7–8).

The first level of intrusiveness is Step 1: Extinction, in which the teacher abruptly withdraws or stops any positive reinforcer that is being given to an inappropriate target misbehavior. Next along this continuum, using minimum procedures, is Step 2: Differential Reinforcement, in which the teacher seeks to lower the rate of the misbehavior by reinforcing an alternative or incompatible behavior to replace the student's misbehavior.

Next on the intrusiveness continuum is Step 3: Response-Cost Procedures, in which reinforcing objects and stimuli are removed. In Step 4: Time Out, the student is removed from a stimulating environment. Time out can be performed itself along a continuum from nonseclusionary time out to contingent-observation, followed by exclusionary time out, and finally seclusionary time out. The final location on the Degrees of Intrusiveness continuum is Step 5: Aversive Stimuli,

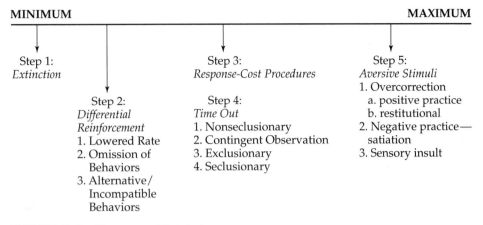

MINIMUM   MAXIMUM

Step 1:   Step 3:   Step 5:
Extinction   *Response-Cost Procedures*   *Aversive Stimuli*
                                                                  1. Overcorrection
          Step 2:   Step 4:   a. positive practice
          Differential   *Time Out*   b. restitutional
          Reinforcement   1. Nonseclusionary   2. Negative practice—
          1. Lowered Rate   2. Contingent Observation   satiation
          2. Omission of   3. Exclusionary   3. Sensory insult
             Behaviors   4. Seclusionary
          3. Alternative/
             Incompatible
             Behaviors

FIGURE 7–8   Degrees of Intrusiveness

involving the application of some form of discomfort directed at the student who is evidencing a behavior dangerous to himself or herself.

Step 1: Extinction

Extinction is simply stopping the positive reinforcers that have been maintaining an inappropriate target behavior.

Peggy fails to raise her hand and cover her mouth at circle time, which is the proper procedure for being called on by the teacher. Instead, she shouts out the answer. During the first few days of school, the teacher mistakenly accepts her shouted answer. Without realizing it, the teacher is positively reinforcing Peggy's behavior. By the fourth day of school, the teacher understands her mistake and decides to use *extinction* to stop Peggy's shouting out. The teacher will not provide any reinforcement when Peggy shouts, and instead will call on those with their hands in the air, then state the rule and reinforce those complying. When Peggy shouts out, the teacher acts as if the student does not exist. When the teacher's reinforcement stops, Peggy's shouting gets louder and she pushes her way to the front of the circle. When the teacher continues to ignore her, Peggy even goes to the extreme of using her hands to move the teacher's head so the teacher is forced to look at her. The teacher physically but gently moves her aside and out of her view. Peggy drops to the floor and has a full-blown temper tantrum. The teacher continues to ignore Peggy's tantrum and moves her own chair to another section of the circle, so that all the students are looking at the teacher and their backs are to Peggy and her tantrum on the floor.

Extinction is most effective to decrease classroom behavior when the student finds the teacher's attention and approval to be reinforcing. When extinction—the abrupt stoppage of reinforcement—is used, you may anticipate a number of behaviors to occur:

1. The student's behavior will get worse before it gets better. When Peggy did not get the teacher's attention, she escalated her shouting and behavior into a full-fledged tantrum.
2. Extinction can induce aggression by some students. The next day, Peggy again fails to follow the rule of raising her hand to speak, and the teacher withholds all attention or reinforcement. Peggy walks forward and strikes the teacher (or a classmate).
3. Other students might begin to imitate the very misbehavior you are ignoring, thinking, "If she can get away with it, so can I." Normally, dealing with these "copycat" students through an assertive command will desist the copied behavior quickly.

One of the criteria for determining if the teacher can use extinction is whether she can put up with this increased disruption for a period of time. Extinction will be effective only if the teacher "holds tough" and does not give in.

Step 2: Differential Reinforcement

Differential reinforcement employs the procedure of reinforcing certain dimensions of behavior selectively. This process can utilize three techniques: (1) reinforcing lowered rates of the misbehavior, (2) reinforcing the omission of the misbehavior, and (3) reinforcing incompatible behavior and alternative behavior.

Lowered Rates of the Misbehavior

The school rule for students' safety is that young students remain seated while eating, and especially when chewing a mouth full of food. (At a neighboring school, a student stuffed an entire peanut butter sandwich into his mouth and then ran outdoors to play. The peanut butter lodged in his throat and could not be easily freed, almost resulting in a terrible tragedy.) Event recording done by the teacher shows that Kevin was out of his seat at snack time 15 times in a 30-minute period, and nearly every one of those times his mouth was full of food. The teacher decides to use the Step 2: Differential Reinforcement procedure involving *the reduction of the rate of the misbehavior*. The teacher establishes a specific objective: "While at the snack table, Kevin will leave his seat five times or less during the 30-minute period."

Since the teacher has identified a baseline of 15 out-of-seat behaviors in 30 minutes, she knows that requiring Kevin to stop out-of-seat behavior completely is not practical. She begins a system in which Kevin obtains a positive reinforcer—being able to take the large plastic trash bags to the back of the school with the male janitor—if he gets out of his seat five times or less. Every time Kevin leaves his seat, the teacher makes a mark on a 3" × 5" filing card she keeps in her pocket. She also reinforces Kevin every 5 minutes for being in his seat by commenting on how he is remembering the rule, touching him on the shoulder and smiling. At the end of the 30-minute snack period, the janitor appears—and so does Kevin. The teacher has Kevin count the marks that indicate the number of times he was out of his seat.

On Monday, he counts five marks, on Tuesday nine marks, on Wednesday four marks, on Thursday six marks, and on Friday three marks. As a result, on Monday, Wednesday, and Friday, Kevin is permitted to help the janitor. During the second week of the differential reinforcement process, the teacher drops the number of permitted out-of-seat behaviors to three, and the third week to one. At the beginning of the fourth week, the teacher does not need to count any out-of-seat behaviors because Kevin is now able to follow the rule, getting out of his seat only for appropriate reasons and frequency, and never with his mouth full of food. This method requires the student to reduce the behavior to a set number of times in a preestablished time period.

At times, the teacher does not totally wish for all forms of a target behavior to be reduced. On the playground, Mary appears before the teacher and, like a machine gun, breathlessly begins to tell the teacher whatever is going though her mind at the moment: what she did in the past, what her parents have done, a list of trivial items of interest to her, and more. She does not stop to permit an interchange or give-and-take conversation with the teacher. Mary keeps up this verbal barrage for the entire recess period. The teacher would not wish totally to eliminate Mary's enthusiasm for talking, but would want to bring it to a more reasonable level. Therefore, the teacher uses the strategies of differential reinforcement.

The teacher states, "Mary, you have lots of wonderful things to tell me at recess, but sometimes I get tired and I need to talk to other students. (Teacher holds up five fingers.) You may tell me five things that interest you today, and then I will need to be with other students and you will need to go off and play." As Mary speaks, the teacher closes one finger at a time, visually counting off the five items Mary tells her. Two days later, the teacher holds up four fingers, and listens only to four of Mary's tales. The limit now changes in following days to three, and then finally to two. The teacher verbally reinforces Mary when the girl stops herself when no more fingers are up. From then on, when Mary appears to be going off into one of her self-centered monologues, the teacher simply holds up two fingers and says, "Two, Mary, two!" Finally, the teacher does not need to speak, but gains Mary's compliance simply by holding up two fingers. Finally, Mary can come to speak to the teacher in a normal fashion, without any finger prompts from the teacher.

Omission of the Misbehavior

A second method of differential reinforcement is omission of the misbehavior. Applying this method to our earlier example of Kevin, the teacher could establish six time intervals of 5 minutes each over the 30 minutes of snack time. The teacher lightly tapes a 3" × 5" card to the table in front of Kevin and places a check mark on the card if Kevin has *not* gotten out of his seat (omission of the misbehavior) for that 5-minute time interval. The student turns in the card to the teacher at the end of the snack period, and if there are two checks on the card during the first week, he earns the activity reinforcer. The next week, the criterion changes and Kevin must have three checks; later the standard is four, until finally Kevin stays in his seat for the entire 30 minutes of snack period.

One difficulty is that in requiring the student to omit a behavior, the teacher can create a problem if the student does not have a repertoire of other behaviors he can perform instead. For instance, Jimmy comes to the edge of the block area and watches for most of the morning as Robert and his friends build a structure with blocks. Finally, without provocation, Jimmy kicks out and knocks over the blocks or grabs a particular block most needed by the boys. He then runs off to hide in a corner. Jimmy has just shown a behavioral vacuum. Differential reinforcement of omission can be applied, but Jimmy is still left without an understanding of how to behave to join Robert and the other boys in the block construction. He needs to know not only how to stop kicking, snatching, and running, but also how to make social overtures to be an associative player.

Both these methods accept the position that the student cannot go "cold turkey" and stop his misbehavior immediately and completely. However, by changing the criteria, the teacher can place more and more demands on the student until the final terminal behavior is reached.

Incompatible Behavior and Alternative Behavior

In the use of differential reinforcement of incompatible behavior, a response is chosen and reinforced to make it physically impossible for the student to engage in the inappropriate behavior. In differential reinforcement of alternative behaviors, an appropriate behavior is reinforced. This behavior is not one that, when performed, eliminates the physical possibility of exhibiting the target behavior. An example of incompatible and alternative behavior involves the teacher's practice of requiring each student to raise a hand to be called on after the teacher asks a question. This wait-time permits all students to have a few seconds to think about the answer. However, Peggy impulsively shouts out the answer again and again. In response, for a few weeks the teacher gives the students new instructions: When they have the answer and want to speak, they are to cover their mouth with their left hand (incompatible behavior making it impossible to speak) and raise their right hand (alternative behavior). The teacher ignores anyone who does not have his or her mouth covered and hand raised—including impulsive Peggy. In her desire to be heard, Peggy quickly learns the proper procedure, and soon her impulsive responses are less frequent and then, finally, stop. Before long, the requirement for the left hand over the mouth will be dropped and the class returns to simply raising hands. Often, alternative behaviors are differentially reinforced since there is not always a physically incompatible behavior available for every target behavior (see Figure 7–9).

Step 3: Response-Cost Procedures (Removal of a Desirable Stimuli)

Paul, a most unruly student, treasures wearing the school's police officer outfit consisting of a hat, a badge, and a large thick belt on which is snapped a set of handcuffs. The teacher tells Paul that police officers are bosses and that he needs to be the boss of his own behavior—no hitting, no destroying others' products, and

Target Behavior	Incompatible/Alternative Behavior
When traveling through a large museum (or zoo, etc.), the students wander off and don't stay with the group.	A soft 1½ inch rope is used with a "train engine" (leading student) at the front of the rope and a "caboose" at the end. All students are taught to be a "train car" by holding the rope with one hand—a practice that is incompatible with wandering off.
The students are screaming at the top of their voices on the field trip bus.	The teacher leads the students in soft singing of familiar songs. Singing is an alternative to screaming.
Susan reunites poorly with her father at the end of the day, kicking and refusing to put on her coat.	The teacher gives Susan a small envelope containing a surprise. It is her father's job to open this envelope, which contains a sticker Susan treasures. The father places the sticker on Susan's coat once the student is wearing it (alternative behaviors).
The boys are throwing stones over the school fence at passing cars.	The teacher brings out a basket and ball and sets up a target at the opposite side of the playground. She encourages the boys to throw the balls at the target (incompatible/alternative behaviors).
Some of the boys, when urinating, are having much fun aiming everywhere but into the bowl.	The teacher adds some liquid soap to the "residual water" in the toilet bowl and when the boys aim properly, bubbles appear. Over time, liquid soap is only occasionally placed in the bowl; eventually it is phased out completely.
Some of the students have been seen playing with the pet gerbil too vigorously.	The students are shown how to pet the gerbil slowly and softly. They are permitted to handle the gerbil more if they pet it gently.
Graham comes to school and immediately goes to Ms. Smith, the aide. He follows her and remains close at all times, not interacting with any other adults.	Ms. Smith is seated with Ms. Seay at the start of class. When Graham first approaches, Ms. Smith and Ms. Seay conduct the morning's activities together while Graham follows along. Ms. Smith is "called" to the school director's office. Ms. Seay now engages Graham in a new activity and reinforces him with verbal and eye contact while Ms. Smith is away. Ms. Smith now interacts with Graham only if he is with other caregivers.
At mealtimes, Billy constantly demands to be served first.	The teacher tells Billy that if he uses an inside voice to ask, "May I be served first today?" he might be served first. However, she also points out that someone else who asks with the same inside voice might be first instead.

FIGURE 7–9   Examples of Incompatible Behaviors/Alternative Behaviors

obeying the school rules. If he cannot be the boss of his own behavior, he will lose the privilege of wearing the police outfit. By 9:30 A.M., Paul has taken another student's toy. The teacher removes the handcuffs from Paul's belt and states, "If you want to wear these items—the belt, the badge, and the hat—you must obey school rules." By 10:00 A.M., Paul has kicked a neighbor during circle time and he loses the belt. At snack time, he throws food and loses the badge. While washing his hands to get ready for lunch at 12:00 noon, he is found throwing water at peers and loses the police hat. This produces a temper tantrum. After nap time, all four items are given back to Paul, but the process of removing this desirable stimuli can be repeated if necessary. It is important that the teacher also reinforces Paul by "catching him being good" and reminding him to be the boss of his own behavior (like the police officer). During the afternoon, Paul loses no items. The second morning, he loses only one piece of the police outfit, and in the afternoon, he is able to go the entire time without losing an item.

What we see the teacher doing is removing a desirable stimulus. This requires that the student have within his possession and control certain tangible items that he treasures and that serve as reinforcers for him. The question or dilemma for the student is: How much is he willing to pay—in terms of losing these reinforcers—in order to continue with his misbehavior? In technical terms, this is called a *response-cost procedure*, in which the teacher has the ability to take away a reinforcer once given. As an example of the use of response-cost procedures, consider the following: All students have five tokens pinned to their shirts as they depart on a field trip. The students are taught rules of desirable behavior for the trip, and remaining tokens will be redeemed for a treat. The teacher removes one token each time a student breaks a rule. If the student has all his or her tokens taken away, he or she is unable to receive a treat through token redemption.

Step 4: Time Out

Time-out procedures serve as punishment by denying a student, for a fixed period of time, the opportunity to receive reinforcement. This removal of stimuli is actually *time out* from positive reinforcement. Time out generally is used when the social context is so reinforcing that the teacher's application of other reinforcers is ineffective. In the illustration of Jimmy "El Zorro," this reinforcing social context can be seen in the approach of Robert and the attack squad or the lure of the multicolored paint pots. The next option for the teacher is to remove the student from some or all reinforcement. There are four categories of time out, each of which will be discussed next (see Figure 7–10).

Nonseclusionary Time Out
To deal with a minor disturbance, the teacher takes some physical intervention to deny the student reinforcement by removing the materials that are being used inappropriately (eating utensils at snack time, water play toys, or paints and brush—as in our earlier example), or by having the students put their heads down on their desks and turning off classroom lights. This time out is called nonseclu-

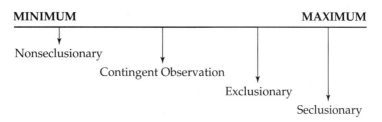

FIGURE 7–10   Time Out and Degrees of Aversion

sionary because the misbehaving student is not removed from the classroom or immediate environment.

For instance, after a visit by a local police officer, a police hat is introduced into the classroom's dress-up corner. Paul, an aggressive and difficult student, clearly desires to wear the hat. Paul is given a second police hat with his name taped in it, and the teacher tells him, "Police officers are bosses, and if you want to wear the police officer's hat you must be the boss of your own behavior. If you hit, destroy, or disrupt the activities of other students, then you will lose your hat." (This is called an *if-then statement*: "*If* you do X behavior, *then* Y consequence will happen.")

In the first two or three days, when Paul forgets and is disruptive, the teacher takes away his police hat, places it within his view on a hook too high for him to reach, and sets a timer for three to five minutes. When the bell rings, the hat is returned to him. On the first day, Paul loses the hat (nonseclusionary time out) on six occasions. On the second day, it drops to two occasions, and in the remaining three days of the week, the hat is removed only once.

Contingent Observation

In contingent observation, the student is removed to the edge of an activity so he can still observe the other students being reinforced. For example, the school has a narrow circular tricycle path with painted arrows pointing the direction in which the students are to ride (visual prompt). The arrows guide the students so they will not collide with each other by going in opposite directions. The rule has been explained and taught to Harold, but he repeatedly seems to enjoy going in the opposite direction and colliding with playmates, who then complain in the strongest of terms. The teacher pulls Harold and his tricycle to the school steps at the edge of the cycle path, removes Harold from his tricycle, and requires him to sit passively and watch others obeying the rule and having fun. The teacher reinforces the other students (models) as they correctly obey the direction rule. After four minutes, she asks Harold, "Do you now see how our rule works? Can you ride your tricycle following the direction of the arrows?" If Harold answers *yes*, he is permitted to return to his tricycle; if he answers *no*, he stays on the steps (the time out) for another two minutes and is again asked whether he is ready to comply.

The contingent observation is nonseclusionary because the student is not removed totally from the environment, such as being required to go inside the school or leave the section of the playground. Instead, he is placed at the edge of the activity so he may observe others being reinforced. Following are some other examples of contingent observation:

- The student is splashing others while he is supposed to be washing his hands. He is removed to the side to watch others washing. When the line of students has finished he is allowed to wash his hands.
- The student's behavior is disrupting her peers at the snack table. Her chair is pulled away to approximately four feet from the table and out of reach of her food. After four minutes, she is able to return to snacking.
- The student is being reckless on the tire swing (or slide, or any other playground equipment). He is removed from the apparatus and asked to sit nearby and watch. After four minutes, he is allowed to return.
- While seated on the floor at circle time, the student repeatedly disturbs others seated nearby. She is removed from the circle and seated on a chair in the doorway. After three minutes, she is allowed to return.

Note: The criterion for returning or being released from the contingent observation nonseclusionary time out, such as those described above, is contingent on the student maintaining nondisruptive behavior for a minimum time requirement. Normally, the student is asked, "Do you know and understand the rule?" and "Will you obey it when you return?"

When the techniques of nonseclusionary time out have been tried but have failed, the teacher may recognize that the student's behavior is so serious that it demands a stronger form of response. Two other forms of time out are available in such a situation: exclusionary and seclusionary.

Exclusionary Time Out

This involves the removal of the student from an activity as a means of denying access to reinforcement but generally not access to the classroom. While the contingent observation and modeling were used in the nonseclusionary time out, *none* of these procedures is used in exclusionary time out. The student may be placed near a corner facing the wall or in an area of the classroom that is screened off from the room activities so the student's view is restricted.

Seclusionary Time Out

This is the complete removal of the student from the classroom or environment to a time-out room because of the student's misbehavior, usually aggression or noncompliance. This denies the student access to any reinforcement from the classroom, including peers, adults, objects, or activities.

Note: The justification for the use of any of the forms of time out is not for purposes of retribution based on the idea that the student has failed morally or has not lived up to the adult's values and expectations. From a behavior analysis standpoint, the justification is that the environment and social context are so strongly reinforcing the student to continue his or her misbehavior, and the objective is to remove that reinforcement, that the only way to accomplish this is to use one or more forms of time out. Time out and time-out rooms have historically been misused or mismanaged by teachers, causing great distrust of this technique by parents and the general public. (Figure 7–11 presents some guidelines for the time-out room.) Students of any age are not to be put in time out for a long period. The student should be in time out for 1 to 6 minutes; it is clearly doubtful that any period beyond 10 minutes would be effective for the young student. A time-out record form documenting the procedure (giving witness names, circumstances, times and dates), such as the one in Figure 7–12, should be required for each staff member who uses time out.

It should be remembered that when a student is told that time out is over and she may return to the classroom activities, the teacher should do so in a calm and low-key manner. No anger or extended conversation should take place, or the teacher may actually set up a chain of events in which the student learns to misbehave and then be placed in time out in order to then get into a conversation with the teacher when time out is over. Some teachers use a bell timer to indicate when time out is over, and the student is informed that she can rejoin the group when the bell sounds. The teacher interacts minimally with the student. The bell signals the student that it is time to rejoin the class. From that point forward, the teacher should treat the student the same as any other member of the class.

Let us now relive the opening vignette and see the teacher correctly using the Rules and Consequences face, with *positive reinforcement* and *punishment* provided under the control of the teacher.

> Jimmy stands before the paint easel. Using a large, thick paintbrush, he dips the end into the paint pot. Soon the brush reappears, dripping with a large glob of paint. As Robert walks by, Jimmy turns and sticks out the brush as if it is a sword and attempts to "stab" his schoolmate. The peer screams and runs off, much to the delight of Jimmy. Smiling, Jimmy "El Zorro" dips his brush into the paint pot and looks about for a new target.

The following are basic requirements for the space and procedures for a time-out room:

1. The "room" (or space) should be at least 36 square feet (or approximately 6 × 6 feet).
2. Adequate light must be provided (never use a darkened or unlit room).
3. Be certain that the room is properly aired (not an enclosed space such as a large refrigerator box).
4. The room must not contain objects that the child may use to hurt himself when he is angry.
5. The adult must be able to see and hear the action of the child at all times.
6. Locking the room is forbidden.

FIGURE 7–11   Guidelines for Time-Out Room

Student's Name	Date	Time of Day	Total Time in Time Out _____ number of minutes
Teacher's Name Other Adult Witness			Type of Time (check one) ____ Nonseclusionary ____ Contingent Observation ____ Exclusionary ____ Seclusionary
Description of the Situation		State Behavioral Change Wanted	

FIGURE 7–12   Time-Out Record

The teacher moves to Barbara, who is painting at a nearby easel, and states, "Good painting, Barbara. I see you have remembered our rule about keeping the paint on the paper." The teacher gently touches Barbara's back and smiles at her warmly. The teacher gives no sign of acknowledgment or awareness to Jimmy. (The teacher is using positive *social reinforcers* with Barbara, who is *modeling* the appropriate behavior that the teacher wishes Jimmy to perform. She ignores, or gives no reinforcement of any type for, Jimmy's misbehavior, attempting through the removal of reinforcement to place Jimmy's destructive actions on extinction.)

Robert joins two friends in the block corner to tell them of Jimmy's "paint stabbing." The three classmates smile broadly as they move as a group, much like a military assault squad, tentatively and defensively approaching Jimmy to see if they can get the same results. The teacher steps in front of the "assault squad" and tells them in a soft voice that Jimmy cannot hear, "Boys, do you see that box on the shelf? In that box are new outdoor sand toys, and I believe you might find some new cars and trucks in that box. I want you to choose one of our inside toys to play with now, and after that when we go out to the playground today, you may open the box and be first to select one of the new sand toys." The boys move to the block area and begin cooperatively building a castle. (The teacher has established a *contingency* [*if-then statement*] with the boys and diverted their attention from Jimmy's "brush stabbing," thus preventing Jimmy from receiving *social reinforcement* from the boys.)

Jimmy stands holding his paintbrush "sword," waiting for a new victim. The teacher again moves to Barbara, touches her warmly and smiles, "Barbara, you sure have been working hard on your painting today. I would like to invite you to bring your painting to circle time today to share it with the other students." (The teacher *positively reinforces* the *model*, Barbara, who is correctly performing the behaviors that the teacher wishes Jimmy to perform, and at the same time gives no reinforcement to Jimmy in an attempt to place his inappropriate behavior on extinction.)

Jimmy touches the brush to his easel and paper and makes a red circle. The teacher quickly moves to him, places a hand gently on his shoulder and smiles warmly, "Jimmy, you have chosen red, an exciting color. It looks like you are also on the way to making a painting that we may all wish to see. Let me know when you have completed your picture and I will come back to see it." (The teacher has "caught" Jimmy being good, and when he has performed the desired behavior she immediately provides *social reinforcement*. She also has established an *if-then statement*: When you finish a painting *[behavior]* I will come back to see it *[consequence]*.)

Jimmy adds a mouth, eyes, nose, and ears to his circle and calls it a "doggie." He looks around and catches the teacher's eye. The teacher moves quickly to his side and states, "Great job, Jimmy!" (*social reinforcer*). She writes his name and date on the back of the paper and includes his description of a dog. "You may use the clothes pins and clip your painting to the rope line until it dries (*activity reinforcer*). We must remember to have you bring that painting to circle time to share today." (The teacher promises another *social reinforcer*.)

Jimmy begins a second painting with a clean sheet of paper. He now holds the brush as one would use a knife and slashes up and down, heavily matting paint over the paper and slightly tearing the paper. With this same knife-like grip on the handle of the brush, he begins to pump the paintbrush up and down in each colored paint pot, rotating his paint-covered brush from one pot to the next until the colors in all four pots become a blended mess of muddy brown. The teacher removes all but one "mud"-colored paint pot from Jimmy's easel, applies a strip of masking tape on the remaining pot, and labels the pot by writing the boy's name on the tape. "Jimmy, this is the color you have chosen to make and use for painting. I have written your name on it, and we will save it when you are done today for you to use tomorrow." (By removing the three paint pots, the teacher has used *nonseclusionary time-out*[1] procedures to deny the student access to reinforcers through a temporary manipulation of the environment—removing the materials, herself, and her attention for a brief period contingent on the inappropriate behavior.)

The teacher turns to Barbara, who is still painting next to Jimmy, and states, "Barbara, let us see what you have painted. (The teacher gently touches the student and smiles.) Great, I can clearly see that you are giving this second painting much care! (*social reinforcer*) And look (points to the student's fingers holding the brush)—you have remembered the rule of how to hold the brush and use it correctly. (The teacher's pointing is a *visual prompt* to clearly show what behavior is desired by the teacher. At the same time, the teacher socially reinforces the *model* Barbara.) It looks like you're going to have a second painting to share with us this morning!"

Jimmy also begins his second painting in a similar manner, creating a circle with two eyes. Suddenly, he stops and dips his brush into the paint pot. He brings out his brush, inspects it closely, and then reaches over to Andy's easel and makes a mark down the right side of this student's paper. Andy screams at Jimmy, and the teacher appears. Without saying a word, the teacher takes away Jimmy's brush and paint pot but permits him to continue wearing his smock.

Jimmy is placed on a small chair at the edge of the painting area and told to watch and see how others paint. Four minutes later, the teacher approaches and asks if he feels he can now return to painting and use the brush for painting only. He says he can, and is permitted to return to the painting *(nonseclusionary time out with contingent observation)*.

What we have just seen is the teacher reinforcing those students who were models of the correct use of materials, attempting to reinforce Jimmy while he showed "cooperative behavior" and using punishment in the form of time out to control the reinforcement Jimmy was receiving after a misbehavior.

Step 5: Aversive Stimuli

Overcorrecting

When Johnny is through the classroom door, he seems incapable of stopping himself from running down the hall and stairs to the playground. This practice is dangerous and should be stopped. Once the teacher has deposited the other class members safely on the playground under another teacher's supervision, Johnny's teacher takes him by the hand and walks him back to the classroom. The teacher verbally states the school rule to "walk in the halls and on stairs" and, still holding his hand, walks Johnny out to the playground in a correct manner. She then returns him to the hallway, repeats the rule and now makes Johnny walk down the hall and stairs without holding her hand. He is made to walk the hall and stairs three more times, each time returning to the classroom. This demand for rewalking is a behavioral procedure called *positive-practice overcorrection*, and is educational because it teaches the student how to perform correct behavior through an element of aversion. Another example would involve a student who drops his coat on the floor when he enters the classroom instead of putting it on his hook; the student is now required through positive-practice overcorrecting to repetitively "come in and hang it up" three or four times as the teacher repeats the rule.

Mark has just finished eating his juice popsicle and discards the used stick by simply dropping it on the playground. He has a history of dealing with nearly all waste materials in such a manner. The teacher now takes him by the hand and states, "When we have trash, we throw it in the waste can," and she has him pick up the stick and throw it in the can. She now walks him to a second piece of trash laying about and has him pick up this trash and throw it in the trash can. The teacher then takes him around the playground, requiring him to pick up trash on six more occasions as she verbally states the rule. This is a procedure called *restitutional overcorrection*, which requires the student to make amends by restoring the object, materials, or environment he may have destroyed or disrupted back to its original and proper condition and then going beyond that to do more—thus *overcorrecting*. Other examples of this technique are shown in Figure 7–13.

Positive Practice	Restitutional Overcorrection
Student urinates on floor; must help clean up.	Student puts inappropriate or dirty object in mouth; must brush teeth.
Student bites; must practice kissing.	Student bites; must wash affected area, apply antibacterial cream, and dry surrounding area carefully.
Student steals; must return object and practice borrowing.	Student steals; must help gather all misplaced objects and return them to proper place.
Student throws food; must help clean up and must practice proper eating techniques.	Student throws food; must clean up all spills and wipes all tables after snack.

FIGURE 7–13   Examples of Overcorrection

Negative Practice-Stimulus Satiation

Lisa has a problem with spitting at inappropriate times. When she does not get her way in most matters with classmates or the teacher, she will predictably spit at them. The teacher decides to use *negative practice-stimulus satiation* to deal with Lisa's spitting. She takes Lisa to the toilet and gives her a large cup filled with water, then asks her to take a large mouthful and spit it into the toilet. The girl complies, with a little giggle. She is then asked to continue taking water from the cup and spitting, until the cup is empty. A second cup of water is then presented to her, and her demeanor changes to reflect a sense of drudgery. At this point, the teacher begins each discharge by stating, "Spitting is against school rules." With the use of negative practice-stimulus satiation, there is no intent to be educational or to teach new behaviors; instead, the idea is to have the student repeat the inappropriate behavior over and over until the act becomes tiresome and punishing, and the student becomes satiated and does not wish to do this action again. Figure 7–14 gives other examples of this technique.

Sensory Insult

In the vast majority of cases, the techniques previously discussed will be sufficient to put an end to most forms of misbehavior. However, there are occasional extreme cases that call for extreme measures. These measures will not be necessary for most students; when they are required, they must be used with the utmost care and with the full participation and approval of the parents of the student with the problem behavior.

Martha is a new student in the classroom. During her first two weeks, the teacher discovers that Martha will bite and chew her right hand until the flesh is actually torn and bleeding. This self-abusive act occurs repeatedly throughout the

Target Behavior	Example
Student runs down stairs.	Student must repeatedly run up and down stairs.
Student hits playmate.	Student must repeatedly hit a pillow.
Student kicks over classmate's block construction.	Student must assemble simple block structure then kick it down and repeat.
Student will not share toy.	Student must play with only that toy the rest of the period, as well as the next play period.

FIGURE 7–14   Negative Practice-Stimulus Satiation

day and creates a serious physical danger to the student. Using techniques described previously in this chapter, the teacher determines that the self-abusive behavior occurs for 6 to 7 hours per day over a five-day period, and Martha's behavior of biting herself is on the increase. The teacher attempts a host of positive reinforcers, as well as the first three steps of the Degrees of Intrusiveness process (extinction, differential reinforcement, and response-cost) without success.

A meeting is called, bringing together Martha's classroom teachers, a school administrator, the student's parents, a special education teacher (when possible), and a local psychologist (or school counselor or social worker). The teacher passes out records she has kept on the aversion steps attempted, including various forms of time out and positive reinforcement, and graphs she has made to track Martha's biting. Also, with the permission of the parents, a videotape of Martha's typical self-abusive biting behavior is shown to this committee of professionals. The group recommends approval of the final component of Step 5: Presentation of Aversive Stimulus, *sensory insult*. The group—including the parents—approves and signs an individualized educational plan (IEP), stating a new goal (e.g., reduction of self-abuse). The members of the group permit the teacher to use such aversion stimuli as (1) putting a lemon into Martha's mouth when biting (aversive taste stimulus); (2) using bright food coloring to paint the area of her hand that Martha tends to bite (possible visual aversion); (3) painting Martha's hand with a quinine liquid, which would create an aversive taste when she puts her hand in her mouth; and/or (4) if necessary, putting the hand into a leather glove Martha could not remove, which would protect her from most of the force of the biting. The IEP indicates that any or all of these aversion techniques may be used for a period of 10 days, with the teacher recording data and graphing the results. A second IEP meeting is set for the end of this 10-day period.

The classroom teacher has come to the point where she feels required to deliver an aversive stimulus, in the form of sensory insult, in order to stop a student's behavior that is endangering herself and others. However, this teacher is considering a dangerous series of strategies with a high risk of being accused of student abuse or exposure to possible legal assault charges. When allegations of aversive tactics (see Figure 7–15) are brought in court and possibly circulated by the news media, the general public might be shocked and feel as if the teacher is being inhuman and using excessive punishment. In reality, however, it would be no less inhuman to permit Martha to suffer the potential physical pain and health risks of repeatedly abusing herself by biting her hand and disfiguring her body, which will likely cause the need for expensive medical care. It is highly recom-

Target Behavior	Sensory Insult	Procedure
Head/Self Injury: • striking own head with hand or object • pulling out large amount of own hair	Hearing Touch	Blow a whistle to distract the student. Apply and require wearing of restraining devices (plastic or leather helmet).
Limbs/Self Injury: • biting hands or feet or other parts of body	Touch Smell Sight Taste	Apply and require wearing of restraining devices. Apply ice cube or cold water. Touch smelling salts to student's nose. Paint the area being bitten with bright food coloring. Put lemon into student's mouth.
Climbing poles or support beams to dangerous heights on the playground	Touch	Cover reachable area with axle grease.
Eating materials such as clay, modeling dough, paints, etc.	Taste	Add or spray quinine to the materials.
Sucking or biting play objects	Taste	Spray objects with diluted water and tabasco sauce.
Kicking others	Touch	Remove the student's shoes on rough or textured floor surface.
Scratching oneself to the point of bleeding	Touch	Cover the area with heavy petroleum jelly.
Repetitive behaviors (excessive head rocking, repeating nonsense phrases, etc.)	Hearing Touch	Blow a whistle to distract the student. Apply and require wearing of restraining devices (plastic or leather helmet).

FIGURE 7–15 **Examples of Sensory Insult Aversion Procedures**

mended that if a teacher is faced with the need to utilize such aversive techniques, the student should immediately be referred to a psychologist or behavioral specialist, as this student's needs might be beyond the classroom teacher's skills and abilities. In the example that follows, the teacher has consulted with a psychologist or behavioral specialist, and as a team they have agreed on the approach the teacher will take in dealing with the disruptive student.

> The teacher observes Martha constantly for three days, and when biting occurs, the teacher uses the lemon and issues a sharp verbal "No!" Martha stops her biting for approximately 2 minutes the first day. When these events are played out again on the second day, the no-biting period increases to 45 minutes. On the third day, the lemon and command are needed on only two occasions. On the fourth day, since the sharp verbal "No!" has been *paired* with the lemon, the teacher needs only to say "No!" to Martha and she stops the biting. (Note that these time periods are for purposes of illustration; reaching this level of progress may take more or less time, depending on the individual learner.)
>
> By the end of the second week of intervention, Martha can go an entire day without biting herself. Finally, during the following four weeks, there are two occasions when the sharp command "No!" and the use of lemon stop Martha's biting. Since it was previously paired with the lemon as an aversive consequence, the sharp verbal "No!" has now become a learned or conditioned aversive stimulus. For the remainder of the school year, with the exception of returning after long holidays, Martha almost completely stops the biting as a daily occurrence. When it does appear, only the conditioned aversive stimulus ("No!") is needed to stop the target behavior of self-biting. The collected data and graphing (described earlier in this chapter) clearly demonstrate the effectiveness of the aversive stimulus to help Martha reach the goal of reduced self-abuse. Success! But not all stories, of course, have such a pleasant or simple ending.

To summarize, such strong aversive stimuli should be used rarely, and only when adhering to strict guidelines requiring that:

1. The failure of alternative nonaversive procedures to modify the target behavior is demonstrated (possibly through videotaping) and documented (data collection and graphing).
2. Informed written consent is obtained from the student's parents or legal guardians, through due process procedures and assurance of their right to withdraw such consent at any time.
3. The decision to implement an aversive procedure is made by a designated body of qualified professionals.
4. A prearranged time table for reviewing the effectiveness of the procedure is established as soon as possible.
5. Periodic observation is conducted to ensure staff members' consistent and reliable administration of the procedure.

6. Documentation of the effectiveness of the procedure and evidence of increased accessibility to instruction is maintained.
7. Administration of the procedure is performed only by designated staff member(s), who should be knowledgeable and skilled in behavior analysis.
8. Incompatible behavior is positively reinforced whenever possible, as a part of any program using aversive stimuli.[2]

Note to the wise teacher: Never use aversive stimuli as punishment techniques without strictly following all of these guidelines, as well as any adopted by school administrators.

SUMMARY

When the teacher feels it necessary to use the techniques of the Rules and Consequences face, he typically is faced with very serious and difficult inappropriate behavior, usually including aspects of aggression or destruction and a general disruption of the ongoing classroom activities. In applying these techniques, the teacher would begin with an assertive command, making quite clear the behavior he wishes to see. If that command does not work, the teacher would begin a behavior analysis process based on data gathering, positive and negative reinforcement, and perhaps various steps in the application of the escalating use of reduction procedures. Application of behavioral principles requires the teacher to state a target behavior and behavioral objectives, and the target behavior must be observed through a variety of assessment processes (with event recording the method of choice due to ease of implementation). The teacher uses a host of positive reinforcements with students who demonstrate or model proper behavior, catching them acting appropriately. This increases the likelihood of obtaining desired appropriate behavior, while at the same time documenting behavior changes by repeated observations through various methods. If the behavior does not change in the desired direction, the teacher must modify the intervention.

Finally, the teacher can use shaping to teach new behaviors to students while gradually thinning the use of reinforcers until little or no teacher-delivered reinforcement is needed. The experiences of life itself are now rewarding to the well-adapted student, and the student is reinforced naturally. For very destructive behavior that the teacher wishes to stop, various steps involving increased degrees of intrusiveness may be used—but only with much caution and preparation to minimize the potential negative side effects of punishment.

ENDNOTES

1. P. A. Alberto and A. C. Troutman, *Applied Behavior Analysis for Teachers*, 3rd ed. (New York: Merrill-Macmillan, 1990).

2. Ibid., pp. 276–277.

RELATED READINGS

Alberto, P. A., and Troutman, A. C. *Applied Behavior Analysis for Teachers,* 3rd ed. New York: Merrill-Macmillan, 1990.

Engelmann, S., and Carnine, D. *Theory of Instruction: Principles and Application.* New York: Irvington, 1982.

Madsen, C. H., and Madsen, C. K. *Teaching/Discipline: A Positive Approach for Educational Development.* Raleigh, NC: Contemporary Publishing, 1981.

INSTRUCTIONAL MEDIA: BEHAVIOR ANALYSIS

Name	Minutes	Format	Sound	Address of Distributor
Behavior Control	60	video	yes	PBS Video 1320 Braddock Place Alexandria, VA 22314

While not always conscious of the process, everyone is to some extent affected by behavior modification. When is it proper to modify human behavior, who decides whose behavior should be modified, and how can you tell when it's being done? Investigates techniques used to influence people's behavior, from subliminal messages to work with the mentally ill.

Behavior Modification	15	16 mm	yes	Educational Coordinates 625 Ellis Street Mountain View, CA 94043

Explains how tokens are used to reinforce appropriate behavior and learning in an elementary school setting. Shows how students, teachers and parents are involved in a token economy behavior modification type of program.

Behavior Modification	15	16 mm	yes	Hubbard Scientific Co. P.O. Box 104 Northbrook, IL 60062

TDemonstrates behavior modification techniques and concepts as approaches to language learning. Examines such techniques as prebase rate observations, positive reinforcement, scheduling, and negative reinforcement. Emphasizes the value of behavior modification in changing verbal and nonverbal responses of children with learning disabilities.

Behavior Modification in the Classroom	24	16 mm	yes	University of California Extension Media Center 2176 Shattuck Avenue Berkeley, CA 94704

Demonstrates the use of rewards and other positive reinforcement techniques to modify the behavior of elementary and junior high schools or classes whose performance suffers because of their distracting behavior, lack of attention, or poor motivation.

Name	Minutes	Format	Sound	Address of Distributor
Peer-Conducted Behavior Modification	25	16 mm	yes	Media Guild 11722 Sorrento Valley Road Suite E San Diego, CA 92121

Explains that the behavior of a disturbed or mentally retarded child often causes rejection by parents, siblings, and peers. Parents suffer extreme frustration watching this ostracizing process. This film, with commentary by Dr. Gerald Patterson, dramatizes such a situation and shows steps to solve the problem.

Name	Minutes	Format	Sound	Address of Distributor
Catch'em Being Good—Approaches to Motivation and Discipline	30	16 mm	yes	Research Press Co. Box 3177, 2612 Mattis Champaign, IL 61821

Presents research-based methods for dealing with students who have academic and social difficulties. Contrasts the more rewarding application of positive discipline based on warm teacher/child interaction with traditional but ineffective ways of responding to common behavioral and performance problems.

8

SKILLSTREAMING
Teaching Prosocial Skills

Theorists/Writers: Arnold Goldstein and Ellen McGinnis

- *Skillstreaming the Elementary School Child*
- *Skillstreaming in Early Childhood: Teaching Prosocial Skills to the Preschool and Kindergarten Child*
- *Skillstreaming the Adolescent: A Structured Learning Approach to Teaching Prosocial Skills*

A young teacher-in-training sees her favorte teacher from high school at the local mall, and approaches to reintroduce herself as a former student and to tell her that she, too, is now becoming a teacher. The veteran high school teacher responds unenthusiastically with, "Oh, well! I retired last year, and thank goodness! Students today are not what they used to be, and I am very glad to be out of the classroom."

The writers and designers of Skillstreaming suggest that this attitude is seen and heard more and more often from today's seasoned and experienced teachers. We hear about students' noncompliance, their confrontations with one another, their failure to work and show interest in their studies, the decline in their joining and supporting activities, and a host of other complaints. In addition to this list is the new concern about violent and aggressive students and passive introverted students who are socially isolated with little sense of belonging.

John is a student who constantly interrupts the teacher's instruction and directs put-down remarks to other students when they are talking. He is disliked by his peers and is unwanted for classroom cooperative groups. The teacher's overtures and discussions with John are met with claims that "you are picking on me."

Kate cannot focus and stay in her seat long enough to do her work. Her body—especially her arms and legs—are constantly in motion. When she is free to interact with her peers, she pushes and takes similar physical actions that produce fights with others. At the same time, the teacher knows that Kate is bright and academically capable, but her work does not show it.

Mario is an introverted boy who sits passively slumped down into his chair behind his desk. He tends to be bored, and complies with the teacher's requests only grudgingly. Other students are fearful of him; on one occasion, when he was accidentally jostled by a fellow student, he drew a knife.

These are some examples of misbehaving or problem children that classroom teachers are facing today. Discipline models discussed in other chapters of this book have provided various theoretical positions on how to view these children and their behavior, and differ dramatically on how to intervene or deal with such children. Skillstreaming also makes a clear claim to being able to help teachers and have an impact on such children so that the classroom—from preschool to kindergarten to secondary schools—improves. Skillstreaming is a psychoeducational intervention program that draws on both psychology (primarily behavior analysis) and education (mainly direct instruction).

DEFINING SKILLSTREAMING

To describe it in abbreviated form, Skillstreaming is a skill-deficit model. Designers of this model view misbehaving students as lacking the necessary social skills—which they call *prosocial*—to function well with peers and adults. This lack of skill in handling potentially stressful social interactions and conflicts leaves these children with only the stereotypic responses of passivity, isolation, or violent actions toward others. The Skillstreaming designers developed a list of 60 necessary prosocial skills they believe most students absorb through incidental learning. They believe that students today—in significantly greater numbers than in the past—are not acquiring these social skills. Thus, Skillstreaming attempts to teach the following skills directly:

- Classroom survival skills (asking for help, saying thank you, listening, etc.)
- Friendship-making skills (introducing yourself, beginning a conversation, joining in, etc.)
- Dealing with feelings (expressing your feelings; recognizing another's feelings, dealing with anger, etc.)
- Alternatives to aggression (maintaining self-control, responding to teasing; avoiding trouble, staying out of fights, etc.)

• Dealing with stress (dealing with boredom, reacting to failure, saying no, accepting no, etc.).

Figure 8.1 list these skills and compares them across categories at the early childhood, elementary, and adolescent levels.

Early Childhood[1] (ages 3 to 7)	Elementary Years[2] (1st to 5th grades)	Adolescence[3] (middle and secondary school)
I: Beginning Social Skills	I: Classroom Survival Skills	I: Beginning Social Skills
• Listening • Using nice talk • Using brave talk • Saying thank you • Rewarding yourself • Asking for help • Asking a favor • Ignoring	• Listening • Asking for help • Saying thank you • Bringing materials to class • Following instructions • Completing assignments • Contributing to discussions • Offering help to an adult • Asking a question • Ignoring distractions • Making corrections • Deciding on something to do • Setting a goal	• Listening • Starting a conversation • Having a conversation • Asking a question • Saying thank you • Introducing yourself • Introducing other people • Giving a compliment
II: School-Related Skills		II: Advanced Social Skills
• Asking a question • Following directions • Trying when it's hard • Interrupting		• Asking for help • Joining in • Giving instructions • Following instructions • Apologizing • Convincing others
III: Friendship-Making Skills	II: Friendship-Making Skills	III: Planning Skills
• Greeting others • Reading others • Joining in • Waiting your turn • Sharing • Offering help • Asking someone to play • Playing a game	• Introducing yourself • Beginning a conversation • Ending a conversation • Joining in • Play a game • Asking a favor • Offering help to a classmate • Giving a compliment • Suggesting an activity • Sharing • Apologizing	• Deciding on something to do • Deciding what caused a problem • Setting a goal • Deciding on your abilities • Gathering information • Arranging problems by importance • Making a decision • Concentrating on a task

(continued)

FIGURE 8–1 A Comparison of Prosocial Skills: Early Childhood, Elementary Years, and Adolescence

Early Childhood[1] (ages 3 to 7)	Elementary Years[2] (1st to 5th grades)	Adolescence[3] (middle and secondary school)
IV: Dealing with Feelings	III: Dealing with Feelings	IV: Dealing with Feelings
• Knowing your feelings • Feeling left out • Asking to talk • Dealing with fear • Deciding how someone feels • Showing affection	• Knowing your feelings • Expressing your feelings • Recognizing another's feelings • Showing understanding of another's feelings • Expressing concern for another • Dealing with your anger • Dealing with another's anger • Expressing affection • Dealing with fear • Rewarding yourself	• Knowing your feelings • Expressing your feelings • Understanding the feelings of others • Dealing with someone else's anger • Expressing affection • Dealing with fear • Rewarding yourself
V: Alternatives to Aggression	IV: Alternatives to Aggression	V: Alternatives to Aggression
• Dealing with teasing • Dealing with feeling mad • Deciding if it's fair • Solving a problem • Accepting consequences	• Using self-control • Asking permission • Responding to teasing • Avoiding trouble • Staying out of fights • Problem solving • Accepting consequences • Dealing with an accusation • Negotiating	• Asking permission • Sharing something • Helping others • Negotiating • Using self-control • Standing up for your rights • Responding to teasing • Avoiding trouble with others • Keeping out of fights
VI: Dealing with Stress	V: Dealing with Stress	VI: Dealing with Stress
• Relaxing • Dealing with mistakes • Being honest • Knowing when to tell • Dealing with losing • Wanting to be first • Saying no • Accepting no • Deciding what to do	• Dealing with boredom • Deciding what caused a problem • Making a complaint • Answering a complaint • Dealing with losing • Being a good sport • Dealing with being left out • Dealing with embarrassment • Reacting to failure • Accepting no • Saying no • Relaxing • Dealing with group pressure • Dealing with wanting something that isn't yours • Making a decision • Being honest	• Making a complaint • Answering a complaint • Showing sportsmanship after a game • Dealing with embarrassment • Dealing with being left out • Standing up for a friend • Responding to persuasion • Responding to failure • Dealing with contradictory messages • Dealing with an accusation • Getting ready for a difficult conversation • Dealing with group pressure

FIGURE 8–1 (continued)

[1]McGinnis and Goldstein, 1990, pp. 59–62.

[2]McGinnis and Goldstein, 1997, pp. 88–89.

[3]Goldstein, Sprafkin, Gershaw, and Klein, 1980, pp. 84–85.

Sources: Ellen McGinnis and Arnold P. Goldstein, *Skillstreaming in Early Childhood: Teaching Prosocial Skills to the Pre-school and Kindergarten Child* (Champaign, IL: Research Press, 1990); Ellen McGinnis and Arnold P. Goldsein, *Skill-streaming the Elementary School Child: New Strategies and Perspectives for Teaching Prosocial Skills* (Champaign, IL: Research Press, 1997); Arnold P. Goldstein, Robert P. Sprafkin, N. Jane Gershaw, and Paul Klein, *Skillstreaming the Adolescent: A Structured Learning Approach to Teaching Prosocial Skills* (Champaign, IL: Research Press, 1980).

The prosocial skills are structurally taught by selecting students in need of these skills and enrolling them in a group-training session that meets three to five times a week. Two adult leaders use modeling, role-playing with the help of skill cards, performance feedback, and homework activities in an attempt to transfer the training to real-life situations for these students. The instructional principle is based on behavior analysis principles, so rewards and incentive systems are used; therefore, the classification of this model is Rules and Consequences. *Note:* The writers provide an adequate review of the research, data, and theories that support and define the use of the preceding four activities (modeling, role-playing, performance feedback, and homework activities) as well as the 60 prosocial skills.

SKILLSTREAMING AND DISCIPLINE

Skillstreaming was first used with children with special needs who had to be taught social skills to be able to leave protective care as adults and live in independent self-care homes and situations. The national trend toward more and more violence, and the increasing numbers of very difficult children who require excessive disciplining in classrooms, prompted the designers to reshape their model. They created direct instructional programs appropriate for children of normal functioning, as well as children with special needs, in public school classrooms who had not yet acquired many of the most basic and simple social skills.

Skillstreaming is a proactive model, not a reactive one. Such discipline models as those of Glasser (Chapter 5), Dreikurs (Chapter 4), and the Canters (Chapter 10) provide direct and concrete actions for the teacher to use in reacting to a misbehaving child. Skillstreaming is a program that is initiated with a student *before* the misbehavior occurs, enabling the student to acquire the prosocial skills that can help him become more effective. As a result, the student would not be getting into or causing trouble, not only at school but also at home and in the wider society. Thus, Skillstreaming is proactive—in this sense, similar to the *peer mediation*[1] model. How is the Skillstreaming model carried out?

GETTING READY FOR SKILLSTREAMING

The first step in Skillstreaming is to select group leaders. When possible, the leaders should be two experienced teachers or a teacher and another adult paraprofessional. The selection process requires an understanding of cultural diversity and methods of motivating students through behavior analysis constructs and actions. The program suggests methods of selecting students who have difficulties with interpersonal relations, aggression management, and related problems. These students are evaluated, through direct observation or a skills checklist, based on the prosocial skills mentioned previously to determine their level of proficiency regarding the needed skills. Students with similar skills needs are then placed together and taught as a group for periods of 25 to 40 minutes three to five times a week, in a set-aside space that may contain a chalkboard or easel pad, chairs, and a few selective props related to the theme of the role-play. The program may last as little as two days or as long as three years, depending on each individual student's progress. The instructional system uses skill cards that cue the role-playing student in practicing the skills. For example, for the skill *listening*, the card will require the student to:

1. Look at the person who is talking.
2. Sit quietly.
3. Think about what is being said.
4. Say yes and nod your head.
5. Ask a question about the topic to find out more.

The program also utilizes two booklets: a Skillstreaming Student Manual that introduces Skillstreaming to the student, along with the procedures of modeling, role-playing, performance feedback, and transfer training (homework); and a Program Form booklet that provides essential program forms, checklists, and charts that may be reproduced.

SKILLSTREAMING TEACHING PROCEDURES

In order to carry out the program's teaching principles of modeling, role-playing, performance feedback, and transfer, the teacher (as group leader) follows an orderly nine-step program (see Figure 8–2).

Step #1: Define the Skill

The group training session begins with the teacher defining the skill, showing the skill card, stating why the skill is needed, and engaging the students in some discussion about the skill.

1. Define the skill.
2. Model the skill.
3. Establish student skill need.
4. Select role-players.
5. Set up the role-play.
6. Conduct the role-play.
7. Provide performance feedback.
8. Assign skill homework.
9. Select next role-player.

FIGURE 8–2   Skillstreaming Teaching Steps

Step #2: Model the Skill

Once the skill is defined and introduced, the teacher moves to modeling the skill. *Modeling* is defined simply as learning through imitation. The modeling permits the student to learn new behaviors (observational learning) by imitating others. Peers who model aggressive behaviors and see this behavior go unpunished during routine daily living will learn to become aggressive, as well. On the other hand, modeling of altruism and care by peers under the training of Skillstreaming can help inhibit these same negative aggressive behaviors. Through modeling, a child who deals with a confrontational peer in a positive effective manner may enable the classmate to approach future confrontations in a similar positive manner.

The teacher/leader of the training group understands and uses the various modeling stages of attention, retention, and reproduction. He or she minimizes distractions and keeps the students focused and alert so their attention is on the model. The retention—that is, remembering the behaviors after the modeling stops—is achieved through *covert rehearsal.* This is done by having the student perform activities under the questions and guidance of the teacher in a way that requires the student to verbally retell the actions he saw or to role-play the actual behaviors. Finally, *reproduction* is the process of arranging reinforcing rewards to get the student to show not just that he knows the skill but also that he can use it in a real-life social situation.

The guidelines for Step #2 are:

- Do two examples for each skill demonstrated.
- Select themes and situations related to the real life of the student.
- Have a modeling student or adult leader resemble the real-life antagonist as much as possible.
- Model positive outcomes and reinforce them.
- Use modeling that follows and depicts the list of actions on the skills cards.
- Use modeling that depicts one skill at a time.

Step #3: Establish Student Skill Need

The student is asked to describe where, when, and with whom he will need this skill in the future. (On the chalkboard or easel pad, write the student's name and future person as well as theme.) Relevance must be established for the use of this skill in real life.

Step #4: Select Role-Players

Generally, every member of the group gets to role-play each skill. The reluctant student usually goes last. (*Note:* Writers offer guidelines and techniques for dealing with reluctant students.)

Step #5: Set Up the Role-Play

Once the need for the skill is established in Step #3, a main actor in the role-play is appointed, and a second person (co-player) with characteristics of the real-life person is chosen. The teacher/leader then questions the main actor to set the scene and context for the situation. The leader requests additional information to set the stage and describe the physical setting, to be aware of events immediately preceding the situation, and to be familiar with the mood or manner of those being portrayed.

Step #6: Conduct the Role-Play

The role-play now begins. The main actor is asked to follow the behavioral steps on the feedback cards, as the second teacher/leader near the chalkboard points to various behaviors on the cards to cue the actor. The audience is also assigned a role to observe the skills and describe them later. An unusual technique of "think aloud" is requested of the main actor: Rather than thinking internally about what is happening, the actors are asked to speak their thoughts out loud for all to hear.

The actors are coached to stay in their roles, and prompts are given if needed. Each member gets to role-play, and the actors' roles may be reversed or the group leader may play a role. For performance feedback purposes and to reinforce actions after the role-playing, the "production" may be videotaped.

Step #7: Provide Performance Feedback

After the role-play is completed and as part of the performance feedback, the students are asked to react to how the (1) co-actors, (2) assigned observers, and (3) group leaders followed the skill steps. The leaders will use praise, approval, and encouragement statements. After hearing what has been said, the main actor may comment on the feedback he has received. Finally, it may be helpful to have the actors repeat their roles after hearing the feedback.

Step #8: Assign Skill Homework

After the successful role-play, the students are given the homework assignment of using that skill at some future date in a real-life situation. Through questioning and coaching by the leaders, the students decide when, how, and with whom they will use the skill in a future context ("I'll use this with my older sister, after dinner, when we normally argue about clean-up duties!").

The homework, as the transfer training activity, is viewed at three levels, depending on the age and capabilities of the student. It assumes a level of increased difficulty as the levels progress.

Homework Level 1: Preparation

The teacher helps the student fill out Homework Report Form 1, which requires the student to name the person with whom he will attempt to practice this skill in the future. On the form, the student indicates the date, skill, and steps he will perform. After completing this homework assignment, the student is asked to indicate on the form what happened and how well he did, using the criteria of *Good, OK,* and *Not so good.* Since these activities can be done at the preschool/kindergarten, elementary, and adolescent levels, these forms vary in the amount of writing required of the student. For example, the evaluation done at the preschool/kindergarten level requires the student to evaluate how he did by circling one of three "smiley faces"—one with a smile, another with a mouth as a straight line, and a third with a down-turned mouth. Finally, the teacher discusses the form with the student to see why he evaluated his actions as he did.

Homework Level 2: Documentation

The student at Level 2 has achieved mastery of a particular skill and is now ready to document his homework independently. The Homework Report Form 2 requires the student to record a short documentation of "When did I practice?" Note that at this level, the child uses the skill many times, but always just the same one skill. The student turns this homework in to the leader, who writes comments on the report and returns it to the student.

Homework Level 3: All Skills

Finally, at Level 3, the child documents his practice as homework by writing not just one but all skills practiced that week, making tallymarks for each time a skill is used.

Each new training session begins with a homework report, with the leader reinforcing the student's performance positively or negatively. The teacher also uses a Group Self-Report Chart (the student places a sticker or indicator when the skill was used) that lists all the students' names as a continued reinforcer and reminder. Skill Contracts, Self-Recording Forms, and Skill Awards are also used. (These are included and described in the booklets.) The written materials also provide guidelines and procedures for handling student behavioral problems while conducting the training sessions. These actions are based on behavior analysis principles, which are discussed in Chapter 7 of this book.

Step #9: Select Next Role-Player

The next student is selected to become the main role-player and the steps are repeated.

SUMMARY

Skillstreaming is a structured approach based on behavior analysis. It works to teach prosocial skills directly to students at all age levels through modeling, role-play, performance feedback, and transfer (homework). The teacher follows step-by-step procedures, permitting a Teacher Behavior Continuum comparison (see Figure 8–3). The philosophical position is that the misbehaving student has a skill deficit and if she is taught these skills, she will be able to transfer this training to

Looking On	Nondirective Statements	Questions	Directive Statements
		Step 1: *Define the skill.*	
		Step 3: *Establish student skill need.*	
		• Student describes where, when, and with whom they will need this skill in the future. (Write the student's name with future person and theme.)	

FIGURE 8–3   Teacher Behavior Continuum (TBC) Skillstreaming

her school and daily life, thus becoming a socially skilled and well-behaved productive person. Books and other written documents, including training videos, demonstrate to teachers how they may carry out such training in their schools. The philosophy here is that by spending "pennies" of time up front, you can save "dollars" of time in the future. In other words, Skillstreaming activities are very time consuming in the course of the schoolday, but if you identify the students in need of these skills and train them beforehand, being proactive, you will eliminate the need for reactive discipline actions that are very time consuming for you, the administrators, and the school system in general. Prosocial skills may be as important—or even more important—to some children as reading, writing, and arithmetic, because as well-functioning children with these skills, they will have greater life successes.

Modeling	Reinforcement	Physical Intervention/ Isolation

Modeling

Step 2: *Model the skill.*

Step 4: *Select role-players.*
- Everyone role-plays each skill; the reluctant student goes last.

Step 5: *Set up the role-play.*
- Actor chooses second person (co-player) with characteristic of real-life person.
- Request additional information to set the stage.
- Describe the physical setting.
- Describe events immediately preceding the situation.
- Describe mood or manner of those being portrayed.

Step 6: *Conduct the role-play.*
- Follows behavioral steps on feedback cards.
- "Thinks aloud."
- All others are instructed to watch for behavioral steps (may assign a step to be observed to an audience member).
- Coach actors to stay in roles.
- One group leader points to behavioral steps on chalkboard as they are enacted.
- Repeat with other group members.
- Do two of each skill each session.
- Actors' roles may be reversed or group leader plays role.

Reinforcement

Step 7: *Provide performance feedback.*
- React to role-play (1) co-actors, (2) assigned observers, (3) group leaders (using praise, approval, and encouragement) of following skill steps.
- Main actor comments on feedback received.
- Actors may repeat role after criticism.

Step 8: *Assign Skill Homework.*
- Decide when, how, and with whom the student will use the skill in future context.
- Use Homework Level in order of difficulty:
Level 1: Preparation: fill out homework report form (name, date, skill, steps, who?, when?). After completed: What happen? How did I do? (evaluation Good, OK, or bad) Why did I evaluate as such?
Level 2: Documentation: Uses Homework Report Form 2 independently, turns in to leader who writes comments and returns it.
Level 3: All Skills: Listed on 3 × 5 index card, tallies each time a skill is used.
(Each session begins with homework report with leader reinforcing positive or negatively.)
- Teacher uses Group Self-Report Chart (students place "sticker" or indicator when Skill was used).
- Continued reinforcers and reminders: Skill Contracts, Self-Recording Forms, Skill Awards.

FIGURE 8–3   (continued)

ENDNOTE

1. Fred Schrumpf, Donna Crawford, and H. Chu Usadel, *Peer Mediation: Conflict Resolution in Schools* (Champaign, IL: Research Press, 1991).

RELATED READINGS

Goldstein, Arnold P., Sprafkin, Robert P., Gershaw, N. Jane, and Klein, Paul. *Skillstreaming the Adolescent: A Structured Learning Approach to Teaching Prosocial Skills.* Champaign, IL: Research Press, 1980.

McGinnis, Ellen, and Goldstein, Arnold P. *Skillstreaming in Early Childhood: Teaching Prosocial Skills to the Preschool and Kindergarten Child.* Champaign, IL: Research Press, 1990.

McGinnis, Ellen, and Goldstein, Arnold P. *Skillstreaming the Elementary School Child.* Champaign, IL: Research Press, 1997.

INSTRUCTIONAL MEDIA: SKILLSTREAMING

In addition to the textbooks on Skillstreaming, both print and video materials are available to help teachers learn and implement the program. These materials may be purchased by contacting Research Press, 2612 North Mattis Avenue, Champaign, IL 61821, (217) 352–3273 or (800) 519–2707; fax (217) 352–1221.

Name	Authors	Level	Format	ISBN
Skillstreaming in Early Childhood: Teaching Prosocial Skills to the Preschool and Kindergarten Child	Ellen McGinnis & Arnold Goldstein, 1990	Preschool/ Kindergarten Program Text	Paperback, 200 pages	0-87822-320-7
Skillstreaming the Elementary School Child: Teaching Prosocial Skills to the Preschool and Kindergarten Child— Program Forms (rev. ed.)	Ellen McGinnis & Arnold Goldstein, 1990	Preschool/ Kindergarten Program Forms	Paperback, 80 pages, 8½ × 11	0-87822-321-5
Skillstreaming the Elementary School Child: New Strategies and Perspectives for Teaching Prosocial Skills—Program Forms (rev. ed.)	Ellen McGinnis & Arnold Goldstein, 1997	Elementary Program Forms	Paperback, 64 pages, 8½ × 11	0-87822-374-6
Program forms for the elementary level include the following: Teacher/Staff, Parent, and Student Skillstreaming Checklist; Skillstreaming Grouping Chart; Homework Reports; Group Self-Help Chart; School-Home Note; Parent/Staff Skill Rating Form; Skill Awards; Skill Contracts; and Self-Recording Forms				
Skillstreaming the Elementary School Child—Student Manual	Ellen McGinnis & Arnold Goldstein, 1997	Elementary Student Manual	Paperback, 80 pages	0-87822-373-8
Skillstreaming the Elementary School Child—Skill Cards	Ellen McGinnis & Arnold Goldstein, 1997	Elementary Skill Cards	480 cards	--
People Skills: Doing 'em Right!	Ellen McGinnis & Arnold Goldstein, 1997	Elementary Student Video	17 minutes	--
Shows an elementary-level Skillstreaming group in progress and teaches the group members what is expected of them.)				
Skillstreaming the Adolescent: New Strategies and Perspectives for Teaching Prosocial Skills (rev. ed.)	Arnold P. Goldstein & Ellen McGinnis, 1997	Adolescents Program Text	Paperback, 352 pages	0-87822-369-X
Skillstreaming the Adolescent: New Strategies and Perspectives for Teaching Prosocial Skills (rev. ed.)	Arnold P. Goldstein and Ellen McGinnis, 1997	Adolescents Program Forms	Paperback, 48 pages, 8½ × 11	0-87822-371-1
Skillstreaming the Adolescent—Student Manual	Arnold P. Goldstein & Ellen McGinnis, 1997	Adolescents Student Manual	Paperback, 64, pages, 8½ × 11	0-87822-371-1
The Skillstreaming Video: How to Teach Students Prosocial Skills	Arnold P. Goldstein & Ellen McGinnis, 1988	Teacher Video	26 minutes	--

9

THE POSITIVE DISCIPLINE MODEL

Theorist/Writer: Fredric Jones

- *Positive Classroom Discipline*
- *Positive Classroom Instruction*

The following is a classroom discipline incident involving a teacher using the *positive discipline*[1] techniques of Fredric Jones. Italicized words highlight the techniques or processes being utilized, and will be defined later in this chapter.

Ms. Dumas has just finished teaching a new concept to her algebra class and has assigned the class to do seatwork to practice applying this concept. She moves around the room *(working the crowd)* and checks each student's work. She hears muffled whispers and the slight movement of a chair coming from the far side of the room. She looks up *(check it out)* to see Nancy's eyes appear above her textbook and then disappear behind it. Again there are whispers, and Ms. Dumas sees Nancy physically turn toward Martha, her neighbor. Nancy is busy giggling and talking to Martha, who appears to be writing. Nancy is clearly off task, requiring Ms. Dumas to take some action to get her to use the seatwork time constructively.

Ms. Dumas (1) stands fully erect, (2) turns her body and feet so that she is *squared off* with Nancy, (3) takes two controlled *relaxing breaths,* and (4) attempts to make eye contact with Nancy, who is not looking in her direction. Ms. Dumas's voice (5) broadcasts across the classroom, "Nancy," but there is no response from the girl. Again she calls, "Uh-h, Nancy." The neighbor hears and sees Ms. Dumas's cues, and signals Nancy to look in the teacher's direction. Nancy now makes eye contact with Ms. Dumas and sees the teacher looking straight at her. She wiggles in her chair and turns her upper body toward Ms. Dumas, but her lower body (knees and feet) still face her neighbor. She picks up her pencil *(pseudo-compliance: pencil posturing)* and places it on her paper as if to write. She looks again to see Ms. Dumas still holding the same unwavering eye contact. Nancy meets Ms. Dumas's eye contact directly and smiles at her with an open-mouth-and-teeth smile, with a slight cock of her head and raised eyebrows *("smiley face")*. The endearing smile is one that would encourage anyone to automatically or reflexively smile back, but Ms. Dumas holds her same upright posture. She maintains the same visual lock with Nancy but returns Nancy's smiling overture with a flat facial expression that clearly communicates, "I am not amused!" or "I am bored!" while taking two more *relaxing breaths.*

What we see Ms. Dumas doing is applying Fredric Jones's visual *limit-setting* techniques to deal with student misbehavior. The Jones model of classroom discipline is premised on the belief that teachers should not get bogged down in the use of language and negotiations with backtalking students, but should use the powers of proximity and vision to assert their will. The Jones model features four legs to the "chair of discipline and management," and each leg must be intact and functioning to make the positive discipline process work: (1) limit setting, (2) responsibility training, (3) omission training, and (4) a back-up system (see Figure 9–1). In addition, Jones asserts that classroom structure, although not one of these four legs, sets a foundation that allows good discipline to occur. We will first discuss details of limit setting and back-up systems, followed by discussion of the remaining two legs; however, you should keep in mind that all four systems must be running in parallel if the full discipline program is to work.

Jones draws theoretically and conceptually from the knowledge bases of behavior modification, proximity research from anthropology as a study of animal behavior, and neurobiology as to how the human brain functions. Each set of techniques and practices is grounded in a justification drawn from these three knowledge sources, as well as the practical teacher folklore and classroom traditions Jones has gathered from his many years of observation in classrooms at all grade levels. The model is surprisingly void of traditional psychological behavioral terminology but is chock full of "Fredisms," coined by Fredric Jones to describe techniques, philosophies, or personal wisdom statements drawn from his rural Kansas upbringing and his high interest in athletics. For example, his "Pay now or pay later" means that you first take the time to get control of your classroom or it will later cost you even more time to remediate a bad classroom situation.

LIMIT SETTING

The objective for all limit setting is to calm the students and get them back on task. Jones's research shows that 80 percent of all discipline problems involve the off-task behavior of students talking to others when they should be working. The second most common is out-of-seat behavior, or goofing off (15 percent), followed by such misbehaviors as note passing, playing with items smuggled into class, and

Part	Definition	Knowledge Base	Examples of Techniques
Limit Setting	Actions taken by the teacher to control the students' natural reflexes and prompt students back to work while (1) students are doing seatwork or (2) teacher is lecturing	• Neurobiology (brain functioning) • Fight or flight • Modality functioning Proximity	• Relaxed breathing • Slack jaw • Speed of movement • Inhibit talking Body-telegraphing • Working the crowd • Eye contact • Posture • Facial expression • Closing distance (far, near, and intimate, "in the face")
Responsibility Training	The use of an incentive system for obtaining new behaviors or increasing existing ones	Behavior modification	Group incentives Preferred activity time (PAT) Differential reinforcement
Omission Training	Getting very difficult student to desist misbehavior	Behavior modification	Differential reinforcement, group incentives
Back-up System	Three levels of intervention from private to public sanctions	Traditional school practice Behavioral discriminate teaching	Office referral, time out, expulsion, suspension, staffing, parent conferencing
Classroom Structure	The arrangement of objects and furniture, and the teaching of rules and procedures		3-step lesson: Say, Show, Do Over-practice

FIGURE 9–1   Positive Discipline: Parts, Definitions, Knowledge Bases, and Examples of Techniques

tying shoelaces. However, when most teachers think of discipline problems, we usually think of the "big ticket" items of physical aggression, overt defiance, and destruction of property. Jones uses time as a central variable for justifying and thinking out the value of the teacher's action, asking: How much does this teacher technique cost in time? We may have wonderful discipline procedures but if they eat up so much of our time that none is left for instruction, the techniques are of no value.

To follow Jones's reasoning, these "big ticket" discipline actions normally are very rare occurrences. These incidents take five minutes or less, and generally are seen by teachers no more than five times in a school year. By multiplying the five incidents by five minutes, we see that we may spend a great deal of time worrying about the major discipline incidents that might actually involve 25 minutes or less of our teaching time in an entire school year. What is more important is to watch the "nickel-and-dime" actions of talking and out-of-seat behavior, which might eat up one-third or more of our total class time if there is poor discipline. At the same time, it is these nickel-and-dime misbehaviors that consume the teacher's energies and eventually wear the teacher down. Nancy and Martha's talking may be seen as a minor incident on its face, but it caused the teacher to stop her instruction. Multiply that by 8 to 10 of these incidents in a relatively short span and they will add up, wear the teacher out, and cut deeply into "time on task" which is corre-lated to academic achievement.

Jones sees the Nancys and Marthas of the classroom as playing a power game and doing penny-ante gambling. When these girls face Ms. Dumas for the first time, they ask themselves, Does she really mean what she says? Do we have to work in this classroom or can we play? Nancy, as a low roller (or gambler) has a "Ph.D." in the Teacher Game to see who will hold the power in this classroom—to see how far she can go and to test this teacher to see if she means business. She has learned from her "Ph.D." a host of pseudo-compliance behaviors to sidetrack the teacher during power plays. If she can get the teacher to buy into these behaviors when the teacher asks her to "stop playing and go to work," the teacher will lose the game and control will shift to the student's game playing. Although they look different and take various forms of being negative or positive, the techniques are all labeled as *back talk*. All of the students know the power game that is proceeding, with the ultimate prize being to see the teacher "lose her cool" and signal a com-plete victory for the students and a total lack of control of the classroom. Remem-ber: "Your life is in the hands of any fool who makes you lose your temper." Calm is strength. Upset is weakness.[2]

Fight or Flight Response

Think back to a time you may have tried hard to forget. You were driving your car and stopped at a red light. The light changed and you slowly pulled into the inter-section, but another driver ran the light and barreled through the intersection at excessive speed. If you had not suddenly jammed on your brakes and turned your wheel quickly, you would have had a very serious accident. The adrenaline pumped through your body, your heart was in your throat, your face was warm, and you clenched your teeth. For a moment you weren't sure if you were going to throw up, and 15 minutes later as you got out of your car your legs were still wob-bly. You were experiencing the results of a fight or flight response.

Let's look at a second example, one most people are likely to have seen. Your 3-year-old child has broken away from your hand and has just run into a busy street, or pushed over the white-hot charcoal grill, or released the parking brake on dad's car, or some similar action that could clearly be life threatening for the child or others. Moments later you are nose to nose with the child, screaming at the child never to do that again. Your emotional state and inside feelings are just as you felt when you almost had an auto accident. For all intents and purposes you—under-standably—are hysterical and out of control, and the child will be lucky to avoid being shaken harshly or hit. We as teachers in schools and classrooms, of course, cannot deal with students in such a manner as the parent deals with this misbehaving child.

What your body has experienced is an *adrenaline dump,* causing a reflex body action triggered by an external stimulus. You are out of control as long as you are in this hyper-alert state, meaning that for a short period, you have lost your use of rational reasoning and are functioning as an automatic defensive being. Rational thinking is too slow for sudden emergencies, and your body has a built-in survival process that shuts down higher-order thinking so the defensive reflexes can act to save you. When animals are cornered, their lack of language skills and rational thinking leaves them with only two choices—they can fight or they can flee. Humans experience a similar response when events push them out of rational thinking. This fight or flight response exacts a high price in our level of stress and burned-up energy.

Theoreticians suggest that humans have what may be thought of as three brains. This *triune brain* contains (1) a reptilian brain located at the base of the brain stem; (2) a paleocortex, an ancient cortex or "doggy-horsey brain;" and (3) a neocortex, or new cortex of higher intelligence. The triune brain theory (see Figure 9–2) suggests that each of these three brains has its own functions, but under stress the brain downshifts to lower primal centers for purposes of survival. Under moderate arousal, the management of behavior shifts from the neocortex to the paleocortex. Under extreme arousal, the management of behavior shifts from paleocortex to the reptilian brain. This means that when we are angry, frightened, and upset, we are a noncortical, animal-like being and that higher thinking in our cortex is unavailable

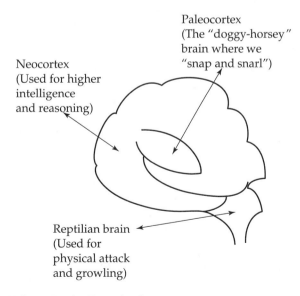

Paleocortex
(The "doggy-horsey"
brain where we
"snap and snarl")

Neocortex
(Used for higher
intelligence
and reasoning)

Reptilian brain
(Used for
physical attack
and growling)

FIGURE 9–2   Triune Brain Functioning

to us until we calm down. The downshift occurs in two forms: an *adrenaline dump* or a *slow "bleeding"* of adrenaline into our body system, maintaining us in a constant defensive stressful state.

In the automobile near-miss and the reprimanding of a child for a dangerous action, we have seen a full regression or downshifting to the reptilian brain as a result of a full adrenaline dump. In classrooms, we may have discipline incidents that are extremely confrontational toward us, possibly Nancy's implicit verbal aggression of, "I'll return to my talking once I get you out of my face, so f--- off!" Other examples, admittedly less frequent, may include a student who has a weapon, or is spiteful and hurtful to others, or exhibits a willful destruction of school property. More likely for most teachers are the day-in, day-out moderate arousals that cause the *slow bleeding* of adrenaline into our system. This constancy, because of small "nickel-and-dime" discipline incidents such as Nancy's chatting and off-task behavior, causes us to constantly teach and function at a moderate arousal level. For the teacher partially in a fight or flight stance with its accompanying stress, classroom life has been compared with the soldier who begins to suffer battle fatigue—a constant draining of energy.

The central contribution to the general field of discipline techniques of the Jones discipline model is the acknowledgment of this "slow bleed" phenomenon caused by stress, and clear practical actions to control this stress and maintain the teacher's classroom power and effectiveness. In the student power game, the ultimate way of winning control of the classroom is to have the teacher regress to a state where she has "lost her cool," meaning that the teacher is so emotional that she is reflexively acting from her reptilian brain and her higher-order thinking is unavailable. There is a high probability that the teacher, because of the lack of cortex thinking, will do something very dumb. When the teacher has regressed, *going brain stemmed,* it is for students what Jones calls "show time"—the teacher is now out of control and the students are in control, and the teacher's behavior will be quite amusing to the students as she struggles in an attempt to regain classroom control.

Let's take a look at how another professional handles a high-stress situation: a baseball umpire. It's the last of the ninth inning, and the home team is down by two runs. There are two outs and the bases are loaded. The batter hits a single to right field and the player on third base scores; the runner on second base rounds third and heads for home with the tying run as the right fielder makes a powerful, accurate throw to home plate. It's a close play. As the dust clears, 50,000 fans in the stadium, a few million watching on television at home, and the players (with their multimillion dollar contracts depending on the outcome of games such as this) are all waiting for this one individual—the umpire—to call the play. The umpire looks, points his thumb to the heavens, and shouts, "You're out!" All hell breaks loose. The home team's players and manager pour from the dugout and descend on the umpire—a lone man in a stressful situation who now needs to live with his decision. A power game begins with the manager shouting in the umpire's face. The manager's power game is to see if the umpire "means business" or if he can get the umpire to back down.

Now let's clearly see what the umpire does. He removes his face mask, plants his feet firmly on the ground and squares off to the manager, who is screaming in his face as the TV cameras zoom in for a close-up. The umpire puts his hands behind his back and crosses them, while he maintains unwavering eye contact with the hostile manager. He takes on a facial expression that says, "I am bored. I wonder what I'll have for dinner tonight," and appears to mentally leave the ball-park. If he is skilled, he says nothing but stands his ground with that unwavering eye contact with everyone who is *back talking* to him. He simply stands there and breathes, waiting for the manager and players to wear themselves out with insults, blame, and questions of his professional competence. Doing nothing is an act of power and control. If he cannot control the adrenaline rush moving through his body, he *goes brain stemmed* or loses his "cool" and begins to talk back to the manager and players. If this happens, he is doomed and loses control, and real violence may erupt causing the most dangerous of situations among the players and fans. Jones would say there is a very important lesson for the classroom teacher to learn from the baseball umpire's behavior. The teacher will find herself in confrontational situations with students that will involve heated and stressful interaction and back talk, but just like the umpire, the professional teacher must control her behavior and maintain power. Calm is strength. Upset is weakness.[3]

Following is an example of the behavior of a teacher who has "gone brain stem" or "gone chemical" (meaning physically full of adrenaline and overcome by a fight or flight posture), as Jones would label it.

> In a harsh voice one step short of actually shouting, Ms. Hopkins says, "If I have told you once, Linda and Brenda, I have told you a hundred times. (The teacher stands with left hand on left hip, balancing on one leg and hip and tapping the toe of her right foot, as she points and shakes her index finger across the room at the girls in an action called *pheasant posturing*). This is work time and I don't want to see you two talking, and I don't want to have to come over there! This is valuable class time and you, young ladies, are losing it. I am sick and tired of having to stop my work because of you two girls."

This teacher is a nagging person who is under stress and has regressed to a fight or flight position, probably with only her paleocortex, or doggy-horsey brain, in gear. The teacher, much like an animal, "snaps and snarls" and does what Jones would label *silly talk*, meaning that the words she says mean nothing and are even poor examples of threats. The hand pointing and similar physical actions are non-verbal territorial actions, used in the animal kingdom by creatures such as the male pheasant, to intimidate and scare off a rival (thus Jones's term, *pheasant posturing*). The screaming baseball manager is a good user of pheasant posturing as he gestures and shouts, but these are a part of the manager's powerlessness and game playing. The fans, however, are entertained because it is "show time." Students see these behaviors in teachers and are not fearful but are entertained by the sight of a teacher who is so weak that the students can "push her buttons" and get such an entertaining action from this adult who is supposed to be mature and in charge.

Eye Contact and Proximity

In animal species and also among humans, contact with another individual is done by reading nonverbal body messages. The eyes are the most expressive nonverbal communication process. An unswerving eye lock with an individual is the most powerful confrontational stance involving real power and subservience. Eye contact with another individual is a direct challenge or exercise of power, and when the other individual breaks the visual lock, it is read as capitulation and subservience ("I don't wish to fight; I yield to your power"). The dominant person looks and the other person smiles back as a signal of capitulation, or "I wish to be your friend." If the dominant person smiles back, the offer of friendship is accepted. If the other person does not smile back or break the heat of looking, then we have a direct power challenge.

> Nancy meets Ms. Dumas's eye contact directly and smiles at her with an open-mouth-and-teeth smile, with a slight cock of her head and raised eyebrows (*"smiley face"*). The endearing smile is one that would encourage anyone to automatically or reflexively smile back, but Ms. Dumas holds her same upright posture. She maintains the same visual lock with Nancy but returns Nancy's smiling overture with a flat facial expression that clearly communicates, "I am not amused!" or "I am bored!"while taking two more relaxing breaths.

The "heat" that the other person will feel emotionally from being visually confronted will depend on the spatial distance between the two people or a *concept of proximity.* Across the classroom the challenge can be very strong but can be fended off by many game-playing students. But when the teacher moves to the edge of the student's desk and leans over it, the visual heat is turned up dramatically and the student's inner-kettle of emotions begins to bubble—fueled by the output of adrenaline and stress within the student. The student is now in a fight or flight confrontation with the teacher.

> Ms. Dumas now leans or eases over in a slow controlled manner and places the palms of her two hands flat on the far sides of Nancy's desk and paperwork, and takes two relaxing breaths. The teacher remains palms-down on Nancy's desk and watches with unwavering eye contact.

Most people have around them personal space, much like an invisible three-foot bubble, in which they feel safe. When this space is invaded by others, the person becomes emotionally uncomfortable and potentially threatened. When we touch students, place our hands on what they touch, or place our face inches from theirs, we burst their bubble and the protective safety of their personal space. We force them to back down or resist (fight or flight). This will be especially true for adolescents filled with raging hormones, who are struggling with their own sexual and physical body changes and their new interest in intimacy with members of the opposite sex.

Ms. Dumas, in a slow controlled manner, stands erect, does her best imitation of Queen Victoria, takes two relaxing breaths, and then slowly moves behind and between the two girls. Ms. Dumas eases between them, placing her elbow on Nancy's desk. She leans over, meeting Nancy in a face-to-face, eyeball-to-eyeball fixed stare, with her back to Martha. She creates a wall between Nancy and Martha, and points to Nancy's paper.

When visually confronting a misbehaving student, space distances may be classified as *proximity-far* for across the room, *proximity-near* when we are within three feet or at the edge of the student's "comfort bubble," and *proximity-intimate* when we are inches from the student's face. The teacher actually uses these three distances as a technique of signaling the student to desist and return to work, and escalates the intrusion by doing a slow *High Noon* walk. The teacher begins a process of "closing space" and begins to turn up the heat in the confrontational process. The slow movement of walking and all other easing movements are to permit the student to have much time to recognize and understand the challenge, and to enable the teacher to maintain and body-telegraph a calm message of "I am in charge" and "I mean business."

STEPS IN LIMIT SETTING

Step 1: Eyes in the Back of Your Head

Ms. Dumas has just finished teaching a new concept to her algebra class and has assigned the class to do seatwork to practice applying this concept. She moves around the room *(working the crowd)* and checks each student's work. She hears muffled whispers and the slight movement of a chair coming from the far side of the room. She looks up *(check it out)* to see Nancy's eyes appear above her textbook and then disappear behind it. Again there are whispers, and Ms. Dumas sees Nancy physically turn toward Martha, her neighbor. Nancy is busy giggling and talking to Martha, who appears to be writing. Nancy is clearly off task, requiring Ms. Dumas to take some action to get her to use the seatwork time constructively.

Effective teachers have "with-it-ness," meaning that at all times they are perceptually and cognitively aware as to what is occurring in their classroom. They repeatedly check out what students are doing. To be effective in doing this, the teacher must be careful where she "parks her body." If Ms. Dumas is helping Mark and is bent over with her head down and her back to 80 percent of the classroom, she will not hear Luis tearing out a piece of notebook paper to make spitballs, or see Stan creep among the desks to snatch Harold's ball cap from his back pocket, or notice Angelica abandoning her math problems to snap open her purse in order to put on more makeup for the thousandth time.

The with-it teacher "parks her body" with her back to the closest wall so that with her peripheral vision she can see as much of the classroom as possible. A good classroom arrangement will facilitate the teacher's body positioning. Additionally, the teacher must never get "lost" perceptually in the one student she is helping. If one student is standing before you, you may step back, take him by the shoulder, and turn him around so you are able to look at him and over his shoulder at the class at the same time. If you are bending down looking at a student's papers on his desk, you must heighten your hearing awareness to make up for your loss of vision. You should then periodically bob your head up like radar to make a 270-degree scan of the classroom so that you can make quick eye contact with any student who is giving some thought to gambling on a fun off-task behavior. If the desks and other classroom furniture are arranged properly, and if you position your body with your back to the wall and facing students, you are now in the best position to see what is happening in the classroom.

Jones's use of the term *check it out* means simply that the teacher needs to keep her broad perceptions running, even when she is focused on one student or activity, and she must "surface" regularly to scan and check things out (see Figure 9–3).

Step 2: Terminate Instruction

With her body still bent over the student's desk, Ms. Dumas takes two more relaxing breaths and stretches her neck up to scan the classroom, only to discover that Nancy is again off task. Staying down, she (1) excuses herself from Mark, the student she was helping; (2) takes two more relaxing breaths, and (3) straightens at a deliberate pace, slightly faster than slow motion, to an upright position, where for the second time she takes on the "I am not amused" facial expression. She then (4) stares directly at Nancy across the room while (5) placing her hands behind her back *(body-telegraphing)*.

Proximity: Far			
Start: "Working the crowd" (eyes, modulation of voice, and moving)	Step 1: Eyes in the back of your head (with-it-ness)	Step 2: Terminate instruction	Step 3: Turn, look, and say name. Student response: smiley face or back talk
Modality (felt by student)	Hearing	Visual	Visual and auditory

FIGURE 9–3 Jones Positive Discipline Model: High Profile (Visual) Desist

Discipline comes before instruction is the Jones model's cardinal rule. The teacher is instructing Mark at his seat and is just getting to the point of closure on her mini-lesson when a discipline situation surfaces. The teacher may think, "I will just ignore Nancy for another minute until I finish this instruction with Mark, and then I will go and take care of the problem involving Nancy." No, no, no! The students will then learn that instruction is more important than classroom discipline, and once learned, they will take every opportunity to misbehave with nickel-and-dime misbehavior; they will gamble that they can get away with it, and the teacher will get little instruction done in the future. Pay now with small change, or pay later with big dollars to remediate the problem. Step 2 requires the teacher to apologize to the student (i.e., Mark) and tell him you are done with him for the moment, and then "announce" that you are about to escalate your power by dealing with the misbehavior.

Step 3: Turn, Look, and Say the Student's Name

Ms. Dumas (1) stands fully erect, (2) turns her body and feet so that she is *squared off* with Nancy, (3) takes two controlled *relaxing breaths,* and (4) attempts to make eye contact with Nancy, who is not looking in her direction. Ms. Dumas's voice (5) broadcasts across the classroom, "Nancy," but there is no response from the girl. Again she calls, "Uh-h, Nancy." The neighbor hears and sees Ms. Dumas's cues, and signals Nancy to look in the teacher's direction. Nancy now makes eye contact with Ms. Dumas and sees the teacher looking straight at her. She wiggles in her chair and turns her upper body toward Ms. Dumas, but her lower body (knees and feet) still face her neighbor. She picks up her pencil *(pseudo-compliance: pencil posturing)* and places it on her paper as if to write. She looks again to see Ms. Dumas still holding the same

Proximity: Near		Proximity: Intimate		
Step 4: Walk to the edge of student's desk (closing space)	Step 5: Prompt, break the "comfort bubble" of omnipotence (what they touch)	Step 6: Palms (what they touch)	Step 7: Camping out in front elbow down	Step 8: Camping out from behind (one may also consider "Moving Out" as a Step 9) elbow down, put up wall
Visual	Visual and touch	Visual and touch	Visual, touch, and smell	Visual, touch, smell and hearing

FIGURE 9–3 (continued)

unwavering eye contact. Nancy meets Ms. Dumas' eye contact directly and smiles at her with an open-mouth-and-teeth smile, with her head slightly cocked and her eyebrows raised *("smiley face")*. The endearing smile is one that would encourage anyone to automatically or reflexively smile back, but Ms. Dumas holds her same upright posture. She maintains the same visual lock with Nancy but returns Nancy's smiling overture with a flat facial expression that clearly communicates, "I am not amused!" or "I am bored!" while taking two more *relaxing breaths.*

Nancy is far from being an endearing student and would not be at the top of Ms. Dumas's list for an "Outstanding Citizen" award. In fact, she has just disrupted the very hard and important work the teacher was doing with Mark. If there was any legal possibility of getting away with it, at this moment she would march over there and tear Nancy's face off. This is Ms. Dumas's reptilian brain speaking!

The teacher in Step 3 is now fighting biology, trying to control herself so that she does not *go brain stemmed* or *go chemical* and lose out to a fight or flight reflex triggered by Nancy's behavior. This step requires the teacher to act out a drama with clearly defined choreographed movements, but with no lines—*this is a non-speaking part.*

Turn and Face

The teacher is to stand and turn around completely and face the student in a square stance, which means that the teacher's feet are parallel and facing the student. If Ms. Dumas has one foot pointed to Nancy and the other foot pointed in a second direction, making an L shape, experts in nonverbal behavior would say this body posture is ambivalent and will body-telegraph that the teacher is not committed to the confrontation with Nancy.

Look Them in the Eye

Make unwavering eye contact with the misbehaving student and do not drop the stare. If she is not looking, say her name in a flat nonhostile voice. Again, in contrast, if Ms. Dumas drops her eyes, she communicates subservience and fear.

Teacher's Facial Expression

The smiling exchange between two individuals speaks volumes. If one person makes eye contact and the second smiles, this smile is seen in the animal kingdom as a submission response that occurs when one signals capitulation. The dominant individual smiles back and the communication is "I want to be a friend" and "Yes, I wish to return your friendship." When a smile does not occur, we have a power confrontation between two individuals. The teacher using positive discipline wishes to communicate that the classroom is her territory, she means business and is in control, and she will use the eye signal to establish this dominance.

Again, in confronting Nancy, Ms. Dumas is struggling to control the fight or flight response, which causes her eyes to widen and her teeth to clench, producing a fight or flight face. To stop this from occurring, Jones suggests that the teacher permit her face to relax and unclench the teeth by becoming "slack-jawed." The teacher is advised, while standing and staring, to take her tongue and curl it back in her mouth until she can touch the beginning of the soft tissue at the back of the mouth. This opens up the jaw and creates the "slack jaw" effect, ensuring that in a confrontation the teacher will not grit her teeth as a result of fight or flight reflex.

The student, under the heat of eye contact, does a "silly" smile, which is described as an open-mouth-and-teeth smile with a slight cock of the head and raised eyebrows, much as a baby might smile at his parents. The *smiley face* communicates to the adult from the child, "Look at me! Aren't I cute and adorable and don't you just love me!" The teacher is advised to return the silly smile with a flat facial expression to send a message, "I am not amused" (a sentiment often associated with the staid face of Queen Victoria of England) or "I am bored and will wait right here until you comply." At the same time, the teacher should maintain eye contact, providing the visual heat.

Additional Body Cues
Every part of the body communicates and telegraphs, and it is difficult to hide internal tension. Jones suggests taking a wide foot stance and placing the hands, which are normally a give-away for tension, behind the body and clasping them together. Simply stand as relaxed as possible. The teacher resembles a baseball umpire at this point.

Saying the Student's Name
If Ms. Dumas cannot get the acknowledgment and attention of the misbehaving student, she broadcasts to the student across the classroom by saying only her first name, using a flat nonhostile manner: "Nancy. Uh-h, Nancy."

Ms. Dumas now has the Queen Victoria stance established. She stands, turns, squares off, goes slack-jawed, and says the student's first name. What is critical in this is that all of these actions are taken at a speed just slightly faster than if in slow motion. Normally, when the teacher wants to "rip off Nancy's face" she would march off in sudden, quick, and intense actions, which are not actions communicating confidence and control. *Slower is better. Calmness is strength and communicates power.*[4]

Relaxing Breaths
Any teaching of how to self-master tension and control emotional and physical action—such as relaxation therapy, stress management, and prepared childbirth training—involves teaching the person to breathe properly during a stressful situation. This is done by taking two controlled, slow, shallow breaths, filling about 20 percent of your lung capacity and letting it out slowly, then resting for a few seconds and repeating the sequence. Normally, a breathing coach counts while you inhale and exhale. The exhaling is critical, relaxing the body and mind and slowing down the pace of all actions.

As you read this, you may have little appreciation of the value of controlled breathing, or even find it humorous. ("Wha-at? I need to be taught how to breathe? Ha!") However, controlled breathing is the anchor and central technique on which is based all control in a stressful confrontational Jones discipline situation.

In on-site training sessions taught personally by Fredric Jones, all of the techniques—including relaxed breathing—are taught to teachers through a process of *Say* (describes the technique), *Show* (models it), and *Do* (has groups of two teachers enact the techniques). Considerable time is spent on training "how to breathe." If you wish to put the Jones positive discipline techniques into practice, you are advised to find a person who has had prepared childbirth training and have that person explain, model, and coach you through the process until you feel comfortable and in command of these techniques. The vignette with Ms. Dumas and Nancy shows how the teacher needs to punctuate every new action by first taking two relaxing breaths and then moving slowly in a controlled manner.

To Move In or Not to Move In

Nancy sees Ms. Dumas and quickly returns to her *"pencil posturing."* Ms. Dumas takes two more relaxing breaths and waits. Minutes, or more likely seconds, click by with Nancy being aware of receiving visual heat from Ms. Dumas. Like a boiling pot, Nancy becomes active in an array of actions—she tears out a sheet of paper, takes a second pencil from her purse, folds the paper, and appears to put her pencil to paper *(pseudo-compliance),* all for the purpose of convincing Ms. Dumas that she is now working and that the teacher can turn off the visual heat.

This time Ms. Dumas is not fooled. She takes two more of her controlled breaths and then—while still not breaking her visual stare—begins to walk slowly across the room straight toward Nancy. She moves with a gait straight out of *High Noon.* She stops and squares off inches in front of Nancy's desk, again assuming *the* posture with her hands behind her back and her face with the flat Queen Victoria "I am not amused" expression. Finally, her eyes are fixed and are looking directly down at Nancy. Ms. Dumas takes her two relaxing breaths and waits. Nancy responds, "Wha-a-t?"

Once you have broadcast the student's name and made eye contact, your next decision is to determine whether the student has "gotten the message" and is complying or whether you need to escalate the confrontation by "closing space"—moving spatially closer to the misbehaving student. The student will perform a host of *pseudo-compliance* actions, such as *pencil posturing,* paper shuffling, or pretending to read, in an attempt to convince you that he or she is now working and to get out of your visual fix. One way of determining if the student is complying is to compare the positions of the student's upper and lower body.

Nancy now makes eye contact with Ms. Dumas and sees the teacher looking straight at her; she wiggles in her chair and turns her upper body toward Ms.

Dumas but her lower body (knees and feet) still face her neighbor. She picks up her pencil *(pseudo-compliance: pencil posturing)* and places it on her paper as if to write. She looks again to see Ms. Dumas still maintaining the same unwavering eye contact.

Ms. Dumas notices that under the table Nancy's lower body, especially her knees, is still pointing to the neighbor who was the target of her talking. This position seems to say, "I'll return to my talking once I get you out of my face."

The student's upper-body position is for show and attempts to convince the teacher that the student is cooperating, but the lower body—with the knees still pointing to the neighbor—nonverbally shows the student's real intention. Until the student moves her legs under her desk, real work will not be started.

Nancy turns her lower body so her legs are now fully under her desk, and does a second, third, and fourth algebra problem while Ms. Dumas is *camped out*. When Nancy is halfway through the second line of problems, Ms. Dumas speaks to her for the first time, "Thank you, Nancy." The teacher smiles.

The teacher will need to read the student's posture messages and not be fooled by the pseudo-compliance behavior in the discipline poker game. If the student does comply and returns to work, the incident is over and the teacher returns to her previous activity. The basic goal, always, in limit setting is to *calm the students and get them back on task*. We would like to avoid any behaviors that would cause an *adrenaline dump* or a *fight or flight response* in the misbehaving student or other class members, because after such negative incidents it can take 20 to 30 minutes for them to clear this adrenaline from their bodies and be relaxed enough to do real work. *Do not go any further with the limit-setting sequence than is required to produce the desired result.*[5] However, if the student does not comply, and is playing a game of discipline poker with you, you may be forced to escalate your intervention by *closing space—moving in*.

Step 4: Walk to the Edge of the Student's Desk

This time Ms. Dumas is not fooled. She takes two more of her relaxing breaths and then—while still not breaking her visual stare—begins to walk slowly across the room straight toward Nancy. She moves with a gait straight out of *High Noon*. She stops and squares off inches in front of Nancy's desk, again assuming *the* posture with her hands behind her back and her face with the flat Queen Victoria "I am not amused" expression. Finally her eyes are fixed and are looking directly down at Nancy. Ms. Dumas takes her two relaxing breaths and waits.

The teacher now does a slow walk to the student, never breaking eye contact. She stops when her legs are touching the front of the student's desk, and then assumes the Queen Victoria posture and facial expression. Repeated relaxing breaths are used. Once in front of the desk, the teacher simply waits and permits the student to sizzle in the teacher's visual heat. At any time during the limit-setting steps, if the teacher feels that the student has now learned that the teacher means business and has gone back to work, the teacher stops the escalation and advances to the process of *moving out.*

At this point the teacher is most likely to get varying forms of *back talk* (helplessness, denying, blaming, etc.), with the student playing a host of recognizable games to divert the teacher from her real behavior and intent. Do not be taken in by these student maneuvers, especially the helpless statements that suggest the student does not understand the assignment and needs your help—this is a distracting ploy.

One of the most difficult forms of back talk is profanity. It is stressful to deal with, but you must not permit the student to control you with such offensive language. Stay with your passive but unwavering eye contact, and deal with the profanity later, being certain that the offending student is not allowed to get away with it.

> Martha, the neighbor, now joins Nancy's power team and attempts to gang up on Ms. Dumas, stating, "Yeah, get out of her face. Are you queer or something? F--- off!!" *(back talk: profanity).*

When students become verbally abusive, hold your Queen Victoria stance and eye contact. Keep repeating your relaxing breaths, but now add a *focal point* in order not to hear the harsh words the student is hurling at you. Select a small point (focal point) on the student's forehead and stare at that point. This permits your mind to bring forth a pleasant scene and mentally leave this confrontational situation—in essence, allow your mind to take a brief vacation. Remember the baseball umpire. Do not respond to any form of back talk no matter how clever or offensive, but stand your ground and be prepared to "camp out." *Camping out* means a willingness, communicated by nonverbal actions, to spend as much time as needed to win in this power game and to get the student back to work. (*Note:* If in your judgment there is any chance that closing space is likely to cause the student to assault you, stop and drop the limit-setting approach. You will need to move to a back-up system, which will be described later.)

Teachers, by their nature, are verbal people. We make our living by talking, but Jones would say, "No, not at this time!" Do not speak—say nothing—shut up—keep quiet. There are no words that we can use to be effective in this confrontation. It is the power of the teacher's calmness, eye contact, and use of spatial proximity that will induce the student to capitulate and get back to work. Jones says, "Any fool may speak, but it takes two people to speak foolishly." If we venture to verbally debate or discuss using words to answer the student's back talk, we will be foolish and will be hooked by the student into playing the game on his or her ground. We would produce "silly" talk and lose the confrontation. Keep quiet—do not speak—shut up!

Step 5: Prompt

Nancy whines, "I wasn't doing anything. Wha-a-t? *(back talk: denial)* Martha wanted a pencil *(back talk: blaming)*, that's all." Ms. Dumas maintains her posture and stares. Nancy drops her eyes and becomes passive. Ms. Dumas reaches out with her right hand, turns Nancy's textbook to page 45, and points to the first problem *(prompt)*. She then returns to the same upright Queen Victoria stare.

Having moved across the room to stand before the student's desk, the teacher is now in new territory *(proximity-near)*. She is standing at the edge of the student's *comfort bubble* but has not invaded it. The teacher now breaks that comfort bubble by reaching in with her hand and signaling a prompt to an action that she wants. She touches objects that are the student's possessions. "Ms. Dumas reaches out with her right hand, turns Nancy's textbook to page 45, and points to the first problem." With the nonverbal action of hand gestures, she prompts the student to get to work. Again, Ms. Dumas is still holding the unswerving eye contact, repeatedly taking relaxing breaths, and maintaining her posture. If she is successful and the student does begin to work, she can start her steps for *moving out* (described later), but if Ms. Dumas is not successful, she will continue her spatial escalation.

Step: 6: Palms

By reaching into the student's comfort bubble to *prompt,* the teacher now gets into that bubble with the student.

Ms. Dumas notices that under the table Nancy's lower body, especially her knees, is still pointing to the neighbor who was the target of her talking. This position seems to say, "I'll return to my talking once I get you out of my face." Nancy now appears passive and fails to continue. Ms. Dumas leans or eases over in a slow controlled manner and places the palms of her two hands flat on the far sides of Nancy's desk and paper work, and takes two relaxing breaths.

The teacher remains palms-down on Nancy's desk and watches with unwavering eye contact with Nancy *(camping out in front)*. Ms. Dumas is still looking when Nancy again whines, "I don't know how to do this" *(back talk: helplessness)*. Still, Queen Victoria waits before her subject *(camping out in front)*.

The teacher leans over and places her hands palms-down on each side of the student's desk with the student's papers and work between these hands. The *palms* on the desk say to the student, "I am planted here and I will stay until you get back to work." Thus, you are saying you are willing to *camp out in front* as long as it takes. Remember to keep taking your relaxing breaths and maintaining your eye contact, now from a distance of approximately one foot from the student's face (nose to nose). At this point the new modalities of smell and even the sound of your breathing join the modality of looking. This *proximity-intimate* is generally very unnerving for the adolescent student.

Caution: The female teacher must be careful to wear high-buttoned blouses so that when she leans over she does not reveal herself. The male teacher dealing with a female student wearing an open-top blouse should stop at the previous step and not use palms down or get closer, in order to avoid the improper appearance that he is looking down the student's blouse. The adolescent will find this close spatial proximity unnerving and will blame your actions on voyeurism. We don't want to give the student this type of excuse. The teacher who cannot advance further on the steps will be forced to go to the back-up system, which will be described in detail later.

Step 7: Camping Out in Front

We are now at *palms* and the student is "mouthing off" with a barrage of *back talk*. After a period of time, the teacher now eases in by lifting one hand, bending an elbow, and placing weight on that elbow, which is now on one edge of the desk top *(camp out in front)*. The teacher maintains the relaxing breathing, keeps the unwavering eye contact, keeps quiet, and waits.

Step 8: Camping Out from Behind

If there is a second neighboring student involved—and there usually is when talking is involved—most likely the second student will join the first student's *back talk* to gang up on you.

> "Martha asked me for a pencil. I was only giving her a pencil" *(back talk: blaming)*. Martha, the neighbor, now joins Nancy's power team and attempts to gang up on Ms. Dumas, stating, "Yeah, get out of her face. Are you queer or something? F--- off!!" *(back talk: profanity)*.
>
> Ms. Dumas, in a slow controlled manner, stands erect, does her Queen Victoria, takes two relaxing breaths, and then slowly moves behind and between the girls. Ms. Dumas eases between the girls, placing her elbow on Nancy's desk. She leans over and meets Nancy in a face-to-face, eyeball-to-eyeball fixed stare, with her back to Martha *(camping out from behind)*. She creates a wall between Nancy and Martha, thus splitting up the gang of two.

When two students gang up on you in a power game, you will not win if you deal with both of them at the same time. You must divide and conquer, by putting up a wall between them and dealing with one student at a time.

Walk slowly, remembering always to take two relaxing breaths between any action, and ease in between the two students, placing your elbow and weight on the desk of the originally misbehaving student. Then move slightly between the desks, showing your back to the second student, who is now walled off from the power interaction between you and the first student. You are now *camping out from behind*. Keep up the relaxing breathing, keep the unwavering eye contact, keep quiet, and wait.

By this point—though often long before now—the student has capitulated and begins to work. You then need to begin *moving out*, which is also a controlled process of steps. Before we move out, however, let's deal with the second student.

> Nancy turns her lower body so her legs are now fully under her desk, and does a second, third, and fourth algebra problem while Ms. Dumas is *camped out*. When Nancy is halfway through the second line of problems, Ms. Dumas speaks to her for the first time, "Thank you, Nancy." The teacher smiles, then picks up her elbow and turns around to face Martha. She places her other elbow and weight on Martha's desk. Martha does not look up and is obviously working like an eager beaver on her algebra problems. Ms. Dumas smiles and says, "Thank you, Martha." Queen Victoria-Dumas begins to ease out from this confrontation; she slowly stands erect (*moving out*), breathes, turns, and walks to the front of Martha's desk. She takes two relaxing breaths, assumes the royal poise, and looks directly at Martha. Ms. Dumas slowly walks away from the girls (*moving out*), but first she takes five or six steps, stops, turns, takes two relaxing breaths, and looks at Nancy and then Martha. Both students are now too busy to look up.

You thank the first offender for her compliance—a technique in the moving-out steps—and now turn around by changing elbows and placing the second elbow and your weight on the second student's desk. You begin with eye contact with the second student, and prompt her if necessary. Keep up the relaxing breathing, keep the unwavering eye contact, keep quiet, and wait. Once you are assured that the second student has gone back to work, you may now follow your moving-out steps, thanking the second student before you leave.

Step 9: Moving Out

If you are relieved that you have won the confrontation and go rushing back to the student you were originally helping, this quick departure can be interpreted by Nancy and Martha as, "Well, she was a big fake after all. Look at her running away from us!" You must use the moving-out process step by step, in a slow, skilled manner or you will lose everything you have established to this point.

In a pace just faster than slow motion, stand and begin to move back to your original position (where you were working with a student across the room). But stop, posture, breathe, and make eye contact at each of the proximity points of *near* (at the edge of student's desk) and *far* (across the room).

> Ms. Dumas slowly walks away from the girls (*moving out*), but first she moves to the front of each girl's desk, stops, turns, takes two relaxing breaths, and looks at Nancy and then Martha. Both students are now too busy to look up. Ms. Dumas walks back to Mark, the student she was helping, but before bend-

ing over to help, she again assumes the Queen Victoria pose and looks at Nancy and Martha. After finally being reassured, she takes two more relaxing breaths and bends over to help Mark, placing herself beside Mark but again in direct view of Nancy and Martha, as well as the remainder of the class *(tail-hook)*.

The visual proximity confrontation process is now completed, but will continue to be maintained through the teacher's walking about the classroom looking and checking on the students' work *(working the crowd)*. When confronted for compliance in our example, Nancy and Martha began a conscious and unconscious series of back-talk maneuvers to take Ms. Dumas down a blind alley toward powerlessness and defeat. This back talk took the following forms:

- *Helplessness:* "I don't know how to do this."
- *Denial:* "I wasn't doing anything. Wha-at?"
- *Blaming:* "Martha wanted a pencil—that's all!"
- *Accusing the teacher of professional incompetence:* "You went over this so quickly I didn't understand it."
- *Excusing the teacher to leave:* "Yeah, get out of her face."
- *Insult:* "Are you queer or something?"
- *Profanity:* "F--- off!"

Other forms of back talk that do not appear as such to most teachers include:

- *Crying:* The student attempts to get our sympathy.
- *Compliments:* The student makes flattering statements to the teacher.
- *Tangential statements:* The student asks a question about a topic not under discussion.
- *Pushing you aside:* When the teacher puts her hands on the desk, palms down, the student pushes them aside and off the desk.
- *Romance:* The student actually kisses the teacher or makes a sexual overture.

Let's review the summary points:

- Move slowly (slightly faster than slow motion).
- Take two relaxing breaths before and after each action.
- Maintain unwavering eye contact.
- Escalate your power by closing space but be prepared to stop when compliance is established.
- Do not respond to back talk.
- Prompt if necessary.
- Be prepared to use as much time as needed.
- If you must deal with more than one student, put up a "wall" and deal with one at a time.
- Exit or move out in a slow predetermined manner.

- If you anticipate an assault, or any sexual interpretation of your actions by the student, drop limit setting and begin the back-up system.

The steps are:

Step 1: Eyes in the Back of Your Head
Step 2: Terminate Instruction
Step 3: Turn, Look, and Say the Student's Name
Step 4: Walk to the Edge of the Student's Desk
Step 5: Prompt
Step 6: Palms
Step 7: Camping Out in Front
Step 8: Camping Out from Behind
Step 9: Moving Out

Limit Setting on the Wing

Proximity is accountability. Distance is safety.[6] The teacher who has been trained in positive classroom discipline will not be found lecturing from in front of her desk, seated on top of her desk, or seated in a chair. This style of teaching requires the teacher to be on her feet, slowly walking and *working the crowd,* moving among the students who are seated at desks or tables. When walking, or *on the wing,* the teacher is aware of and uses eye contact and proximity to maintain the attentiveness or work activity of each and every student. The walking and looking combination creates a conscious ballet of movement that will bring the teacher in *proximity-far* (as far as 10 feet) and *proximity-near* (at the edge of the 3-foot *comfort bubble* of each student). Periodically, when the teacher bends over to help one student for a few moments, the teacher is in *proximity-intimate.* Throughout the entire class period, students will always feel the presence of the teacher, while the teacher is instructing or even while the student is doing independent seat work.

> After she has helped Mark, Ms. Dumas slowly walks through the students' prearranged desks, traversing an *interior circle* around the classroom as she passes among the working students. She checks on students' work, and passes again before Nancy and Martha. She stops, looks, checks, and, in a voice soft enough that a neighbor cannot hear, makes comments about a particular student's work before moving on *(working the crowd).* In all, she speaks to five to seven students. When she comes to Martha, three minutes before the bell is to ring, she appears to stop, look, check, and comment in a similar fashion *(camouflage),* but this time she whispers a different nonacademic statement: "Martha, after the bell rings, I would like you to stay behind—we need to talk."

In order for the teacher to perform this walking ballet in which she is working the crowd, it is critical to have well-designed staging of the student's desks, chairs, or tables. Traditionally, we think of all classrooms as six rows of five or more chairs, with the teacher's desk before a chalkboard in the front of the classroom. Such a room arrangement, however, puts walls between the teacher and the students and always maintains the teacher at the *far proximity*. Jones arranges the students' desks with an interior loop as a pathway for the teacher to walk through (see Figure 9–4). The use of an interior loop of free floor space where the teacher can walk without obstruction permits easy teacher movement and excellent supervision through the use of proximity and eye contact.

Guidelines for Room Arrangement/Space Use

- Don't let the janitor dictate the desk arrangement.
- Furniture arrangement is best when it puts the least distance and fewest barriers between the teacher and students.
- Place the teacher's desk on the side or in the rear and get the entire class as close as possible to the chalkboard.
- Compact the students' desks together as much as possible.
- The teacher goes to the students; students are not to come and wait for the teacher.
- Place well-behaved, cooperative students in the most distant seats from the teacher.
- Place misbehaving students in the middle of the interior loop and as close to the teacher as possible.[7]

THE BACK-UP SYSTEM

When one student is a chronic discipline problem and the limit-setting techniques fail despite being correctly applied, you are now required to drop limit setting and move to something else. That something else is the use of either a back-up system or omission training (OT). The back-up system will be discussed here. Omission training, as well as the incentive program and responsibility training—the final legs of the discipline "chair" necessary for the total Jones discipline program to work—will be discussed later.

Typically, most schools by default have a back-up system that is neither systematic nor well thought out, but applies certain traditional sanctions to students, generally arranged in increasing severity. They typically are, in sequence:

- Warning
- Conference with student
- Time out, being sent to the office, detention
- Conference with parent
- Conference with teacher, parent, and principal or vice principal
- In-school suspension
- Out-of-school suspension (1 day)
- Out-of-school suspension (3 days)
- Expulsion and/or a special program such as "continuation school"

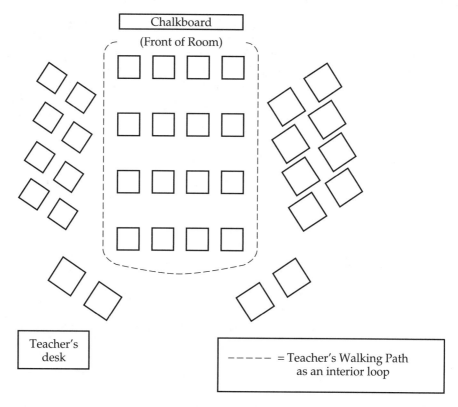

FIGURE 9–4   Positive Discipline Classroom Arrangement

Most of these progressively punitive sanctions are overused by the majority of schools, and simply do not work. They are self-perpetuating and do not "self-eliminate." On pages 260–265 of his book, Jones gives a solid description of why these sanctions fail based on behavioral theory, reinforcement scheduling, and reinforcement error.[8] His explanation is a "must read" for any teacher and school continuing to use such useless traditional practices. Jones simply and concisely summarizes what these practices are really saying to a chronically misbehaving student. Jones's message can be paraphrased as, "You know what we're going to do to you? We're going to send you to the office, where you'll have nothing to do but watch all the activity that goes on there. And then we may have to suspend you—to deprive you of the opportunity to sit in your math class, your English class, your social studies class, your science class. In other words, we're going to punish you by making you go out and have a good time."

Essentially, this says to the misbehaving child that if he escalates the level of his obnoxious behavior, authorities will have no choice but to grant him freedom. The sanctions basically fail because the teacher and school have little or no system or technology and they are blundering through the application of these sanctions.

Jones proposes a methodology by defining three levels of the back-up system as Level 1: Small Back-Up Responses, which take place in the classroom and are private between the teacher and student; Level 2: Medium Back-Up Responses, which are mostly carried out by the teacher but are now more public; and Level 3: Large Back-Up Responses, a time-costly process that will involve high public visibility and the participation of others such as a counselor, the principal, or even the judicial system.

Back-Up Responses in the Classroom

After she has helped Mark, Ms. Dumas slowly walks through the students' prearranged desks, traversing an *interior circle* around the classroom as she passes among the working students. She checks on students' work, and passes again before Nancy and Martha. She stops, looks, checks, and, in a voice soft enough that a neighbor cannot hear, makes comments about a particular student's work before moving on *(working the crowd)*. In all, she speaks to five to seven students. When she comes to Martha, three minutes before the bell is to ring, she appears to stop, look, check, and comment in a similar fashion (camouflage), but this time she whispers a different nonacademic statement: "Martha, after the bell rings, I would like you to stay behind—we need to talk" (moved to *Back-up System Level #1: Small Response—"Ear Warning"*).

Minutes later, the bell rings and the students depart, passing Ms. Dumas as she stands at the door. When Martha approaches, the teacher signals her to move to a nearby desk, then closes the door to the now empty classroom *(private meeting)*. It is time for Ms. Dumas to deal with Martha regarding her use

---

Out-of-School-Suspension

Kid, if you gross out a teacher, do you know what we are going to do? The teacher is going to give you a reprimand, and we know how much respect you have for those. And, kid, if you do it again, we are liable to involve your parents, and let you know how supportive they usually are. And, kid, if you gross out the teacher again, do you know what we are going to do? We are going to send you to the office! And you know what happens down there? Well neither does anyone else. But wait a second, kid! If you persist in this behavior and gross out another teacher again, do you know what we are going to do with you? We are going to have no choice but to suspend you for a whole day. You will have to give up learning in favor of hanging around the streets, playing video games to your heart's content, and perhaps making some money on the side. But wait a second, kid! That's not the end of it. If you keep up this behavior, do you know what you are going to force us to do? You are going to force us to give you 3 days off! Do you hear that? For 3 solid days you will be denied access to your math class, your English class, your social studies class, your science class and all study halls. Our ultimate weapon is to force you to go out and have a good time.

Source: F. Jones, *Positive Classroom Discipline.* New York: McGraw-Hill, p. 265. Reprinted with permission.

of profanity. Ms. Dumas has not forgotten Martha's words, "Yeah, get out of her face. Are you queer or something? F - - - off!!"

After-Class Meeting: Example 1

MS. DUMAS: "Martha, the use of such harsh language toward me today suggests to me that you may be angry or that there is some problem occurring with you. Can I help?"

MARTHA: "Well, things are not good at home these days. My father was arrested last night. We were at the jail all night, and I'm really exhausted. I don't know what got into me today."

MS. DUMAS: "Well, sometimes no sleep and such problems do rattle our nerves and make us edgy. An apology would be welcomed by me!"

MARTHA: "Well, I am REALLY sorry. I don't know why I acted so rude to you."

MS. DUMAS: "Your apology is accepted, and if things continue to be rough for you, I can extend your deadline for the class project. You also may wish to stop by and talk with the school counselor, Mr. Evans. I'll write you a pass to get out of study hall so you can talk to him."

After-Class Meeting: Example 2

MS. DUMAS: "Martha, the use of such harsh language toward me today suggests to me that you may be angry or that there is some problem occurring with you. Can I help?"

MARTHA: "F - - - off, Dumas, get out of my face!"

MS. DUMAS: "Martha, I will not accept such rudeness from you. This is your warning. If you swear at me again, I will need to take actions that you will not like and that I would prefer not to take. It is now your choice. I would prefer to settle this calmly between the two of us. But it is your choice. Do you wish to talk to me about anything that can be causing you to be so angry?"

MARTHA: "NO!"

MS. DUMAS: "Okay, you have had your warning. You may now go to class. I will be watching your behavior in the future, and I hope that we have settled this matter with this warning."

(Martha departs.)

Small Back-Up Responses

The Level 1: Small Back-Up Response is a quiet and private confrontation between the teacher and the misbehaving student. The teacher continues to *work the crowd,* walking around the classroom to supervise and using eye contact and proximity to keep the students working. The teacher periodically speaks softly to the various students about their work, which is her standard routine. When the teacher wants to use a back-up response by warning the student about the misbehavior, she first camouflages her intent by stopping at three or four students' desks to talk about academic matters. But when she comes to the misbehaving student, she issues a nonpublic warning: "Nancy, this is the second time class has been disrupted by your talking. If this occurs again, I will need to think about taking some actions to get you to stop this." *(ear warning)* The teacher stands, makes eye contact, assumes the Queen Victoria pose, and then moves on to another student. The *ear warning* is not heard by any neighbors, thus is done in such a *nonpublic manner* that the student does not need to act back in order to save face. There are a number of methods of warning the student without going public.

Examples of Ear Warnings

1. "I am sorry that I have to be back here again regarding your note passing (relaxing breath, and eye contact). If I have to return again, I will take action. This is your warning; do you understand?"
2. "I want this behavior to stop immediately (relaxing breath, and eye contact). This is your first and only warning. I will be watching to see if this will occur again."
3. "Stop (the action) now and I will say no more. Do it again and I will return to deal with it."

Three more examples may be useful.

1. Mr. Granger has a filing box on his desk with 3" × 5" cards containing the addresses of the students' parents. The teacher meets the misbehaving student's eyes, removes the student's card from the box, sets it on the edge of the desk, and points to the card as a warning (as if to say: "Stop or I will call your parents").
2. A student has misbehaved. Mrs. Arthur goes to her desk, takes out two sheets of paper, and writes a short note to the parents telling of the student's misbehaviors. The note is placed in an addressed envelope and then taped to the front of the student's desk. "Michael, this is a letter to your mother regarding your behavior today. I will leave it here all week, and if you can stop this behavior, I will let you tear it up in front of me. If this behavior occurs again, I will mail the letter and telephone your mother two days later."
3. Mr. O'Brien places a folded 3" × 5" card on a student's desk. When the student opens it, it simply reads, "Stop!"

The idea of the ear warning is to get the student to stop while still saving face. If necessary, a *private meeting* would be held between the student and the teacher out of the view and hearing of peers, as Ms. Dumas did with Martha regarding her swearing. In these conferences, we teachers have two choices: either think and talk or warn and deliver. In the after-class meeting with Martha in example 1, we see the teacher talking to Martha supportively and listening and thinking about what she is hearing from the girl. In example 2, we see the "warn and deliver" actions by Ms. Dumas; she warns Martha about the swearing and is prepared to "deliver" if it occurs again.

Quiet Time.　Quiet time, different from time out (which will be explained under Level 2: Medium Back-Up Responses), is a technique that requests that the student go to an out-of-the-way area and become quiet and reflect on his or her actions and decide to change. The time should not exceed 5 to 10 minutes, and it is hoped this physical action will serve as another form of warning for the student.

> As part of the her working-the-crowd supervision techniques, the teacher whispers in Nancy's ear "Nancy, you are having a hard time staying at your work and you're about to get in deep 'doggy doo' with me. I would like you to have some quiet time, to think this over and decide to change your behavior. Go to that chair at the back of the room to have some quiet time, and I will signal you in five minutes. Then I want you to return to your seat ready to work."

Medium Back-Up Responses

> Mrs. Alda has arranged to have a professor of ornithology from a local university give a guest lecture in her biology class this morning. Bird study is Mrs. Alda's passion, and she is both excited and a little nervous about having such a renowned national expert in her classroom. During the lecture, the guest demonstrates a number of bird calls to the class, to the amusement of Robin. In the middle of each call, Robin erupts into a large belly laugh that stops the demonstration. She then leans over to her neighbors and makes odd whistling and mouthing sounds, causing everyone on that side of the room to "crack up." Mrs. Alda walks to the classroom door and signals with one finger for Robin to follow her. Robin, a freshman, is quickly escorted to the end of the hall and placed on a lone chair at the back of Mr. Fox's senior advanced Latin class. She is now in time out.

Medium back-up responses are those sanctions that have traditionally been used in schools, including time out, loss of privileges, parent conferences, and detention. The processes of the medium back-up responses are still primarily carried out by the classroom teacher, without the aid of school administrators. These methods are considered risky. They may produce feelings of hostility and nonacceptance in students, they are time consuming, they have a high probability of failing, and they are much more public. So, before the teacher moves to a medium back-up response, it is best to revisit the practices of limit setting, omission training, and incentive program to see if those processes are working; if they are, the teacher should make all efforts not to advance to the more risky medium back-up. Medium back-up responses are not ray guns that we quickly pull out when the occasion arises and zap the misbehaving student. They must be well thought out, used systematically, and done in as *private or semi-private* a manner as possible.

The rule of thumb is to deliver a nonpublic warning to students in preparation for a medium back-up response, as far as it can be done. Don't go public; stay private. Putting the student's name on the board as a warning, for example, would be public and destructive to the student-teacher relationship, and eventually will cost the student. Use private talks out of the view and hearing of peers. When creeping up to an escalation to medium back-up responses, always reexamine to see if your entire management system is working—perhaps you are moving too fast and short-cutting your other systems.

The following are some medium-level sanctions listed by Jones:

1. Time out in the classroom
2. Time out in a colleague's classroom
3. Public warning
4. Threat
5. Being sent to the hall
6. Detention after school
7. Loss of privilege
8. Parent conference

Items considered to be very poor practice are:

9. Lowering the student's grade
10. Extra homework[9]

Let's see how Jones would view each of these sanctions.

1. and 2. *Time Out in the Classroom/in a Colleague's Classroom:* Time out is the temporary removal of a student from an activity as a consequence of his inappropriate behavior, usually not to exceed 5 minutes. Normally, the place of time out is a neutral isolated chair. Jones feels this is an overused and misused process, with many teachers unaware of the requirements for time out to be truly effective. They are:

a. *Rules and expectations spelled out clearly in advance:* We cannot sanction a student for rules that we have not taught or spelled out to them. Mrs. Alda would have been advised to have introduced the concept of how guests are treated when they visit the classroom, with specific rules taught in a Say, Show, and Do lesson. Many teachers may have an attitude of "Well, they are freshmen. They should know how to act by now." This is not necessarily true; rules governing behavior must be taught.

b. *Consequences for unacceptable behavior described and demonstrated in advance:* Again, as part of the teaching of the rules, specific consequences need to be clearly described in advance, giving basic *prior notice-due process* requirements and consideration (see Chapter 6).

c. *Selection of an appropriate time out place that denies the student substitute means of reward:* Placing the student on a seat in the front office, with a jolly talkative receptionist and the interesting comings and goings of parents and visitors, is not an appropriate location because it rewards the student by providing interesting actions to observe. The time-out location should not be a hostile or uncomfortable environment—it should be boring.

d. *Early response to the problem behavior with limit setting followed by warning:* The ornithologist has made his first bird call, and Robin's laughter is excessive and disruptive. Unnoticed by the guest and most of the students listening to the lecture, Mrs. Alda stands, takes two relaxing breaths, moves to catch Robin's eye, puts on her Queen Victoria face and posture, stares, and breathes again *(limit setting)*. Robin sees Mrs. Alda 's nonverbal communication but continues to ignore it and disrupts again. Mrs. Alda takes two more relaxing breaths and slowly moves around the room, stopping behind Robin *(moves in—closes space)* at the edge of her *comfort bubble* and waits while taking two more breaths *(camping out)*. Again, Robin disrupts, this time by putting her hand under her arm pit and making a distracting sound, to the delight of her neighbors. Mrs. Alda takes two relaxing breaths, leans over, and gives Robin an *ear warning:* "This is your only warning. Stop the noise making and silly laughing and stop disrupting our guest. If this occurs again, I will point to the door, and I want you to get up quietly and go to the hall and wait for me at the water fountain. This is your choice" (dumps *limit-setting* and escalates to *small back-up response*).

Five minutes later, the guest is making duck calls with a wooden block, which at first brings normal minor giggles and smiles from the students and the guest. But Robin does not stop at that, continuing her silly laughter and attempting to bring the class's attention to herself. Mrs. Alda moves to where she can make eye contact with Robin, and, without anybody in the room seeing her action, points one finger at the door *(prompting)*. A few minutes later, Mrs. Alda quietly exits the classroom, collects Robin from the water fountain, places her in Mr. Fox's senior Latin class, and then returns to the bird lecture (uses *small back-up response*).

e. *Follow through the next time (consistency):* Since the teacher has had to escalate to a middle back-up response, she is no longer required to give any more warnings before she takes consistent actions to deal with any of Robin's future misbehaviors.

f. *Effective delivery of the student to time out if she resists:* If Robin has resisted—requiring the teacher to go public and have her removed from the class—the confusion would cause more disruption to the guest lecturer than did Robin's misbehavior. We must realize that when time out is initiated, we are placing our back against the wall; if the student refuses, we are into a time-costly and emotionally charged confrontation that will cause much damage to the teacher/student relationship. Don't take middle back-up responses lightly.

g. *Effective response to problems that the student might cause while in time out:* What if Robin, sent to a Latin class, acts out in Mr. Fox's classroom, and he loses large amounts of his class time attempting to "put the lid" on Robin? Our response if the student disrupts while in time out must be clearly thought out beforehand. Normally, this will involve a process leading to a costly large back-up response. In order to use time out in a colleague's classroom, called the "lend-louse" program, a number of guidelines must be followed:

- The colleague must be a strong disciplinarian and be willing to accept this responsibility without feeling imposed on.
- The colleague should put the student to work. (Previously Mrs. Alda has created a workfolder for Mr. Fox, which he gives to time-out visitors.)
- The student should stay in this time out for 15 to 30 minutes.
- The classroom accepting the student should be as many years as possible from the age of the time-out student, either much younger or much older, in order to isolate the misbehaving student from peers as much as possible. If this is a high school with departmentalization, the student should be put in an advanced class with high achievement-oriented students, such as Mr. Fox's advanced Latin class.
- Either physically escort the student to the time-out location or have the student carry a "time-out card" with the time of departure so the receiving teacher will know that the student was not wandering the halls for the last 15 minutes. Be careful of runners who, when put out on their own, will leave the school grounds.

3. and 4. *Public Warning and Threats:* Public warnings and threats in which the teacher uses pheasant posturing, nagging, and silly talk are costly to the teacher, ineffective, and destructive, and they will eventually require an escalation to a large back-up response. Don't use them.

5. *Being Sent to the Hall:* This is a time-honored practice that takes a dangerous gamble. The student is humiliated by being seated in the hall, is reinforced by activity going on in the hall, is unsupervised, and can wander about causing real mischief or can run away. Don't use it!

6. *Detention after School:* Jones questions the real value of after-school detention. Only the students who don't really need it show up for detention, and it teaches them that being in a classroom and in a school setting is punishment. As a result, through associative learning, all school attendance becomes a punishment. In addition, the use of detention is a quick ray gun to zap students, is overused by many teachers, and is self-perpetuating. Rarely—preferably never—use it, but Jones says if it is necessary it should be used in a well thought-out systematic manner.

7. *Loss of Privilege:* On the surface, this looks like a good sanction, but it will cause high resentment from the student, and eventually the student will seek to make the teacher pay. An escalating battle will develop and eventually lead to a large back-up response.

8. *Parent Conference:* Many of today's teachers are angry at parents and feel they get very little support from them. A parent conference used by the teacher costs much time and hardly ever produces meaningful results. Jones feels that the misbehaving student is one who has learned to misbehave at home under the ineffective discipline techniques of parents. What makes a teacher think that if he or she cannot control the student at school, the parents have the parenting skills to effectively get the child's behavior to change? To help parents remediate the negative behaviors of their child requires professional counseling or therapy, and the teacher does not have the necessary skills or time to be effective with parents. You may try parent conferences, but don't expect much help from this approach. Jones, who is a family psychologist and therapist, says, "Get what you can out of a parent conference and keep your hopes modest. In most cases it's cheaper to fix it yourself."[10]

9. and 10. *Lowering Student's Grade/Assigning Extra Work as a Discipline Sanction:* Lowering a grade and giving extra work as a discipline sanction are widely used but highly destructive practices that condition students to hate school work (extra work) and resent the teacher (lowering grades).[11] Don't do it.

Large Back-Up Responses

The large back-up response to discipline situations is the very public action of sending the student to the office, which has a high probability of escalating to more extreme sanctions, including in-school suspension, out-of-school suspension, or expulsion.

Sending Students to the Office.   Jones would say, "Indeed sending a student to the office may have the dubious distinction of being the most overused and overrated discipline technique in education."[12] It is time that we give up the myth that the vice principal or the school counselor has a magic ritual that will change the misbehaving student into a angel. Let's also give up the idea that being sent to the office is or can be a punishment. It is not and cannot be. In the student's mind, the message is: If I get sent to the office, I escape for an entire period of American History, and I am entertained by the office social happenings. I get rewarded by being able to talk to my friends who are also sitting on the bench waiting to talk to the administrator. When I return, I'll swagger into class and put my feet up, and my peers will say, "How was it?"

So, what can the professionals in the office—the principal, assistant principal, and counselor—do to help the teacher? The answer is that they usually do have behavioral and counseling skills that can be useful to the teacher, but they rarely get a chance to use these skills. Jones reports that in a typical large high school, the office referrals, counting tardies, run between 2,500 and 5,000 per school year. The vice principal is running a revolving door referral service with no time to really counsel the students, who receive a bunch of "silly" talk and are sent back to their classrooms.

Why are so many students referred to the office, creating this gridlock? Jones says it is because of the "bouncers." Excluding tardies, 90 percent of all office referrals are sent to the office by the same 5 percent of teachers, and the effective teachers who rarely use the office don't know the facts regarding this overuse by the "bouncers." The teachers who are not willing to take the time to use limit setting, omission training, an incentive program, and responsibility training are the very ones who, in the face of some minor misbehavior, "bounce" the students down to the office. The bouncer is rewarded by being rid of the difficult student for the remainder of the period. It is easy for the bouncer-teacher: Just zap them with a pink slip, send them to the office, and you are done with it.

Sometimes the committed teacher with a genuine discipline system in place does rightfully need the office's help. For example, Larry in Mr. O'Donald's class has been back talking and appears irritable. Mr. O'Donald is aware that Larry's father is an alcoholic and is violent with Larry. Last night his father fought with Larry and literally kicked him out of the house, and as a result Larry slept in the bus station. Today, as he arrived for second period English class someone had taken his normal seat. When the classmate refused to move, Larry slugged him. Mr. O'Donald sent Larry to the office, and now needs help from the office staff regarding what to do about Larry. This is a legitimate problem, and the school structure must serve Mr. O'Donald's need. So, for office referrals, we have two objectives: (1) set up an omission-training program that makes it costly for the bouncers to cause gridlock by sending students who are performing minor misbehaviors to the office in order to dump them on the administration and (2) create a system whereby the office staff can help teachers such as Mr. O'Donald who really are conscientious and have a legitimate need for assistance.

Office Referral System.   The administration, typically the vice principal, establishes the guidelines for referring students to the office:

> *First referral* (during a six-week period): The teacher referring the student not only sends a pink slip with the student to the office but also, before departing the school that evening, must complete a Background of Referral form. This is a one-page form asking such questions as what happened, what steps the teacher tried previously with this student, the teacher's plans for future action, and what help the teacher expects from the office.

> *Second referral* (during a six-week period): The referring teacher completes a Background of Referral form and must meet to talk with the vice principal in the principal's office during the teacher planning period, or for a period of 30 minutes after school. The principal discusses with the teacher what future actions can be taken.

> *Third referral* (during a six-week period): A one-hour staff meeting regarding this student will be called (see Chapter 2 and staffing procedures for a structure for carrying out such meetings). The meeting will be held after school and attended by the referring teacher, the vice principal, the school counselor or any other person who might be helpful, and will also include any other teacher who has also referred this student within the same six-week period.

This system, with its paperwork and meetings, will be viewed by the bouncer as a punishing and costly disincentive, but will be seen as a real way of getting office help for the committed teacher (such as Mr. O'Donald, who really wants to get help for Larry). The principal's procedure after the second office referral and during the after-school meeting with the bouncer is: "Tell me about the limit-set-ting actions you have taken with the student you referred. Tell me about your omission training and your responsibility training. Oh, you don't have one and haven't done this! Well, here is Jones's book called *Positive Discipline;* take it, read it, and use it in your classroom, and I will be by to see if you still need my help in implementing such a discipline program. By the way, until we have all four legs of this discipline system working well, please do not refer any students to the office. Thank you very much, Ms./Mrs./Mr. Ex-bouncer."

In contrast, the committed teacher now has a structure for getting the real help that is needed. The disincentive system has stopped the bouncer's trivial referrals, the office gridlock has been broken, and the principal and counselors can now do the job they were really trained to do. Other large back-up responses may also be addressed as a part of the staffing process, including notifying parents, in-school suspension, expulsion, or involving the police or juvenile authorities, all of which Jones feels are highly destructive and ineffective. "Are we going to pull out all the stops to keep this student in public education, or are we going to call it off?"[13] The staffing process is a system for working as a group to "pull out all the stops."

Corporal Punishment.   Jones does not mince words when discussing the use of corporal punishment: "If the technology of discipline management could be lik-ened to an animal, then corporal punishment would surely be its ass end. Of all the discipline techniques in existence, corporal punishment distinguishes itself as hav-ing the fewest assets and the greatest number of liabilities. In terms of locking adult and child into a series of coercive cycles, it is the all-time champion. Those who rely on it swear by it—testimonial to the addictive properties of quick short-term cures."[14]

Many teachers and administrators use the question, Where do you stand on corporal punishment? as a litmus test for whether the discipline system being sug-gested is a "soft" model or whether it really "means business." Jones uses his behavior analysis construction regarding reinforcement, and demonstrates that the whole process of sending a student to the office for corporal punishment is full of reinforcement errors. Unknowingly, those who use corporal punishment fail to see that the student receives constant and positive reinforcement as the process unfolds. The "bad" student gets the entire class to stop and focus on him; he passes classmates in the hall and they give him acknowledgment by their smiles of recog-nition and comments; the office atmosphere changes when he arrives; he gets to interact with the principal; and he returns to the classroom as a "hero," one who has been through it and lived. One school so clearly failed to see how the student was really being positively and socially reinforced that it actually permitted the student to sign the paddle.

Corporal punishment is the granddaddy of large sanctions. As a part of the back-up system, these sanctions will likely (1) be destructive to the school-student relationship, (2) cause the student to feel resentment and withhold all future coop-eration, (3) make the student irresponsible, (4) make the student dependent on an external authority, and (5) cause the student to become counter-coercive to "get even" with the school or teacher.[15]

RESPONSIBILITY TRAINING

Limit setting is for the purpose of stopping misbehavior—to calm the student and get him or her back on task—but it has its limitations. In order to run a productive classroom, the teacher needs cooperation from students, such as showing up on time, walking in an orderly fashion as they enter the classroom, bringing books and pencils, taking their seats right away, being ready to work when the bell rings, and a host of similar behaviors. The teacher cannot force students to do such cooperative behaviors; they are a gift. Cooperation is always voluntary and under the control of the student. Students choose to cooperate or not cooperate. Responsibility training is *positive discipline's* system for helping the teacher obtain such positive cooperation. When the teacher seeks cooperation from students, they naturally ask, Why should I? or What's in it for me?

Let's look at two toddlers—one lucky to have warm effective parents, the other an unlucky child who has been neglected and not nurtured. The parents of Lucky see her holding a valuable, breakable knick-knack, and mother asks, "Careful dear, give that to Mommy, please. That is not a toy." Lucky, who has learned to trust and depend on adults in her work, complies and is kissed and hugged by her parent. Unlucky is asked to "give it to Mommy" but there is no trust. He does not trust that he will receive hugs, kisses, and warmth, so he thinks, "I will keep what I have and get as much pleasure as I can from this." He refuses to give it up, throws a temper tantrum, and breaks the item. Unlucky has no trust in the future, and so we see no cooperation.

Many students coming to our schools today are like Unlucky. They don't have sufficient trust in adults and teachers to accept the demands made of them for school and classroom cooperation. "I will goof off and take as much pleasure with my friends now because I am sure that it will not come to me in the future." These students need to be given to, at the human relationship level, before they can give back with cooperation. Traditionally, schools and teachers nag, punish, and coerce these children at a great price, but with no results. Jones says that every classroom needs an incentive system to teach cooperation. Limit setting can be very helpful for stopping misbehavior, but responsibility training is needed to develop cooperative behavior in students.

To put it simply, students have to be given something that they value, something they will strive to conserve once it is in their possession. Jones uses the analogy of teaching a teenager to be responsible with money. The teenager is given a sum of money to spend and take care of necessities, including his school lunch money. He has not earned it, but his parents have given it to him. He is (1) responsible for this finite amount of money, (2) responsible for the control of how the money is spent (consumption), and (3) made responsible for living with the consequences if he overconsumes and runs out of the resource (money). By Wednesday,

"He's one of those get-tough-on-the-first-day types."

Cartoon by Ford Button.

the teenager has used up all of his monetary resources, and asks his Dad, "Could you spare some change for my lunch money for the remainder of the week?" Good old Dad says, "No!" He is teaching his child to be responsible, and there is real-life stress in the situation. (It is important to note, however, that the teenager would not starve if he misses lunch, or he can take some fruit or other items from home to eat at lunchtime.)

This is the basis for Jones's responsibility training. Let's see this in action:

"Good morning, eighth-graders, and welcome to second-period English class. I am your teacher, Mr. Hansen. I have a surprise gift for all of you. Is there anyone here who does not enjoy watching videos? (No hands go up, but a few giggles are heard.) I am going to start this class off with a video gift to you. (The teacher then shows 25 minutes of the motion picture *To Kill a Mockingbird*, which is the first book the class will read.) I can see by your faces that you enjoyed that and are curious to see the rest. Well, you will see it this Friday. In the future, you and I will negotiate on future videos that you might like to see, or other enjoyable activities. Every Friday I will give you a PAT. (laughter) No, not that kind of pat. My PAT means Preferred Activity Time. I have chosen the preferred activity this week as a video, but in the future you will help me decide what PATs you like and how you want to use your time. Now, the *T* in

PAT stands for *time*. I am awarding you a gift of 15 minutes of class time (writes 15 on the corner of the chalkboard) on Friday this week for you to see more of this video. In the future, you can earn even more time to be added to this 15 minutes by your cooperation in here.

"Now, you may add more 'free' time to this 15-minute PAT in a number of ways, including hurry-up bonuses, automatic bonuses, bonus contests, and individual bonuses. Hurry-up bonuses are given when you hustle. Okay, let's try to see if you can win some hurry-up bonuses right now. On the board I have written jobs that we need to accomplish quickly this morning. They are:

Directions

1. The last person in the row get a textbook for each person in that row.
2. Write your name in the book, at the proper location on the inside front cover.
3. Place your book ID number on the master list that is being passed around.
4. Read the three-paragraph introduction to *To Kill a Mockingbird* on page 7.
5. No talking or goofing off.

"Now, you can see that in my hand I'm holding a stopwatch. My calculation is that the jobs on the board can be accomplished in five minutes. I will click the stopwatch and you will begin. When all these jobs are accomplished, you will signal by turning over your textbook. When I see everyone done, I will stop the watch and whatever amount of time is left on the watch will be added to your PAT gift of 15 minutes. During the week you may continue to add more free time for your Friday PAT. Begin now!"

The teacher clicks the stopwatch. During the activities, Jim, who sits in the front row and was one of the last students to get a book, begins to mentally drift off. His book is now in front of him and so is the master list, but he is "spaced out." Quickly, those students around him see that the master list is stalled on his desk and he is not working. The neighbors gently poke him, frown, and point to the list. Startled, Jim quickly "gets with the program."

This example uses peer pressure rather than teacher nagging, threats, or coercion. Several minutes later, Mr. Hansen says:

"Oh, I see you are all done. Let me check my watch. Ha! One minute and twenty seconds remaining! You have earned this time. I will write it here on the board under the 15 so we will remember, and on Friday we will add up the minutes. By the way, no cheating. I keep a record of this in my grade book, so I don't want anyone changing times up here. (laughter) Now, you will also earn time through automatic bonuses. For example, if each of you is in your seat and working when the bell rings, this will be an automatic two minutes added to your PAT. You will see that cooperation will result in other ways to earn automatic bonuses. I am also going to keep the time awards up here for all three of my English classes, so you can see how your competitors are doing. Whichever of the three classes has scored the highest points will receive a bonus of five minutes, and second place will get three extra minutes. So we have a bonus contest going on here among my three eighth-grade English classes."

What we have just seen is Jones's responsibility training and the use of incentives (the PAT, or preferred activity time). Time is the currency that students will earn. Just like the teenager learning to be responsible with money, the students are given 15 minutes of time-currency as a gift from the teacher. They are (1) responsible for this time-currency and there is a finite amount, (2) responsible for controlling how the time-currency is spent (consumption), and (3) made responsible for living with the consequences if they overconsume and run out of the resource (time).[16] This spending of the time-currency may occur in two ways: through penalties or use of the PAT.

Penalty

Let's continue with Mr. Hansen and his eighth-graders:

> "Students, you now have your time. All the other time during our class period is mine for instruction. Your job is to work hard during my time. Sometimes, some students like to play games and use up their time before the end of the week, which is when most PATs are done. When they poach on my time like this, they are penalized by losing some of their time."

Here is an example of the awarding of penalties by the teacher.

> It is the second day of English class, and the students are busy working when Laverne decides to get a dictionary. She stands, but instead of walking straight to the shelf holding the dictionary, she takes the "scenic" route past a friend and drops off a note on the friend's desk. She then flips through the dictionary for a number of minutes. Mr. Hansen stands, takes two relaxing breaths, assumes his best Queen Victoria posture, and calls across the classroom, "Laverne." The girl looks up at him. He holds up the stopwatch and states, "Laverne, you are on your own time," and clicks the watch. Laverne freezes like a deer caught in headlights, but the students nearby whisper, "Sit down, Laverne, you're wasting *our* time. Sit down, now!" Laverne scurries to her seat, opens her book, and begins the work. Mr. Hansen clicks the timer off, goes to the chalkboard, and writes –45 seconds.

Through her behavior, Laverne began to play a game of noncooperation by killing time and not working. Rather than nag her, Mr. Hansen simply starts the stopwatch, which makes a small beeping sound all can hear, and begins counting the off-task student's penalty time. This is then displayed on the board and sub-

Example of a Preferred Activity Time (PAT)
Academic Baseball (Grades 4–12)

Subject Area

Math, History, Foreign Languages, Science, Vocabulary Development, Spelling, etc.

Objective

Test review

Materials and Preparation

- The teacher or students prepare questions in four degrees of difficulty: single, double, triple, home run.
- Two baseball diamonds will be needed in order to use a ping pong game format (described below). Mark the bases on the floor.

Student Grouping

Two teams.

The Play

1. The batter is asked by the pitcher to pick the level of difficulty for the question (single, double, triple, or home run).
2. The pitcher selects and asks a question from the single, double, triple, or home run stack. If, however, the teacher is "pitcher" and does not have stacks of questions already prepared, the teacher just asks the questions "off the top of her head."
3. If the student answers correctly, the student walks to the appropriate base and other runners advance the same number of bases.
4. If the question is answered incorrectly, a "fly ball" is called, and the question goes to a player of the opposite team.
    - When the teacher says "fly ball," she should wait before calling on a student so that everyone in the field must dig for the answer.
    - If the player in the field answers the question correctly, the fly ball has been caught and the batter is out.

- If the outfielder misses the question, the fly ball has been dropped, and the batter goes to first base on an error. All runners advance one base on an error.

5. When using the ping pong game format, the questions alternate between teams. So, the second question goes to the team that was in the field (i.e., playing defense) during the previous question. The ping pong format guarantees that both teams get to bat an equal number of times, that everybody plays all the time, and that both teams are continually engaged in scoring runs.
6. The ping pong format does away with innings. In order to make outs meaningful, the final score is computed as *runs minus outs*.

Team 1: _____   **Team 2:** _____

Score   *Score*
  Runs _____   Runs _____
– Outs _____   – Outs _____
  Total _____   Total _____

Fine Points

- Most games follow a ping pong format with the question going to the opposite team if missed. It is best to play such games open-book. The teacher will find the players on defense digging for the answer as soon as the question is asked. Since youngsters hate doing nothing, the rest of the students on the team that is "at bat" can usually be found digging for the answer as well.

- Football is similar except that the defense can "sack the quarterback" for a 10-yard loss when the student picks a 10-yard question, or they can intercept a 20-, 30-, or 40-yard pass play.
- If the teacher has any question about rules, it can be turned over to the students. They will make sure the rules are fair. Speaking of keeping things fair, a perennial preoccupation with teenagers is how to choose teams fairly. Four students of roughly equal scholastic ability can be chosen as captains. They do not need to be fast students; in fact, this is a nice chance for the teacher to honor some of the slower students. The teacher should give the captains a class list and say: "I want you to take this class list to the table in the back of the room and make equal teams for me. Horse-trade until they are equal because you will have to live with them." If the teacher wishes to add a further guarantee of fair play, the students can be told: "It is your job to choose and trade until the teams are equal. After you give me equal teams, you will draw lots to see which team you will captain."

Source: F. Jones, *Positive Classroom Discipline: Training Manual.* © 1993 Fredric H. Jones and Associates, 103 Quarry Lane, Santa Cruz, CA 95060. Reprinted by permission.

tracted from the total time accumulated to that point. Since the "free" time or PAT belongs to all class members, Laverne is selfishly using up everyone's time. This creates social pressure, but not from the teacher as an authority figure toward whom Laverne could target her anger. Instead, it comes from her peers. Thus, the class, rather than enjoying one student's challenge to the teacher's authority (*show time*), now becomes a part of the socialization process; misbehavior is just too expensive for the individual student to engage in because she is hurting herself (loss of free time) and must endure the wrath of her peers. Jones would say that social pressure is very strong among peers, but through this incentive system, the pressure is rendered benign and harnessed to support productive cooperative behavior. Penalties are used in conjunction with bonuses to give the teacher considerable control in obtaining cooperation from the students. Jones says, "It allows the teacher to combat the countless scams and flim-flams which students devise with a calm that can only come from having discovered the perfect antidote."[17]

Coming to Class without Materials

Through responsibility training, the teacher can now use bonuses and penalties to begin to teach students to be responsible—to show up on time (deduct PAT time if a student is late), bring their books and pencils, take their seats, and begin work before the bell rings. These are all behaviors missing in many middle and high schools today. By way of example, let's see how the teacher can manage the example of the forgotten pencil:

> Mr. Hansen tells the class, "Students, take out a sheet of clean notebook paper and put your heading on, and then get ready to take down this sentence." He is interrupted by Larry, who informs him, "Teacher, I ain't got no pencil." Mr. Hansen stands, takes two relaxing breaths, and holds up the stopwatch. But

before he can tell Larry that he is on his own time until he gets a pencil, a classmate pushes one into Larry's hand. By standing and holding up the stopwatch, the teacher has become a warning prompt and the students have learned to act quickly so they will not suffer the penalty of lost PAT time.

But Larry is a sly fox and a gambler. Five minutes later, he has broken off the end of his pencil. He says, "Mr. Hansen, my pencil is broken." Larry knows that Mr. Hansen has preestablished a set of rules that prohibits using the pencil sharpener while class is in progress. As part of this preestablished routine, Mr. Hansen has deposited two cans on his desk, one labeled *Yours* and the other *Mine*. The teacher has asked the janitor to save him all the old pencils he finds laying on the floor, the grungier the better. In fact, if some pencils in the *Yours* can look too nice, Mr. Hansen deliberately breaks them into short stubby pencils. Larry is holding his broken pencil in the air. Mr. Hansen nods (*prompt*) and clicks on the stopwatch. Larry jumps up quickly and moves to Mr. Hansen's desk, puts his good but broken pencil in the *Mine* can and takes out a grungy sharpened pencil from the *Yours* can. He then moves quickly to his seat and starts to write. Mr. Hansen takes two relaxing breaths and slowly moves to the chalkboard, where he writes –18 seconds penalty under the PAT minutes. Larry's peers scowl at him. Later, Larry asks if he can go to the bathroom, and Mr. Hansen replies, "Sure, Larry, but you are on your own time," and holds up the stopwatch. The classmates look at Larry and groan, and Larry says, "Never mind!" and sits down. Mr. Hansen also uses this technique for handling behavior when moving the students through the halls and during school assemblies.

The incentive system with the use of time as a currency is an economy system where the students are permitted to learn responsibility by the way they spend their resources (time). This is a total group management program where everyone is in the system and it is "all for one and one for all." If one person is uncooperative, he or she hurts everyone by the selfish stealing of time. As a result, this individual will feel social pressure from the other class members. The students discover (as did the teenager who was learning to handle money) that (1) the time is a finite resource, (2) they have control over its consumption, and (3) they must live with the consequences when the resource is used up.

The "Rule of Penalties"

Let's look at an example where penalties are abused by a negative, personal teacher.

> "Class, I am counting to ten. I want everyone in their seats, all paper off the floor, and the desks in neat, orderly rows. For each number I count before this is accomplished, you will lose that much time from this afternoon's pep rally. One...two...."

This is not what Jones is proposing in his incentive system. Therefore, he has created a rule to eliminate teacher abuse of this system by teachers who repeatedly zap students with more and more penalties, until the students know they will not win a PAT. This rule is simple: *Every penalty implies a corresponding bonus.* This is done to prevent the system from degenerating into negativism whereby the students begin to feel resentment, undermining their relationship with the teacher. This will also cause rebellion and very negative peer pressure. The idea is that students should and must accumulate PAT time for the fun of it, in order for it to serve as an effective incentive.

Types of Preferred Activity Time

Preferred activity time is not "kicking back" time that allows students to hang out with each other and do nothing. If adolescent students are given the freedom to do nothing, that is exactly what they will do. Jones would clearly admit that the use of PAT with students is really a "shell game." Activities such as a popcorn party would be permitted as PAT but would be considered a poor or weak use of PAT. Under Jones's definition, PATs are fun activities that hold high interest for students but have embedded in them a routine of drill and practice, or even content review of the subject matter. In short, they are process activities involving elements of learning. The PAT of watching the video of *To Kill a Mockingbird* involved a book the students will read this semester; seeing the video is a motivating, high-interest activity that the teacher simply turned into a PAT—thus the shell game.

The book *Positive Discipline* contains a host of starter games to get teachers started at all age levels. The suggested PATs involve:

1. *Team Competitions* (games with lineups, such as a classroom game of baseball that uses knowledge of any material being taught)
2. *Team Competitions* (games without lineups, such as classroom baseball, volleyball, or college bowl that modifies the game so there is no lineup)
3. *Team Competition with Complex Work* (math teams and cut-throat)
4. *Path Games* (spelling, typing, bingo)
5. *Enrichment Activities* (permitting the students to break from the tradition and try advanced applications of the subject area)
6. *Fun and Games* (simple party time, which the teacher will rely on the least as the students gradually learn to use the academically mixed games above)

Particularly for high school students, such games might be seen as "uncool." Jones permits much feedback from students in choosing and modifying the activities for their own interest. Historically, games with rules are passed down from one generation of children, beginning in the upper elementary grades, to the next generation of children. They normally are not taught by adults but are strictly dependent on the child-culture (remember Red Light-Green Light and Red Rover?). Because of television, mall arcades, computer games and chat lines, and the general marketing of childhood leisure activities, these traditional games are being lost and not passed down to many children today. The commercial games, such as Nintendo or its sibling Game Boy, are isolated activities; therefore, children are losing out on the very valuable social interaction that traditional games have long taught them. According to Jones, children—especially adolescents—simply do not know how to have fun, because that fun for hundreds of years has been centered around group games. Jones's PAT approach is literally attempting to save children's cultural heritage and get teachers and students to socially enjoy themselves, while at the same time slipping in some academic training and review. Historically, when a group of people worked hard on a laborious task (picking corn, cutting forest timber, or shucking oysters), they would fill their free time engaging in games of competition involving these same activities (so we have corn-husking, log-splitting, and oyster-shucking contests).

Finally, this incentive system of awarding time-currency and using a stopwatch to give bonuses and penalties will gradually fade. Once the students have developed normal classroom habits that will begin on the first day of school, the stopwatch can be put away—but not the PAT. The PAT should continue throughout the year with normal classroom teaching and learning becoming more fun and game-like until Jones's wish is met: Teaching and having fun begin to blend into one activity.

OMISSION TRAINING

The positive discipline system is a four-legged chair, and we have reviewed three of those legs: limit setting, back-up systems, and the incentive system as a part of responsibility training. The fourth and final leg is omission training. It is important to remember, however, that all four systems are interrelated and all must be functioning in order for the system to work. (To review, limit setting is the daily classroom practice used to stop minor nickel-and-dime misbehaviors and time off-task, to calm the students and get them back to work. A back-up system is used when the student escalates the power confrontation to the point that limit setting is ineffective; the teacher attempts to keep back-up system actions as nonpublic as possible, starting with small back-up responses, escalating to medium back-up responses, and, on rare occasion, advancing to the use of large back-up responses.)

Omission training is used with the one or two students who are chronically provocative toward the teacher or toward peers, who take the attitude, "I don't care about PAT and you can't make me!" By his behavior, this difficult student is causing penalties for his classmates; he is alienated and typically has few or no social skills or friends. He is bitter and revengeful, and wishes to get even with others for the social isolation he feels. His behavior clearly provokes rejection. This student is taken to a private conference and permitted to move out of the responsibility training process. Then, if he misbehaves, his actions will not penalize classmates and destroy the incentive system set up by the teacher. The teacher continues to calmly use limit setting for minor off-task behaviors with this student. By taking this student out of the PAT system, the teacher removes a control lever the student has been using to get even with peers. By creating an alternative omission training system for this student, the teacher has a face-saving course of action that simultaneously deprives the student of the class as an audience.

Omission training is an individualized program of incentives for the very defiant student, encouraging him to earn rewards through the omission of unwanted behavior. We arrange this reward to provide bonuses in time added to the class PAT, thus making the student a hero within the classroom if he is able to control himself. The student may not be interested in adding to the PAT itself, but the "hero" status it will give him among his peers is a strong incentive. This process is established in three ways:

1. *Private Meeting:* Larry is told that he may drop out of the normal responsibility training and he may choose to skip the PAT, or he may individualize his PAT to his liking. Either way, a special rewards program is set up for him. A kitchen timer will be set for a period of time, and if he can control himself for this time by not performing certain general categories of behaviors (hitting others, swearing, putting others down, or a host of other unwanted behaviors), he will earn one minute of extra time for everyone. *Note:* He does not earn it individually, but by his actions is able to give bonus gifts to the entire class and is rewarded with feelings of being a hero.

2. *Class Meeting:* A class meeting is held, with the teacher pointing out that Larry has been causing the entire class to lose time because he has had trouble controlling his behavior. From this point on, Larry cannot hurt the class as a whole but can only help it. When the kitchen timer goes off, a bonus of one minute will be added to the class PAT. So it now becomes the class's responsibility to help Larry. Classmates should not provoke him but should help and invite him into their activities, because they help themselves by helping Larry control himself. This control will bring bonus points to the entire group.

Through the omission training program, the revengeful student who lacks social skills and acceptance is now placed in the best position for social pressure to help him find this acceptance. Many of these problem students have learned to be the best bad kid, and have a sense of status by being the class outcast. He cannot improve his behavior or get better until the class changes its actions toward him, and the omission training system places the incentives in front of the group to help change its actions toward him.

3. *Process:* Once the kitchen timer rings, the teacher announces that Larry has given the class bonus time. The teacher writes it on the board and encourages the class to applaud Larry. With Larry able to maintain good behavior for 30 minutes (as an example), the timer is now set—unknown to Larry—to 35 minutes; it is gradually increased to require longer and longer intervals of good behavior from Larry.

Finally, Larry's behavior has changed so dramatically that the teacher needs to phase out the omission training process. First, the timer is eliminated. The teacher begins class by announcing, "Class, Larry has been doing so well that I will give you Larry's gift of 7 minutes right now, because I am confident he will be able to control his behavior today." Finally, after a private meeting with Larry, he is brought back into the regular responsibility training process.

The central concept of omission training for the very difficult student is: (1) remove her from the responsibility training program so that she cannot use her misbehavior as a power lever to hurt peers; (2) permit her to earn bonus points for the entire class, which includes her; (3) challenge class members to help the difficult student succeed and in turn help themselves; and finally (4) gradually phase out the omission training process.

CLASSROOM STRUCTURE

Mr. Fox's Latin class has been in session for 15 minutes when Carol's pencil breaks, leaving her unable to do the written assignment. She thinks, "Can I just get up and go over there and sharpen my pencil? In the past, some teachers have permitted me to do this and some have not." Carol stands, makes eye contact with Mr. Fox, points to the pencil sharpener, and takes five steps toward it. Mr. Fox demands, "Young lady, where do you think you are going? I did not give you permission to get out of your seat! Sit down immediately!"

All the students tense up and think, "Ah, Mr. Fox is going to play the game of 'minefield' with us." The students realize that Mr. Fox is going to keep his class rules a secret at the beginning of the semester, and they will have to break a rule ("step on a mine"), causing Mr. Fox to explode and "slam dunk" that person in order for them to learn the particular rule and how to avoid breaking it (to not step on that mine).

The game of "minefield" will create battle fatigue among the students in this class and war will be declared between teacher and student, because they will never be able to feel comfortable or relaxed within a predictable structure. The students realize that it may take all semester to learn all of Mr. Fox's rules, and the moment they think they know them all, a new one will pop up from out of nowhere. If Mr. Fox is erratic and inconsistent based on his mood, the students will have a tremendously difficult time dealing with him. If one day a student breaks a rule but Mr. Fox does not explode, yet a similar violation by another student the next day makes him erupt and threaten 10 years of detention, the students quickly recognize that this will be a tense, hateful school term. They could easily assume the position that if Mr. Fox is going to play such punitive games with them, they will also play their own game of war, escalating their use of power in order to get even with the teacher. After all, they know he is only one individual and there are 25 to 35 of them; Mr. Fox is outnumbered, and reinforcement troops will be sent in every semester or year. The students figure it won't be long before administrators will be giving Mr. Fox a "Section 8" discharge as emotionally unfit—the students will drive him crazy.

Structure—class routines, the organization of desks and furniture, and general rules—give students a sense of predictability. Once they learn this structure, they are free to act within defined boundaries and have the sense of security that they will be safe and can relax. Many teachers, especially upper-level high school teachers, adhere to a number of myths about structure and rules, including:

1. Students, especially in middle or high school, should already know how to behave. Wrong! Each class is different and every student wants to know where this teacher's "mines" are located.
2. It takes too much time to teach rules and structure. Wrong! The teacher will pay a higher price in time later in remediation—and perhaps with a stomach ulcer—if she does not take the time up front.
3. Rules are general guidelines and need only to be announced. Wrong! Rules must be taught like any other concept in a lesson; they cannot be just verbally announced, but must be specifically taught in the form of what motor actions are needed to comply with this rule.
4. Teach rules well at the beginning and then you can forget about them. Wrong! Rules need to be monitored and retaught after long holidays, when spring weather breaks out, when new students are enrolled, and periodically throughout the year. Rules need maintenance!
5. Teaching rules equates to undue strictness. Wrong! Rules are like the guardrail on a high bridge: They show us where to stop, show us where we may safely maneuver, and keep us on the proper path.
6. Students hate rules. Wrong! Mr. Fox's students would love to know what the rules are. Students appreciate a certain amount of rules, so they may know how to avoid out-of-bounds behavior.

From the moment the students enter the classroom managed by Jones's positive discipline techniques, the teacher shows that he means business and teaches through structure. Here are Jones's recommendations for the first day of class:

1. The teacher greets each student by shaking the student's hand, saying his own name and asking the student's name. The teacher then gives the student a card with a number corresponding to the seat she will take, and asks the student to begin working, following the directions on the board.
2. The board directions will ask the students to fill out a 3" × 5" card with their name, address, and phone number and their parents' names, places of work, and work phone numbers. These cards will be used as a part of the back-up system if and when a student needs to be warned.

In this way, the student has learned that rules begin the moment she walks into the classroom. The message delivered by the teacher is: I care who you are and I want you to care for me, to walk into my class, to take your seat, and to begin working. The teacher now plays a game (a variety of choices is included in Jones's book) so that everyone in the classroom gets to know everyone else's first and last name.

Later, the teacher will pass out a seating chart to test whether each student knows everyone else's name. Once everyone passes the name test, bonus points are added to the PAT. Anonymity creates within the student a distance toward the teacher and classmates ("If he doesn't even know my name, he doesn't care about me, and I don't care about him!"). This personalizing of each student is critical for establishing a relationship between the teacher and class members and must be accomplished immediately.

Teaching Rules and Structure

The teacher actually teaches all rules and the structure of the classroom—the use of furniture and equipment—just as any other lesson is taught through a Say, Show, and Do process. "Students, in this chemistry class it is critical that all test tubes are absolutely clean or contaminants will destroy new experiments. Let me show you how they are to be washed out each and every time we are done using them. First we get the water hot, then . . . *(Say)*. Now watch me do it, as I repeat the directions *(Show)*. Now pair up in groups of two, and one of you will become Professor Einstein and the other will be Dr. Schweitzer. Dr. Schweitzer, cross your arms across your chest and Professor Einstein will show you how to do this. Professor Einstein will teach you the lesson of 'cleaning test tubes' and bring the cleaned-out tube to you. Now, Dr. Schweitzer, you teach this same lesson with a new test tube to Professor Einstein *(Do)*." What we see is the teacher not just announcing rules or telling rules, but actually teaching all rules and procedures needed in this classroom before any instruction can begin. Each teacher will need to establish rules for the particular type of classroom, but here is an example of those for a chemistry class:[18]

- How to use gas and water jets on the lab table
- How to fill out a lab manual
- How to check out glassware
- How to check out elements and consumables
- How to operate the weights and measures
- How to operate the microscope
- What to do in case of fire at the lab table
- What to do in case someone's clothing catches fire
- What to do in case of cuts from glass
- What to do in case of contact with acids
- What to do in case of caustic substances in the eye
- How to clean a test tube
- What to do with unconsumed elements
- How to clean up your lab table
- Who to talk to during lab
- How loud to talk during lab
- What to do if you need help
- What to do if you are done with your experiment before the end of the period

This chemistry teacher's list is long, and each of these rules will be taught in a three-step lesson of Say, Show, and Do. All teachers will need to make similar lists and teach the rules they need in their particular classroom.

SCHOOLWIDE DISCIPLINE MANAGEMENT

Most schools do very little planning on how out-of-classroom management will be done. Therefore, when misbehavior does occur, the tendency is for the school to jump right to medium or large back-up system sanctions, which are self-perpetuating and destructive to the school environment. The positive discipline approach presents very valuable procedures for dealing with supervision in these areas (although in very abbreviated form). Primarily, Jones is suggesting the use of limit setting (with eye contact and proximity) and responsibility training for these areas.

First, the principal must be the leader, just as the teacher is in the classroom. There must be a commitment by all teachers that when students are in the school, but out of their classrooms, "every student belongs to every teacher"[19] and they are willing to give their time to teach responsibilities and limit setting in these areas.

Assemblies

School assemblies are not times for teachers to retreat to the teachers' lounge, leaving 1,000 middle school or high school students undersupervised in an auditorium. Teachers must be on site, perhaps seated with their homeroom classes, and using limit-setting procedures just as they did in the classroom. Special area teachers and school administrative staff should also participate. Procedures for assemblies include:

1. Students are assigned seats, with friends separated.
2. Homeroom teachers discuss proper behavior before the students leave the homeroom for the assembly.
3. The teacher seats herself on an aisle and in a position to see all of the students in her class.
4. Students who tend to misbehave are seated as close as possible to the teacher.
5. The teacher uses limit-setting techniques to prompt students who are not attentive or who are being disruptive.
6. If a student dramatically disrupts, he is removed immediately.
7. The principal opens the assembly, using a lavaliere (clip-on) microphone to move up and down the aisles "working the crowd" and getting as close as possible to the students.
8. After the assembly, the students are dismissed in groups rather than as a mass.
9. The vice principal might position himself at the favorite exit (often near the student parking lot) to find and deter skippers.
10. In the class immediately following an assembly, the teacher should take roll.

Halls and Lavatories or Supervision of the Yard and/or Playground

Jones does not approve of hiring hall or playground monitoring staff. However, if they are used during the first three weeks, after long holidays, and periodically throughout the year, Jones says teachers should be assigned a section of hallway, stairs, or lavatory to monitor, and they should model limit-setting techniques for the hired personnel before finally phasing out their presence.

Fire Drills

Each homeroom teacher should teach students how to evacuate the classroom and the building, and how and where to wait outside. The teacher should use limit setting outside to monitor the group. This would be taught in a Say, Show, and Do process. If the practices are not done properly, the teacher would have the class return and redo it properly until the seriousness of the actions are understood. If one or two students still are "messing up" the procedures, they would be told to report to the homeroom teacher before lunch and the teacher would practice with them individually.

Cafeteria

In many schools, cafeteria monitors are hired to supervise the cafeteria area. When this practice is used:

1. The teacher should be present for the first two to three weeks and at certain times thereafter, joining the hired supervisors in modeling limit-setting procedures.
2. The principal or vice principal should be present and greet the students at the entrance, and should attempt to learn the students' names.
3. During the first days of school, the hired supervisor and/or the principal can use an instant camera to photograph large groups of students eating, being sure to include particularly disruptive students (*camouflage*). With the use of these photos, they can then learn the students' names and establish a talking relationship with them before any misbehavior begins. Use and teach the hired monitors to use limit setting, including *ear limits, eye contact, working the crowd,* and, to the extent possible, *not to go public.*

JONES AND THE TEACHER BEHAVIOR CONTINUUM

In the early 1990s, an automobile manufacturer made the claim that "Quality is Job 1." For quality classroom teaching, the Jones model of *positive discipline* would say that Job 1 is discipline—discipline before instruction. For most middle school or high school teachers, their passion is their subject area, be it history, physics, music, or the array of other subjects. They would love to step into their classroom each day and just deal with content. However, because of a host of home, community, and societal pressures, fewer and fewer of today's students come with the attitude of really wanting to learn what teachers would like to teach them. When they butt their heads against a wall of resentful students, most teachers will take one of two routes: either they lower their standards and make do or they leave the teaching profession. The Jones model, however, presents a discipline method designed to help teachers reclaim their students' interest and enthusiasm.

In many ways, parts of the Jones model parallel elements of the Teacher Behavior Continuum (see Figure 9–5). From the beginning, the teacher informs the students about the structure and rules he wants in the classroom, following the pattern of the TBC's *modeling*. This sets the stage for the future classroom drama of limit setting (TBC's *directive statements*) for the high-rolling misbehaviors, and then responsibility training (TBC's *reinforcement*) for all students with an incentive program that creates new cooperative behavior. Finally, for those one or two students with major emotional and social adjustment problems, the teacher piggybacks an incentive system for the purpose of omission training (again, TBC's *reinforcement*).

SUMMARY

Good classroom discipline and management start the minute the first student walks through the classroom door at the beginning of the semester. Either the teacher sets the agenda or the students will set it for her. From the first day, the teacher must be clearly in charge and mean business by "owning the classroom and furniture." The teacher immediately teaches the classroom structure she will use, and is prepared to use the Jones techniques of limit setting, back-up system, and responsibility training to deal with most behavior problems. For the more serious, less frequent problems, the teacher uses a process of omission training. In these limited cases, the teacher wishes to stop the unwanted behavior and get peers to help the misbehaving student find social acceptance.

The Jones model is centered on the general principle that the teacher will not take any action to hurt the teacher/student relationship, and that the control of behavior is in the hands of the student, within the context of peer pressure. Through an incentive process, Jones harnesses and channels this peer pressure to help all students learn cooperation. A covert set of values lies hidden within the discipline system through the use of PATs, giving the teacher and students some time to enjoy each other, cement their relationships, and simply have fun.

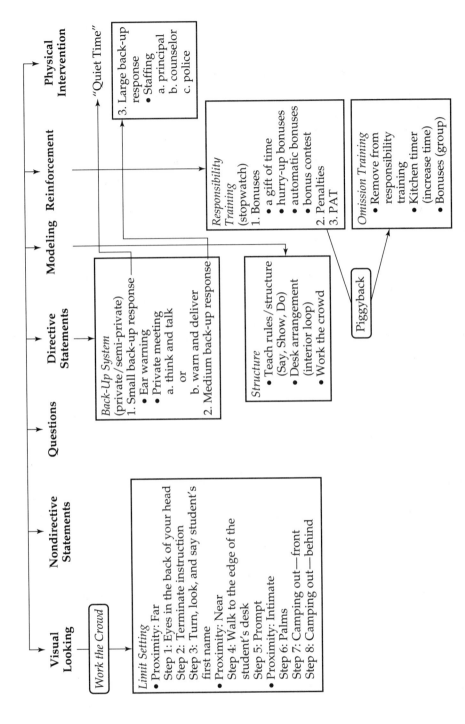

FIGURE 9–5   Teacher Behavior Continuum: Jones Positive Discipline Model

ENDNOTES

1. F. Jones, *Positive Classroom Discipline* (New York: McGraw-Hill, 1987).
2. Ibid.
3. Ibid.
4. Ibid.
5. Ibid., p. 93.
6. Ibid., p. 57.
7. Ibid., pp. 56–65.
8. Ibid., pp. 260–265.
9. Ibid., p. 281.
10. Ibid., p. 285.
11. Ibid., p. 281.
12. Ibid., p. 289.
13. Ibid., p. 301.
14. Ibid., p. 344.
15. Ibid., p. 342.
16. Ibid.
17. Ibid., p. 170.
18. Ibid.
19. Ibid., p. 312.

RELATED READINGS

Jones, F. *Positive Classroom Discipline.* New York: McGraw-Hill, 1987.

Jones, F. *Positive Classroom Instruction.* New York: McGraw-Hill, 1987.

INSTRUCTIONAL MEDIA AND WORKSHOPS:
POSITIVE DISCIPLINE

The Jones Positive Discipline Trainer
of Trainers Master Workshops

Dr. Jones offers school and districtwide workshops, as well as summer workshops throughout the United States and Canada, to teach trainers to work with their home school staff. Here is his explanation for his workshops:

Training Format.   A trainer of trainers program can accommodate up to 10 teams of three: two master teachers and an administrator. To provide an adequate concentration of effort at target schools, they recommend at least 1 team from a medium-sized elementary school, 2 from a middle school or junior high, and 3 from a high school. The training sequence includes four sets of training days separated by a month, during which time trainees work together in collegial work groups to solidify newly acquired skills. The focus of the training days is:

- Round 1 (3 days): *Positive Classroom Discipline*
- Round 2 (2 days): *Positive Classroom Instruction*
- Peer Training (3 days): One day of trainer preparation and two days of supervised peer training
- Follow through (2 days): Completion of *Positive Classroom Instruction* and development of the school site support structure

A Video Course of Study.   After the completion of *Positive Classroom Discipline, A Video Course of Study*, the trainee can use a series of prepared videotapes to disseminate Jones's classroom management training through large-group workshops. (The tapes must be purchased and used by the districts.)

Name	Time	Format	Sound	Address of Distributor
Positive Classrom Discipline, A Video Course of Study	Eight 1.5-hour tapes, involving 3 hours of training	Video game interactive	yes	Fredric H. Jones & Associates, Inc. 103 Quarry Lane, Santa Cruz, CA 95060 408 / 425-8222 Fax 408 / 436-8222
Positive Classroom Discipline, A Video Course of Study is designed to help school site training teams make the transition from trainee to trainer. On the tapes, Dr. Jones takes a group of teachers through the entire training process. The tapes are interactive so you can replicate the frequent live interactions that make training work.				

Positive Classroom Discipline and *Positive Classroom Instruction*, published by McGraw-Hill Company, represent the training program in hard copy. The trainees also receive a Trainee's Manual.

- Jones, F. *Positive Classroom Discipline.* New York: McGraw-Hill, 1987.
- Jones, F. *Positive Classroom Instruction.* New York: McGraw-Hill, 1987.

10

ASSERTIVE DISCIPLINE

Theorists/Writers: Lee Canter and Marlene Canter

- *Assertive Discipline: Positive Behavior Management for Today's Classroom*
- *Assertive Discipline: A Take-Charge Approach for Today's Educator*

The following scene takes place in an eighth-grade classroom with a teacher who uses the assertive discipline approach to discipline:

Scattered around the classroom are five students who are off task. They are talking and generally failing to do the seatwork they were assigned.

TEACHER: "Class, we should be working on the six problems on page 32" (*limit setting—Warning: Hint*).

(Three of the five off-task students return to their work, while the other two continue to talk.)

TEACHER: "I can still see people who are not working. What should you all be doing now?" (*limit setting—Warning: As a Question*).

(The two students are quiet for a few minutes before returning to their off-task behavior.)

TEACHER: "Janet and Noreen, I want you to return to your seatwork assignment!" (*limit setting—Warning: I-Statement*).

(The students again fail to comply.)

TEACHER: "Janet and Noreen, that is your warning." (The teacher writes the two girls' names in her gradebook as a *tracking system*. This is the first step on the Discipline Plan—*Warning*.)

(At first, both girls comply, but then once the teacher turns his back to write on the board, Janet passes a note to a neighbor and begins making whispering overtures to those around her.)

TEACHER: "Janet, you were warned. Now you have chosen to stay after class one minute after the bell rings." (The teacher places a *tracking system* check mark by Janet's name in his gradebook for the second step on the Discipline Plan—*Consequence: Stay after Class One Minute.*)

JANET: "Aw, s---! I didn't do anything."

TEACHER: "That is your third time breaking a rule— this time, swearing. Janet, you were warned. Now you have chosen to stay after class two minutes when the bell rings." (The teacher places a *tracking system* check mark by Janet's name in his gradebook for the third step on the Discipline Plan—*Consequence: Stay after Class Two Minutes.*)

JANET: "Christ, I am not staying after school. You're out of your mind if you think I'm going to waste my time like that!"

TEACHER: "Janet, that is the fourth misbehavior. I want you to call your parents." (This is the fourth step, *Consequence: Call Parents;* the teacher intends to take Janet to the office and have her call her parents to inform them about her behavior.)

JANET: "No way, man! I'm not going to the office to make any phone calls!"

TEACHER: "Janet, you knew the rules and you have chosen to break them. Now you must experience the consequences (moves to a position in front of the student). Janet (states the student's *name*, points a finger at her, and then *gestures* toward the door and makes *eye contact*), I want you to stand, go out the door, and go straight to Mr. Hall's office" (*limit setting—Assertive Command* and fifth step: *Go to the Principal's Office*).

JANET: "I wasn't doing anything!"

TEACHER: (moves to a position in front of the student) "Janet (points a finger at her and then toward the door and makes eye contact), I want you to go to Mr. Hall's office" (*limit setting—*first initiation of a *"broken record"*).

JANET: "Noreen was talking and you didn't say anything to her!"

TEACHER: (moves to a position in front of the student) "Janet (points a finger at her and then toward the door and makes eye contact), I want you to go to the office" (*limit setting—*second example of a *"broken record"* by repeating the *assertive command*).

JANET: "I don't know how to do this work."

TEACHER: (moves to a position in front of the student) "Janet, to the office" (*limit setting*—third example of a *"broken record"*).

JANET: (drops her eyes but doesn't move)

TEACHER: "Janet, this is your last chance. Move now or I will need to get Mr. Hall to come here and we will escort you to the office. This is a promise—you choose!" (*promise of a consequence*).

JANET: (makes quick eye contact, drops her head, and begins to grind her teeth)

TEACHER: (takes two envelopes from his gradebook and addresses himself to a well-behaved student seated near the door) "Gwen, please take this letter to Mr. Coats across the hall, and then this second letter to Mr. Hall in the office." (Mr. Coats and Mr. Hall [the *Who-Squad*] soon appear in the classroom and ask, "Who?")

TEACHER: "Janet, seated here" (points to Janet). (The principal approaches Janet, takes her by the elbow, and escorts the student to his office. Mr. Coats stands nearby ready to help if needed.) (*send to principal*)

This teacher/student interaction is an example of the teacher practicing assertive discipline techniques. The teacher has determined his own right to teach, has developed a clear punishment system, and will not back down with a student who violates a rule.

The teacher is not concerned with Relationship-Listening or Confronting-Contracting approaches with the student. Instead, the assertive teacher clearly is aligned with the Rules and Consequences approach to discipline. The teacher holds maximum control while the student has minimum control over correction when discipline problems occur. Shortly, I will discuss the range of Rules and Consequences that an assertive teacher can use, but first let's review the assertiveness model.

THE ASSERTIVENESS MODEL

The assertiveness model approach to discipline has been populized by Lee Canter and Marlene Canter in their book *Assertive Discipline*. After the book was published in 1976, Lee and Marlene Canter and their associates began conducting discipline workshops, primarily on the West Coast of the United States. Since then, the assertive discipline approach has been disseminated across the United States by additional consultants, videotapes, and workbooks. It is rare to find a locality in the United States where the assertive discipline approach is not known.

The Canters' approach to discipline is derived from the application of assertiveness training to various forms of human conflict. Such books as *Stand Up, Speak Out, Talk Back* (Alberti & Emmons, 1975)[1] and *When I Say No, I Feel Guilty* (Smith, 1975)[2] are examples of the human conflict literature that were forerunners to the Canter approach.

"Mrs. Eggleston has been quite successful with reluctant readers."

Cartoon by Ford Button.

Assertiveness training is based on the premise that humans can respond to conflict in one of three ways: nonassertively, hostilely, or assertively. For example, if an employer at the last minute asks her employee to stay after work to do an extra assignment and the employee already has family commitments, the employee can respond in one of three ways.

1. The first way is *nonassertively,* by not telling the employer of his previous commitments and instead passively complying, such as, "OK, boss, I don't mind staying after work."
2. The second is the *hostile* way, by telling the employer in a vindictive and emotional tone what he thinks of such a request, such as, "You may be my boss but I don't care! That's the most inconsiderate request I've ever heard! Don't you have any feelings for others?"
3. The third is the *assertive* way, by telling the employer in a calm but serious manner of the previous commitment and suggesting a solution that is within an employee's right's, such as, "I'm sorry, but I have family obligations after work. If it's a real emergency, I could arrange to start work early tomorrow morning, let's say 7:00 A.M. But I would want to finish work at 3:00 P.M. instead of the usual 5:00 P.M."

The assertive person states what his reasonable rights are without being obnoxious, aggressive, vengeful, apologetic, or "wishy-washy." As the assertiveness writers state, every person has the perfect right to express his or her own needs and desires.

Using the opening teacher/student classroom incident, examples of nonassertive, hostile, and assertive responses would be seen as follows:

1. A *nonassertive response* would be for the teacher to deal with Janet by pleading ("Janet, could you be more quiet and try to get back to your work?") or even failing to ask Janet to stop and simply choosing to ignore her behavior.
2. A *hostile response* would be for the teacher to yell, "Janet, shut your mouth! I have had enough of you already. I am sick and tired of you and your actions."
3. An *assertive response* would be many of the actions we saw in the opening vignette, including such a statement as, "Janet, I want you to be quiet. I will not tolerate disruption in my classroom. You know the rules, and if you talk again, then you have chosen to go to the principal's office."

The Canters and their associates have applied these assertiveness training concepts, borrowing some elements of behavior analysis to create their assertive discipline model. They base their philosophy on the following value statements as they relate to the classroom teacher:

- You have the right and the responsibility to establish rules and directions that clearly define the limits of acceptable and unacceptable student behavior.
- You have the right and responsibility to teach students to consistently follow these rules and directions throughout the schoolday and school year.
- You have the right and the responsibility to ask for assistance from parents and administrators when support is needed in handling the behavior of students.[3]

The Canters believe that teachers must attend to their own needs and not become confused by other approaches to discipline (such as the supportiveness model of Thomas Gordon or the reality model of William Glasser), which they believe attend more to student than teacher needs. The assertiveness model of discipline is therefore a systematic combination of verbal assertiveness training combined with teachers using the everyday rewards and punishments that they have at hand. Let us turn to the Teacher Behavior Continuum and see how a teacher would apply the assertive model to his or her classroom.

PREPLANNING (COVERT TEACHER ACTIONS)

The teacher writes out a discipline plan, gives a copy to the principal for approval, and sends it home to the parents, asking for feedback and suggestions. The teacher also teaches the plan, with its accompanying rules, to the students.

The plan must contain a clear statement of *classroom rules*, which are also posted on the chalkboard; *positive recognition* actions that the teacher will take to positively reinforce those students who follow the rules; a statement of *consequences* if the rules are broken; and a *severity clause* allowing the teacher to jump past other steps if the misbehaving student is endangering himself, fellow students, or property. An example of such a plan for a Middle School or High School teacher might be as follows:

1. *Classroom Rules*
   Follow directions.
   Be in the classroom and seated when the bell rings.
   Do not swear.
2. *Positive Recognition*
   Give praise.
   Send positive notes home to parents.
   Award with privilege pass.
3. *Consequences*
   First time a student breaks a rule: Warning.
   Second time: Stay in class 1 minute after the bell.
   Third time: Stay in class 2 minutes after the bell.
   Fourth time: Call parents.
   Fifth time: Send to principal.
4. *Severity Clause*
   Send to principal.[4]

Classroom Rules

Although assertive discipline suggests rules that most teachers typically need in running their classrooms, Canter would state that it is the teacher who ultimately must decide what rules are needed for running a particular classroom, and that the teacher's power to create her own rules must be defended.

Other typical rules seen in many classrooms may be:

- Follow directions.
- Keep hands, feet, and objects to yourself.
- No profanity or teasing.
- No eating.
- Walk in the classroom.
- Do not leave the classroom without permission.
- No yelling or screaming.[5]

Canter sets out a number of principles to follow in creating rules. First, the rules must be observable. Vague rules such as "show respect" or "no fooling around" are poor examples because they do not spell out clearly the behavior that the teacher wants. An observable rule such as "keep your hands to yourself" would replace such vague rules as "show respect at all times," and "be in your seats" would be better than "no fooling around." Also, rules created and published by the teacher for the classroom should not involve academic or homework issues because they are not related to observable classroom behavior.

Second, each rule that is posted—ideally no more than four, and never more than six—must be enforceable all day long. Canter would not like a rule that states "Raise your hand and wait to be called on before you speak" because he would suggest that many times throughout the day the students cannot fully comply with this rule and a teacher should not really expect them to do so. "No swearing" is a good rule because this rule would be observable and relevant all day long.

Finally, Canter would suggest that, when possible, students should be involved in the establishment of rules, although the final say *must* belong to the teacher.

Positive Recognition

The second part of a classroom plan is positive recognition that will motivate students to follow rules that the teacher creates. Canter suggests that a well-developed and executed plan of positive recognition for students' productive behavior will encourage most students to behave appropriately, increase their self-esteem, reduce discipline problems, create a positive classroom climate, and create and establish a positive relationship between the teacher and the students. The basic recognition process is: (1) praise, (2) positive notes and phone calls home, (3) special privileges, (4) certificates and awards, and (5) tangible rewards.

Praise

The nonassertive teacher fails to see and give recognition to appropriate behavior. Some teachers believe appropriate behavior is simply to be expected from students, and so it goes unreinforced. But an assertive discipline system requires repetitive and large amounts of praise for appropriate behavior. The praise must be personal and genuine, and, for middle and high school students, it must be given quietly out of the hearing of peers or in such a manner that it will not make the older student look as if she is "sucking up" to the teacher. Most importantly, praise must be descriptive and specific. Comments such as "Good work, Carol" are too vague and do not point out what behavioral actions the teacher is recognizing. "Carol, I have noticed that for the last two weeks you have been doing all your seatwork and your grades have jumped one grade level. Keep it up!" is a specific and discipline value praise statement.

Since teachers are busy and can get distracted and forget to give positive recognition, assertive discipline would recommend *positive reminders* (prompts) on the classroom clock or the teacher's lesson plan or gradebook. In essence, the teacher makes a specific agreement with himself to make a specific number of praise statements within a classroom period. Such structure begins to help the teacher shift into a habit of being positive. In the *Assertive Discipline: Secondary Workbook*, a Positive Parent Communication Log is provided that enables the teacher to record and keep track of praise, positive notes, phone calls, and other parent communication. (See Figure 10–1 for similar workbook helpers.)

The *Assertive Discipline Workbook,* in an edition specifically for the secondary teacher, provides examples and "fill-in-the-blank" helpers that give a practical structure to the assertive discipline guidelines. Most of these can be copied by the teacher. This workbook contains:

- Classroom Rules Worksheet
- Posters
- 50 Opportunities to Say "You're Terrific"
- Example of positive notes to parents
- Positive Parent Communication Log
- Positive Memo
- Form for "A Note from the Teacher"
- A postcard from the teacher
- Quick Notes to Parents
- Clock Buster (coupons give special privileges)
- Privilege Pass
- Raffle Ticket (book markers)
- Message from the Teacher (forms)
- School-Community Positive Recognition (forms)
- Wish List of Special Privileges
- You Earned It! (forms)
- Positive Recognition (forms)
- Forms for playing a touchdown classroom game

FIGURE 10–1   Workbook Helpers

Positive Notes Home and/or Phone Call to Parents

Often parents hear from the classroom teacher only when their child has done something wrong. Assertive discipline believes that teachers must quickly (at the beginning of the school year or semester) begin to acquire good relationships with the parents of students so that parents will give their full support to the teachers' teaching and discipline efforts. Assertive discipline requires that as a part of the discipline plan the teacher send positive notes home and make phone calls to parents telling about authentic behaviors that the child performed in the classroom. Assertive discipline workbooks contain scripts for the phone calls and notes, as well as forms to practice making original feedback statements to parents. This sounds very time consuming for the middle school and high school teacher who instructs a large number of students each semester, but, again, the teacher must commit to a structure to make a specific number of calls or send a specific number of notes home per week.

Behavior Awards, Notes to Students, Privileges

Notes of a personal nature to students, about a job well done or how their appropriate behavior is valued by the teacher, are recommended. Also suggested are awards such as a *Clock Buster,* a ticket that the student may earn and later use to turn in a paper late or to take a test at a later day (or even be excused completely from taking a test). A raffle-ticket combination is suggested whereby the teacher awards a marker or ticket as a recognition award, which the student saves. Then, periodically a raffle is held with one or two markers drawn and the winners receiving a Clock Buster credit. Finally, assertive discipline suggests getting the community involved by contributing free passes (a coupon for free popcorn at a movie theater, free skates at a rink, free shoes at a bowling alley, etc.) to use as recognition for properly behaving students. Again, the assertive discipline workbooks provide examples of awards and coupons that may be copied.

Finally, a number of in-school special privileges are suggested. This list includes, but is not limited to, the following:

- Be the first one excused from class.
- Choose any seat for a day (or week).
- Listen to a cassette with a headset.
- Get 10 minutes free time.[6]

Consequences

Assertive discipline views a consequence for breaking a rule as a student's choice, such as when the teacher says, "Harry, the rule is no profanity, and you have chosen to break the rule. Therefore you have chosen the consequence of staying one minute after class."

In the discipline plan, the consequences must be made clear to the students so they will know the choice they are making through their behavior. These consequences do not have to be severe. Canter points out that one of the most effective consequences for middle and high school students is simply requiring the student to remain in the classroom for a few minutes after all other students are dismissed. Children this age seem very much to dislike this rather simple consequence, and it is used extensively with these older students.

The consequence should be listed in a *discipline hierarchy*, moving from a warning, which includes writing the student's name in a gradebook or a discipline folder carried by the teacher, to a second violation, which entails a minor consequence with another check mark beside the student's name (all future infractions for that day, along with the teacher's subsequent actions, are recorded in the gradebook or discipline folder). The student starts anew each day, getting a "clean sheet" with no infractions or penalties carried over. The third violation generally increases the consequences (wait two minutes after class), and the fourth violation requires the student to call her parents at home or at work and tell them about the inappropriate behavior. Finally, with the fifth violation, the student is sent to the principal's office and typically is given some consequence by the principal. Canter's book provides this particular plan, but suggests that each teacher is free to design his own plan using a discipline hierarchy whereby the consequences become increasingly severe or place greater demands on the student.

It is important to note that Canter urges that when the teacher is carrying out this discipline plan hierarchy, students should be treated alike. The teacher should not be confused by what Canter refers to as *roadblocks*. Roadblocks are thoughts by the teacher that individual students cannot behave properly because of factors beyond the teacher's control, ranging from emotional illness or hyperactivity to family conditions and socioeconomic background. Such a defeatist attitude becomes a self-fulfilling prophecy. If the teacher excuses the student from following the rules, then he is accepting a discipline problem that will probably affect the entire class for the entire year. Instead, a teacher should expect the same standards from all students, and the teacher should expect to succeed. He may have to call in the help of such other resources as parents, counselors, juvenile authorities, and administrators, but this is the teacher's right. The teacher has the right to teach and to have students behave.

Putting Names on the Chalkboard

In the first assertive discipline book and training, it was recommended that the teacher *not* stop teaching when a student was misbehaving, but simply place the student's name on the board as a visual warning and record check marks beside the student's name in a similar manner. This has been widely criticized as humiliating to the student.[7] As a back-up position, Canter now recommends writing the name in a discipline folder or the gradebook, with an accompanying verbal warning. (The workbook provides a well-developed Behavior Tracking Sheet, which may be copied.) *Note:* Canter does suggest that names be put on the chalkboard by the teacher for good behavior and positive recognition, even recommending that a game be played to see how many names in one day or period can get on the board for appropriate behavior, perhaps earning some sort of reward.

Corporal Punishment/Isolation

During the final step on the discipline hierarchy, the student is sent to the principal's office. Many schools have interpreted this step as indicating corporal punishment (as paddling or getting "your licks") by the principal or in- and out-of-school suspension/isolation for days at a time. This has resulted in a number of high-profile court cases in which principals have used corporal punishment or long periods of isolation, claiming they were only carrying out a nationally known and respected assertive discipline plan. Canter clearly states that this was a total misinterpretation of the assertive discipline philosophy, and has issued a clear disclaimer that corporal punishment is not a part of the assertive discipline techniques. Canter also recommends that time out or isolation be used in a very cautious manner; if it *is* used, the student should be in isolation (a classroom across the hall or the principal's office) for no more than a few minutes, not exceeding an hour at the middle school or high school level. (Criteria for a room or location for isolation are given, and are nearly identical to those previously presented in Chapter 7.)

TEACHER BEHAVIOR CONTINUUM

The Teacher Behavior Continuum can be applied as a way of viewing the power techniques inherent in the assertive discipline process. Refer to the following items displayed on the TBC in Figure 10–2.

Visual Looking	Nondirective Statements	Questions
a. Establish/publish discipline plan to: • Students • Principal • Parents b. Post rules—must: • Be observable • Apply all day • Relate to teaching style • Involve students • Be age appropriate	The Assertive Process After 1st misbehavior (give warning): (1.1) Warning: Hints "Class, we should be..."	(1.2) Warning: As a Question "What should you be doing now?"
Redirection 1: The "Look" 2: Physical Proximity	3: Mention off-task student's name 4: Proximity praise (praise the appropriate behavior of students on each side of off-task student) 5: Praise the student later (when he or she is on task)	

(numbers) = overt behaviors
(letters) = covert behaviors
4 = five steps on the discipline plan

FIGURE 10–2   Teacher Behavior Continuum: Assertive Discipline

Looking On

Before using the classroom actions and techniques, through preplanning the teacher covertly (1) establishes a discipline plan that is published to students, the principal, and parents; (2) posts the rules on the chalkboard; and (3) teaches the discipline plan to the students through a Say, Show, and Check process using the TBC's *directive statements* or directive teaching.

Directive Statements	Modeling/Reinforcement	Physical Intervention
(c) Teach the discipline plan Step 1: Say (1.3) Warning: I-statement "I want you to stop talking now and...!"	Step 2: Show (model) Step 3: Check (have student model or demonstrate) • Use positive repetition (teach this four times the first month)	4(5) After 5th misbehavior: Consequence (5.1) Go to office ("Who-Squad" if needed)

4(1.4) Warning: "This is your warning." (write name in tracking book)

4(2) After 2nd misbehavior: Consequence
(2.1) Stay after class one minute (write a check in tracking book)

6. Assertive command
   • say student's name
   • gesture
   • touch (not for secondary grades)
   • eye contact

4(3) After 3rd misbehavior: Consequence
(3.1) Stay after class two minutes (write another check in tracking book)

6. Severity clause (send to the principal)

7. Broken record
(repeat assertive command three times, then follow through with consequence)

4(4) After 4th misbehavior: Consequence
(4.1) Call parents (write another check in tracking book)

8. Promise: "Be quiet now or you'll have chosen to (experience a negative consequence)!"

The Recognition Process

a.) Positive recognition
   • Praise
   • Notes/calls home
   • Certificates/awards
   • Tangible awards
b.) Reminder for teacher
   • Classwide recognition
   • Use + behavior chart

Go to office (for recognition/praise)

FIGURE 10–2   (continued)

Nondirective Statements/Questions

The first step in an assertive discipline plan is to give the off-task student a warning. This will use minimal power in the form of a warning such as a hint ("Class, we should all be doing... !") (*nondirective statement*)[8] or a similar warning in the form of a question ("What should you be doing now?") (*questions*).

Directive Statements

Next, the warning becomes quite directive as an I-statement, such as, "I want you to stop talking now and ... !" Finally, this warning is labeled as the student's last signal to change the off-task behavior—"This is your last warning"—before a consequence will occur.

Modeling/Reinforcing

In the discipline plan hierarchy, the teacher must follow up a warning with a consequence. This is generally a negative minor consequence (e.g., stay after class one minute). After a third violation, the hierarchy moves to an increased negative consequence (stay after class two minutes). Finally, with the fourth infraction, the parents are called by the student. The student is taken to the office, the teacher dials the phone to get the parent at work, and the teacher states, "Hello, Mr. (Mrs.) Parent, this is Mr. (Ms., Mrs.) Jameson, your child's teacher, and we are having some difficulty with his (her) behavior in class today. I now will put him (her) on the phone so he (she) can tell you about it." The telephone is then turned over to the student to tell the parent what has occurred.

ASSERTIVE COMMAND

At times, a desist process between teacher and student becomes confrontational, which undoubtedly will challenge the teacher. Assertive discipline would not want the teacher to retreat to a nonassertive passive stance and behavior or to a hostile response in these taxing interactions. Canter provides clear guidelines for how to give an *assertive command*—say the student's name, gesture, touch (not for secondary teachers), establish eye contact, and tell the student exactly what to do.

TEACHER: "Janet, you knew the rules and you have chosen to break them. Now you must experience the consequences (moves to a position in front of the student). Janet (states the student's *name*, points a finger at her, and then *gestures* toward the door and makes *eye contact*), I want you to stand, go out the door, and go straight to Mr. Hall's office" (*limit setting—Assertive Command*).

At times, the student will not comply, instead giving the teacher back talk or playing games to distract the teacher from this assertive position. When this occurs, the teacher does not fall into the student's trap by arguing or trying to reason with the student, but moves to a *"broken record"* response by saying the assertive command over and over, like a broken record, at least three times before following through with a consequence.

JANET: "I wasn't doing anything!"

TEACHER: (moves to a position in front of the student) "Janet (points a finger at her and then toward the door and makes eye contact), I want you to go to Mr. Hall's office" (*limit setting*—first initiation of a "*broken record*").

JANET: "Noreen was talking and you didn't say anything to her!"

TEACHER: (moves to a position in front of the student) "Janet (points a finger at her and then toward the door and makes eye contact), I want you to go to the office" (*limit setting*—second example of a "*broken record*" by repeating the *assertive command*).

JANET: "I don't know how to do this work."

TEACHER: (moves to a position in front of the student) "Janet to the office" (*limit setting*—third example of a "*broken record*").

JANET: (drops her eyes but doesn't move)

Enough is enough. There comes a point where the teacher has escalated to the top of his or her discipline hierarchy and now must follow through with physical intervention by removing the student to the principal's office. Before this occurs, the student is given a clear choice through the use of a *promise of consequence*, which permits the student a final choice.

TEACHER: "Janet, this is your last chance. Move now or I will need to get Mr. Hall to come here and we will escort you to the office. This is a promise—you choose!" (*promise of a consequence*).

JANET: (makes quick eye contact, drops her head, and begins to grind her teeth)

The Who-Squad

After the fifth infraction or breaking of the rule, the student is sent to the principal's office. If the student refuses to go and directly challenges the teacher's authority, the teacher makes use of two previously prepared letters, one addressed to the principal in charge of discipline and the other to the teacher across the hall. These have been stored in the teacher's lesson plan book or gradebook. A well-behaved student seated near the door is asked to take these envelopes, which contain letters that state, "Help. I need your help to escort a defiant student out of my room." The fellow teacher and principal appear at the classroom door and ask, "Who?" and the teacher points and says the student's name—hence the title, *The Who-Squad*. The squad then escorts the student to the office, where the principal will counsel the student and possibly give some negative consequence.

TEACHER: "Janet, this is your last chance. Move now or I will need to get Mr. Hall to come here and we will escort you to the office. This is a promise—you choose!" (*promise of a consequence*).

JANET: (makes quick eye contact, drops her head, and begins to grind her teeth)

TEACHER: (takes out two envelopes from his gradebook and addresses himself to a well-behaved student seated near the door) "Gwen, please take this letter to Mr.

Coats across the hall, and then this second letter to Mr. Hall in the office." (Mr. Coats and Mr. Hall [the *Who-Squad*] soon appear in the classroom and ask, "Who?")

TEACHER: "Janet, seated here" (points to Janet). (The principal approaches Janet, takes her by the elbow, and escorts the student to his office. Mr. Coats stands nearby ready to help if needed.) (*send to principal*)

The Severity Clause

If the student is endangering property, himself, or others, the teacher obviously would not take the time to progress slowly up this hierarchy. Instead, the teacher would invoke the severity clause and send the student directly to the principal.

Modeling/Reinforcement

Also, under the reinforcement column of the TBC, we would place the recognition process of our assertive discipline plan. This would involve a teacher relating to one student through recognition actions of praise, positive notes/calls home, certificates/awards, and tangible awards. Again, the teacher would place reminders to himself to give recognition daily, and these teacher actions would be tracked.

The teacher would also use a teacher-to-all-students (entire class) recognition system. This might involve a game of "classroom football" in which the entire class gains points through the appropriate behavior of all students or by just one student; when the game is won, the whole class wins by having a special privilege (e.g., no homework for one evening) or getting free time to do whatever they want.

Canter recommends a series of other techniques to create an accepting climate and positive relationship with students, all designed to be reinforcing:

- Take an inventory of student interest and attempt to bring this interest into the classroom activities. (A form for a Student Interest Inventory is included in the text and workbook.)
- Greet students at the door.
- Spend a few special minutes with students in small talk.
- Make home visits.
- Make a phone call to a student who had a difficult day in your classroom to let her know that you care.
- Make a phone call to a student when he has had a good day.
- Send a get-well card to sick students.

Teach the Discipline Plan and Rules

Assertive discipline maintains that a discipline plan, and especially the rules, need to be directly taught to the class just as the teacher would instruct any new knowledge in the subject area. Even in middle school and high school, we cannot assume that just because the students have been in school for many years and are older, they will automatically understand and follow the rules after we have explained them once. Canter provides a teacher lesson plan for teaching discipline to the total class with the lessons covering such points as (1) explain why you need the rules, (2) teach the rules, (3) check for understanding, (4) explain why you have consequences, (5) explain how you will reinforce students who follow the rules, and (6) check for understanding.[9] These direct instructional strategies generally follow the Madeline Hunter[10] approach of instructional procedures as seen in Jones's positive discipline model following the basic three-step lesson of *Say* (verbally explain), *Show* (physically model and demonstrate), and *Check* (test for comprehension). Canter would also point out that the teaching of rules, even when following direct lesson procedures, cannot be done on a one-shot basis, but instead needs positive repetition. At the middle and high school levels, this means that once a new rule has been taught, it must be retaught, through positive repetition, at least four times during the month in order to truly reinforce the learning.

Other Suggested Classroom Procedures

In his newest book, Canter has added a number of general classroom practices that look quite similar to those first described in Jones's positive discipline model.

Scanning
This technique is used to get students to maintain a working behavior at their desks or while working in groups. While working with a group of students, the teacher periodically looks up and over the remaining students in the classroom and gives praise statements to those who are actively working. This alerts the students to the fact that the teacher is still observant.

Circulating the Classroom
"Don't stay seated behind your desk!" directs assertive discipline. Get on your feet and move around the room—in other words, circulate.

Redirection
When a student is off task, Canter suggests a series of low-profile correction techniques, again similar to those used in the Jones model. In visually looking, the teacher gives the off-task student a "look" to signal that the teacher is aware of the off-task behavior. Next, the teacher may mention the off-task student's name during the discussion or lecture, again signaling the student. Also, the teacher would use proximity praise by praising the students on each side of the off-task student for their appropriate behavior, thus attempting in a subtle manner to cue the off-task student. Finally, whenever the student does comply and gets back to work, the teacher finds the earliest opportunity to praise the student for the cooperative behavior.

SUMMARY

The underlying premise of the assertiveness model is the right of the teacher to teach and to expect students to obey, with the full support of parents and administrators if needed. An assertive teacher clearly conveys her rules for compliance and the actions that will greet noncompliance. The assertive discipline teacher does not back down. She covertly makes a discipline plan for all students and teaches this plan directly to the class through an instructional process. The teacher gives warnings, and then, if needed, follows up with preestablished consequences, making it clear that the misbehaving student has chosen this negative consequence by his own behavior.

Although the plan clearly delineates negative consequences, Canter has outlined a positive recognition system whereby praise is used and documented by the teacher. The system attempts to train the teacher to repeatedly give reinforcing positive actions toward the class and individual students.

ENDNOTES

1. R. E. Alberti and M. L. Emmons, *Stand Up, Speak Out, Talk Back* (New York: Pocket Books, 1975).

2. M. J. Smith, *When I Say No, I Feel Guilty* (New York: Bantam Books, 1975).

3. L. Canter and M. Canter, *Assertive Discipline: Positive Behavior Management for Today's Classroom* (Santa Monica, CA: Lee Canter & Associates, 1992), p. 5.

4. Ibid., p. 45.

5. Ibid., p. 50.

6. L. Canter, *Assertive Discipline: Secondary Workbook* (Santa Monica, CA: Lee Canter & Associates, 1992), p. 37.

7. D. Hill, "Order in the Classroom," *Teacher Magazine* (April 1990): 70–77.

8. L. Canter, "Be an Assertive Teacher," *Instructor* (November 1978).

9. Canter, *Assertive Discipline: Secondary Workbook*, p. 60.

10. M. Hunter, *Teach for Transfer* (El Segundo, CA: TIP Publications, 1971).

RELATED READINGS

Teachers

Canter, L. *Homework without Tears for Teachers— Grades 1–12.* Santa Monica, CA: Lee Canter & Associates, 1989.

Canter, L. *Back to School with Assertive Discipline: Grades 1–6.* Santa Monica, CA: Lee Canter & Associates, 1990.

Canter, L., and Canter, M. *Assertive Discipline: A Take-Charge Approach for Today's Educator.* Los Angeles, CA: Canter & Associates, 1976 (the original text).

Canter, L., and Canter, M. *Assertive Discipline: Positive Behavior Management for Today's Classroom.* Santa Monica, CA: Lee Canter & Associates, 1992.

Canter, L., and Canter, M. *Succeeding with Difficult Students: New Strategies for Reaching Your Most Challenging Students.* Santa Monica, CA: Lee Canter & Associates, 1993.

Parents

Canter, L., and Canter, M. *Assertive Discipline for Parents*. New York: Harper & Row, 1988.

Canter, L., and Canter, M. *Parents On Your Side: A Comprehensive Parent Involvement Program for Teachers*. Santa Monica, CA: Lee Canter & Associates, 1991.

Canter, L., and Hausner, L. *Homework without Tears: A Parent's Guide for Motivating Children to Do Homework and to Succeed in School*. New York: Harper & Row, 1987.

Difficult Students

Canter, L. *Succeeding with Difficult Students: Workbook—Grades K–12*. Santa Monica, CA: Lee Canter & Associates, 1993.

Workbooks

Canter, L. *Teacher's Mailbox: A Collection of Reproducibles to Facilitate Communication Between Teachers, Students, and Parents—Grades K–6*. Santa Monica, CA: Lee Canter & Associates, 1988.

Canter, L. *Assertive Discipline: Elementary Workbook—Grades K–5*. Santa Monica, CA: Lee Canter & Associates, 1992.

Canter, L. *Assertive Discipline: Middle School Workbook—Grades 6–8*. Santa Monica, CA: Lee Canter & Associates, 1992.

Canter, L. *Assertive Discipline: Secondary Workbook—Grades 9–12*. Santa Monica, CA: Lee Canter & Associates, 1992.

Auxiliary Staff

Canter, L. *Assertive Discipline for the Bus Driver: A Step-by-Step Approach for Managing Student Behavior on the School Bus*. Santa Monica, CA: Lee Canter & Associates, 1987.

Canter, L. *Assertive Discipline for Paraprofessionals*. Santa Monica, CA: Lee Canter & Associates, 1987.

INSTRUCTIONAL MEDIA: ASSERTIVE DISCIPLINE

Name	Minutes	Format	Sound	Address of Distributor
Assertive Skills: Tintypes	20	16 mm	yes	Salinger Educational Media 1635 12th Street Santa Monica, CA 90404

Shows that assertive training is based on the premise that meekness and aggressiveness are undesirable behavior patterns and that assertive skills and behavior may be learned. Will help audience recognize these modes of behavior in themselves and create the desire for change.

Assertive Discipline in Action	22	16 mm	yes	Films Incorporated Video 5547 N. Ravenswood Avenue Chicago, IL 60640-1199 (800) 343-4312 Ext. 388 (312) 878-2600 Ext. 388

Shows elementary- and secondary-level teachers using Lee Canter's assertive discipline strategies in the classroom and on the playground. Summarizes the technique's main points as the formulation of fair, consistent rules; the development of consequences for breaking rules, as well as rewards for following the rules; and the cooperation of administrators and parents. Emphasizes that everyone involved must know the rules, consequences, and rewards, and the necessity for consistent action.

Assertive Discipline in the Classroom	29	Video ¾ inch	yes	Films Incorporated Video 5547 N. Ravenswood Avenue Chicago, IL 60640-1199 (800) 343-4312 Ext. 388 (312) 878-2600 Ext. 388 FAX: (312) 878-0416

Lee Canter presents his approach to school discipline, which adapts the principles of assertive training for classroom application. This "no-nonsense" approach shows teachers how to gain self-confidence and master specific competencies necessary to manage a classroom effectively. Assertive discipline strategies are demonstrated through role-play and in documentary classroom scenes.

Name	Minutes	Format	Sound	Address of Distributor
Assertive Discipline Workshop: *Session #1—What Is Assertive Discipline?* *Session #2—Roadblocks to Assertive Discipline* *Session #3—Limit Setting in the Classroom* *Session #4—Positive Consequences in the Classroom* *Session #5—How to Start the First Day of School; School Wide Discipline* *Session #6—Follow up*	29	16 mm	yes	The Arthur Canter Film Collection 2113 Broadway, Suite 400 New York, NY 10023

Assertive discipline is a competency-based approach to discipline developed by Lee Canter, director of Lee Canter & Associates. His unique program will provide an educator with the skills and confidence necessary to "take charge" of behavior problems in a firm and consistent, yet positive, manner. Provides the background to assertive discipline and describes nonassertive and hostile teachers.

Because of the controversial nature of the assertive discipline model, research and discussion literature regarding this model is provided here as a resource to the reader:

Research and Discussion Papers Related to Assertive Discipline

Allen, R. D. "The Effect of Assertive Discipline on the Number of Junior High School Discipline Referrals." *Dissertation Abstracts International, 44* (1984): 2299A–2300A.

Barrett, E. R. "Assertive Discipline and Research," 1987. Unpublished manuscript available from Canter & Associates, P.O. Box 2113, Santa Monica, CA 90406.

Barrett, E. R., and Curtis. K. F. "The Effect of Assertive Discipline Training on Student Teachers." *Teacher Education and Practice* (Spring/Summer 1986): 53–56.

Bauer, R. L. "A Quasi-Experimental Study of the Effects of Assertive Discipline." *Dissertation Abstracts International, 43* (1982): 25A.

Canter & Associates. "Abstracts of Research and Validating Effectiveness of Assertive Discipline," 1987. Unpublished manuscript available from Lee Canter & Associates, P.O. Box 2113, Santa Monica, CA 90406.

Canter, L. "Competency-Based Approach to Discipline—It's Assertive." *Educational Leadership, 8* (1979): 11–13.

Canter, L. "Taking Charge of Student Behavior." *National Elementary Principal, 58,* 4 (1979): 33–36, 41.

Canter, L. "Assertive Discipline: A Proven Approach." *Today's Catholic Teacher* (October 1983): 36–37.

Crawley, K. E. "Teacher and Student Perceptions with Regard to Classroom Behavior Conditions, Procedures, and Student Behavior in Classes of Teachers Trained in Assertive Discipline Methods." *Dissertation Abstracts International, 43* (1983): 2840D.

Ersavas, C. M. "A Study of the Effect of Assertive Discipline at Four Elementary Schools." *Dissertation Abstracts International, 42* (1981): 473A.

Fereira, C. L. "A Positive Approach to Assertive Discipline," 1983. Martinez, CA: Martinez Unified School District. (ERIC Document Reproduction Service No. ED 240058).

Henderson, C. B. "An Analysis of Assertive Discipline Training and Implementation on Inservice Elementary Teachers' Self-Concept; Locus of Control; Pupil Control Ideology; and Assertive Personality Characteristics." *Dissertation Abstracts International, 42* (1982): 4797A.

Mandelbaum, L. H., Russell, S. C., Krouse, J., and Gonter, M. "Assertive Discipline: An Effective Classwide Behavior Management Program." *Behavior Disorders, 8,* 4 (1983): 258–264.

McCormack, S. L. "Students' Off-Task Behavior and Assertive Discipline." *Dissertation Abstracts International, 46* (1985): 1880A.

Moffett, K. L., Jurenka, D. J., and Kovan, J. "Assertive Discipline." *California School Boards* (June/July/August 1982): 24–27.

Parker, P. R. "Effects of Secondary Level Assertive Discipline in a Central Texas School District and Guidelines to Successful Assertion and Reward Strategies." *Dissertation Abstracts International, 45* (1985): 3504A.

Render, J. F., Padilla, J. M., and Krank, H. M. "Assertive Discipline: A Critical Review and Analysis." Paper presented at the annual meeting of the Northern Rocky Mountain Educational Research Association, Park City, UT, October 1987.

Render, G. F., Padilla, J. M., and Krank, H. M. "Assertive Discipline: A Critical Review and Analysis." *Teachers College Record,* 1996.

Smith, S. J. "The Effects of Assertive Discipline Training on Student Teachers' Self-Perceptions and Classroom Management Skills." *Dissertation Abstracts International, 44* (1984): 2690A.

Ward, L. R. "The Effectiveness of Assertive Discipline as a Means to Reduce Classroom Disruptions." *Dissertation Abstracts International, 44* (1984): 2324A–2325A.

11

MANAGING STUDENT VIOLENT ASSAULTS AND BREAKING UP STUDENT FIGHTS

Regrettably, today's schools increasingly are the scenes of worsening violence. Assaults occur with greater frequency and ferocity than ever before, posing a serious threat to teachers and the students whose lives they hope to improve. This unhappy trend creates a new set of difficult challenges for today's classroom teacher.

Revengeful, assaultive, and violent students are simply "reflex" beings, their negative behavior automatically triggered by external stimuli or situations and by internal fears. To help such a student requires strong intrusion and controlling techniques from the teacher. He or she must first be assertive, and then plan a systematic shaping, behavioral process to help the student gain self-control and a reawakening sense of trust. If necessary, in order to keep the student and others safe from the student's violent and raw aggressive actions, the teacher will need to nonaggressively restrain the student. Let's see an example of such a student and the teacher's response with the use of Rules and Consequences techniques.

Crisis Level 1: Potential Crisis[1]

Mrs. Monroe is supervising the campus area near the cafeteria when she comes upon James, a fourth-grader who is standing before the school wall and bouncing a golf ball off the bricks. Each time the ball hits the wall, it makes a white circle on the bricks and is coming dangerously close to nearby windows.

> *TEACHER:* "James *(name)*, stop!" She points to James's hand holding the ball *(gesture)* and moves face to face *(eye contact)*. "The ball is causing damage and may break a window. Put the ball in your pocket or I will need to take it."

JAMES: (stands still, holds the golf ball tightly with both hands, glares directly at the teacher, and then looks down at the wall and throws and catches again.)

TEACHER: "James *(name)*, stop!" (points to the ball *[gesture]*, moves face to face *[eye contact]*, and places herself between James and the wall). "Put the ball in your pocket or give it to me" *(broken record).*

Crisis Level 2: Developing Crisis—(a) Ventilation and (b) Defiance

JAMES: (screams) "You bitch! You bitch! Keep your bitch hands off me! Keep your bitch hands off me! No, let me go—don't touch me!"

TEACHER: (lets 45 seconds pass) "James *(name)*, stop! Put the ball in your pocket or in my hand *(broken record)*. If you cannot, then I will need to take the ball from you" *(preparatory)* (moves toward James).

Crisis Level 3: Imminent Crisis (Assault)

James turns and with both hands—including the one still holding the ball—forcefully pushes the teacher at shoulder level, causing her to fall back three full steps. The teacher quickly catches her balance.

TEACHER: "James *(name)*, stop! Put the ball in my hand or your pocket" *(broken record).*

JAMES: "No—f- - - off, old lady!" (James screams at full volume, and again attempts to push the teacher with both hands; the teacher grasps both his arms at the wrist to prevent him from throwing the ball again. He drops the ball and attempts to butt her with his head. He now lashes out with his right leg in three quick kicking motions, one of which strikes the teacher squarely on the shin, causing her definite discomfort.)[2]

Mrs. Monroe now releases James to see if he will quiet down; instead, he runs in the door to the band room. The teacher physically prevents him from exiting the band room by holding the exterior door. He kicks the door, to his discomfort, and runs his arm across a storage shelf holding musical instruments, knocking most of the instruments to the floor with a great crashing noise. He now moves to the window and violently strikes it with a fist; it cracks, but the window pane stays intact. This action carries the real potential for James to injure himself, so before a second blow lands, the teacher again grasps his wrists and pulls him away from the window. He now runs out the open door and into the arms of Mr. Harrison, a male teacher significantly bigger than James.

Mr. Harrison puts his arms around James, grasping the boy's right wrist with his left hand and left wrist with his right hand, and pulling toward him in a way that causes James's arms to cross over the front of his body (see Drawing 10, page 284). Mr. Harrison moves his body sideways to the student, at a 45-degree angle. This places James's back or hip on Mr. Harrison's right thigh, and the teacher then pulls James's arms back toward him and lightly lifts up.

This causes James's heels to come slightly off the floor, forcing him to stand on his tip-toes with his weight supported by the teacher's thigh, thus preventing him from kicking, biting, or struggling free.

While holding James in the *basket restraining hold*,[3] Mr. Harrison parallels his physical action with accompanying verbal explanation and reassurance to James.

> MR. HARRISON: (now whispers) "James, I am not going to hurt you, and I am not going to let you hurt me. You are safe—I will keep you safe. I will not hurt you *(broken record)*. I am the teacher. I keep students safe; I will not hurt you! James, I am holding you with my hands to keep you safe. See my hands? They are holding you but they are not hurting you *(broken record)*. (James attempts to struggle free but Mr. Harrison holds him firmly.) See my hands? They are holding you but they are not hurting you *(broken record)*. I need to hold you until you can relax. I am holding you but I am not hurting you!"

James attempts to bite Mr. Harrison, but the teacher moves to prevent this; James screams a list of profanities at the teacher, but Mr. Harrison continues to speak to him in a whisper: "I am not going to let you hurt me, and I am not going to hurt you. I am not hurting you. These are helping hands that do not hurt students! You are safe; I am going to keep you safe. I am the teacher, I am the boss, and I can keep students safe. I am going to keep you safe!" (James now begins to cry and slowly stops struggling.)

Crisis Level 4: Reestablishing Equilibrium

> MR. HARRISON: "James, I can see by your face that you are very angry. But look—here are my hands and they are holding you to keep you safe. I will not hurt you—you are safe now."

James's body now goes limp in Mr. Harrison's arms. He permits James to be released and to be seated on a nearby chair.

We have just witnessed one of the most demanding teacher/student interactions—one that involves a clear assault on the teacher and a danger to the student. As a teacher dealing with such a student, your heart is pounding and the adrenaline is rushing through your body, pushing you to a state of hyperalertness and creating a defensive stance for your own protection and for the student's safety. Out of your own understandable fright, you yourself may emotionally flood, thus causing real difficulty in thinking correctly and acting constructively as these sudden and quick actions unfold.

Experts who have studied such violent actions by students recognize a general level-by-level progression in the child's behavior and actions. If we as teachers understand these levels of crisis progression, then when sudden quick developments do occur, as just seen, they can be better understood and thus be less frightening. Previous *thought rehearsal* will permit us to respond constructively.

There are generally four Levels of Crisis Development leading to possible violent acts by the student : Level 1: Potential Crisis; Level 2: Developing Crisis—(a) Ventilation and (b) Defiance; Level 3: Imminent Crisis (Assault/Revengeful); and finally, Level 4: Reestablishing Equilibrium. (These levels parallel the passive-aggressive construct explained in Figure 11–1.[4])

LEVEL 1: POTENTIAL CRISIS

As a result of some source of frustration, in Level 1: Potential Crisis, the student appears as if he is a tightly wound spring, ready to snap. Inner-emotional energy and tension are mounting. His hands may be clenched into a fist with white knuckles, and he may drop his eyes or glare intently, his gaze either focusing sharply on a peer or teacher or, instead, alternately focusing on his subject and then darting away. He may become physically restrictive, pulling inside of himself and turning away, or actively pacing like a caged cat and exhibiting nervous ticks. His actions clearly attract the *attention* of peers and observant adults. Students will ask, "Why is James acting funny?" whereas adults will say, "It looks like James is going to have one of his bad mornings."

The student, if caught quickly, is still rational enough to respond to the teacher's use of language. Our goal is to take this built-up internal energy and have the student ventilate it externally in one of two ways: through the use of language *(talk it out)*, discussed below, or through the use of physical activity *(play it out)*.

Talk It Out (Verbal)

If possible, we bring into use all the Relationship-Listening techniques we have learned. We use *door openers* ("James, I can see that you are very unhappy this morning. Tell me what is bothering you"). If the student does speak, we use *acknowledgments* and *active listening,* and encourage the student to externalize or ventilate these strong pent-up feelings through language and words, keeping in mind that some of these words may be aggressive and hostile. If this "talking it out" is effective and we begin to hear the student tell us the root cause of his heightened emotional condition, we might use the Six Steps to Problem Solving to help him resolve his problem or dilemma.

Let's repeat our earlier teacher/student example. Remember that the first time we encountered Mrs. Monroe and James, she immediately directed him to stop bouncing the ball against the school or she would take it from him.

> *TEACHER:* (nondirective statements) "James, the golf ball is doing damage to the school building. That is fun and exciting for you, but part of my job as a teacher is to keep school property safe."

> *JAMES:* "Damn it!"

> *TEACHER:* "You're angry?" *(active listening)*

Crisis Level	Student Behavior Characteristics	Teacher Goals and Techniques
1: Potential Crisis— Attention Getting	As a result of some frustration, the student appears as if he is a tightly wound spring ready to snap. His hands may be clenched into a fist with white knuckles, and he may drop his eyes or glare intently, his gaze either focusing sharply on a peer or teacher or, instead, alternately focusing on his subject and then darting away. He may become physically restrictive, pulling inside of himself and turning away, or become active— pacing like a caged cat and exhibiting nervous ticks. His actions clearly attract the attention of peers and observant adults.	The student, if caught quickly, is still rational enough to respond to the teacher's language. Have the student ventilate representationally through language (talk it out). Redirect the student away from social interaction, giving him his "personal space." If possible, make few or no demands. With the use of the teacher's language, employ Relationship-Listening techniques.
2: Developing Crisis— Power (a) Ventilation and (b) Defiance	In order to maintain his power over a teacher or peer, the student now screams or shouts verbal aggression in the form of swearing, name calling, and similar verbal outbursts that appear as a release or ventilation of stored-up tension. This may quickly escalate to threats against peers and teachers and/or definite defiance of the teacher.	The teacher positions herself in an alert supportive stance and permits the child's ventilation through verbal aggression. If the verbal aggression turns to defiance, the teacher moves to provide an assertive command (assuring the student of potential consequences) and promises of safety. Give the student time and space to ventilate, and do not physically intervene if possible.
3: Imminent Crisis— Assault/ Revengeful	The student now becomes totally revengeful and nonrational, and cannot control his own actions. He physically strikes out in a direct assault toward a peer or teacher by choking, biting, or hitting/ throwing.	In response to the assault, the teacher defends herself with restraining techniques (head down, basket hold), and accompanies her physical actions with an assertive command sending two messages: an order to desist action in a way the teacher desires, and verbal reassurance through a promise of safety and nonaggression toward the student.
4: Reestablishing Equilibrium	After the violent action, the student is deflated and becomes passive with little energy. He has feelings of guilt and feels helpless as to how others might respond to him.	Help cognitively recapitulate the happenings for the student, first by having him verbally talk about it with the teacher using Relationship-Listening techniques, and then, if unsuccessful, advancing to Confronting-Contracting techniques. Reestablish the relationship verbally and by touch.

FIGURE 11–1   Levels of Crisis, Student Behavior, and Teacher Techniques

JAMES: "That bastard!"

TEACHER: "You are very angry with someone?"

JAMES: "Yeah, I'm one of the best players, and he let Robert play first string and cut me!"

TEACHER: "You're angry because you were cut from the team" *(active listening).*

JAMES: "Yeah, it ain't fair. I'm better than Robert. And I was only late three times."

Mrs. Monroe's efforts to determine the cause of James's aggressive throwing of the golf ball has exposed a deeper problem that James is facing, and she can begin dealing with him from a new perspective.

Six Steps to Problem Solving

TEACHER: "Ah, you have a problem, and that problem is, you were late to practice three times and were cut from the team. How can you deal with this? *(Step 1—Defining the Problem).* Let's think together of ways that you might solve this problem. What are your ideas?" *(Step 2—Generating Possible Solutions).*

JAMES: "I could have my old man talk to Coach."

TEACHER: "That may work, but let's think of a lot of other ways, too."

JAMES: "The 'Y' is putting together a team and I could play over there. Or I could apologize to Coach Michaels and tell him I won't be late again."

TEACHER: "There are other teams to play on, or apologizing might get you back on the team" *(active listening).*

JAMES: "Maybe, but the 'Y' team has a bunch of losers."

TEACHER: "Which one of your ideas is best?" *(Step 3—Evaluating the Solutions).*

JAMES: "I think I'll keep my father out of this. He might screw things up and make it worse between Coach and me. But I have a hard time talking to Coach—he makes me nervous and I can't speak" *(Step 4—Deciding Which Solution Is Best).*

TEACHER: "OK, you have decided that is not a good solution. What actions will you take?"

JAMES: "I will go by the 'Y' after school and see who's on their team, and maybe write Coach a note, apologizing and asking for a second chance."

The next day Mrs. Monroe watches James, who appears less tense *(Step 5—Implementing the Solution).* After lunch, she talks to James.

TEACHER: "Was your solution to your problem a good one?" *(Step 6—Evaluation of the Solution)*.

JAMES: "Yes, it was *great*. There are some good players on the 'Y' team and they said I could play on their team. Coach also accepted my apology and said I could come back next week. Now I have to decide between two teams!"

With quick and early intervention, the teacher has headed off an aggressive situation with James by having him talk it out through language, with the teacher using Relationship-Listening techniques.

If the root of the student's stress is beyond the immediate and manageable confines of the classroom setting, such as having been punished by a parent that morning, we would not be able to turn to the Six Steps to Problem Solving, but would instead continue with *active listening* and allow verbal ventilation for the student. If we are unsuccessful at resolving the problem in Level 1: Potential Crisis because we caught it too late or the intensity of the student's emotional flooding was excessive, most likely the student will regress to a more severe Level 2: Developing Crisis, with its two substages of ventilation and defiance.

LEVEL 2: DEVELOPING CRISIS— (A) VENTILATION AND (B) DEFIANCE

In order to maintain his *power* over a teacher or peer, the student enters Level 2: Developing Crisis. He uses ventilation, screaming or shouting verbal aggression in the form of swearing, name calling, and similar verbal outbursts, which appear as a release or ventilation of stored-up tension. This verbal aggression, no matter how it frightens us and classmates, is a good release or ventilation. We *do nothing*. We *do not* challenge his display of power as the student screams, shouts, and swears, because after many minutes of doing so the student will have no anger energies left for a more physical assault. The longer the student ventilates by being verbally aggressive, the better, because he is simply wearing himself out and dispersing his stored-up tension. Don't be frightened by the verbal aggression, but do be cautious. This verbal aggression may quickly escalate into threats to peers and teachers and/or definite defiance toward the teacher.

"You bitch! You bitch! Keep your bitch hands off me! Keep your bitch hands off me! No, let me go—don't touch me!" *(ventilation)*.
"No, it's my golf ball! I'm going to break your face!" *(defiance)*.

In this Level 2: Developing Crisis situation, the student is not rational, but a defensive reflex has set in and he is not capable of controlling his own behavior. While in this state of hypertension, the student will have great difficulty in hearing the teacher's words, but will depend visually and auditorily in assessing nonverbal actions for any hint of action toward him, which he will interpret as hostile and aggressive. Once the defiance and threats are heard, the teacher should signal to a fellow adult or send another student to get the principal, any security personnel, or the teacher across the hall—in short, *get help*. This second or third adult is helpful both in restraining the assaulting student and later as a witness to any actions that may occur in the event of any administrative evaluation. Also, the teacher should take actions to remove onlookers by either having the other students moved to another room, sectioning the area off from the view of other students, or, if possible, moving the student to another room. Witnessing an outburst by the revengeful, flooded student can be very frightening for classmates, and may cause the assaultive student not to back down because he would feel he is losing face among his peers. Later in this chapter will be a description of how to explain the assaulting student's behavior and the teacher's restraining actions to onlooking students through a *problem-solving class meeting*.

When the Level 2: Developing Crisis event does occur, we have two ways of responding: assertive demand with its parallel assertive stance, and supportive demand with its parallel supportive stance.

Assertive and Supportive Demands

The *assertive demand,* as a part of the assertive discipline techniques, and assertive stance should be used with students whose behavior is a problem because of their need for attention. The *supportive demand* and stance are used with flooded power-seeking and revengeful students who may pose a danger to themselves or others or to objects.

Both the assertive and supportive demands are made up of two parts: the teacher's verbal *directive statement,* and a follow-up *preparatory command* if the student does not desist. We add one more important verbal statement said repetitively as a broken record—a *promise of safety:*

> "James, I am not going to hurt you, and I am not going to let you hurt me. You are safe—I will keep you safe. I will not hurt you and I will not let others hurt you. I want to help you be safe!" *(promise of safety).*

The nonverbal actions that are a part of the assertive and supportive stances differ dramatically, but the manner in which verbal commands are delivered should have certain common characteristics. While issuing an assertive or supportive command, the teacher uses a well-modulated voice (controlled tone, volume, and cadence)—neither too fast nor slow, neither too loud nor soft. In the most normal voice possible, the teacher tells the student the *motor actions* or behaviors he or she wants performed. Remember—we do not tell the student what *not* to do.

An assertive demand can be seen as:

> "James (*name*), stop!" (points to the ball James is holding [*gesture*]; moves face to face [*eye contact*]; and places herself between James and the wall). "Put the ball in your pocket or give it to me" *(broken record).*

The parallel nonverbal behavior, or assertive stance, of the teacher to accompany the assertive verbal command is to gesture with her hands and fingers, move squarely in front of the student and make fixed eye contact, and touch the student. When accompanying the verbal assertive demand, these actions are most confrontational. By these actions, the teacher challenges the child's power directly. This assertive demand, with its accompanying stance, may be used effectively with the student who is motivated by attention getting and may be having a difficult moment. However, this approach will be disastrous with the power and revengeful student who is flooded and has taken this general life-stance position toward his world. *We do not use an assertive demand with a flooded, revengeful student* at Level 2: Developing Crisis because the challenge will set him off and he will assault, especially if his personal space is violated (see Figure 11–2).

The teacher technique that is used with these students at this level of crisis is the supportive demand, with the verbal techniques described previously and its accompanying stance. The nonverbal behavior, or stance, used for the supportive demand includes:

1. Stand still and do not get closer than three feet from the student. Do not touch the student, for this would be considered an invasion of his private space, or "bubble." A circle of space exists around all individuals—a hypothetical "bubble" in which they feel safe until others close in. When others do close into this space, it is typically for purposes of expressing intimate affection (cuddling) or for purposes of aggression. The hyperalert Level 2: Developing Crisis student will clearly interpret closing space as an aggressive act, which will arouse his aggressive instincts. This is why you beckon the student in Level 1: Potential Crisis to come to you ("Walk to me and give me the golf ball").

2. Turn your body at an angle, with your preferred foot pointed toward the student (see Drawing 1) and the other foot at a 45-degree angle. Do not square yourself shoulder to shoulder with the student. The angled stance toward the flooded student is interpreted as nonhostile, whereas a squared shoulder is a position one would choose for confrontation and fighting. The foot pointed toward the student may be raised to deflect or block the kicking action of a youth's foot. The other,

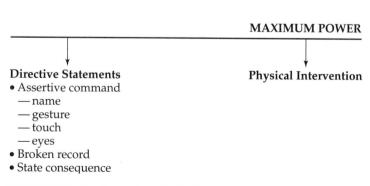

FIGURE 11–2   Assertive Techniques

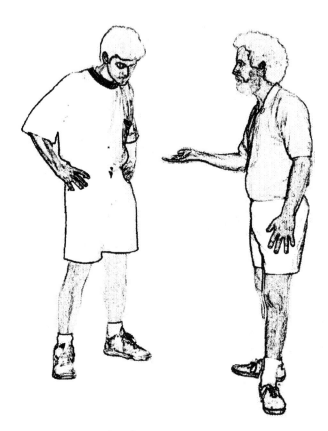

DRAWING 1   The Supportive Stance

angled foot can be used for temporary balance; a stance with parallel feet leaves you flat-footed and prone to being knocked off balance by any minor assault.

3. Your eye contact should not be fixed or glaring.

4. Place your hands behind your back but be ready to use them to block an assault. (Do not gesture or make any threatening moves with the hands, such as pointing.) If assault appears imminent, hold both hands open, one at stomach level and the other in front of your chin, with the palms open and showing the flat face of your hands to the student. Do not put your hands on your hips, clench your fists, or point.

While employing the supportive stance, state a supportive verbal command and repeat it two or three times (broken record), attempting to have the student hear you. If you do not get a change in the student's behavior, clearly state a preparatory directive statement for possible consequences, followed by a promise of safety:

"James, lower your voice, put the ball in your pocket, and go to the cafeteria (*supportive command*; teacher is also in a supportive stance). Lower your voice, put the ball in your pocket, and go to the cafeteria (*broken record*). If you do not, I will need to (teacher chooses one) call your mother and father and tell them of your behavior/have you go to the principal's office/have another teacher remove you from the campus to the office. James, I am not going to hurt you, and I am not going to let you hurt me. You are safe—I will keep you safe. I will not hurt you and I will not let others hurt you. I want to help you be safe!"

The standoff between the flooded Level 2: Developing Crisis student and the teacher's supportive demand and stance should not be rushed. Do not be in a hurry; what you are trying to do is prevent an assault by the student. You may permit many minutes to go by in hopes that the student will desist, back down, and comply. If he does not and instead regresses further, the next action is likely to be physical flooding and an assault.

Also, at this level you will hear verbal defiance:

"You bitch! You bitch! Keep your bitch hands off me! Keep your bitch hands off me! No, let me go—don't touch me!"

Although these words are unpleasant to hear, it is ventilation and the "pouring off" of stored-up anger. Permit this to occur, because the student can only do this so long, until all of his energy is used up.

LEVEL 3: IMMINENT CRISIS (ASSAULT/REVENGEFUL)

If the incident escalates further, the student now becomes totally *power-revengeful* and nonrational, and cannot control his own actions. He physically strikes out in a direct assault against a peer or teacher by choking, biting, kicking, grabbing, or hitting/throwing. In response to the assault, the teacher should defend herself with *restraining techniques* described on pages 280–282 (using the help of a second or third adult if one is nearby). The teacher should accompany her physical actions with an assertive command sending two messages: a directive to desist the unwanted action, and a promise of safety and nonaggression toward the student.

Assault by Choking [5]

When a student assaults you by a front choking—placing his hands around your throat and squeezing—respond by standing erect, thrusting both arms upright above your head, stepping back one step to put the student off balance, and turning suddenly to the right or left so the child's hands will be pulled. Do not try to grab the child's hands and pull them off your throat; this will simply be inefficient or ineffective, and the student might dig his fingernails into your throat (see Drawings 2 and 3).

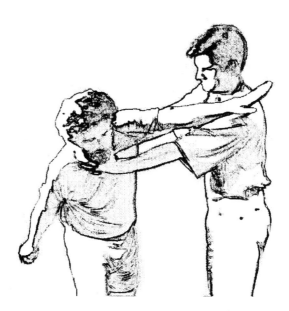

DRAWING 2 **Front Choke Release**

DRAWING 3 **Rear Choke Release**

Assault by Biting

If the student has caught you off guard and has sunk his teeth into you (most likely an arm), you can get yourself free from the biting hold by putting the edge of a flat free hand under the child's nose and against his upper lip and quickly vibrating your hand up and down with sufficient force to free yourself without injuring the student. Do not pull away from the bite but lean into it, as your pulling can cause more damage than the bite itself. If the student has turned in such a manner that you cannot immediately get to his lip-nose area, take the fingertips of a flat free hand and push them firmly into his cheek, finding the teeth between the upper and lower jaw and again vibrating your hand in an up-and-down motion to free yourself (see Drawing 4).

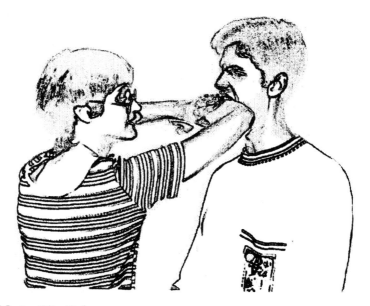

DRAWING 4   Bite Release

Assault by Kicking

From a supportive stance with your feet at a 45-degree angle, you will be able to lift the foot pointing toward the student while balancing on the other foot. While holding up your foot as a barrier, attempt to block the kick with the back of your foot or shoe. When you have a strength advantage over the student, you may remove his shoes and he will desist or else feel the natural consequences of his action (pain). If this kicking continues, a restraining hold might be required (see Drawing 5).

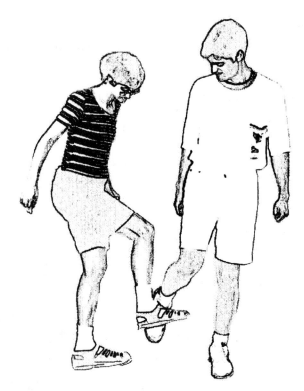

DRAWING 5   Kick Block

Assault by Grabbing

The assault by grabbing will usually be the student doing a one- or two-handed grab of either your arms or hair.

One- and Two-Arm Grabbing Release

When the student uses either one or two hands to grab your arm, there is a weak link in the grab between the child's thumb and forefinger. Simply take your free hand, lock the fingers of your two hands, and pull in the direction that the child's thumb is pointing, normally up (see Drawings 6 and 7).

One- and Two-Hand Hair Pulling Release

If the student grabs your hair, either with one hand or two, clasp his hand and push it into or against your head, while at the same time turning toward the student and bending your upper body down in a 45-degree angle. The child's wrist is bent backwards, causing a loss of strength in his hands and enabling you to break free. Then physically move away (see Drawings 8 and 9).

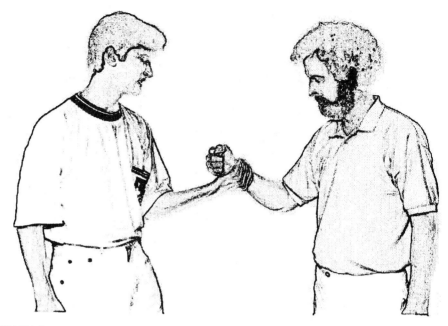

DRAWING 6   One-Hand Grab Release

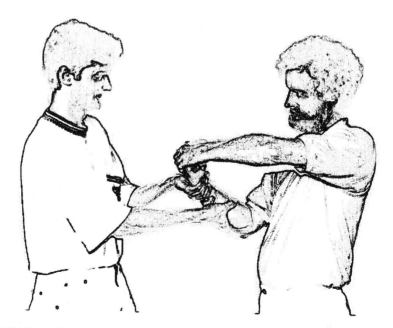

DRAWING 7   Two-Hand Grab Release

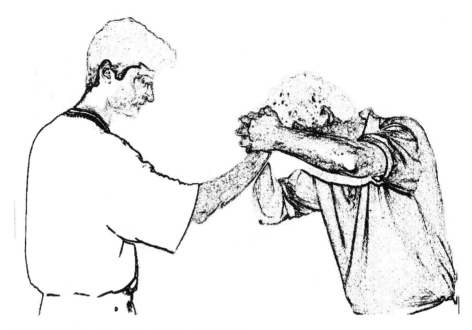

DRAWING 8   One-Hand Hair Grab Release

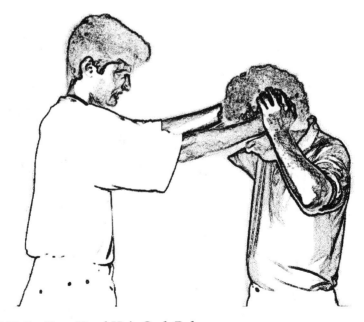

DRAWING 9   Two-Hand Hair Grab Release

Assault by Hitting and Throwing

When the student is hitting or throwing, there are two ways of handling an object moving toward you that has the potential to do you bodily harm. Either move out of its path and dodge, or block and deflect. If you have time and the student is strong enough to do you serious harm, you may pick up an object—such as a book or small chair like a "lion tamer"—and use it to block and deflect the blow or object thrown. The three-foot spacing in the supportive stance may give you the room to use such an object. If the student catches you off guard and has closed in on you, striking with his right fist, then block and deflect this blow with the edge of your right arm by holding it across your body. (The reverse would occur with a left-hand blow.)

If, after an incident of choking, biting, kicking, grabbing, or hitting/throwing, the student retreats and moves to a protective corner or space out of the way of classroom activities, presenting no danger to himself or others, simply leave him alone. Consider him to have moved to Level 4: Reestablishing Equilibrium, and use the techniques explained below. However, if the student still is endangering others, property, or himself, you must now use nonviolent restraining techniques on him.

Nonviolent Restraining

Basket-Weave Hold Restraint [6]

If the student is small enough and you have the advantage of strength over him, you may choose to use the basket-weave hold. This is a preferable restraining technique for a small student. This hold is accomplished by getting behind the assaulting student and putting your arms around him, grasping his right wrist with your left hand and his left wrist with your right hand, and pulling toward you in a way that causes the child's arms to cross over the front of his body (see Drawing 10). As you stand, move your body sideways to the student, your feet at a 45-degree angle. This places the child's back on your right hip, and you then pull his arms back toward you and lift up. This causes the child's heels to come slightly off the floor, forcing him to stand on his tip-toes with his weight supported by your thigh. You also may hold or restrain the student in a seated position. Remember to use only the minimum amount of force needed, so that no injury is done to the student.

Note: The basket-weave restraint is the most powerful hold suggested for a small student where the teacher has a substantial physical strength advantage. If the child is too big and strong, the teacher may be required to use a wrist-shoulder hold.

Wrist-Shoulder Hold Restraint

Once a full blow has been thrown by the assaulting student, quickly step behind the student and grasp his right wrist with your right hand, with the thumb side of your hand facing in. At the same time, take your open left hand and place it on the child's right shoulder from behind. The thumb of your left hand should be posi-

DRAWING 10   Basket-Weave Restraint

tioned in the "V" formed by the child's arm and rib cage (see Drawing 11). Now push down with your left hand on the child's shoulder, while you turn the child's wrist clockwise with your right hand. Be careful to apply only the needed pressure—you do not want to hurt the child. These are to be nonviolent restraining techniques. The child is pushed head-down until his head is below his waist line, and from this position it is impossible for him to pick up his feet to kick. If his head is not down far enough, he can take his free left hand and move it across himself with a blow that can strike you in the face. Take your left foot and place it in front of the child's body and between his two feet, thus preventing the child from walking out of the restraining hold.

Team (Two Adults) Wrist-Shoulder Hold Restraint
With the very strong assaultive child, when a second teacher or adult is available, the wrist-shoulder hold is more safely accomplished. The helping team member takes the child's free arm and does parallel wrist turning and shoulder pushing. Both you and your helper must face the same direction as the student, and both of you place your inside legs in front of the student (see Drawing 11).

DRAWING 11   Wrist-Shoulder Pull-Down Restraint

Transporting Techniques

Keep the child in the wrist-shoulder restraint position until he has stopped struggling. Permit the child to rise very slowly, watching for any signs of renewed struggle, including the possibility that the free hand might strike you in the face. If struggling occurs again, push the child's head below the waist and reestablish the original restraint. Never try to transport a struggling child.

   If the child does stop struggling and you now have him in an upright position, quickly take the hand previously holding the child's shoulder and move it under his arm. Being careful not to release the child's wrist, use your free hand to grasp the inside of the elbow of the child's other arm (see Drawing 12). Now walk quickly, bringing the child with you at the fastest manageable pace.

   This transporting might be done with a team helper (a second adult) holding the child's free arm in a similar manner. A third helper can get behind the child and place both of his or her hands on the student's shoulder blades and push (see Drawing 13). If at any time during the transporting process the child excessively struggles to get free, simply reapply the wrist-shoulder hold.

   IMPORTANT: Physical restraint should be accompanied by parallel language of supportive command, preparatory directive statement, and promise of safety.

DRAWING 12   Single Transport

"James, I want you to stop hitting and relax (*supportive command*). When you do so, I will let you go (*preparatory*). You are safe. I am not going to hurt you, and I will not let you hurt me" *(promise of safety).*

Also, repeat the entire verbal sequence over and over as a *broken record* to attempt to get the student to hear you from within his state of flooding.

Some teachers state that when they are hit, kicked, or bitten by a student, they hit, kick, and bite back, so that the student "knows how it feels."

WARNING: Do not *ever*, under any circumstances, hit, kick, or bite a student who has done this to you. This could rightly be defined as child abuse, and you could properly be charged under the law. When a student is flooded and carries out an assault, he is no longer rational and capable of stopping himself; returning his aggression does not teach him "how it feels" but simply confirms his unreasonable concern that you are a person to fear. When you use nonviolent restraining techniques and parallel supportive demands and promise of safety and you do *not* return the student's aggression, the student gradually learns to trust you and give

DRAWING 13   Two-Person Transport

up his aggression and fears. Remember that during each of these levels of crisis—and especially during the assault action—the student is terribly frightened. He actually scares himself when he is out of control.

Again, if the student becomes passive after an assault, retreats to a protective corner or space out of the way of the classroom activities, and no longer presents a danger to himself or others, simply leave him alone and consider him to have moved to Level 4: Reestablishing Equilibrium.

LEVEL 4: REESTABLISHING EQUILIBRIUM

After the violent act, the student is deflated and becomes passive, with little energy. He has feelings of guilt and feels helpless as to how others might respond to him. Some students will retreat so far back into passivity that they fall asleep or begin self-abusive activities, such as pulling out their hair, biting themselves, or some similar act of physical abuse on themselves. We as teachers will intervene if the student retreats too deeply into passivity by sleeping or beginning physically self-abusive activities.

Since the student is now rational, we wish to help him cognitively recall what has happened, for he may not actually remember what started the flooding incident or what occurred once it began. We will primarily use the Confronting-Contracting techniques.

JAMES: (slouches down into the chair, drops his eyes, pouts with a frowning face for a period of four to six minutes, and then begins to sit up in the chair watching other students)

TEACHER: (approaches) "I need to talk to you about what occurred. What did you do?" *(Step 2—Confronting: "What" Question).*

JAMES: "I don't know" (or the student might say, "I was angry and hit!").

TEACHER: "Well, I saw what you did, and you were using the golf ball and throwing it against the wall, causing damage. You could have hit one of the school windows with the ball. What is the rule? *(Step 2—Confronting: "What" Question,* requesting a verbal statement of the rule). You got so angry that you wanted to hit and bite, but I stopped you and kept you safe."

JAMES: (eyes drop) "Uh-h-h, keep school property safe."

TEACHER: "Yes, when balls are bounced, they need to be bounced on the pavement where they will do no damage. Also, the rule is that hitting and biting are not allowed, and when someone is angry they need to use words to tell the other person. When you got angry and did hit and bite, I needed Mr. Harrison to help hold you tightly to keep you safe. We did not hurt you; I didn't let anyone hurt you. Mr. Harrison kept us both safe. These are helping hands, not hurting hands, and these hands keep students safe[7] (restates the rule so it is very clear). Now you and I must work this out *(Step 3—Contracting).* We must have an agreement (moves to James, takes him gently by the hands, and makes eye contact). What will you do to change?" *(Step 2—Confronting: "What" Question,* requesting change).

JAMES: "Bounce the ball on the pavement and learn to not hit."

TEACHER: "Yes. Do we have an agreement on this? Can I depend on you to remember the rule?" *(Step 3—Contracting: Verbal Agreement).*

JAMES: "Yes" (looks up and makes eye contact with the teacher).

TEACHER: "What will you do when someone makes you angry?"

JAMES: "Words."

TEACHER: "Yes. Do we have an agreement on this? Can I depend on you to remember the rule?" *(Step 3—Contracting: Verbal Agreement).*

JAMES: "Yes" (looks up and makes eye contact with the teacher).

TEACHER: "Good, we now have an agreement. If you agree, I want to shake hands to show a special agreement between us" (holds out her hand to James and smiles warmly) *(Step 3—Contracting).*

JAMES: (returns the teacher's smile and shakes her hand)

TEACHER: "Good, we now have an agreement! You can now remember rules regarding the care of school property. But if you forget the rules, your behavior will say that you do not know how to use the outdoor campus and you will not be able to go outside after lunch *(Step 3—Consequence).* Now, you may feel free to come back to class and work with us, when you feel that you are ready" *(handling isolation).*

It is recommended that during Level 4: Reestablishing Equilibrium, the student and teacher be eye to eye in a very close, intimate space. This can be done by seating the student on an adult chair, with the teacher sitting on a small student-size chair.

To summarize, during this level it is important that the student be able to cognitively state—or the teacher be able to describe—the events that have occurred in a way that imparts no guilt, and for the relationship between the teacher and student to reach a new emotional equilibrium free of hostility. Both the student and the teacher need this reunion.

I would caution against the teacher forcing a verbal apology that requires the student to say "I'm sorry." The verbal statement may be something the teacher needs, but if forced, the student will begin to have feelings of guilt. If the equilibration goes well, students will have feelings of remorse and wish to apologize, but they may express it in a nonverbal form. The student meets the teacher's eyes, saying nothing but smiling affectionately. We as teachers must also learn during the interaction to nonverbally express our "forgiveness" back to the student through similar smiling, but we must also do it in the form of verbal expression as a statement of *promise of safety.*

CLASSMATES AS ONLOOKERS TO THE ASSAULT

It has been recommended previously that steps should be taken to remove onlookers by either having the other students move to another room, sectioning the area off from the view of other students, or, if possible, moving the assaultive student to another room. Witnessing the revengeful, flooded student is very frightening for some classmates; others may "get a kick" out of it. Our restraining actions on the assaulting student may appear to some students as if we are hurting this student ("Mr. Harrison hurt James's arm!").

It is quite important to deal with the classmates who were onlookers to an assault by the revengeful student. Witnessing such aggression can cause an individual student or an entire group of students to move to Level 1: Potential Crisis, whereby they become highly anxious with accompanying behavior that might escalate through these crisis levels. We may deal with this by doing the ventilating techniques previously suggested in working with Level 1: Potential Crisis students. We now view the entire class, if the incident occurred in our classroom, after these violent incidents as being in Level 1: Potential Crisis, so we want the students to "talk it out." This involves holding one or more class problem-solving meetings, as suggested and described by Glasser, using the Relationship-Listening techniques.

Class Meetings (Verbal Ventilation)

The entire class is seated on student-size chairs along a circular line. The assaulting student is included in the meeting. Just as the Confronting-Contracting techniques were used for Level 4: Reestablishing Equilibrium to enable the teacher to establish an emotional equilibrium with the previously assaulting student, this equilibrium will also need to be reestablished with the child's classmates. They have seen or heard the frightening event, and have identified themselves as a part of the action. Through verbal ventilation in the class meeting, we attempt to reach the point where the teacher and students have gotten rid of any feelings of hostility. If we do not do this, the classmates—out of their fear of the acting-out student—will begin to make him the *outside aggressor*.

Let's watch the meeting unfold. Notice that the process begins with the teacher wearing a Relationship-Listening face with its accompanying techniques, and then moves to Confronting-Contracting:

TEACHER: (opens the meeting) "Friends, I'd like to talk about some upsetting and frightening things that happened this morning" *(door opener).*

STUDENTS: (no one speaks for a few minutes, but then a discussion begins)

HARRIET: "James was a mean dude—he really lost it!"

PAUL: "Man, he tried to deck the teacher. Definitely uncool."

TEACHER: "James was very angry. And when he gets angry, he explodes" *(active listening).*

DIANA: "He frightens me when he gets like that—you never know what he's gonna do next!"

TEACHER: "When people hit, it can be hard to like them or feel safe around them."

JOHN: "What bothered me was that Mr. Harrison hurt James's arm."

TEACHER: "When he held James, you thought he was hurting him" *(active listening).*

PAUL: "Mr. Harrison didn't hit James."

TEACHER: "What else did you see and feel?" *(door opener).*

NANCY: "I saw James hit you and try to bite Mr. Harrison. He cried, screamed, and cussed."

This verbal ventilation may continue for 5 to 10 minutes with the teacher maintaining a Relationship-Listening face and techniques. Now the teacher moves to Confronting-Contracting and does not hesitate to deal with the realities of the situation and explain misinformation.

TEACHER: "What happened first? Harriet?" *(Confronting: "What" questions).*

HARRIET: "James was throwing the ball against the school."

TEACHER: "What happened next?" *(Confronting: "What" questions).*

JOHN: "You told James to stop. He pushed you and ran into the music room."

TEACHER: "What happened next?" *(Confronting: "What" questions).*

DIANA: "James screamed, knocked over the musical instruments, and tried to break a window."

TEACHER: "What happened next?" *(Confronting: "What" questions).*

JOHN: "Mr. Harrison hurt James's arm."

TEACHER: "No. Because James got so mad that he could hurt me, he could hurt others, and he could hurt himself, I needed to have Mr. Harrison hold him tightly to keep him safe. Being the teacher puts me in charge, but I don't hurt students. I am a friend, but sometimes when students get very angry I need to hold them tight to keep them safe" (a reality explanation and *promise of safety*).

JOHN: "Well, it sure looked like he hurt James's arm."

TEACHER: "No, John. Mr. Harrison was holding his arm and hands tightly so that his hands would not hurt me. He did *not* hurt James. He was keeping him safe. Come up here, John. (John stands before the teacher.) Let me show you how safely he was holding James." (The teacher now demonstrates the basket-weave restraint on John and two other students. John chuckles as if it is a game, and now a number of other students want a chance to see how their classmate was held.)

TEACHER: "When people get very angry, they sometimes try to hurt other people. But I am a teacher, and no matter how angry students may get, I will not hit them, I will not hurt them, I will not kick them, and I will not bite them. We teachers will hold students to keep them and others safe" (reality explanation and *promise of safety*). Now we need to have an agreement. What should we do when others make us angry?"

Various members of the class volunteer: "We need to talk it out."

TEACHER: "Right. When others make us angry, we need to talk it over, and you can come to a teacher to get help. But *don't* try to straighten things out by hitting, biting, kicking or spitting—this will only make things worse. Use your head to come up with a solution instead. Can we all agree to that?"

Almost in unison, the class members nod their heads in agreement.

TEACHER: "Great, now we all have an agreement. We are going to deal with these kinds of problems with our heads, using language to resolve things" *(contracting).*

This vignette, of course, is for purposes of modeling teacher techniques, and is certainly somewhat artificial. This ventilation process and the confronting and contracting might take many minutes, or even many meetings, and may need to occur throughout the year if aggression is high in your classroom. But the techniques to be used, and the general attitude and processes to be employed, should develop in a direction much as the one demonstrated in the vignette.

This class meeting will serve a number of purposes: (1) it ventilates any pent-up anxiety and feelings that any student might have after witnessing such aggression; (2) it helps both for James and his classmates to reestablish an emotional equilibrium, potentially preventing him from becoming the *outside aggressor;* (3) it helps students understand that if they, too, should become angry (and they will), the teacher will not aggress against them but instead will help; and (4) it dispels any misinformation and misperceptions the students might have ("Mr. Harrison hurt James's arm").

VERBAL AGGRESSION

Verbal aggression is defined as any vocalization, such as crying to get one's own way, shouting, whining, swearing, name calling, verbal threats, and similar actions. We can decide what action we should take toward such verbal aggression by asking the question, What is the motivation of the student for such verbal aggression? The answer will be one of the following: attention getting, power, or revenge. When dealing with students who are swearing, we can apply the Three Faces of Discipline, as discussed next.

Relationship-Listening

"Harold, when that swear word is said, I am afraid that other students will begin to say those words, and those are not school words that I can permit students to use in our classroom." Before delivering such an I-message, we take Harold by the hand and move him out of the hearing and possibly the vision of the other students.

Confronting-Contracting

If the I-message fails to work, we may move to confronting-contracting techniques. "Harold, come with me (take him out of the hearing of classmates). I need to talk to you about these harsh and aggressive words. What are you doing? Well, I think what you are doing is trying to get other students to see you when you use those words so you can have everyone look at you *(attention getting),* or these words can make you the boss *(power)* and feel strong. The rule is that they are not school words and they will not be permitted."

Rules and Consequences

We approach the attention-getting or power-seeking student who is swearing, take him off to the side out of the hearing of others, and deliver an assertive demand. "Harold *(name)*, stop (holds Harold's hand—*touch*). This is not a school word *(eye contact)*. If this word is said again, I will need to call your mother or father and I will send you to time out *(preparatory)*." In the alternative, we may take a behavior analysis response to Harold's swearing.

If the student is motivated by attention getting or power seeking, he may use the "Big F" word or similar swearing so that others will see him and respond in a way that makes him the center of attention. In such an instance, we may behaviorally deal with this by *not* giving attention and by acting as if we do not hear it. We refuse to give our attention *(extinction* by withdrawing *social reinforcement)*, thus the student has no payoff. When we do withdraw our attention, a number of actions will occur. The attention-getting and power-seeking student will intensify the action, since his motivational payoff is to get attention and experiencing the opposite prompts him to escalate the swearing action. We may be able to "tough it out" by refusing to respond to the swearing, and after it gets worse it will dissipate *(extinction)*.

At times, we as teachers might observe unwanted reinforcement and attention for the swearing student from classmates who might giggle and begin saying the same word. This provides the swearing student with a very powerful social reinforcement. We then isolate the student (time out) in such a space that classmates will not socially reinforce him. We enforce this isolation each and every time the attention-getting student acts out through swearing. The power-seeking student will refuse to stay in this isolation, and it might require us to restrain him in the isolated, screened off space; it certainly will require that we remain with him in this space. When we are restraining in time out, we do not speak to the student or give him any other form of verbal or nonverbal acknowledgment. It is helpful to set an egg timer for 5 to 15 minutes, and when it goes off the student is permitted to return to classroom activities. (See Chapter 7 on behavior analysis and the guidelines for the use of time out.)

Swearing is a very different matter for the revengeful student regressing through the levels of crisis. When such students are flooded emotionally in Level 2: Developing Crisis, their verbal aggression in the form of swearing, threats, and other hostile verbal actions is considered ventilating. As odd as it might seem, the more verbal aggression the better, because it means that the child's internal anger, anxiety, and related energy are being ventilated.

CRYING TO GET ONE'S OWN WAY/WHINING

Crying to get one's own way, sometimes called "water power," and whining are both auditorily abrasive expressions that grate on our nerves to such a point that we often give in to the student's demand just to get these sounds to stop. To deal with it, we again may follow the escalation of power techniques of the Three Faces of Discipline continuum.

Relationship-Listening

The I-message contained in the Relationship-Listening face is a particularly helpful technique to use both for "water power" crying and for whining.

> *Crying:* "When I hear crying, I cannot understand what the person wants, and crying hurts my ears."
> *Whining:* "When I hear a squeaky little voice, it hurts my ears, and I have a very difficult time listening to what the squeaky voice wants. People who want me to hear them must use an adult voice for me to hear."

We do not give the student what he wants while he is crying as a use of "water power" or whining, nor shortly after, and the behavior will soon dissipate.

Confronting-Contracting

TEACHER: "What are you doing? What is the rule?" (use words to tell your needs; possibly apply a logical consequence). "That 'squeaky voice' hurts our ears and we are not able to be comfortable at the work table. If that 'squeaky' voice is used again, it is showing us that you do not know the rules for being with us, and I will need to ask you to work at a table by yourself where that 'voice' will not hurt others' ears."

Rules and Consequences

TEACHER: "Carol (*name* and *gestures*), stop (*eye contact, touches*), move now to choose a new table, and begin."

The teacher may choose to reinforce another student who is not crying or whining, use extinction to attempt to withdraw reinforcement given to these acts, or use forms of time out.

BREAKING UP A FIGHT

The National Crisis Prevention Institute, which does much training on the restraining techniques described in this chapter and prepares educators to deal with aggressive students, states that in general a fight occurs between students for one of the following reasons:

Saving Face

People will commonly risk their personal well-being to maintain their dignity. *[This is, of course, especially true for the adolescent child who has peers looking on.]*

Defending Property or Territory

Concern for material objects of real or imagined value will occasionally cause people to sacrifice their safety or even their lives.

Fear (Fight or Flight)

The emotional physiological response of fear can be great enough to impair rational thought. In peak fear response, the body can switch to self-defense mode which demands fleeing or fighting.

Testing the Pecking Order

One person may become jealous over the status of another and respond by picking a fight or generally looking for trouble.[8]

One of the best ways of dealing with fights is to attempt to stop them before they start. This can be done by:

- Responding to early warning signs
- Getting assistance (call principal/other teachers)
- Removing peers (order students out of the area)
- Approaching calmly and confidently (don't rush in)
- Using a supportive stance (see above)
- Using distraction (blink or shut off lights, make a loud distracting noise)
- Using firm nonverbals and paraverbals (control your voice and actions, and use assertive commands)
- Setting and enforcing reasonable limits (use assertive command)
- Separating, if necessary (move the students so they cannot visually see each other to let them calm down)[9]

When a fight between students is in progress, our first critical response is to get help. We may send a student to bring the principal or neighboring teachers to help us deal with this disruption. If possible, remove any obstacles and weapons, and quickly order peers as onlookers to move out of the area. Next, start with verbal intervention by using the supportive demand.

We would not step into the middle of a fight unless we are absolutely certain that we can manage the size and strength of all participants—never intervene alone. If two students are fighting, their behavior will change over time, being either combative or defensive. Try to identify which position each is taking as the fight is progressing. It will be easier to physically restrain the students if they both have taken a defensive stance because this will signal that they really want to stop.

Also, the energy levels will fluctuate between highs and lows. Never grab to restrain a student at the maximum energy upswing; wait until a lull. Team-restraining actions by teachers should occur only as a last resort. The teachers will now use verbal commands in the form of assertive demands, grabbing at each student and putting both into a team (two adults) wrist-shoulder hold restraint (see Drawing 11), keeping their heads down until they stop struggling and agree to stop their fight. Move the students to different rooms and out of visual sight of each other with the use of the transporting techniques. Once control is established, permit the students to cool down and then, by talking to them individually, move to Level 4: Reestablishing Equilibrium through Relationship-Listening and Confronting-Contracting techniques. Then bring both students together, normally with a table between them, and counsel them with the Confronting-Contracting techniques for the purpose of attempting to reestablish a positive working relationship between the two students. The meeting should end with a contract or agreement. If hostilities remain, more discussion should occur, permitting ventilation of issues, or both students may be kept in isolation until they are ready to work it out.

SUMMARY

At times we are faced with a student who is so flooded that he or she acts out in an assaultive and violent manner that endangers himself and others. We must understand the levels of crisis through which the student will move, and first make attempts to get the student to ventilate inner tensions through language. We will also be required to mediate for classmates who have witnessed violent behavior through the use of classroom meetings. We may use any of the techniques previously learned from the Three Faces of Discipline to deal with many other forms of verbal aggression, including swearing, whining, and crying.

ENDNOTES

1. T. McMurrain, *Intervention in Human Crisis* (Atlanta: Humanics Press, 1975). *Nonviolent Crisis Intervention for the Educator: Volume III, The Assaultive Student* (Brookfield, WI: National Crisis Prevention Institute, Inc.).

2. *Note:* After reading the full explanation to follow, you will see that the teacher in this example made a number of mistakes in handling this incident and dealing with a revengeful child. She should have used *supportive demand and stance* rather than *assertive demand and stance* (soon to be explained). However, if the teacher has had little past experience and does not know the history of this child, she might judge his actions as an attempt to grab attention or power, and then might find herself handling the revengeful incident as best she can once it begins.

3. *Nonviolent Crisis Intervention for the Educator: Volume III, The Assaultive Student.*

4. This is also a reconceptualization of the Crisis Development Behavior Levels as developed by the National Crisis Prevention Institute. The Institute's training videos and training workshops are to be highly recommended; more detail on them may be found at the end of this chapter.

5. National Crisis Prevention Institute, Inc.

6. Ibid.

7. Often it is adult hands that do hurt children and create great fear in them.

8. D. Rekoske, and G. T. Wyka, *Breaking Up Fights—How to Safely Defuse Explosive Conflicts* (pamphlet) (Brookfield, WI: National Crisis Prevention Institute, 1990), p. 3.

9. Ibid., pp. 3 and 4.

RELATED READINGS

Freud, A. *Normality and Pathology in Childhood: Assessments of Development.* New York: International University Press, 1968.

McMurrain, T. *Intervention in Human Crisis.* Atlanta: Humanics Press, 1975.

Nonviolent Crisis Intervention for the Educator: Volume III, The Assaultive Student. Brookfield, WI: National Crisis Prevention Institute, Inc.

Wolfgang, C. H. *Helping Aggressive and Passive Preschoolers through Play.* Columbus, OH: Charles Merrill, 1977.

Wolfgang, C. H., and Wolfgang, M. E. *School for Young Children: Developmentally Appropriate Practices.* Boston: Allyn and Bacon, 1992.

INSTRUCTIONAL MEDIA AND TRAINING

Name	Time	Format	Address of Distributor
The Nonviolent Crisis Intervention Instructor Certification Program	24 hrs (6 hours per day)	Video and Role-Play	National Crisis Prevention Institute 3315-K North 124 Street Brookfield, WI 53005 1-800-558-8976 1-414-783-5787

The first phase of the Instructor's Program has you participate in the 12-hour training program just like the staff you will eventually be training. This section is designed to teach you the basic skills and techniques of nonviolent crisis intervention. The next phase focuses on facilitating dynamics. Your professional instructor will train you in teaching techniques that have proven extremely effective throughout the years. Major topics include using CPI materials most effectively, facilitating role-play, class size, teaching physical techniques, answering difficult questions from participants, and dealing with staff resistance. Phase three, instructor practicum, gives you the opportunity to do a presentation of these skills. Four videos are available for purchase:

Volume I—The Disruptive Child
Volume II—The Disruptive Adolescent
Volume III—The Assaultive Student
Breaking Up Fights—How to Safely Defuse Explosive Conflicts

12

STRENGTHS AND LIMITATIONS OF TODAY'S DISCIPLINE MODELS

In the earlier descriptions of the teacher/student interaction models, the theoretical assumptions of student motivation and central overt and covert behaviors were described in the context of the Teacher Behavior Continuum. As yet, however, the individual strengths and limitations of these models have not been compared. In order to make these comparisons, it would be helpful to review these models by scanning the outlines (Figures 12–1 through 12–10), where you will find a more concise summary of the basic assumptions on motivation, overt teacher behaviors, key vocabulary, and educational insights that have been developed in the preceding chapters. With this content in mind, we can now focus on the strengths and limitations of each model.

RELATIONSHIP-LISTENING

Thomas Gordon, Thomas Harris, Eric Berne, and other Relationship-Listening advocates share a belief in the inner rationality of the student. They believe student misbehavior is the result of obstacles that block the full expression of rational thought. Their goal is to use methods to remove those obstacles.

In discussions of the Relationship-Listening models, there are questions common to all. Three such questions are:

1. Do all students, regardless of age or intellectual capacity, have an inherent rationality?
2. Are all students, regardless of language ability, able to verbalize their thoughts and feelings?
3. Inasmuch as an approach predicated on language and reasoning is time consuming, does the teacher have such time to spend with one student?

The Supportive Model of Thomas Gordon

It is difficult to take issue with Teacher Effectiveness Training's (see Figure 12–1) emphasis on a warm, accepting relationship between a teacher and students and the subsequent need to help students acquire healthy, positive self-concepts. Gordon is concerned with the teacher being, foremost, a person who is sensitive, warm, and noncritical. The strength of his model is that he goes beyond the vague descriptions of becoming a "good" person and instead prescribes specific teacher actions and methods to attain that end. He tells the teacher how to use critical listening, acknowledgment responses, door openers, active listening, and I-messages as tools for helping a student verbally reflect on his or her emotions and behavior. He also provides the teacher with *Method III* ("no lose") problem-solving techniques and the six problem-solving steps to resolve conflict in a democratic equalitarian manner. These techniques free the teacher and student from the common outcome of disciplinary actions where one party loses and feels inferior while the other wins and feels superior. Other strengths of Teacher Effectiveness Training are embodied in the concepts of "areas of freedom" and problem ownership. Thus, the teacher need not feel responsible for every student problem that occurs. The teacher can determine those behavioral problems that belong to administrators or legal officials and thus be able to narrow the focus of his or her attention.

The stress on a warm and supportive environment has been mentioned as a strength; yet, as is often the case, a strength can have dimensions of weakness. Gordon gives teachers concrete actions for allowing a student to verbalize his or her actions and feelings, but solutions for dealing with students who are violent are not readily apparent. Gordon's I-messages, or influencing messages, may not be strong enough when a student explodes in rage and strikes another student. Gordon's techniques can be helpful before or after the act, but what can be done during the student's actual act of violence? Doesn't the teacher have to win and the student lose if physical harm is to be avoided?

Another limitation of Teacher Effectiveness Training is that Gordon's underlying assumption of rationality can be questioned. Do students of all ages possess the cognitive structures to make rational and positive social decisions? Cognitive psychologists suggest a student is not truly rational (i.e., considerate of others) until around the age of adolescence. It may be unfair to expect a young pupil or an intellectually limited (i.e., mentally retarded) student to make wise choices. Such students may need the teacher to *tell* them what is best. Furthermore, Gordon's approach of having students verbalize their emotions reflects an obvious problem for the nonverbal student. Some students will refuse to talk, and some may have such a limited vocabulary that they cannot communicate what they are feeling. It would appear that the teacher can use entreaties such as door openers for verbal discourses only with those students who already have a degree of language proficiency.

Finally, perhaps the most frequent criticism of Teacher Effectiveness Training by teachers is that it takes a lot of time to listen and solve problems when working with a misbehaving student. When a teacher has 30 students in a class, is it feasible to use nondirective statements and personal conferences with a misbehaving stu-

Basic Assumptions on Motivation
Child is motivated by internal desire to be good. He or she is helped by a warm, accepting relationship with another that enhances his or her self-concept. The child is rational—capable of solving his or her own problems.

Overt Teacher Behaviors
—Critical listening
—Acknowledgment responses
—Door openers ("Do you want to talk more?")
 1. active listening
 2. I-messages
 3. influencing ("Watch your step.")

Covert Teacher Behaviors
—Method III ("no lose")
—Daily actions
—Reorganizing space
—Reorganizing time: diffused, individual, and optimal
—Six Steps to Problem Solving
—"Areas of freedom"

Key Vocabulary
Ownership of problems
Active listening
I/You messages
Door openers
Method III ("no lose")
Teaching-Learning area

Six steps to problem solving
Twelve roadblocks to communication
Diffused time
Individual time
Optimal time
"Areas of freedom"

Educational Insights
—"Areas of freedom"
—Organizing time as diffused, individual, and optimal
—Organizing space

Strengths
—Child solves his or her problem, thus developing responsibility
—Democratic rule-setting practice
—No bad feelings while solving problems
—Helps teacher to decide problem ownership

Limitations
—At what age is a child rational?
—Is the mentally retarded child rational?
—What about the child without language?
—The time required for the teacher to administer T.E.T. is prohibitive
—T.E.T. cannot be used in every conflict situation (i.e., violent child)

FIGURE 12–1   Outline of Gordon's Teacher Effectiveness Training Model

dent? Would it be simpler to deal with a student in a direct manner and return to the rest of the class?

The Peer Mediation Model by Arnold P. Goldstein, Ellen McGinnis, and Colleagues

More and more of today's children are growing up without the social skills necessary to handle social conflict. As a result, they are left with limited, nonproductive, aggressive acts to try to reach solutions in their interactions with others. The Peer Mediation Model (see Figure 12–2) attempts to teach mediators skills that will last students into adulthood, and, in the short run, to provide skills to lessen peer-to-peer school site conflicts that can lead to violence and other forms of aggression. This rationally based model requires students to cognitively reflect on their actions, to negotiate with others to find alternative solutions to conflicts, and to develop "connectedness" to others. The skills of negotiation, reasoning, and compromise are extremely valuable, and the Peer Mediation process values them as much as it does positive discipline change.

The model draws heavily on a nonjudgmental response by the peer mediators and on summary statements (much like active listening), as well as win-win discussions and negotiation. Thus, we have classified this model in the Relationship-Listening category, which is proactive rather that reactive to specific discipline incidents. Detailed preparation—such as creating and "selling" the program to teachers, parents, and the community; selecting and training mediators; and monitoring and administrating the process—is required or the process is doomed to fail.

The proactive nature of mediation can be seen in child-centered schools and those with a humanistic philosophy and orientation, which view the model as having a potential life-long positive impact on students' lives. The time used for involving students in such activities will most likely come from academic instruction, so the question becomes: How do we use our time in school, and how will educators who understand this model, balance these time demands?

CONFRONTING-CONTRACTING

Confronting-Contracting advocates believe that appropriate behavior is learned as a result of a student coming into contact with the needs of others. The student learns the reciprocal relationship of individuals who accommodate each other in order to live in a social group. The appropriate medium for such learning is interaction with others. The student does not propose solutions that are wholly in his or her own self-interest, but rather finds answers that are acceptable to the teacher and the classmates. The teacher is not the nonjudgmental facilitator as espoused in Relationship-Listening but instead delineates boundaries of behavior. Within those boundaries, choices can be made.

Basic Assumptions on Motivation
The Peer Mediation Model is based on the idea that behavior change of students should not come through a process of coercion related to "don't do's!" but should occur in an education context where students may cognitively reflect on their actions and, with others, negotiate ways, choices, and alternative solutions to work with others while at the same time developing connectedness to others. The skills of negotiation, reasoning, and compromise are highly valued in the Peer Mediation process, as much as positive discipline change.

Overt Teacher Behaviors
Because the mediation model is peer-to-peer process, the teacher and the school are not directly involved in the mediation process.

Covert Teacher Behaviors
Most actions of teachers and school officials who work with Peer Mediation can be classified under the covert category: "selling" the program to parents and the community, selecting and training mediators, and monitoring and administrating the process.

Key Vocabulary

Agreements	Interest
Confidentially	Neutral mediator
Conflict	Peer mediator
Contracts	Principled response
Focus on interest	Soft response
Gather points of view	Summarizing
Hard response	Win-win options

Educational Insights
Few insights are provided for educational practice, although subject areas such as social science studies could use these mediation contracts to role-play historical disagreements between diputants in order to give students a deeper understanding of the subject matter.

Strengths
The model is a proactive process for teaching positive techniques to resolve social conflict. The program field-tested well and consists of clear directions for administering and monitoring the program.

Limitations
The program appears to require a great deal of time for school administrators and staff, as well as out-of-classroom time for students. Although it is suggested that school faculty committees should hold major responsiblilty for implementation and monitoring, one always realizes that eventually the bulk of the work for such activities will fall on one or two educators. Will this be an administrator, such as an assistant principal, or an assigned teacher with release time? There appears little room for the teacher or other adults in the direct mediation process. This is understandable because it is a "peer" mediation process, but could the teacher use similar mediation steps between students and be equally successful? Educators must also be vigilant in keeping an eye out for individual students who acquire the status of the peer mediator role and use it destructively.

FIGURE 12–2   Outline of Peer Mediation Model

Questions of application that critics might raise include the following:

1. If the student and teacher make mutual plans, don't these in reality become merely teacher plans to which students agree?
2. If interaction is based on communication, what happens to the nonverbal student?
3. Do all students want to belong to a group? After all, if it is true that some individuals enjoy being alone, then is social motivation going to work?
4. Isn't using the group to confront and solve a student's problems "heavy-handed," manipulative, and emotionally damaging to a student with an inferiority complex?

The Social Discipline Model of Rudolf Dreikurs

Dreikurs's social model (see Figure 12–3) is based on the underlying assumption that every student (or human) wishes to belong. Misbehavior is a student's misdirected goal of belonging. Therefore, if a teacher can ascertain the student's misdirected goal (attention getting, power, revenge, or inadequacy), he or she can counter with a plan to enable the student to use appropriate behavior to belong successfully.

Basic Assumptions on Motivation
—People are social beings and desire to belong
—People are decision-making organisms
—All behavior is purposeful and directed towards social goals
—People do not see reality as it is, but only as they perceive it to be
—A person is a whole being who cannot be understood by some particular characteristics
—A person's misbehavior is the result of faculty reasoning on how to gain social recognition

Overt Teacher Behaviors
—Confrontation
—Engaging child in friendly conversation
—Disclosing and confirming mistaken goals to the child
—Asking the following questions:
   1. Could it be that you want special attention? (attention getting)
   2. Could it be that you want to be boss? (power)
   3. Could it be that you want to hurt others as they've hurt you? (revenge)
   4. Could it be that you want to be left alone? (inadequacy)
—Class group discussion about all types of behavior (scheduled weekly)
—Confrontation about goals and misbehavior
—Continued encouragement to increase child's confidence (belief in self)
—Avoiding criticism so true motives can be learned and behavior corrected
—Use encouragement techniques, such as:

FIGURE 12–3   Outline of Dreikurs's Social Discipline Model

1. work for improvement, not perfection
2. commend efforts
3. separate the *deed* from the *doer*
4. build on strengths, not weaknesses
5. show your faith in the child
6. mistakes should not be viewed as failures
—Developing logical and natural consequences, logically structured and arranged by the adult, that must be experienced by the student

Covert Teacher Behaviors
—Four goals of child's misbehavior:
1. attention getting
2. power seeking
3. revenge
4. display of inadequacy
—Preventing above behavior by following these steps:
1. conserve child's behavior in detail
2. be psychologically sensitive to your own reaction
3. confront child with questions
4. apply appropriate corrective procedures

Key Vocabulary

Attention getting	Recognition reflex
Power and control	Role-playing
Revenge	Classroom discussion
Helplessness	Sociometric test
Encouragement	Reading stories
Hidden motivation	Informal stories
Natural and logical consequences	

Educational Insights
—Classroom as collective group
—Sociometric tests for analyzing individual's relationship to group
—Classroom operated as a democracy

Strengths
—Develops system of mutual respect (rewards and punishment not needed)
—Allows children time to solve their own problems during class discussion
—Involves whole class in decision making
—Helps to aid in socialization of individual
—Step-by-step procedure according to goals to follow
—Self-worth developed by teacher and child
—Has natural and logical consequences

Limitations
—Teacher may not always be able to determine child's true goal
—Some children refuse to talk about incident
—Passive child is always very difficult to help using this method
—At times, it can be hard to determine consequences

FIGURE 12–3 (continued)

The strength of Dreikurs's model is in the concreteness of application. He tells the teacher how to uncover the student's goal and how to plan according to that goal. Among the techniques a teacher can employ are role-playing, classroom discussions, sociometric testing, and story telling. He advocates a system of mutual respect where natural or logical consequences are used rather than arbitrary punishment or systematic reinforcements. The model is predicated on an optimistic outlook by the teacher who does not "give up" on a student. Rather, the teacher becomes sensitive and appreciative of a student's attempts to improve rather than the improvement itself.

The limitations of the social model are varied. Determining a student's social goal may not be as simple as it appears. What if a teacher has a mixture of feelings toward a student, which include feelings of hurt (revenge), being beaten (power), and inadequacy (helplessness)? What if the teacher asks the student the four verifying questions and receives no recognition reflex? Another problem with verifying the goal lies with a student who does not want to know why she behaves as she does.

The use of encouragement and personal attention also can be viewed as rewarding a student for misbehavior. There are those who believe, for example, that a passive student needs to be drawn out forcefully by physically showing her how to raise a hand, by demanding that the student finish work in a certain length of time, and so forth. Dreikurs's techniques put little pressure on a student to achieve. Another concern is the question of dealing in a caring way with a student who is hurting others. Won't other students see the special attention such students receive for being "bad" and act accordingly?

A further limitation is that the choice of logical consequences is at times difficult to make. What should happen to a student who incessantly talks but still finishes all of the assigned work? What is a logical consequence for this student? Certainly it is *not* having her mouth taped shut, staying after school, or taking a note home. After all, the student is doing all that is expected except for talking too much. It is not readily apparent what the teacher should do.

The Reality Control Theory and Quality Model of William Glasser

Glasser believes that every student has the capacity to be rational and responsible. However, the student does not acquire this capacity by himself. The teacher provides a classroom of relevant activities so that a student will want to succeed. The teacher then confronts the student by asking him to look at the behavior that is keeping him from succeeding. He is then asked to make a commitment to a future plan that will be enforced by the teacher.

Reality therapy (see Figure 12–4) provides the teacher with an understanding of human motivation based on the concepts of love and self-worth. Glasser provides the educator with covert behaviors for assessing the relevance of one's classroom. The strength of the model is in the clear delineation of what a teacher needs to do for every misbehaving student. The student must be confronted with "What"

Basic Assumptions on Motivation
Relevance, responsibility, and reality are necessary for schools without failure. The child is rational. The child has the capability to be responsible, but needs to learn moral or acceptable boundaries of living successfully in society. People must live in a world of other human beings and must satisfy their own needs in a way that does not infringe upon others. Each person has two basic needs, the need for love and the need for self-worth, which must be fulfilled in order to have a successful identity. Behavior problems are a result of these needs not being met. A person must be helped to acknowledge his or her behavior and then take actions in making it more logical and productive. A person must make a commitment to responsible behavior.

Overt Teacher Behaviors
—Confronting transgressions ("Stop that," "The rule is . . .")
—Asking "what" questions ("What are you doing?" "What are the rules?" "In what way is your behavior helping you?")
—Pressing for a plan ("I'll help, but you're responsible.")
—Agreeing on natural consequence of plan
—Failure of plan—isolating in class (repeat 1–4)
—Failure of step 5—isolating in school (repeat 1–5)
—Failure of step 6—isolating outside of school (repeat 1–6)
—Referring to outside agency

Covert Teacher Behaviors
—Observing the student and the situation
—Assessing what the teacher is currently doing and what success the student is having
—Starting fresh by reversing classroom organization and/or activities

Key Vocabulary

Heterogeneous	Signed statement
Reality therapy	Behavior
Identity	Consequences
Nonjudgmental	Value judgment
Class meetings	Tight circles
Intense counseling	Failure
Open-ended	Thinking vs. memorization
Problem solving	Commitment
Responsibility	Relevance
Success	Class meetings
Self-image	Love
Involvement	

Educational Insights
—Class meetings for
  1. problem solving
  2. open-ended
  3. educational-diagnostic
—Superior system of grades; do away with standard A–F
—Upward Bound program
—Strength teaching

(continued)

FIGURE 12–4   Outline of Glasser's Reality Therapy Model

—Seminars for small groups
—Enrichment programs
—Tutors and counseling
—Community contact
—Make curriculum relevant
—No ability grouping

Strengths
—Behavior is student's responsibility
—Has no failures
—Has a step-by-step procedure for all students
—Child must take responsibility for own actions
—Involves all those responsible
—Is a specific use of isolation

Limitations
—Doesn't work well with child who doesn't care
—Class meetings are hard to fit into secondary school schedule
—School changes may be hard to accomplish within school structure
—Difficult to start fresh each day

FIGURE 12–4 (continued)

questions and must be pressed for a plan. The success or failure of the plan becomes the responsibility of the student, not the teacher. Yet, if the initial effort results in failure, the teacher can keep the responsibility on the student by isolating him or her until another plan is developed and agreed upon. Again, if the plan is unsuccessful, the student and teacher can start again. Behavior that is having a detrimental effect on all class members can be handled in a class meeting where all classmates can develop a mutually agreeable plan with the misbehaving student.

The criticisms of Glasser's model first revolve around the educational problem of having to create a relevant classroom environment where a student has successful experiences. There are teachers who teach subjects that they know misbehaving students do not perceive as interesting or relevant. Yet due to external circumstances (i.e., in situations where the principal, superintendent, or school board dictate all policies affecting curriculum and environment), the teacher can do little either to change the subject matter or reorganize the classroom environment. Therefore, these educators have difficulty with the first step of Glasser's approach. They want the students to behave properly in their classroom regardless of whether or not they enjoy what is going on. A second limitation is the use of classroom meetings for a misbehaving student. Again, there are classrooms and class schedules, particularly on the secondary level, that make such meetings improbable. When a teacher meets with a group of 30 students for one 45-minute period a day and has specific learning outcomes for each class, he or she will be hard pressed to find the time to have ongoing meetings that take 20 to 30 minutes to conduct.

Another criticism applies to the student who does not care about school: Making a plan and using isolation with this student are not likely to be successful. A student who would rather not be in school might welcome the chance to be isolated in a comfortable area. Glasser suggests that a student will eventually choose to come out, and the teacher should not allow the student to reenter until a plan is made. If the student does not choose to return, how long is a teacher to wait? Additionally, there is the concern about "making a plan." The strategy is based on the student having a certain degree of organized thought and language proficiency; therefore, it does not address the student who may desire to be in class but does not know how to verbalize or systematize that desire. A final weakness may be the unrealistic hope that a teacher can begin each new plan with an optimistic outlook. It may well be unrealistic to expect a teacher to continue to be optimistic when a student repeatedly breaks contracts.

The Judicious Discipline Model

Models of discipline have been included in this text because they present to the teacher concrete and specific techniques on what to do with a misbehaving student when the misbehavior occurs. Judicious discipline (see Figure 12–5) is not a model that provides help for the teacher on daily limit setting, but does present a framework for possible prevention of discipline difficulties. In addition, it shows how to use a legal framework to create a climate, attitude, and set of procedures for run-

---

Basic Assumptions on Motivation
Because of recent court cases, the concept of *in loco parentis*, which allowed the school and teachers to exercise parent-like authority over students, has been replaced by the position that students do not lose their constitutional rights when they pass through the schoolhouse door. The traditional approach of giving schools nearly unchallenged authority (much like that held by parents) to make rules that fit the teacher's or the school's values is now seen as mis-serving the students. Judicious discipline suggests that the teaching of core constitutional amendments as a basis for establishing classroom and school rules helps the students mature morally and prepares them for citizenship. All discipline practices or sanctions must protect the student's due process rights, in varying degrees, based on the seriousness of the student's actions and the severity of the sanction. Traditional practices such as grading and homework may be viewed very differently when applying a test of liberty as it affects the student's future life-long earnings potential.

Overt Teacher Behaviors
—Teaching principles of individual rights
—Establishing class rules based on three core amendments: teach First, Fourth, and
     Fourteenth Amendments directly
—Posting and publishing rules
—Using "compelling state interest" standard to justify withdrawal of a personal right
—Giving examples of group rights vs. individual rights
—Teaching examples of judicious consequences

(continued)

FIGURE 12–5   Outline of the Judicious Discipline Model

Covert Teacher Behaviors
—Committing to running a democratic classroom

Key Vocabulary

Fear of authority
Judicious consequence
Due process
In loco parentis
Judicious
Liberty
Moral growth
Adequate notice

Student/educator relationship
Individual rights
Feelings and understanding of social
     responsibility
Compelling state interest
Substantive due process
Teachable moment
Tyranny of Fairness

Educational Insights
Requires the teacher and the school to examine policies and procedures that affect traditional school practices related to absences/tardiness, denying credit, suspensions/
expulsions, students with disabilities, withholding privileges, corporal punishment,
student and school property, dress and appearance, public displays of affection,
refusing to say Pledge of Allegiance, locker contents and display, bigotry and free
speech, search and seizure, religious celebrations and symbolism.

Strengths
Gives a legal basis (First, Fourth, and Fourteenth Amendments) for establishing rules,
     procedures, and policies
Gives guidelines for due process
Gives an overall legal construction for broader policy issues

Limitations
—Does not deal with daily problems of limit-setting and confronting students who
     are misbehaving.
—May require a great deal of time if every teacher, especially in secondary school,
     needs to teach amendments and go through an inductive rule developing process.
—Demands that the teacher give up arbitary practices previously sanctioned by *in
     loco parentis,* requiring real change in many teachers' thinking and behavior and
     causing stress and even anger toward such a Judicious position.
—The educational suggestion, such as permitting the student to make up missed con-
     tent and classes, would be expensive and require a fundamental shift in how
     schooling is to be delivered.

FIGURE 12–5 (continued)

ning a democratic classroom based on the principles of the Bill of Rights. Students,
families, schools, and society in general are changing, and teachers have lost their
former *in loco parentis* position of simply creating rules and sanctions based on
their own values and for their own convenience.

   The seasoned teacher sees that judicial actions and court cases have expanded
into playing a significant role in today's daily classroom procedures. Modern
teachers must rethink previous *in loco parentis* practices for two key reasons: (1)
they do not want to find themselves in court as a result of their discipline actions,

and, more importantly, (2) schools and classrooms play an essential role in preparing students for the democratic society in which they live and will fully join as adults. The establishment of rules and due process procedures to be employed by teachers or school authorities when rules are broken provides a practical model for teaching students democratic ways of living. Especially challenging, difficult, and sometimes contradictory is the tension of individual rights versus the rights of the group. Historically, most school practices were created to serve the good of all, with only limited (if any) concern for individual rights.

Again, many seasoned teachers will be angry and surprised to discover that such practices as lowering a student's grade because of repeated absences might be challenged from a legal perspective. However, the suggestions made by judicious discipline for teaching the Bill of Rights, and attempting to use it as a construct for assessing fairness and the justification for various rules, might provide experiences that lead these students to a high moral understanding of society's complex interactions.

RULES AND CONSEQUENCES

The Rules and Consequences writers believe that people are shaped by external stimuli. A teacher needs to be aware of the stimuli a misbehaving student is receiving and should then change the environmental conditions so that appropriate behavior will be more rewarding than inappropriate behavior. The teacher is therefore very much in control and should express explicit standards of conduct for the student.

The basic argument against Rules and Consequences approaches is not whether they work but whether the ultimate consequences for the student are beneficial. For example, reinforcement programs implemented as part of a pilot national experiment in 1972 showed that some severely underachieving and delinquent junior high school students would make drastic changes in behavior if the rewards were great enough. Students who were constantly late and who whistled, moved around, and talked incessantly during class suddenly became the picture of punctuality and docility. They would arrive on time, sit down with folded hands, and be attentive to the teacher when they knew they could earn "tokens" redeemable for record players, transistor radios, bicycles, concert tickets, and the like. The questions debated are whether students should learn to behave for such materialistic reasons, and if so, what happens to a student when the obvious rewards for appropriate behavior end?

The Behavior Analysis Model

The behavior analysis model (see Figure 12–6) is based on the use of positive reinforcement. General behavior is broken down into smaller parts so that students have ensured success. A student can feel successful and competent as he learns appropriate behaviors and receives verbal, social, or material rewards. Standards

Basic Assumptions on Motivation
—Children are not born with self-control—we must help them mold it
—Deal only with outward (external) behavior
—Use scientific techniques to demonstrate effectiveness
—Be concerned with unacceptable behavior the child exhibits and what interventions can be applied to change it
—The cause of the behavior exists outside the child, in the environment
—Motivation-reinforcers:
  Positive—something we like
  Negative—something we dislike
  Primary—relating to basic body needs
  Secondary—abstracts, symbols
—The consequences, more than any other factor, determine the behavior the individual exhibits

Overt Teacher Behaviors
—Teacher controlling the situation, imitation and shaping, fading, and directive statements for contingency contracting
—Explicit modeling for imitation, forward and backward chaining, saturation, time out, rewards for reinforcement of desired behaviors; commands as directive statements
—Using conditioners in the form of material and verbal rewards; child definitely knows what he or she will receive as a result of his or her behavior
—Using variable intervals and variable ratios

Covert Teacher Behaviors
—Reinforcing only the behavior to be increased
—Before beginning behavior modification:
  1. select the behavior to be changed
  2. collect and record baseline data
  3. identify appropriate reinforcers
  4. collect intervention data
—Graphing baseline and intervention data to evaluate effectiveness
—Changing reinforcers periodically

Key Vocabulary

Anecdotal reports	Exclusionary time out
Antecedent stimulus	Extinction
Assertive command	Fixed-interval schedule
Aversive stimulus	Fixed-ratio schedule
Baseline data	Frequency
Behavior	Functional relationship
Behavioral objective	Interval recording
Broken record	Latency recording
Conditioned reinforcer	Modeling
Consequence	Negative practice
Contingency	Negative reinforcement
Deprivation state	Nonseclusionary time out
Differential reinforcement	Overcorrection
Duration recording	Pairing
Event recording	Permanent product recording

FIGURE 12–6   Outline of the Behavior Analysis Model

Pinpointing
Positive reinforcement
Primary reinforcer
Prompt
Punishment
Reinforcer
Response-cost
Satiation
Schedules of reinforcement
Seclusionary time out

Secondary reinforcers
Shaping
Social reinforcers
Terminal behavior
Thinning
Time out
Unconditioned aversive
    stimuli
Variable-interval schedule
Variable-ratio schedule

Educational Insights
—School subjects can be taught in a sequential reinforcement manner
—Stimulation of physical environment (positive and negative) should be considered
—Positive stimuli are most effective in all dimensions of schooling

Strengths
—Is positive oriented, and reinforcers good feelings and self-concept
—Encourages success
—Gives a structured setting for learning
—Eliminates constant/continual contact with child
—Capitalizes on nonverbal communication
—Works (scientifically tested)
—Can work with all children
—Is efficient

Limitations
—Many people feel behavior analysis practices are unacceptable and unethical
—It can have harmful effects if not used correctly; can be abused by insensitive and
    unethical practioners
—Does not accept emotions as important
—Does not let the child use his or her own rational abilities
—Needs precise record keeping to determine its success

FIGURE 12–6   (continued)

of behavior are uniform, consistent, and clear to all students. The teacher does not
need to spend any time in class discussions about rules or to conduct individual
conferences dealing with problem solving, thereby freeing her to spend more time
on instructional matters. Behavior analysis can be used with all students, regardless of their age or cognitive and language abilities. A reinforcement schedule can
be implemented with a nonverbal, passive student as well as with a highly articu-
late, aggressive student. Although, at first, reinforcements need to be used frequently, the teacher can eventually use a random interval schedule. Positive use of
behavior analysis can be scientifically tested by the classroom teacher. This technique usually will work, and it is an efficient way of reversing a student's disruptive actions.

The limitations of the model are both philosophical and practical. Behavior
analysis is an approach that attempts to change a student's observable behavior.

However, some misbehavior may be the result of "inner"-problems. A student who is being physically abused at home may be taking his hostility out on class-mates. A reinforcement program that conditions cooperative class behavior and extinguishes physical aggression may be beneficial to the teacher, but it does not help the student (or parents) resolve the underlying home problem. Therefore, in many cases, behavior analysis approaches may change the symptoms but do little to alleviate the actual problem. There is also the argument that, in a democratic society, it is unethical and unacceptable for schools to control an individual's behavior. Limiting behavior so that destruction or harm can be avoided is neces-sary in any society, but the notion of conditioning specific behavior would be more applicable to a totalitarian society. Educational concerns with behavior analysis are that learning "to behave" is an important cognitive task, just as important as learning such school subjects as reading and mathematics. Therefore, if a student is not allowed to bring her mental operations into use by learning to clarify emo-tions, to weigh alternatives, and to decide on solutions, then a major area of intel-lectual or rational development would be neglected. Another concern is more immediate to teachers in that such a scientific approach is predicated on precise delineation and measurement of a student's pretreatment behavior. To do this, a teacher needs to write down misbehavior in clear terms and to keep an accurate tabulation of frequency. Some teachers would resist spending the time and effort that this ongoing record keeping involves.

Teaching Prosocial Skills: The Skillstreaming Model

Skillstreaming appears to be a well thought-out psychological-education design based on behavioral analysis processes and philosophy. Large numbers of stu-dents today are not learning basic social skills at home, at recreational agencies, or in church settings. The view toward misbehaving students is that you can't just tell them to stop misbehaving (to desist). Rather, you must teach them social skills, so that they may learn appropriate behavioral responses to typical and basic social interactions. If we accept a list of key skills as being central and paramount in chil-dren's lives, we will have a well-developed educational structured system for teaching these skills—that is Skillstreaming (see Figure 12–7).

Methods and procedures for setting up the skillstreaming program—includ-ing setting up the training space, training group leaders, and assessing the stu-dents' social skills—are clearly described through a checklist. Many motivation techniques (homework reports, group self-report charts, skill contracts, self-recording forms, and awards) are used during the transference process. The teacher has a clear and structured lesson, with the support of Skill Cards to carry out the training. The program seems to be well-researched and supported by a clear knowledge base, and has field-tested well. The difficulty lies in the commit-ment of the teacher or school to be willing to implement the program, meeting its time and personal requirements.

Basic Assumptions on Motivation
Large numbers of children are growing up today without obtaining basic social skills, and it is now the role of schools to teach these skills to students. This is done by identifying 60 key skills and teaching these skills through modeling, role-playing, performance feedback, and transference activities (homework). The instructional principles are based on reinforcement theory as defined in behavior analysis.

Overt Teacher Behavior
Clear overt teacher behavior is demonstrated. Since this is behavior and direct instruction approach, the curriculum and procedures can be clearly outlined and followed. The teacher's creativity is her skill in handling the dynamic role-playing process.

Covert Teacher Behaviors
Most preparatory actions of organizing space, training group leaders, and assessing students regarding their lack of social skills is clearly delineated.

Key Vocabulary

Covert rehearsal	Role-playing
Group leader	Skill Cards
Modeling	Social skills
Performance feedback	Transference

Educational Insights
Few insights are provided for educational practice, but improved behavior of the student will save instructional time.

Strengths
The model is a proactive process based on well-established behavior analysis theory, and has field-tested well. The program can be done at the preschool/kindergarten, elementary, and adolescent levels.

Limitations
The program will require a schoolwide commitment by teachers and administrators and a decision regarding the time and personnel committed to the program, which would compete with instructional time and needs.

FIGURE 12–7   Outline of Skillstreaming Model

The Positive Discipline Model of Fredric Jones

The Jones positive discipline model (see Figure 12–8) is based primarily on the concepts of behavior analysis. It is organized around achieving the desired results regarding student behavior by establishing limit setting, a back-up system, an omission system, an incentive system, and responsibility training, and by using the structure of the school time and classroom furniture.

The positive discipline model is clearly based on behavior analysis principles and constructs. Jones's use of "closing space" and eye contact, which are central

Basic Assumptions on Motivation
Jones's Positive Discipline model is clearly based on behavior analysis principles and constructs. His use of "closing space" and eye contact, which are central teacher behaviors for getting behavior back on task, can be considered a mild form of "punishment" under a behavioral definition (see Chapter 7). Jones has also eclectically borrowed elements from neurobiology and anthropology to round out and justify his practices. The difficultly with behavior analysis is the technical skill required by the teacher to place many of these scientifically definable procedures into daily classroom practice with a misbehaving student. The Jones model is a good attempt at making behavioral principles practical.

Overt Teacher Behaviors
—Limit setting
  1. proximity
  2. camping out
  3. relaxing breaths
  4. body movements
  5. moving in/moving out
  6. palms
—Back-up response (private/semi-private)
  1. small back-up responses
—Ear warnings
—Private meetings
—Think and talk
—Warning and delivery
  2. medium back-up responses
  3. large back-up reponses
—Responsibility training (stopwatch)
  1. bonuses
  2. gift time
  3. hurry-up bonus
  4. automatic bonus
  5. penalties
  6. PAT
—Structure (management)
  1. teach rules/structure
  2. say, show, do
  3. desk arrangement
  4. work the crowd

Covert Teacher Behavior
—Controlling the seating arrangement
—Organizing the space and other classroom actions that can be taken before the students arrive

Key Vocabulary

Adrenaline "bleed"	Back-talk (blaming)
Adrenaline dump	Back-talk (denial)
Back-talk	Back-talk (helplessness)
Back-talk (accusing the teacher	Back-talk (profanity)
of professional incompetence)	Back-up system

FIGURE 12–8   Outline of Jone's Positive Discipline Model

Body telegraphing
Camouflage
Camping out from behind
Camping out in front
Check-it-out
Closing space
Comfort bubble
Eye contact
Fight or flight
Focal point
Fredisms
"Going brain stemmed"
Going public
"Gone chemical"
High roller
Incentive program
Limit setting
Low roller
Moving in/moving out
Neocortex
Paleocortex
Palms
Park the body
"Part of a loaf"

Pencil posturing
Ph.D. in Teacher Game
Pheasant posturing
Private meeting
Prompt
Proximity
Proximity-intimate
Pseudo-compliance
Relaxing breaths
Reptilian brain
Responsibility training
Say, show, do
"Show time"
Silly talk
Slack jaw
"Smiley face"
Square off
Structure
Tailhook
Three-step lesson
Triune brain
With-it-ness
Working the crowd

Strengths
—Limit setting, back-up response, responsibility training, omission training, and the
  management structure combine to form a holistic view of how to achieve good
  classroom discipline and classroom management
—The concept of the two dimensions of proximity and helping the teacher maintain
  self-control (to avoid "going brain stemmed")
—Classroom furniture arrangement and the process of "working the crowd" give
  meaning to concepts that many teachers have known and used in limited ways

Limitations
—Fails to explain, in limit setting or during back-up, the use of language between
  teacher and student and tapping the rational capacities of the student
—Since the teacher's use of language is missing in this model, it is unclear how we talk
  to students, especially in doing a conference or private meeting as a part of the back-
  up process
—There is confusion regarding large back-up responses—for example, Jones
  humorously speaks against the use of suspension, but at the same time it is implied
  that the principal will use such techniques
—Fails to deal with the role of parents as a part of the discipline process

FIGURE 12–8   (continued)

teacher behaviors for getting behavior back on task, can be considered a mild form of "punishment" under a behavioral definition (see Chapter 7). Jones has also eclectically borrowed elements from neurobiology and anthropology to round out and justify his practices. The difficulty with behavior analysis is the technical skill required by the teacher to place many of these scientifically definable procedures into daily classroom practice with a misbehaving student. The Jones model is a good attempt at making behavioral principles practical.

By far the greatest strength of the Jones model is that all of its component parts—limit setting, back-up response, responsibility training, omission training, and the management structure—combine to form a holistic view of how to achieve good classroom discipline and classroom management. While most of the previously described models focus on limit setting and confronting to deal with a misbehaving student, the Jones model goes far beyond this to include other dimensions. Jones found that after doing "discipline" training with schools, he could go no further unless he also dealt with the aspect of classroom instruction.

Another contribution of the Jones model is the concept of the dimensions of proximity and helping the teacher maintain self-control (to avoid "going brainstemmed"). At a very practical and specific level, Jones demonstrates how the teacher can gain self-control through relaxing breaths, posture, and movement. Confrontation is the most stressful situation for the classroom teacher, and these relaxing behaviors can be central for a teacher to gain control and remain empowered. The use of proximity, or closing space between the teacher and the off-task student, is new and a significant contribution to the classroom teacher's skills. A teacher's tendency, when challenged by a student, is to react with "flight or fight," and understanding this and having specific techniques to control this reflexive reaction can help many teachers with potentially explosive tempers. Again, the suggestions for classroom furniture arrangement and the process of "working the crowd" give meaning to concepts that many teachers have known and used in limited ways.

A limitation of the positive discipline model is that, true to most behaviorists, Jones does not include teacher actions, especially in limit setting or during back-up, that involve the use of language between teacher and student and tap the rational capacities of the student. The Jones view suggests that if the teacher responds to a student's back-talk, he is falling into the student's trap and is unknowingly reinforcing the misbehaving student. Many teachers may believe that they have a responsibility to express their feelings during an interaction involving possible off-task behavior or misbehavior—perhaps through the use of Gordon's I-messages or Glasser's "What are you doing?" questions. Since the teacher's use of language is missing in this model, it is unclear how to talk to students, especially in doing a conference or private meeting as a part of the back-up process. The Jones position is also confusing regarding large back-up responses—for example, Jones humorously speaks against the use of suspension, but at the same time it is implied that the principal will use such techniques.

Some might also fault Jones for failing to deal with the role of parents as a part of the discipline process. Because he has spent many years doing family counseling with parents, Jones believes that the child most likely acts as she does because of her home experience. Jones fundamentally feels that a request by the school for help with an unruly child is asking parents to do skilled intervention for which they have little or no training—so parents should be kept out of the process. In contrast, other models (such as assertive discipline) use behavioral techniques to move toward including parents in the process.

The Assertiveness Model of Lee and Marlene Canter

Some of the same strengths and limitations of the behavior analysis model apply to the assertiveness model (see Figure 12–9). Canter and Canter believe in the use of positive behavior analysis, but they also emphasize punishment (loss of privileges, detention, notes home). The Canter discipline model is concerned with a teacher asserting his or her rights and putting together a plan of rewards and punishments that will enforce the teacher's authority. Again, many of the behavior analysis advocates take issue with the use of punishment on the basis of research showing that positive and negative reinforcement (systematic avoidance of an undesirable event) works but that punishment does not work. Since punishment is commonly used in schools, most teachers would probably side with the Canter position that even though punishment may not have long-term benefits, it does at least give temporary aid to a teacher to be able to use the threat of punishment with a student.

Basic Assumptions on Motivation
—All students can behave regardless of their family histories, socioeconomic backrounds, or physical/mental exceptionalities
—Student misbehavior continues when teachers do not enforce the same standards for all students
—Teachers have the right to request behavior from students that meets the needs of the teacher and ensures an optimal learning environment
—Teachers have the right to ask assistance from parents, principals, and other school personnel

Overt Teacher Behaviors
—Using hints to alert students that there is a problem with their behavior "Class, we should be doing . . . "
—Disguising directive statements as a question: "Would you stop . . . ?"
—Giving I-messages ("If you don't stop, then you have chosen . . . ") and "broken record" demands to avoid being side-tracked
—Using a steady gaze and low voice when talking to students
—Giving rewards for appropriate behavior (positive notes, calling on a student, token coupons, marble system to reward whole class) and punishments for inappropriate behavior (loss of privilege, detention, note home)
—Using systematic exclusion (to another classroom, principal's office, home)

(continued)

FIGURE 12–9   Outline of Canter and Canter's Assertiveness Model

Covert Teacher Behaviors
—Determining differences among assertive, nonassertive, and hostile behaviors
—Establishing a uniform classroom discipline plan of relatively few but specific rules and consistent actions for enforcing them
—Writing the plan down and sharing it with the principal
—Using mental rehearsal to explain the classroom plan and enforcement procedures and to prepare for handling student violations

Key Vocabulary

Assertiveness	Rewards
Teacher rights	Punishments
Uniform standards	Broken record
Classroom plan	Systematic exclusion
Hints	Roadblocks
Demands	Mental rehearsal

Educational Insights
—A teacher's job is to teach and therefore he or she has the responsibility and right to have his or her own needs met in order to do the job
—The purpose of school is for students to learn; misbehavior keeps students from learning
—Expecting less appropriate behavior from some students because "they simply can't behave" is a self-defeating prophecy
—It is best for students to know that the teacher is in charge

Strengths
—Use of class time is more efficient. Problems are handled quickly and consistently; the teacher can spend more time teaching academic subjects
—A single system of rules, rewards, and punishment can be used for all age levels and kinds of students; there is no need to vary one's approach
—The teacher can be confident and efficient with discipline because he or she has a set program to follow

Limitations
—It may fail to recognize "circumstantial"evidence for misbehavior and the need to give special attention to or plan for an individual student
—It releases the student from personal responsibility and rational decision making
—Punishments may not work
—It is undemocratic and authoritarian; students have little say in rules and procedures

FIGURE 12–9   (continued)

The Canter emphasis on a teacher's being assertive and clear in directions and expectations appears to be a major strength of the model. The use of a uniform plan for all students appears to be the model's greatest liability. Those who believe that a classroom should be a model of democracy, that students should take responsibility for their own behavior, and that misbehavior is often symptomatic of underlying problems will find little comfort with the assertiveness model. Total teacher control, uniform disciplinary actions without regard to individual differences, and a low priority for communicating and understanding a student's behavior are all limitations to those who believe that discipline should include learning about oneself and one's relationship with others, and the attempt to behave according to one's own standards.

Love and Punishment Model of James Dobson

Some of the same strengths and limitations of the behavior analysis model exist with the love and punishment model (see Figure 12–10). Dobson proposes all the

Basic Assumptions on Motivation
—Respectful, responsible children result from families where the proper combination of love and discipline is present
—Developing respect for the adult is critical in student management
—The best time to communicate often occurs after punishment
—Control without nagging
—Don't saturate with excessive materialism
—Avoid extremes in control and love
—The adult is in charge—he or she must win

Overt Teacher Behaviors
—Identifying the rules well in advance; letting there be no doubt about what is and what is not acceptable; when the child cold-bloodedly chooses to challenge those known boundaries, giving him reason to regret it; at all times demonstrating kindness, love, and understanding (discipline is not an antonym of love and discipline is not a synonym of punishment)
—Controlling child behavior by reinforcement (reinforcement must be immediate)
—Using directive statements (contingency contracting): if you do X, then you do or get Y; even though one gains points for following the contract, he or she is also penalized if he or she does not follow it

Covert Teacher Behaviors
—Seeing behavior modification (positivist)
—Reminding yourself to maintain your "power," to use discipline, and to use kindness and love
—Reminding yourself to be immediate and consistent with reinforcers
—Reminding yourself to never let the child have the "upper hand"
—Reminding yourself to be patient

Key Vocabulary	
Discipline	Kindness
Control	Love
Reinforcement	Understanding
Consistency	Respect for authority
Responsibility	Miracle tools
Self-discipline	Family and God
Self-control	Defiance

(continued)

FIGURE 12–10   Outline of Dobson's Love and Punishment Model

Educational Insights
—Discipline needs to be quick with the late bloomer, slow learner, and underachiever
—Grades need to be viewed as reinforcers
—The purpose of school is for students to learn; misbehavior keeps students from learning
—It is better to be strict at the beginning: "Don't smile until December"

Strengths
—Use of class time is more efficient; problems are handled quickly; the teacher spends a lot of time teaching academic skills
—Behavior modification is a scientific method; results can be proven
—Is effective for all age levels and kinds of students

Limitations
—Such techniques need to start very early when the child is young
—Is undemocratic and authoritarian
—May fail to recognize "circumstantial" evidence for misbehaving
—Releases child from personal responsibility and rational decision
—Limits on physical punishment are established by the school board
—Punishment may not work
—Models teacher behavior that is inappropriate for students to engage in

FIGURE 12–10   (continued)

positive behavior analysis approaches, but also includes the use of negative measures such as stern commands, physical intervention, and, at times, physical punishment. He advocates concern and patience with students, but establishes as a firm base that the student must accept a teacher's authority. His premise is that students go to school to learn academics, and therefore a teacher needs to deal with disruption quickly and efficiently. Although positive reinforcement is encouraged, it must be immediately effective or the teacher should directly take steps to make the consequences of a student's misbehavior unpleasant and not worth doing again. In other words, misbehavior should be less positively rewarding than more appropriate behavior. A major strength of the model is in its point of view that discipline is not in opposition to love and respect for students. To provide specific rules and to enforce those rules is to provide a structured environment where love and security can flourish. When teachers take the opposite view that care and sensitivity are shown by allowing students to do and say whatever they wish, the results can often be erratic and even volatile behavior on the part of student and teacher.

The most prevalent concern with this model is whether punishment really works. Scolding or paddling would indicate to a student what she should not be doing, but it does not tell her what should be done instead. Punishment therefore would need to be administered in conjunction with positive reinforcement. If this is so, then why not simply ignore the misbehavior rather than punish it? Also, punishment can have the effect opposite of its intent. To have a student stay after school for refusing to obey the teacher can make the student more resentful and more disobedient. Another concern is that the teacher would be providing a model of behavior to the student that he may not wish the student to emulate. For example, if a teacher believes it is inappropriate for students to use physical means to resolve a conflict and should use calm language to make their needs known, then the use of "punishment" by the teacher would be contradictory. If a teacher grabs or paddles a student for fighting, then he would be clearly showing the student that "might does make right." The student would feel justified in continuing to fight, because she has seen that the teacher has resolved his frustrations in the same manner. Aside from the issues of whether punishment works or whether punishment is a poor model, there is also the reality that the matter of punishment is often strictly regulated by school board policy. Many school systems do not allow, or severely restrict, various forms of punishment (such as paddling or detention after school).

SUMMARY

There are no teacher/student interaction models today that do not have their critics. There is not now, and there possibly never will be, research that provides indisputable documentation that one model is superior to others. It has instead been the purpose here to refresh your memory of the significant features of each model through the presentation of skeleton outlines (Figures 12–1 through 12–10) and then to present some of the debated issues concerning each model.

13

DISCIPLINE AND TEACHING AS A DEVELOPMENTAL PROCESS

For the last 20 years, responsible and well-meaning district or building-level administrators have observed their teachers in classrooms and realized that many of these teachers could benefit from increased training in classroom discipline. The need for discipline training historically has been a political problem that develops after a glaring negative incident—a burned-out high school teacher punching a tenth-grader or an injury stemming from a discipline action—results in a lawsuit or the discipline incident makes the front page of the local newspaper.

The district offices know they have a problem and want a solution. Therefore, they look about to see what is available in discipline training nationally, or in the district next door, and have found *T.E.T.*, or Glasser, or assertive discipline, or the many other models described earlier. It was considered a reasonable action to hire these discipline experts to come in to conduct in-service training workshops, and to purchase their books and media and make the materials available to the teachers. The demand for the teachers, districtwide or schoolwide, to follow these models by one expert ranged from a suggestion to a strong encouragement, or even to a command that everyone *will* do this districtwide model. One superintendent announced, "We have gone *assertive discipline*," meaning his schools had put much money and effort into having the teachers in his district trained in a particular model and he expected every teacher to utilize it.

When one principal heard a presentation involving the Three Faces of Discipline, with its idea that a teacher could select from all three schools of thought and build his or her own model drawing from the seven to eight different models previously presented, he was overwhelmed and stated, "You expect my teachers to do all of that, when we have been doing Glasser for five years and 60 percent of them still aren't using Glasser?" The end-of-the-year testing in one school district showed that "map skills" in the fifth grade were 1.5 standard deviations below the national average. That summer, workbooks on map skills were purchased and given to teachers to use in the following year so that the low scores on the map-skill test would improve.

From "outside the classroom" and from the principal's or district administrator's office, the process is a simple one of question and answer: "What is the problem?" The answer is "poor discipline skills on the part of the teachers; let's buy something to take care of this." Just like the map skills workbooks, administrators are seeking an answer to throw at this problem, so they "buy" one discipline model and "throw" it at all teachers in the school or the entire district. To these administrators, such a move does not seem unreasonable. But if we look closely, we will discover that the majority of the map skills workbooks, much like the science kits and packaged science programs pushed on teachers after the Sputnik national science scare, are hidden in the back of a storage closet, never used. Similarly in discipline, if we return to observe the teachers a year after the discipline model training, we find that the techniques have "decayed." We find a small minority of teachers still using these techniques but never in the pure form, most of them eclectically incorporating a few of the techniques into the basic discipline system they have always used since the time of their student teaching. One answer may be that we teachers are very conservative people and are not motivated to try new things. However, if we ask a group of teachers at any school level what they want from in-service training, *discipline* clearly will be ranked at the top of the list. When Glasser or an assertive discipline presenter appears for workshops, even on Saturday mornings, teachers come to these training sessions enthusiastic, optimistic, and eager for ideas. In short, they are motivated.

I believe the reason that most discipline training historically has failed to have a lasting effect is that (1) the training has been delivered in a verbal modality of teaching as a one-shot deal with no long-term opportunity for practice, and, equally as important, (2) the approach of *one* discipline orientation for all teachers was a failure of *personality fit*.

PERSONALITY FIT

To understand the concept of personality fit, let us look at two mothers as they feed their nine-month-old infants in high chairs. Mother #1 prepares and stores all warm and cold food on a counter nearby, covers herself completely with an apron, has a moist towelet nearby, and places on the infant a bib that would cover Manhattan. Mother #1 feeds the child one spoonful at a time, making sure that all food gets into the child's mouth and goes down properly. Mother #1 is not harsh but uses fun games ("Open up the tunnel, here comes the train") and uses her warm and gracious personality to get the food into the infant with relatively no spills or mess! The infant enjoys the process. Mother #1 demonstrates a need to be in control of all actions, and by her behavior follows a series of rules, or a structure, as to how things should be done.

In contrast, Mother #2, while feeding her infant, covers the floor under the high chair with a sheet of plastic, dresses the child in a diaper and small shirt, places the food on a serving tray attached by suction cups to the high chair's table, gives the infant a spoon, and shows him how to use it. She permits him to feed himself with his hands while she carries on a "conversation" with her child as she works nearby. The child, using mostly his hands, gets one-third of the food in his mouth, one-third on himself, and the other one-third on the floor. The child enjoys the eating experience. Mother #2 is not upset by this messiness; she knows her child and has observed to see that he has had adequate food. She calmly throws the child's shirt into the wash, kisses her child warmly, places him in a bath, and then hoses off the plastic sheet for the next time. Mother #2 grants the infant much autonomy, or self-control, but is not naive or permissive. She has covered the floor with plastic, dressed the child for the occasion, organized the suction feeding bowl so the food would not get knocked from the high chair, and communicated with the child in a warm, supportive manner.

If these two mothers continue their patterns of child rearing for the next 21 years, we can clearly see that these very different mothering techniques would produce very different adult personalities. What if the children were to become teachers and incorporate nearly the exact personality characteristics, techniques, and attitudes toward children, parenting, and teaching of students as their own mothers demonstrated with them? Continuing in this line of thinking, consider what would happen if school administrators forced a model of Relationship-Listening on teacher/child #1, Mrs. Control, whereby the students were to help establish rules and sanctions. Would there be a personality fit with this teacher? Clearly, the answer is no. What if teacher/child #2, Mrs. Autonomy, was required in her classroom to use the obedience model of Rules and Consequences? Would there be a fit here? Most likely, the answer again is no.

Later, in Mrs. Control's classroom, a student's pencil breaks and he needs to use the pencil sharpener. Can he just get up and use the sharpener any time he wishes in class? In Mrs. Control's class the answer is no—students may sharpen pencils at the beginning or end of the period but not during class. Mrs. Control also has a can of sharpened pencils nearby that students may borrow and then return, so students will have a pencil if one of theirs happens to break. Mrs. Autonomy, though, permits students to sharpen their pencils any time they need to, and she does not seem to even notice when it occurs. Both Mrs. Control and Mrs. Autonomy are effective teachers who are loved by their students, but they have very different personalities and run very different discipline and classroom management programs. Observers, such as school administrators, would evaluate them as excellent teachers.

The problem comes when we ask Mrs. (or Mr.) Control and Mrs. (or Mr.) Autonomy to be something that they cannot. We parent the way we have been parented, and we most likely teach the way we have been taught. We as teachers have a personality core that is the "child" in us as to the way we were raised, and we draw on that core when we socially interact with others. We have varying degrees of need for control and of formality of rules to guide our interactions between and among us and others. That core of personality will most likely be who we are for most of our life, but with some minor change as we mature. Establishing rules as a teacher in the classroom, and setting limits with students, is a projection of the personality core of who we are as a person. Forcing us as teachers to practice techniques that are diametrically the opposite of our personal core will make us false, mechanical, and ineffective—it simply won't work. We may then say that some of the discipline models, because of the degrees of power and the development of rules, are a mismatch to our own personality core, and there is a lack of personality fit—this was not our "face." So when the principal says, "We have been doing Glasser for five years and 60 percent of my teachers still aren't using Glasser," what he is really saying is that Glasser was not a personality fit for three out of every five teachers in that school. This was not a "face" or philosophy that they were psychologically comfortable in using.

The Teacher Behavior Continuum, as part of the Three Faces of Discipline construct, takes the position that all of these models are of value, and that teachers cannot be forced to use one model but must find the model or "face" that fits their personality core. Mrs. Control would be called strict by her students, while Mrs. Autonomy might be called a "softy" by the same students, but both of these teachers are effective and well-liked by students and administrators. It is Mrs. (or Mr.) Waffle who has the serious discipline difficulties. One time she strongly disciplines a student for breaking the rules, yet the next day she says nothing when the same rule is broken. She is not fair, firm, and consistent. Her students will tell you that they can never tell where she is "coming from"—she waffles and is unpredictable, and she will be ineffective as a teacher and disliked by her students.

Now we may help Mrs. Waffle by assessing her personality core, possibly by using the Beliefs about Discipline Inventory from Chapter 1, and helping to train her in the one discipline model (or one of the three faces) that best fits her personality. This model will permit her to stop waffling, creating an orderliness to her behavior that students can understand. Thus she becomes predictable and no longer "scary" to the students. We may also use these models and the Three Faces in other ways.

DISCIPLINE AND TEACHING AS A DEVELOPMENTAL PROCESS

The teacher now has a basic understanding of the Three Faces of Discipline as a power continuum from minimum to maximum use of power, as well as an understanding of the host of techniques under each of these philosophies (or "faces") and the concept of *personality fit*. How, then, shall we use these three faces and their techniques?

The use of these techniques will differ widely from teacher to teacher. An undergraduate student beginning to face her first student-teaching or intern experience will respond differently than a first-year teacher attempting to find a footing as a new teacher. A veteran of 15 years teaching middle school will have a different approach than someone who has previously taught kindergarten for many years and now finds himself teaching adolescent students and discovering that what he did for discipline with younger children does not seem to work with older children. Levels of personal and professional maturity vary dramatically among teachers. We may look at teachers along a line of four developmental levels[1] of professional maturity—the Level I: Intuitive-Survival Teacher; the Level II: Reflective-Confident Teacher; the Level III: Prescriptive-Experienced Teacher; and the Level IV: Analytical-Professional Teacher.

Level I: Intuitive-Survival Teacher

The intuitive-survival teacher is the student teacher or beginning teacher—or one who has made a career change—and is now facing a class full of elementary, middle or high school students with whom he or she has had only minimal experience. The immediate goal is to survive[2]—to get through the day without major discipline disruptions to class activities. Such an intuitive-survival teacher works daily with considerable nervous energy and creativity as she or he attempts to "fly by the seat of the pants" when real discipline disruptions occur. These teachers draw intuitively on the "child within themselves," disciplining others as they themselves were disciplined by their parents, teachers, or other significant adults. Sometimes these intuitive techniques are very effective, whereas other times they do not work at all and things go very wrong. Some intuitive teachers feel ashamed that they cannot be more trusting of students to give them more autonomy, whereas others feel that the power they use is comfortable and fits their personality both as an individual and as a teacher. (See Figure 13–1 for all stages.)

There are generally three outcomes to the intuitive-survival teacher's discipline actions:

1. The teacher has a limited repertoire of two or three techniques and methods that work with most, but not all, children. The one student for whom it does not work causes much worry and slight feelings of ineffectiveness.
2. In order to maintain control, the teacher feels forced to use methods and techniques that do not fit her personality or teaching style. She feels that these harsher controlling methods are needed to stop all hell from breaking loose. Because of the disequilibrium between the teacher's values and her contradictory practices, the teacher does not feel a fit with teaching, begins to "waffle" in her discipline techniques, and in turn grows to dislike teaching and students.
3. The teacher cannot seem to get her footing as far as how to discipline in her classroom. When children misbehave, the teacher takes some action that is not powerful enough, and her authority is defied by one or two powerful children; this defiance quickly spreads to most children in the class. Or the teacher is overly harsh in attempting to get control and frightens most children, but one or two (usually boys) push the teacher to perform stronger aversive punishment on them—and it still seems to be ineffective. Soon administrators and fellow teachers begin to communicate to that teacher, in subtle or not-so-subtle ways, that she needs to get "on top" of those children in her class—the teacher's job is threatened and she feels nonempowered.

Level	Characteristics	Use of the Three Faces
I. Intuitive-Survival may be student teacher or new to middle or high school students	Responds intuitively • Has limited repertoire of techniques • Is permissive then harsh (waffles) • Is uncomfortable with the necessary controlling techniques	Select one "face" or methodology and learn to do it well
II. Reflective-Confident may have 3 or more years of teaching at this level	• Has effective discipline methods and a solid feeling of success • Still finds the very difficult child hard to handle and resents the amount of time this child requires	Ready to use all Three Faces of Discipline on a continuum of escalation or deescalation of power
III. Prescriptive-Experienced may have taught for many years	• Is totally confident in his or her own teaching abilities	Can seek help with problem children through staffing and finds time to do a prescribed intervention process
IV. Analytical-Professional may be in midcareer	• Can raise ethical and moral issues regarding school practices as they relate to the welfare of students • Is a leader for students • Mentors younger teachers	Can use all the Three Faces techniques as human relationship skills to become empowered in working with other adults

FIGURE 13–1   Level of Teacher Maturity and Discipline Techniques

The Three Faces of Discipline techniques might help the intuitive-survival teacher. All the techniques from all three philosophies might be too overwhelming for the young or new teacher to master at one time, so it would be advisable for this survival teacher to select one of the three approaches—Relationship-Listening, Confronting-Contracting, or Rules and Consequences—that best fits her personality or value system. The Beliefs about Discipline Inventory (Chapter 1, pages 9 to 11) will help to clarify the teacher's beliefs for her. In other words, if you are having a hard time surviving in the world of discipline, and the Beliefs Inventory and your own judgment tell you that you tend to be a Relationship-Listening teacher, you may temporarily abandon learning the other two systems and attempt to master the Relationship-Listening techniques by reading and rereading that chapter.

You should start by trying out a few techniques each week until you have mastered them and can put them into practice amid the "heat of battle." You may role-play (practice) with others, using these new techniques and getting feedback as to how effective you are in enacting these new techniques. Just because you have learned the techniques through reading does not necessarily mean you can use them in your own behavior—this takes time and practice.

For the intuitive-survival teacher, the best advice is to select one discipline methodology that appears to fit with the teacher's own personality and teaching style, and work to become very effective in using those procedures. The mastery of one "face" will make the teacher's behavior orderly and, therefore, understandable and predictable to students. Thus, this teacher will no longer be waffling and grasping for "something to do" in the heat of the discipline incident.

Level II: Reflective-Confident Teacher

The reflective-confident teacher is normally that teacher who has taught this age youngster for a number of years. She has received signs from her fellow teachers, administrators, and parents of those she teaches, as well as feedback from the students in her classroom, to tell her that she is respected, well-liked, and viewed as an effective teacher. She has a repertoire of discipline techniques that she uses day in and day out that enables her to have a smooth-working and well-disciplined classroom. The problem comes when she has a "time bomb" student. No matter what discipline techniques work with other students, nothing seems to work with this one. This difficult child can ruin an enjoyable year of teaching for the teacher. Even though the teacher is confident about her own abilities as a successful teacher, she resents the amount of time this one child is stealing from other children. The teacher feels the others are being cheated because of the inordinate amount of time she needs to spend putting out this one fire.

The skill for this teacher is to be reflective about past discipline actions and realize that what she is doing is effective with most children, but not with the "walking time bomb." Simply doing more of the same with him will not help and can even make matters worse. After reflection, she must come to realize that she must expand her repertoire of techniques if she is to succeed with the difficult child. This reflective-confident teacher is ideally ready to make full use of the Three Faces of Discipline with a continuum construction that suggests the escalation of power and techniques that may be effective with the one student. Once successful with him, she begins to deescalate the techniques, granting him more autonomy as he shows by his actions that he can handle the freedom. Because of her values, the reflective-confident teacher may not like seeing herself using these more controlling and powerful techniques, but she realizes that this level of intrusion is required for this difficult child and, gradually, the teacher will be able to retreat to techniques more congruent with her own personality.

This suggests that the teacher must read, study, and practice all the techniques on the Three Faces continuum, and then creatively apply these techniques by skillfully escalating and deescalating the amount of power used. (See Figure 13–2, which displays a Three Faces[3] meta-model of some of the best techniques from all models to provide a pathway of techniques, suggesting a movement in power from left to right on the continuum.) The reflective-confident teacher can be highly

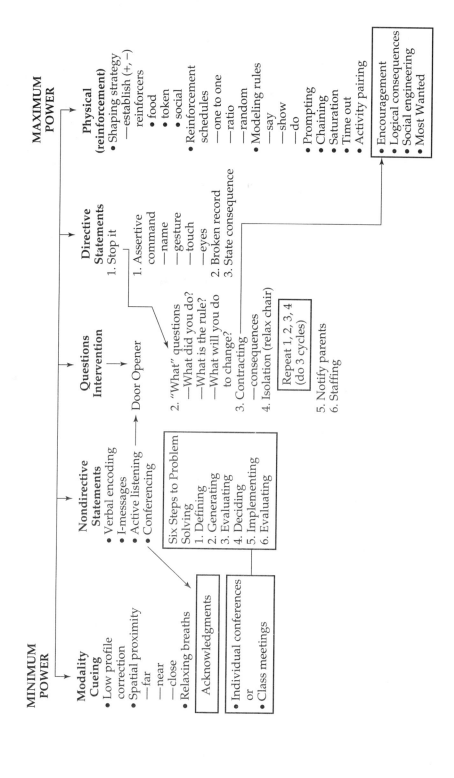

MINIMUM
POWER

MAXIMUM
POWER

Modality Cueing
- Low profile correction
- Spatial proximity
  —far
  —near
  —close
- Relaxing breaths

Acknowledgments

Nondirective Statements
- Verbal encoding
- I-messages
- Active listening
- Conferencing

Six Steps to Problem Solving
1. Defining
2. Generating
3. Evaluating
4. Deciding
5. Implementing
6. Evaluating

- Individual conferences
  or
- Class meetings

Questions Intervention

Door Opener

2. "What" questions
   —What did you do?
   —What is the rule?
   —What will you do to change?
3. Contracting
   —consequences
4. Isolation (relax chair)

Repeat 1, 2, 3, 4 (do 3 cycles)

5. Notify parents
6. Staffing

Directive Statements

1. Stop it

1. Assertive command
   —name
   —gesture
   —touch
   —eyes
2. Broken record
3. State consequence

Physical (reinforcement)
- Shaping strategy
  —establish (+, −) reinforcers
  • food
  • token
  • social
- Reinforcement schedules
  —one to one
  —ratio
  —random
- Modeling rules
  —say
  —show
  —do
- Prompting
- Chaining
- Saturation
- Time out
- Activity pairing

- Encouragement
- Logical consequences
- Social engineering
- Most Wanted

FIGURE 13–2   Three Faces of Discipline Meta-model

effective with many types of children similar to our "walking time bomb." However, in a career of teaching over 25 to 35 years, there will be children with whom even the Reflective-Confident teacher is still ineffective, even though the wide range of discipline techniques is at her command. Other professionals—the principal, school counselors, or psychologist—might need to help this teacher with this particular student. When this occurs, the teacher moves to the level of a Prescriptive-Experienced teacher.

The escalation/deescalation process may progress in three ways (see Figure 13–3):

Pathway 1: starting with Relationship-Listening: The teacher comfortably uses Relationship-Listening techniques, but they are unsuccessful for her with a particularly difficult student. She now moves to Confronting-Contracting, but—still lacking success—escalates to Rules and consequences. Successfully using the strong Rules and Consequences techniques, the teacher then deescalates to the Confronting-Contracting techniques, granting the student increased autonomy. Finally, she is able to deescalate to the Relationship-Listening techniques with a well-functioning student.

Pathway 2: Starting with Confronting-Contracting: The teacher might use Confronting-Contracting techniques naturally, but still find no success with the misbehaving student. She therefore escalates to Rules and Consequences. Once success with the student is attained, she deescalates to Confronting-Contracting. If the teacher's personality permits, she even continue to grant the student increased autonomy by deescalating further to Relationship-Listening techniques.

Pathway 3: Starting with Rules and Consequences: The teacher tends toward a Rules and Consequences personality, and she begins the process with this "face". If her personality lets her grant the student more autonomy, she may

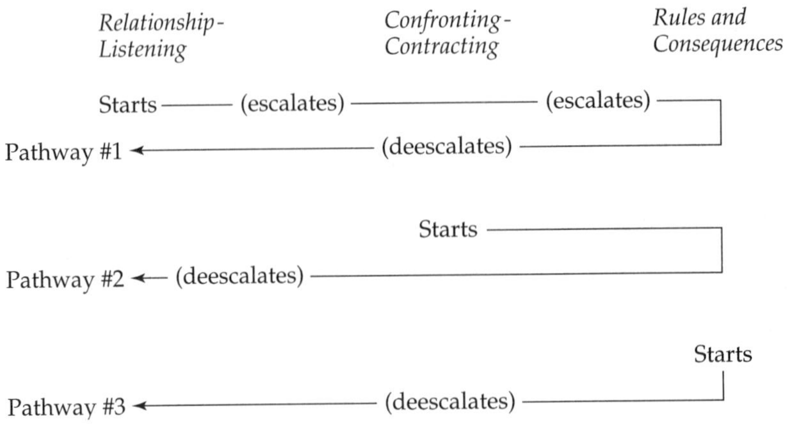

FIGURE 13–3   Pathways

deescalate to Confronting-Contracting, and then to Relationship-Listening if circumstances warrant it. I find that most teachers follow this pathway. At the beginning of the school year, they begin by being quite directive, using Rules and Consequences techniques to deal with problem behavior. By the end of October and into November, the discipline program should be working well and the teacher deescalates to the less controlling techniques of Confronting-Contracting, but she usually does not seem to make it to Relationship-Listening by the December holidays. After the long holiday vacation, the teacher finds it necessary to reescalate to Rules and Consequences. But by the end of January, the teacher has again deescalated to the Confronting-Contractingtechniques, and by March she is completely deescalated to Relationship-Listening techniques. Once good weather arrives in April or May—and with it, a case of Spring Fever among the students—the teacher is back to Rules and Consequences and holds on "for dear life" for the remainder of the school year.

Level III: Prescriptive-Experienced Teacher

The prescriptive-experienced teacher is one who can go beyond simple survival, is so professionally secure that she has few or no questions about her own effectiveness, and is comfortable admitting to difficulty in handling such students as the "walking time bomb." She seeks the help of colleagues and other professionals to assist her in prescribing a proactive intervention strategy for a very difficult student. She can collect data on this student, is comfortable in handling staffings (see Chapter 7) with a team, creates agreed-upon strategies, and writes individualized discipline plans (IDPs). She then finds time during the classroom day to carry out such interventions. Again, the confidence level of this teacher is never concerned with whether she is effective; instead, it tends toward, "I am an experienced teacher faced with a problem (an unmanageable student). How can I use the help of other professionals to learn new ways of becoming effective with this student?"

Level IV: Analytical-Professional Teacher

The highly mature analytical-professional teacher is one who can view the school program and, through her own analytical skill of reasoning, raise ethical issues, value questions, and philosophical questions as to what is best for the students. She can challenge the status quo. She is able to ask questions concerning what life is really like for students in the school and whether rules and procedures have been made for the betterment of the students or for the convenience of the teachers. These analytical-professional teachers can be effective leaders for the teaching profession. They provide leadership in the school by becoming mentors for intuitive-survival young teachers, through involvement in professional teacher associations, and by lobbying school boards and governmental agencies for the purposes of making the school a better place for students. The Three Faces of Discipline techniques are human relationship skills and methods of dealing with others in conflict situations. Not only can the analytical-professional teacher use these techniques and faces with children, she can also use the techniques and skills with adults, including parents, fellow teachers, and administrators. The analytical-professional teacher uses the Three Faces techniques to become fully empowered as a professional.

Note: There will be some teachers, perhaps large in number in a given school, who because of the nature of their personality core may never mature or advance beyond Level I or Level II.

SUMMARY

Just as no group of children can all be disciplined the same way, no large group of teachers can be forced to use and feel comfortable with a single approach to discipline. Each teacher has his or her own personality, and each must therefore work within an approach to discipline that fits with that personality. Levels of professional maturity vary widely among teachers, generally falling into one of four categories. The intuitive-survival teacher is a young professional who may choose one "face" that fits her own philosophy or teaching orientation, and through its use become more skilled and effective. The reflective-confident teacher has established herself as a teacher, but is still struggling with those one or two very difficult students who "pop up" in the classroom. The prescriptive-experienced teacher is so professionally mature and confident that she can admit the need for other professionals to help when she is faced with a very challenging student. Finally, the analytical-professional teacher has attained the most mature level, and becomes a true leader and champion for students; she uses the Three Faces techniques to empower herself and is skilled in dealing with the host of adults who impact the lives of students.

ENDNOTES

1. L. G. Katz, "Developmental Stages of Preschool Teachers," *The Elementary School Journal,* pp. 50–54.

2. K. Ryan, *Don't Smile Until Christmas: Accounts of the First Year of Teaching* (Chicago: University of Chicago Press, 1970).

3. The reader may find a full explanation of The Three Faces of Discipline and the Meta-Model continuum by reading C. H. Wolfgang and M. E. Wolfgang, *Three Faces of Discipline for Early Childhood* (Boston: Allyn and Bacon, 1995).

INDEX